IMAGINING *New England*

Imagining
New England

Explorations of Regional Identity from the
Pilgrims to the Mid-Twentieth Century

JOSEPH A. CONFORTI

The University of North Carolina Press

Chapel Hill and London

Designed by Richard Hendel

Set in Monotype Garamond

By Tseng Information Systems, Inc.

Manufactured in the United States of America

The paper in this book meets the guidelines for
permanence and durability of the Committee on
Production Guidelines for Book Longevity of the
Council on Library Resources.

Library of Congress
Cataloging-in-Publication Data
Conforti, Joseph A.
Imagining New England : explorations of
regional identity from the pilgrims to the
mid-twentieth century / Joseph A. Conforti.
    p. cm.
Includes index.
ISBN 0-8078-2625-1 (alk. paper) —
ISBN 0-8078-4937-5 (pbk. : alk. paper)
1. New England—Civilization.
2. Regionalism—New England—History.
3. New England—Intellectual life.   4. New
England—Historiography.   5. Group identity—
New England—History.   6. New England—
In literature.   I. Title.
F4.C76   2001
974—dc21   2001027027

05   04   03   02   01   5   4   3   2   1

FOR DOROTHY,

with love and appreciation

Contents

Figures & Table

TABLE

Preface

Scholarly books can also be very personal studies. On one level this volume represents an attempt to explain New England to myself. I am a native and lifelong resident of the region. I have lived for long periods of time in three states—Massachusetts, Rhode Island, and Maine. Yet the "real" New England has proved an elusive territory. This book does not pretend to be a comprehensive history of regional identity. Rather, it is in part an effort to demonstrate how I, a native and student of the region, came to imagine New England—that is, how I came to think about and interpret the region without questioning familiar narratives, conventions, and visual icons of regional identity. The real New England of my imagination was a kind of cultural invention, a powerful story that rested on inclusions and exclusions from the regional past. Much of my own experience as a New Englander has defied the dominant narratives of regional identity.

I was born and raised in Fall River, Massachusetts, a gritty New England textile city, a charter member of the Rust Belt long before that term was coined. The so-called Spindle City was filled with Irish, Portuguese, French Canadian, Polish, and Lebanese immigrants and their offspring. Yankee names—Borden, Durfee, Chace, Flint—adorned the hulking granite mills that sprawled across the city. But real-life Yankees were not easily located in the Fall River of the 1950s and 1960s. Indeed, the city's most famous Yankee was the ax murderess Lizzie Borden, who "gave her mother forty whacks and when she saw what she had done gave her father forty-one." In the 1980s a popular watering hole in Fall River, ghoulishly named "Lizzie's," capitalized on the city's notorious historical figure. But in the Fall River of my youth, Lizzie Borden seemed an apt symbol for a city whose Yankee leaders had lost their way, along with much of their money. Fall River declared bankruptcy in 1931 and never recovered from the Great Depression in the postwar decades, the years of my youthful dreams of patrolling centerfield for the Boston Red Sox.

My New England, then, was a gray ethnic city of mills, hills, and dinner pails. From their classroom windows teachers could easily point to half-abandoned factories and warn indifferent students that they would end up in a "sweatshop." Such admonitions failed to stem an inordinately high dropout rate. The teachers and school administrators themselves were more often than not upwardly mobile working-class Catholics who found job security in public education. A longtime superintendent presided over the school system as if it were his papal state. As late as the 1970s he continued to display a large illustration of the Sacred Heart of Jesus in his administrative office—locating the holy icon behind his desk and compelling all visitors to confront the proclamation of his piety.

Ethnicity infused politics in Fall River; the public payroll—and especially the school system—provided a means for rewarding friends, family, and ethnic compatriots. Ethnicity influenced other rewards. In my final year of Babe Ruth League baseball, I learned from my Irish coach that the Most Valuable Player Award, named for a deceased Franco-American war veteran, had to follow ethnic lines. After all, we played games in Lafayette Park, which defined the ethnic makeup of our corner of the city.

Only when Fall Riverites rooted for the Boston Red Sox or Boston Celtics did I feel part of some larger regional community. The real New England seemed to reside somewhere beyond Fall River's hills, mills, and dense triple-decker ethnic neighborhoods. Fabled Plymouth was only forty-five minutes away. Thanksgiving acquired a special aura because of Fall River's proximity to the place where the "Spirit of New England," and of America, was born. My fifth-grade geography book included George H. Boughton's captivating painting of the *Pilgrims Going to Church* (1867). The real New England seemed at once geographically proximate and culturally remote.

After college I left Fall River to attend graduate school in nearby Rhode Island. I came to specialize in the study of Puritanism. Later I realized that my initial scholarly interest in the Puritans represented a search for the real New England and an escape from Fall River and the ethnic Catholicism of my youth that I might now—though it is far too late—embrace for its seeming multiculturalism.

Seventeen years of studying and teaching in Rhode Island were followed by thirteen years in Maine. The move from the ostensible cultural margins of the region to its geographic periphery only enriched and complicated my understanding of New England. I went to Maine because I was offered the opportunity to start an American studies graduate program that would focus on New England. As a teacher, I would finally be able to concentrate exclusively on my scholarly and personal interests and have the time to define New England's essence. In an important sense, this book is a report on thirteen years of research, teaching, and thinking about New England—thirteen years during which I came to realize that Fall River was actually far more a part of the region than I had ever imagined.

My largest debt is to my colleagues in the American and New England Studies Program at the University of Southern Maine (USM). Ardis Cameron, Donna Cassidy, Mathew Edney, Nathan Hamilton, Kent Ryden, and Kenneth Severens have taught me much about social history, art, architecture, archaeology, cartography, geography, landscape and material culture. My good friends in the philosophy and political science departments, Joseph Grange and Richard Maiman, not only have offered personal support and encouragement; they also have stimulated me to reassess aspects of my historical analysis. At USM, I have learned much from our graduate students, who have helped me explore different ways of examining New England. The university granted me a sabbatical in the spring of 1999 to work on this book. I thank Dorothy Sayer, administrative assistant, for working so diligently throughout that semester and during this entire project, even after she moved to another department.

Beyond USM, several scholars have contributed to my work. I owe a large debt to Stephen Nissenbaum, who served as a National Endowment for the Humanities consultant to and evaluator of our master's program. He first provoked me to think in new ways about New England, and, through his writing and lecturing, he has been a continuing source of suggestive ideas. In the spring of 1992 geographer Martyn Bowden held a visiting professorship at USM. He delivered a series of insightful lectures on the cartography and historical geography of New England that helped me organize and clarify my thinking about this study while I was writing a book on Puritan tradition. Jere Daniell kindly agreed to read a copy of the manuscript. He offered many helpful comments, a number of which I incorporated into the final draft. James Leamon read and commented on a draft of the first three chapters and helped me improve my discussion of a period that he knows so well. Robert Lynn and John Woolverton, friends and scholars, have inspired me by their own work and through frequent conversations over lunch. I have greatly appreciated their ongoing interest in this project and their patience as I carried on about New England. With his friendship that is now approaching four decades and his outstanding scholarly achievements, Bill Stueck has done more to keep my study moving forward than he realizes.

Numerous librarians and museum professionals have helped me with source material and illustrations. Three people deserve special mention. Lorna Trowbridge, now retired as archivist at *Yankee,* expressed strong interest in my work, gave me access to the papers of her father, Robb Sagendorph, the founder of the magazine, and kindly made arrangements for the reproduction of illustrations. Irene Axelrod at the House of the Seven Gables directed me to source material on the early history of the museum and thoroughly answered all my questions. Virginia Spiller was especially helpful at the Old York Historical Society.

Once again it have been a pleasure working with the staff at the University of North Carolina Press. Lewis Bateman offered strong support with this manuscript as he did with my previous book. Lew set the review process in motion but then moved on to another press before the readers' reports were submitted. Sian Hunter assumed responsibility for the manuscript and assured me, though we had never met or conversed by telephone, that the review would proceed as planned. She has consistently provided encouragement and sound editorial advice. I am pleased that I had the opportunity to work with her. I also want to thank Ron Maner for his cordiality and efficiency in overseeing the production of this volume and an earlier one. I am grateful for Stevie Champion's superb copyediting.

Finally, I dedicate this book to my wife, ever thankful for her understanding, patience, and love.

Portland, Maine
November 2000

IMAGINING *New England*

Introduction
Region and the
Imagination

In *The Dogs of March* (1979), perhaps the best novel ever writ-
ten about New Hampshire, Ernest Hebert relates the story
of a transplanted Midwesterner. As a young girl living in
Kansas City, Zoe Cutter discovered a picture of an idyllic
New Hampshire town in *National Geographic* magazine: "forested hills, fields that rode the lower slopes, a tidy stone
wall bordering a country lane, white birches in the foreground like two angels, white church steeple just showing behind maples in the background." For thirty years Cutter accepts
National Geographic's image of the "real" New England as if it were "a page
from the Bible." As she enters middle age, her mental postcard of life in
New England inspires her to relocate. She purchases the "Swett Place" in
the fictional town of Darby. Cutter sets out to tidy up her property—to
straighten the stone walls, prune forested fields, and "open a country bou-
tique in the barn."[1] In other words, Cutter uses an old magazine image
to transform the Swett Place and to bring the real New England of her
imagination into existence.

Through Zoe Cutter, a major character in his New Hampshire novel,
Hebert suggests how regions are real locations but also imagined places.
Visual images accumulated over time distill the perceived cultural essence
that defines regional identity and distinctiveness. In turn, as territories on
the ground and countries of the imagination, regions bring geographic
and cultural order to the sprawling continental United States. Regions
help make America geographically comprehensible.

Regions are not only concrete geographic domains but also conceptual places. Humans define regions; they are not geographic entities that
define themselves. Regional identity is not simply an organic outcome of
human interaction with the physical environment—the geology and cli-

mate, for example — of a particular place. Regions are real places but also historical artifacts whose cultural boundaries shift over time.

New England, however, seems like such a "natural" region. Huddled in the nation's Northeastern corner, New England endures as America's smallest region. On a map, size tends to bestow on New England a natural coherence and wholeness that eludes other, more geographically and imaginatively unwieldy regions. The expansive South, Midwest, and West are often divided into subregions, but the more proportioned New England seems to abide intact. "We have so much country that we have no country at all," Nathaniel Hawthorne complained. "New England is as large a lump of earth as my heart can readily take in."[2] This "natural" region stands as a habitable place where life is lived on a human scale. New England embraces the Union's smallest state. New England is a region of towns hived off from larger towns whose boundary signs announce the date of their birth and help create not only a sense of history but also a terrain dense with border crossings. The region's urban landscape is dotted with small to midsize cities. In New England, distances pose few obstacles to tourists bent on exploring seacoast and mountains or to urban-based owners of ski chalets or vacation homes. If one eliminates Maine's Aroostook County, the kind of far-flung, thinly populated district that one finds in other sections of America, even New England's largest state more closely resembles the region's geopolitical norm.

If its six states do not actually comprise a natural region, the scale of life in most of New England suggests that it is a cultural region — a place where people have etched distinctive patterns into the landscape. But to describe New England as a cultural region does not resolve the problem of its distinctiveness; it only offers a basis for examining New England's history and identity. Culture, after all, far from being fixed and holistic, is dynamic, continually changing, and historically contingent. The same is true of regional identities. In fact, for more than three centuries New Englanders have responded to changes like the nineteenth-century ethnic, urban, and industrial transformation of the region's Southern states by revising explanations of regional distinctiveness. Such efforts typically singled out certain cultural patterns and geographic locations and excluded others in the construction of regional identity. Though they did not use the term, the historical architects of regional identity endeavored not only to define but also to delimit and stabilize New England as a cultural region.

Yet much of New England originated and developed as a cultural outpost of a powerful Puritan religious movement. Moreover, as Hawthorne's mid-nineteenth-century stories and novels suggest, Puritanism's imprint on the region persisted long after the collapse of New England's church-state alliance and the demise of Calvinist orthodoxy. Still, the Puritan era too often has functioned as a New England ur-civilization, invoked across time to explain everything from the region's low homicide rate to the fatalism of its Boston Red Sox fans. A scholarly monument enshrines Puritanism as the most studied subject of the American past. And highly trained scholars of Puritanism have not been known for caution in their claims.

In *Albion's Seed: Four British Folkways in America* (1989), David Hackett Fischer offers the most sweeping and controversial interpretation of how Puritanism forever stamped New England's cultural DNA. Influential Puritan founders from East Anglia reproduced in New England the folkways of the world they had left behind. From speech and dress to work, politics, and diet East Anglian founders transferred their religiously informed folkways to the New World. In Fischer's "genetic" history, Puritan folkways not only defined the distinctive culture of colonial New England; they have endured as the shaping elements of regional life down to the present. Similarly, settlers from other parts of Britain carried their folkways to the Delaware Valley, Virginia, and the colonial backcountry, giving birth to what remain historically determined cultural regions that have spread outward from their original hearths.[3]

Fischer's monumental interpretation of the historical origins and persistence of regionalism in American life was greeted with a mixture of praise and criticism. *Albion's Seed* is best understood as a product of the revival of regionalism that gained momentum in the 1980s, a movement that benefited from a new skepticism directed at narratives of a monolithic American identity that Cold War cultural nationalism had generated. America now seemed to be a nation of many stories. American history was miniaturized by the 1980s. Microstudies of communities and particular groups proliferated. A multicultural past was born.

Albion's Seed was a response both to the state of American historical writing and to the renewal of regional studies. If no overarching national narratives could explain America, then a limited number of regional narratives might stave off the "pulverization of the past," the reduction of American history to particles of human experience that comprise no whole.[4] Regional history offered an interpretive middle ground between exclusionary national narratives and endless local stories. Fischer's genetic approach to American cultural regions also coincided with and lent historical support to the revival of regionalism, manifested, for example, in the growth of regional studies centers at academic institutions across the country. *Albion's Seed* repudiated declension models of regional change: the idea that coherent cultural regions may have existed in the past but that they have been in decline for decades as modern and postmodern alterations of American life homogenized the nation.[5]

In *Albion's Seed,* the cultural holism once imputed to the nation is transferred to region. "America" may be destabilized but "New England" persists as a concrete, seemingly static, almost transhistorical cultural whole.[6] *Albion's Seed* ignores differences within regions in the course of emphasizing differences between them. If regional cultures and identities have persisted through time, they have not done so in quite the genetic ways that *Albion's Seed* suggests. Fischer's regional cultures extend across space and time but do not seem to undergo major change within their borders. New England may be older and more conceptually stable than America has been, but it has clearly evolved as a dynamic, constantly changing place. Moreover, new interpretive needs have arisen from social, economic, and political changes that have required continuing revision of New England regional identity. Both persistence and change compel the historian of regional life to ground New England identity and cultural distinctiveness on shifting earth.[7]

Puritanism does loom as a tradition that shaped New England in the colonial era and beyond. From the seventeenth to the nineteenth century, for example, the Puritan commitment to literacy placed New England in the forefront of American education, newspaper publishing, and lyceum founding. Similarly, Puritanism cultivated an interest in the past; from the colonial era through the nineteenth century, New Englanders were America's most prolific producers of historical works. Puritan literacy and historical-mindedness spawned a culture of print that conferred on New England the earliest and, by independence, the most well-developed regional identity of any American region. Along with this regional identity Puritanism propagated a New England sense of moral and intellectual superiority that often irritated outsiders.

But acknowledging such continuities across time that may be traced to New England's founders should not obscure the fact that Puritanism itself was hardly the fixed, cohesive cultural juggernaut that typically undergirds interpretations of regional distinctiveness such as Fischer's. "The Puritanism of the founders was not a stable, reified, and distilled set of ideas ready to be implemented in the pure laboratory of the American wilderness," one of the most recent and astute scholars of the movement argues, "but a complex and sometimes contradictory set of impulses." Similarly, the leading contemporary historian of early New England religion urges us to "move from an essentialist understanding of Puritanism" toward one that recognizes the religious movement as adaptive, evolutionary, "dynamic," "contextual," and "multilayered."[8] The same terms might be applied to New England identity, not only during the Puritan era but also across the arc of regional history that extends from the seventeenth to the twentieth century. Though my analysis acknowledges, indeed traces, Puritan-Yankee continuities in regional culture, it emphasizes how tradition remains, or, rather, becomes, tradition by a continual process of invention and reinvention.

My examination of regional identity also stresses how the landscape of New England life has constantly changed over time, requiring periodic historical and geographic redeployment of region as a country of the imagination. Since David Fischer published his monumental work more than a decade ago, historical study of American regions has gradually moved in new directions that have shaped my approach to New England identity. Scholars increasingly recognize how regions and regional identities are culturally constructed. Some analysts have claimed that a "new regional studies" perspective is emerging. If there is a historical manifesto for a new regional studies movement, it may be found in the editors' brief introduction to *All Over the Map: Rethinking American Regions,* a recent volume of essays on the South, New England, the Midwest, and the West. Edward L. Ayers and Peter S. Onuf draw on contemporary notions of culture as something that is fluid, contested, and negotiated to caution against "attempts to freeze places in time or to define some particular component of a region as its essence, leading regionalists to despair when that essence seems to be disappearing." For Ayers and Onuf, "regions have *always* been complex and unstable constructions, generated by constantly evolving systems of government, economy, migration, event, and culture."[9]

To describe regions as unstable constructions, however, is not to suggest that they are the geocultural equivalent of a false-front Western town. Regions are both historically grounded and culturally invented, components of their identity that change over time. Indeed, regions are rhetorically and conceptually unstable because they are not static worlds on the ground. Historians are increasingly examining both persistence and change in the grounded cultural patterns that confer distinctiveness on

American regions. They are also becoming more aware of how certain patterns and images are singled out and others excluded in the construction of regional identities.[10]

Although this study offers a connected narrative that stretches from the seventeenth to the twentieth century, it is an exploration, not a comprehensive history, of regional identity and regional culture. The chapters do not constitute a survey of New England as symbol and myth. Nor do they attempt to peel away barnacled myths to expose the "real" New England. Rather, this study approaches regional identity as the cultural terrain where the imagined and the historic New England "interpenetrate." As one historian of the West has put it, "The mythic West imagined by Americans has shaped the West of history just as the West of history has helped create the West Americans have imagined. The two cannot be neatly severed."[11]

For most of the twentieth century the West has probably been America's "most strongly *imagined*" region.[12] But New England, with its early historical consciousness and high rate of literacy and cultural production, developed as America's first strongly imagined region. New England, one historian of the colonial era recently observed, was a creation of "stories told about its past" as well as "a place mapped on the ground by settlers."[13] From providential Puritans, to Whiggish antebellum Yankees, to nostalgic colonial revivalists, to partisan academics, New Englanders dominated American historical writing from the seventeenth to well into the twentieth century. New England has been a storied place. Its identity has been encoded in narratives about its past — stories that have been continually revised in response to new interpretive needs generated by the transformations of regional life. *Imagined pasts* have helped New Englanders negotiate, traditionalize, and resist change. To call the changing narratives that have undergirded New England culture and regional identity imagined pasts, however, is not to suggest that they are sheer myth with no empirical foundation. Rather, it is to argue that these narratives are *partial truths,* selective interpretations of New England experience that are held up as the *whole* truth.[14]

My analysis historicizes New England identity and its narrative infrastructure, examining how the discourse of regional distinctiveness attempted to establish cultural and conceptual order on a dynamic place that did not define itself. Religious dissenters, "profane" economic opportunists, and non-English immigrants disrupted the region's Puritan and, later, Yankee culture and identity. Moreover, even the cultural mediators of Puritan-Yankee tradition did not typically speak in one voice. In the antebellum decades, for example, moderate antislavery reformers and more radical abolitionists stirred the regional imagination and appealed to Pilgrim-Puritan tradition in different ways. Moderates invoked the creation and preservation of civic order as the defining cultural legacy of New England's founders, whereas radicals summoned the come-outer moral activism of the Pilgrim-Puritan fathers.

The chapters that follow explore the conflicts and tensions that vexed New England culture and that formulations of regional identity tended to obscure, if not resolve. New England has been a posted territory, where certain people, places, and historical experiences have been excluded or relegated to the cultural margins. Consider Rhode Island. From its emergence as a kind of refugee camp from Puritanism, to the national coercion that was required to end its three-year resistance to joining the Union, to its turn-of-the-twentieth-century distinction as America's most ethnic state, Rhode Island has resided beyond the cultural borders or at the periphery of the "real" New England. In retaliation, Rhode Islanders sometimes have spun their own narratives of regional origins. Taking exception to the nineteenth-century epic account of the Pilgrims and Plymouth, for instance, Rhode Islanders held up the persecuted Roger Williams and the founding of Providence as marking the birth of American civic and religious liberty that then spread to the rest of the American republic, including New England.

Dominant historical narratives of regional identity have performed their cultural work by a process of inclusion and exclusion. Moreover, these narratives have been constructed not only through the written and spoken word but also through a canon of visual markers—icons of regional identity like the townscape enshrined in *National Geographic* that became lodged in Zoe Cutter's imagination. For a region settled by iconophobic Puritans, New England's past inspired, beginning in the nineteenth century, abundant visual and material artifacts of regional identity—statues, monuments, sacred landscapes, prints, photographs, and more. New England identity acquired concrete shape through such material artifacts.

This study proceeds by first examining New England as a changing place on the ground. It then historicizes both the narratives and visual markers of regional identity—the imaginative responses to the new interpretive needs created by the shifting landscape of New England life. Regional identity emerges as far more than an elite construction. Though access to power underwrites successful efforts to affirm regional identity across space and time, the historical agents who appear in the following chapters—New England's changing "cultural custodians" and guardians of the past—do not neatly align on one side of a divide that separates elite from popular culture.[15] Puritan preachers and historians certainly occupied a privileged position in early New England, but they also served as broad, even popular, cultural mediators. Jedidiah Morse, "the father of American geography," drafted texts that were widely used in schools and colleges and readily found in home libraries of the early republic. Lydia Maria Child and Harriet Beecher Stowe were prolific and popular writers of fiction and nonfiction. The enterprising John Barber produced scores of engravings of antebellum New England town scenes. Alice Morse Earle wrote best-selling, extensively illustrated colonial revival histories of early New England. Robert Frost made a career as a popular poet-performer of New England Yankeeness. Robb Sagendorph founded *Yankee* in the depths of the Great Depression and saw it become one of the most popular regional magazines in the country.

In considering these and many other famous and not-so-well-known New Englanders, the following pages analyze how regional identity was both created and culturally transmitted. Settlement promotional literature, Puritan histories, regional geographies, works of fiction, town commemorations, historical pageants, visual artifacts, colonial revival museums, *Yankee* magazine—the texts, institutions, and rituals that supplied the means for the cultural production of New England identity have changed over time.

My analysis begins with Puritan efforts to colonize and exercise imaginative dominion over New England. Chapter 1 explores the founding of New England and how first-generation Puritan migrants took physical and imaginative possession of the region as a "second England." By design this chapter is the shortest in this study, for the founding generation has been the subject of countless books and articles. Chapter 2 analyzes changes in Puritan colonial life and shifts in New England's relationship with the English homeland that required revisions of regional identity. From the second half of the seventeenth century through the first half of the eighteenth century, regional identity was first Americanized and then re-Anglicized. My interpretation of Puritan culture, colonial society, and New England's collective image is rooted in a reading of primary sources, but it also uses the problem of regional identity to synthesize findings from one of the richest bodies of scholarship in American historiography.

Puritanism bequeathed to Revolutionary New Englanders the most well-developed collective identity of any American region. Between independence and the Civil War, the Union served as a national arena where, through political conflict and collective cultural differentiation, New England sharpened its sense of historical distinctiveness from other American regions. Jedidiah Morse's pioneering and widely read geography texts are the focus of Chapter 3. His "American" geographies endeavored to stabilize a rapidly changing New England as the nation's only cultural region and to assert its superiority over other parts of the republic. Morse's influential geographies inscribed the highly politicized regionalism and moralistic republicanism of Federalist New England—a geopolitics that made the Puritan homeland, not the South, the first hotbed of secessionist sentiment.

The antebellum decades witnessed the continuing consolidation of New England identity around narratives and images of the region's distinctive republican past. Chapter 4 examines the emergence of Yankee identity and the growth of a "Greater New England" in the North. Conflict with the South, the missionizing of the West, a regional literary renaissance, town bicentennial commemorations, and the "invention" of the Yankee, the Pilgrims, and the orderly central village—these and other important aspects of the antebellum era shaped New England in ways that have escaped systematic explanation but that continue to influence our understanding of regional identity. The story of this powerful antebellum "reinvention" of New England occupies what is, by necessity, a lengthy and heavily illustrated chapter.

New England's antebellum national regionalism, cultural imperialism, and Whiggish confidence in historical progress appeared to triumph in the Northern victory in the Civil War. Perhaps, the entire nation, including a reformed South, would become a Greater New England. Chapter 5 probes the demise of New England triumphalism and the rise of the nostalgic colonial revival in the decades after the Civil War. The rapid pace of industrialization, urbanization, and, most important, ethnic transformation undermined Yankee confidence in New England's and America's future. When the first federal census had been taken in 1790, New England held 26 percent of the American population. By 1880, that number had fallen to 8 percent, with non-English-speaking immigrants a rapidly growing presence.[16] By then, "Old New England" had emerged as an object of nostalgia and veneration. The rising Midwest increasingly replaced New England as the national heartland, the location of a vital, progressive young America.

Throughout this study I have tried to suggest how regional identities are fashioned relationally. In the colonial era, New England saw itself in relationship to the English homeland and imperial center. Within the national political framework established after independence, regional identities were continually fashioned and revised through a reciprocal process of collective differentiation. The South, the Midwest, and the West were both real and imagined places that helped New Englanders define the cultural boundaries of their own region.

My analysis also shows how the imaginative centers of regional identity have changed over time. Chapter 6 explores how in the twentieth century the imaginative center of the "real" New England migrated northward. The popularity of Robert Frost and the success of *Yankee* magazine reveal how intraregional differences between North and South promoted the imaginative relocation of authentic Old New England to New Hampshire, Maine, and Vermont.

This study is a work of synthesis and original scholarship. The nation's smallest region may also be its most studied one. As a historian who has specialized in New England Puritanism, I am accustomed to feeling both blessed and daunted by what others have written. Throughout this book, especially in the early chapters, my interpretations draw on and extend the work of other scholars. But my examination of New England identity also incorporates large amounts of original scholarship on topics that have received little or no academic analysis—geography textbooks and the new nation, the feminization of the Yankee character, the creation of the House of the Seven Gables Museum, Robert Frost and the regional revival of the 1920s and 1930s, and the founding of *Yankee* magazine, to name several. Such subjects map out my search for post-Puritan sources of New England's cultural distinctiveness.

The Founding Generation and the Creation of a New England

Puritan settlers decidedly shaped the intellectual and cultural history of early New England, but they did not coin the term. Instead, the Puritans wrested imaginative possession of "New England" from more secular promoters and visionaries, principally explorer Captain John Smith, who originated and popularized the name. Laboring to achieve rhetorical dominion over the region, the Puritans proceeded to give it a distinctive colonial birth.

The storied Puritan settlement of New England occurred in one concentrated burst of migration during the 1630s and early 1640s that propelled upward of 21,000 English colonists to the region. The Puritans, who dominated this migration, journeyed to the New World in "companies"—organized bands of kin, neighbors, friends, and fellow church members—that helped sustain both memories of their homeland and persistence in their "new" England.[1] From the early 1640s to the end of the century and even beyond, New England received minimal in-migration. Yet its population surged, driven by a high birthrate and a low deathrate that testified to the region's hearty environment.[2] Thus, New England remained a relatively homogeneous English area from its origins to well into the nineteenth century. History poorly prepared it for the wrenching process of ethnic change that would transform the region beginning in the middle of the nineteenth century.

It was not so much cultural homogeneity, however, that marked New England as a distinctive New World colonial society but other characteristics of the Puritan migration.

Middle-class families filled the ranks of the Puritan hegira to the region; neither the impoverished nor the wealthy migrated in significant numbers. New England began and developed as a middle-class society of wide property ownership, a sharp contrast to the social reality of other New World colonies. Most important for the fashioning of a conceptually and rhetorically dense regional identity, the founding settlers comprised an unusually literate, educated group, especially for a colonial population. The founders' verbal prowess derived from their Puritan faith.[3]

Unlike the small band of Separatists who had settled Plymouth Plantation beginning a decade earlier, the Puritan founders of New England sought not to break away from the Church of England but to "purify" or reform it of entrenched Roman Catholic trappings. The erection of autonomous, nonseparating Congregational churches would preserve the restorationist impulse of the Protestant Reformation until the English homeland was ready to become a spiritual successor to biblical Israel. Puritanism was a religion of the word—of a devotional discipline rooted in literacy, Bible reading, and sermonizing, rather than ceremony, ritual, and such sensualism as churchly icons and instrumental music. From its founding Puritanism conferred on New England the highest rates of literacy in the New World. Puritanism was responsible for the first printing press in colonial America, established at Cambridge in 1640. Puritanism transported a cadre of well over a hundred college-educated intellectual leaders to New England. Graduates of Cambridge and Oxford, the intellectual elite among the founding generation consisted primarily of ministers but also included lawyers such as Governor John Winthrop. Through promotional tracts, sermons, correspondence, and, later, historical accounts, New England's cultural representatives fashioned a collective image for the region. In the seventeenth and eighteenth centuries, they presented a literate population with a torrent of publications focusing on the purpose and history of New England's creation, forging a print culture of regional consciousness unique in the annals of New World colonization.[4]

But creating New England, that is, imaginatively drawing the boundaries of regional identity, involved an ongoing process of cultural negotiation. For New Englanders were both English colonials and Puritan religionists, interwoven underpinnings of their identity that changed over time. As colonials and Puritans, New Englanders in the seventeenth and eighteenth centuries negotiated their identity in response to a shifting relationship with England. They confronted what has been described as the central dilemma of a colonial identity. Colonial societies faced the predicament "of discovering themselves to be at once the same and yet not the same as the country of their origin," a quandary that was complicated by the fact that mother countries held colonies such as New England in disesteem.[5] New England identity from the founding to the eighteenth century may be approached as a rhetorical map that recorded and attempted to impose conceptual order on the changing circumstances of both the region's colonial status and its Puritan religious culture.

The literate middle-class founders of the region conceived of it as a second England and transferred English place-names to the New World. "That it might not be forgotten whence they came," an early Puritan historian observed, the settlers "imprint[ed] some remembrance of their former habitations in England upon their new dwellings in America."[6] The founding generation saw the region as a "new" England where they could re-create ancestral English culture, reform the national church, and generally restore an industrious, pastoral way of life that they associated with an idealized English past. The founders' encounter with the New World served less as a catalyst for an emergent American identity than as a colonial setting for the reaffirmation of their English origins.

Whatever the problems of contemporary England that prompted the Puritans' transatlantic flight, for the pious John Winthrop no less than for the worldly John Smith "New England" announced a quest for cultural continuity with the homeland. Smith, the erstwhile leader and pugnacious Indian fighter of the Virginia Colony, explored the New England coast in 1614 and coined the region's name two years later. For Smith and the Puritan planters who later seized both physical and imaginative possession of the region, New England embodied a vision of the Northeastern coast of the American continent as a cultural and even environmental extension of England. Long before John Locke announced that "in the beginning all the world was America," both Smith and the Puritan patriarchs of New England beheld the region as what England had been in the beginning: a fertile and wooded land waiting to be transformed by industrious English people into a productive pastoral civilization.[7] Of course, the Puritans decidedly inflected Smith's earthly vision of New England with a religious ideology that, among other things, saw the region as the home of the New Israelites—a remnant of the Godly elect.

"Now this part of *America*[,] New England," Smith observed after his first trip to the region, "hath formerly beene called Norumbega."[8] Primarily a French cartographic invention of the sixteenth century, Norumbega had been conceived as both a city of fabled riches — a North American El Dorado — and a broad area that encompassed what would become Smith's New England and that, European fancy speculated, contained fertile land, precious metals, and perhaps the fabled Northwest Passage. The mythical Land of Norumbega lingered in the European imagination as England finally awakened in the late sixteenth century to the promises of New World colonization. But Norumbega barely survived the transition to the seventeenth century, and by the time of Smith's first voyage in 1614 the region he denominated New England was more commonly identified by the English as Northern Virginia, a vague geographic delineation that lay bare the limited knowledge of the area in England.[9]

In 1616 Smith published his influential *Description of New England,* a promotional account of his coastal voyage between Monhegan Island and Cape Cod two years earlier. With "New England" Smith completed the displacement of Norumbega and proclaimed that colonization would require effort, not the easy exploitation of a paradisiacal land. New England also supplanted the designation Northern Virginia, erasing any association between colonization in the north and Smith's disastrous experience with English settlement in the south. For from its establishment as a colony in 1607, Virginia had been promoted as a *new* England — a "Nova Britannia."[10] But instead of the industrious English settlers whom Smith now envisioned for New England, Virginia had attracted gentlemen and ill-prepared adventurers who expected easy riches. Smith had moved to impose order and work discipline on the Virginia settlers only to be driven from the colony in 1609.

Smith's ordeal in Virginia shaped his promotional image of New England, as did the failure of the first English attempt to colonize the region. Sagadahoc, a commercial beachhead with vestigial Norumbega-like hopes of material wealth, was established on the Maine coast in 1607. Poor leadership, economic disappointment, and a severe winter doomed the settlement. In less than a year Sagadahoc collapsed, bequeathing the impression that the region, far from being a mythical land, was a "cold, barren, rocky, Desart" inhospitable to English colonization.[11]

Smith confronted and attempted to deflect the legacy of Sagadahoc. The Maine coast, he allowed, "is a country rather to affright than delight." Casting an eye past numerous islands to the coastal "main," from which the area would acquire its name, Smith suggested that beyond "this spectacle of desolation" fertile valleys might lay in the interior. Still, he reminded his readers, "there is no kingdom so fertile [it] hath not some part barren and New England is great enough to make many kingdoms were it all inhabited." South of Maine, in the land of the Massachusetts tribe, Smith located "the paradise of all these parts." Here, where he saw a resemblance of the coast to Devonshire, Smith imagined the creation of a productive English shire. The territory offered not just fertile soil but impressive stores of fish and timber, all enhanced by the "moderate temper of the ayre." Smith imaginatively assimilated the landscape of his New England to the geography of the homeland, he represented the region as a primitive England, and he exemplified the convention of overstatement that was the staple of promotional literature. "And of all the foure parts of the world that I have yet seene not inhabited," the well-traveled captain enthused, "could I have but meanes to transport a Colonie, I would rather live here [New England] then any where."[12]

Smith included in his *Description of New England* a map that projected the region as a cultural annex of the homeland (Figure 1). Smith's map substituted English toponyms for Native American place-names. Some of these names, such as the Charles River, Cape Anne, and Cape Elizabeth (all chosen by Prince Charles, the future king, in honor of members of the royal family), survived subsequent colonization. As one historical geographer has argued, naming a colonial land is among the first acts of imperialism: "In common with planting the flag or raising the cross, rituals of possession were enacted on innumerable occasions along the shores of America. Naming the land was one such baptismal rite for European colonial societies in the New World."[13]

During the fifteen years between the publication of the *Description of New England* and his death in 1631, Smith remained a devoted publicist for the colonization of the region. He reissued the *Description* and published other tracts that advocated the creation of a "new" England.[14] To promote interest in colonization, he continued to represent the landscape in ways that reassured prospective English migrants. His promotional strategy also accented the economic promise of New over Old England. "For I am not simple, to thinke," he wrote, "that ever any other motive than wealth, will ever erect there a Commonweal; or draw companies from their ease and humours at home, to stay in New England to effect my purposes."[15] Smith, to be sure, miscalculated. His New England, as well as the cartographic and cultural Anglicization of the region that accompanied his promotional vision, served as the prelude to towns and colonies established by English religious dissenters. The most important dissent-

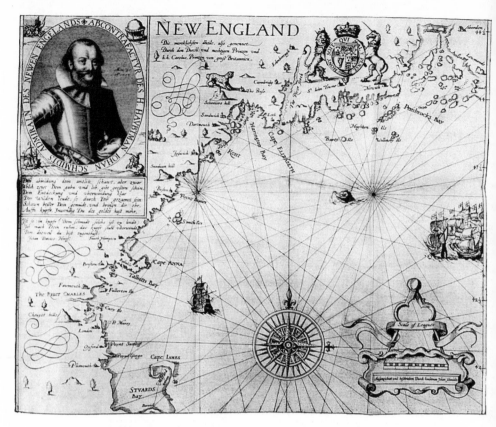

FIGURE 1. John Smith, "New England" (1616, 1635). "New England" originated as a cartographic and promotional idea publicized by Smith. This is a 1635 version of Smith's map, which first appeared in 1616. Courtesy of the Osher Map Library, University of Southern Maine.

ing group, the Puritans, fled to New England in pursuit of a purified, even primitive Christianity that derived from the restorationist aspirations of the Protestant Reformation.

Still, it would be misleading to suggest that the Puritan colonizers of New England inhabited a dualistic universe that separated the sacred from the secular, religion from economics. To the Puritan settlers who created a *new* England on the ground and not just in print, work, improvement, and productivity acquired moral status; economic activity became a way of glorifying God. Smith conferred with John Winthrop before the Puritan leader set sail for New England. Not surprisingly, in his *Advertisements for the Unexperienced Planters of New England, or Any Where* (1631), Smith expressed his hope for the Puritans, who "adventure now to make use of my aged endevours." Unlike the Virginians of his earlier experience, Smith saw the Puritans as the embodiment of "Industry her selfe."[16] Much of their intellectual industriousness would be devoted to explaining New England to outsiders—and to themselves.

To be sure, the Separatists who established Plymouth Plantation preceded the Puritans by nearly a decade. The Plymouth Separatists would be renamed and mythologized in the nineteenth century as the "Pilgrim Fathers" of New England and America. The Pilgrims would become central to a much later imaginative construction—a reinvention of regional identity. But though the Separatists established the first permanent colony in New England, they hardly exerted the cultural effort required to achieve imaginative mastery of the region as a second England. In contrast to the Puritan settlement of New England, Plymouth was a small plantation with the Separatists a minority even at the start. Of the 102 passengers on the *Mayflower,* only 40 were Separatists. The others, including Miles Standish and John Alden, who became legendary figures in the nineteenth century, were "strangers," secular-minded individuals hired for military or economic purposes. Many of the Separatist minority had already rejected the homeland for Holland. Though the sectarian planters of Plymouth read and were influenced by Smith's writings, they seemed not to share his imperial vision of New England or the transatlantic reformist aspirations of the Puritans' New England. Indeed, the *Mayflower* Compact—the agreement enacted by the Separatists in 1620 to establish and submit to laws and ordinances—referred to colonizing "northern Virginia." Moreover, in an important tract, *Reasons and Considerations* for journeying to America, one Plymouth religious leader wrote that "we are all in all places strangers and pilgrims, travelers and sojourners, most properly, having no dwelling in this earthen tabernacle; our dwelling is but a wandering, and our abiding is but a fleeting, and in a word our home is nowhere."[17]

Though the founders of Plymouth subsequently used the name New England, the small plantation acquired neither the intellectual leadership nor the commitment to literacy and education that were so pivotal to the Puritan fashioning of regional identity. Plymouth did not have an ordained minister until 1629, and it would be decades before Plymouth claimed its first graduate of Harvard, the Puritan college founded in 1636. Plymouth's early historical importance stems largely from the support, particularly foodstuffs, that it furnished to the shiploads of Puritan migrants who arrived in the region in the 1630s.[18] In contrast to the early Separatists, these nonseparating Congregationalists began to domesticate and dominate their new world by imagining it as a second England.

Until recently, historical scholarship on the founding of New England has tended to stress how the New World environment challenged and ultimately eroded inherited patterns of thought and action. Such a line of analysis may reflect the abiding influence of a frontier model of American historical development that has emphasized the "experimental, adaptable, and innovative" features of pioneering settlements in the nation's past.[19] The founders of New England quickly established decentralized civil, religious, and military institutions that grew out of the new context of their lives. Local self-government, covenanted churches that required a testimony of spiritual conversion for membership, town-based militia— these and other seeming innovations suggest that the doctrinally rigid Puritans adapted to New World circumstances.

Yet recent scholarship documents persuasively that though significant adaptations were made over time, the founding generation saw itself as a "transplanted English vine."[20] Wherever and whenever they could, first-generation Puritan New Englanders reaffirmed loyalty to their English heritage. Even the celebrated local institutions of early New England were understood as the restoration of an idealized English past. In America, the Puritans overturned the innovative centralizing reforms of the Stuart monarchy in civil, religious, and even military affairs. The familiar persecution of religious dissenters such as the Puritans represented only one consequence of a newly intrusive monarchy. New England emerged as a New World outpost for the reconstruction of English local customs associated with an idealized ancestral past.[21] Moreover, like immigrants and refugee groups who fill the pages of later American history, the Puritan settlers responded initially to the New World by reasserting the inherited culture of the Old. They clung to and even became newly conscious of their "ethnic" identity in ways that would have been unnecessary at home. Furthermore, the founders' heavy investment in the preservation of their English heritage and traditions rested on common seventeenth-century fears that colonization in a new environment away from the "civilized" homeland would result in cultural and even physical degeneration—an unsettling prospect that seemed to be borne out by the English experience in Virginia.[22] Thus, for a complex of reasons, New England represented to the first generation of Puritans a quest for cultural continuity that was inscribed in print, in local practices, and in the landscape.

The Puritans not only transferred English town and county place-names to America; they also imposed cultural order on their new physical world by applying familiar geographic terms and classifications. Through the use of descriptive categories such as brook, pond, marsh, orchard, and fen, the Puritan settlers assimilated the landscape of New England to the physical world they had left behind. Indeed, this imaginative and cultural imperative to homologize the geography of homeland and colony even encouraged settlers to cleave to the notion that New England was an island. Though John Smith had expressed skepticism that New England was an island, the Puritan founders' very limited geographic grasp of the region enabled the seemingly reassuring image to persist well into the 1630s.[23]

Following Smith, Puritan promoters of colonization represented the New England landscape as a second England in fertility and pastoral promise. Early settlements clustered along the coastal lowlands, where Native Americans had cleared large tracts of land—a development that ironically furnished objective support for the promotional image of the region as a second England. Through contact with traders well before permanent settlement, the Native American populations of coastal New England had been devastated by European diseases to which they had not been previously exposed. One traveler into the country of the Wampanoags south of Boston reported that "skulls and bones were found in many places lying still above ground, where their houses had been, a very sad spectacle."[24] Native American depopulation helps explain the testimonies to the openness of the New England landscape that one finds in Puritan promotional literature of the 1630s. Francis Higginson, for example, a minister who had arrived at the former Native American village of Naumkeag (which would be renamed Salem) in 1629, noted that a few miles inland "a man may stand on a little hilly place and see divers thousands of acres of ground as good as need to be, and not a tree in the same." Farther south, in the area that later became the town of Quincy, promotional writer William Wood described a "great store of plain ground without trees." "Near this place is the Massachusetts Fields," Wood continued, "where the greatest sagamore in the country lived before the plague, who caused to be cleared himself."[25] By the time the Puritans swarmed into the land of the Massachusetts in the 1630s, the decimated tribe could offer only token resistance. Abandoned Native American villages like those of the Massachusetts became particularly attractive locations for the development of communities that would be part of a *new* England.

Of course, Native American village sites, like all of the New England landscape, required transforming "improvement" before settlements that resembled the English countryside could emerge. Native Americans migrated among temporary, often seasonal, villages; they did not raise livestock, they failed to bound their land, and women usually performed agricultural labor. In both their physical appearances and cultural conventions, Native Americans were "un-English"; they struck one early New Englander as akin to "English gypsies."[26] Habits of migration, the refusal to impose bounded order on the landscape, and unexploited English-like meadows all rendered Native Americans obstacles to the reconstitution of new English communities. The Puritans' God intervened to advance the cause of English civilization in the New World. The diseases that ravaged tribal populations came to be understood as a providential instrument— God's "fatal broom," as a Puritan poet put it, that provided His people "elbow room."[27]

Diminished native populations and tribal indifference to English standards of improving the land thus encouraged Puritan leaders to represent New England as a *vacuum domicilium,* an empty New World home that belonged, legally and morally, to those who subdued and improved it.[28] Where intact tribes resisted such a reading and seizure of the landscape, Puritan leaders could not wait for "God's broom" to do its work; gunpowder assisted the opening of Native American territory to Anglicization. In 1637 the Pequots of eastern Connecticut fell victim to the first tribal massacre in New England's history. The town of New London on the Thames River announced the triumph of transplanted English settlers and their colonial agenda.

But the bloody victory of 1637, in which the Pequot fort was set ablaze and fleeing men, women, and children were slaughtered, posed a dilemma for English colonial identity. The Puritans were well aware of the "Spanish Cruelties" that Conquistadors had inflicted on the native populations of New Spain. The torture, killing, and enslavement of native people had been perceived in England as evidence both of the Spanish character and of New World barbarism. The Puritans saw themselves as civilized English colonists, who, with the history of New Spain in mind, would resist the threat of cultural degeneration in a new, undomesticated land. "New" England articulated this cultural ideal, but English behavior in the Pequot

War disrupted it. The colonists, for example, reported that the Narragansetts, who had allied with them against the Pequots, "much rejoiced at our victories, and greatly admired the manner of Englishmen's fight, but cried Mach it, mach it; that is, It is naught, it is naught, because it is furious, and slays too many men." As they would with later Indian wars, the English turned to print to revisit the cultural battlefield. In historical accounts, Native American treachery and savagery were recorded in detail alongside a triumphalist narrative of the progress of English civilization, a conquest that proceeded through God's "special providences."[29]

During the years of sustained English migration surrounding the Pequot War, Puritan writers represented New England as a region that resembled the homeland and that held the promise of becoming a second England in pastoral, ordered beauty and productiveness. But Puritan promoters did not lose sight of the industry and travail that migrants would confront as they subdued a fertile but primitive land, molding it into a second England. Far more than for John Smith, New England became to Puritan writers a place for labor in the pursuit of "competency" or "sufficiency"—a middling, but not indulgent or excessively worldly economic ambition. Industry and competency undergirded the middle-class English social ideal that writers projected onto New England—a family-based, regional aspiration shaped by Puritan religion.[30]

"If men desire to have a people degenerate speedily, and to corrupt their mindes and bodies too . . . ," minister John White suggested in *The Planters Plea* (1630), "let them seeke a rich soile that brings much with little labour." New England would not be a seductive earthly paradise, but an environmentally hospitable land for Puritanism and for the restoration of middle-class English social values. White put it succinctly: "If men desire that piety and godliness should prosper, accompanied with sobriety, justice, and love, let them choose a country such as this [New England], which may yield sufficiency with hard labour and industry." Similarly, John Winthrop saw the potential moral and spiritual bounty that would accrue to colonists who labored to bring forth a *new* England. When critics of migration warned of the consequences of abandoning an already "fruitful" homeland, Winthrop argued that the comparatively "meane condition" of New England offered "more freedom to dye . . . [to] the things of this world . . . [and] to laye up treasure in heaven."[31]

Puritan writers and promoters envisioned New England not just as a second England for fertility but as a place of the moral imagination. Industry, improvement, competency would be imprinted on the landscape. New England would be a moral terrain, a terra firma for glorifying God and preserving English culture and tradition. To underscore the urgency of institutionalizing both the biblical injunction to increase, multiply, and subdue the earth and the colonial imperative to Anglicize their New England, Massachusetts authorities established policies that discouraged land speculation. In 1634 it was decreed "that if any man hath any great quan[tity] of land . . . and doeth not builde upon it or imp[rove it] within three years," the Massachusetts General Court had the right to "disp[ense] of it to whome they please."[32]

The Puritans' middle-class moral vision of New England, which enshrined industry, improvement, and competency, suggests that colonization involved a selective transfer and replication of English culture. The Puritans, after all, were reformers disaffected by the real and perceived excesses of contemporary English life. "Oh Newe England, Newe England," one visitor wrote to his brother in the homeland in 1635, "how much am I bound to the Lord for granting me so great mercy as to tread on thy grounds and to enjoy and partake of thee many sweet examples and holy practices thou has afforded me." To this Puritan correspondent, England appeared "disfigured" with social ills, including "so many beastly, barbarous, belching drunkards."[33] New England was not imagined by its founders as an uncritical cultural reproduction of contemporary England. To the contrary—the Puritan creators of New England held a restorationist vision that looked back to an idealized English past. "New" England identified a moral precinct where a *reformed* English way of life would be installed.

Though images of a peculiarly, even pathologically, repressive Puritanism persist, we appreciate the founders of New England as both religious reformers *and* English folk. The killjoy, fanatic, sometimes freakish Hawthornesque attributes imputed to the Puritans now seem more a projection of the nineteenth-century imagination than central elements of the seventeenth-century world inhabited by migrants who were simultaneously religious reformers and pragmatic *English* colonists. Still, the middle-class founders of New England renounced the seeming profligacy of the contemporary homeland. "Merry Old England" would not be reproduced in the New World. Rather, a more nostalgic attachment to the English past, particularly to the reformist promise associated with the Protestant Reformation, informed the Puritan social aspiration for New England. Not only did "Saint Monday" find no sanction in the disciplined, work-centered culture of early New England; the English ecclesiastical calendar was also radically revised. New England authorities discountenanced—even forbade—the celebration of saints' days, Easter, and Christmas. Having failed to restore a biblically based, strict Sabbatarianism at home, the Puritans institutionalized the sanctified Sunday in their *new* England. Yet, not just Sunday but every day offered Puritans the injunction to glorify God by sacred work in the world. Hence, traditional "holy" days represented human contrivances that artificially disjoined the sacred and the secular.[34]

Perhaps early New England meetinghouses best suggest both the Puritan resistance to dividing the world into the sacred and the secular and the Puritan longing to reconstitute familiar and reformed English ways in America. The Puritan founders of New England called their places of worship meetinghouses, not churches. Meetinghouses doubled as civic buildings where nonreligious assemblies gathered. Meetinghouses were not sacred space—worship-centered hallowed ground fenced off from secular Puritan life. The meetinghouse stood as a locus of communal devotion, but the glorification of God—through private prayer, Bible reading, and self-denial as well as through work, improvement, and productivity—invaded everyday life. Not surprisingly, given the Puritans' organic, worldly understanding of glorifying God, English ecclesiastical architecture was not replicated in early New England. The Puritans erected square or, more often, rectangular, steepleless, unpainted structures that were a far cry from the famed white churches of later New England. Though they rejected the ecclesiastical architecture of the homeland, the Puritans still drew on familiar English models in constructing their meetinghouses. Early New England meetinghouses resemble civic buildings, particularly town houses, in the English communities whose names the Puritans transferred to the New World.[35]

Of course, the moral regimen of Puritanism with its strict Sabbatarianism, its renunciation of Merry Old England, and its culture of work proved to be oppressive to certain social elements in early New England. Servants and other migrants who sought economic opportunity and who did not embrace Puritanism often found themselves in conflict with Puritan authorities. Remigration became far more common than the fabled accounts of early New England acknowledge. Perhaps up to one-sixth of the approximately 21,000 colonists who journeyed to New England in the 1630s and early 1640s abandoned the region, many returning to England, others seeking a new start in different parts of America. As early as 1631, Thomas Dudley reported that at least 100 colonists who had ar-rived a year earlier sailed away from New England, "partly out of dislike of our government, which restrained and punished their excesses, and partly through fear of famine." [36]

Hundreds of devout Puritans joined more secular-minded migrants in forsaking New England. Numerous committed Puritans continued to own property in England, reinforcing ties to home and providing a hedge against disillusionment with the New England experiment. Homesick-ness afflicted many migrants who returned as well as those who stayed. The Reverend Peter Bulkeley of Concord, Massachusetts, wrote to a fel-low minister pouring out his affection for "my dear native country whose wombs bore me, whose breath nourished me, and in whose arms I should desire to die." [37] Yet the homogeneity of the migrants to New England, the bonds of kin, neighbors, friends, and church members that were trans-ported across the Atlantic, the shared commitment to a Reformed English Protestantism — all these social and cultural adhesives encouraged recon-stitution of a new English world in America that counteracted massive remigration. Though one-sixth of the founding generation of migrants may have deserted New England, that number does not begin to approach the rates of remigration — often reaching 50 percent — that characterized later groups of American immigrants. [38]

For migrants from a temperate climate who sought to re-create an English way of life in the New World, the New England climate pro-pounded challenges both for daily life and for the imaginative conquest of the region as a second England. Weather has resided at the center of New England identity from the beginning of the region's history. New England was hotter than Old England, though not nearly as menacing to English settlers as the summers of Virginia. In *New England's Prospect* (1634), William Wood reminded his readers that Virginia's "extreme hot summers, hath dried up much English blood and by pestiferous diseases swept away many lusty bodies, changing their complexion not into swar-thiness but into paleness." [39] New England publicists evoked memories of the colonial graveyard that early Virginia had become, thereby pro-moting the healthy summers of New England that were hotter than in the homeland but nevertheless moderate compared to the tobacco South. But migrants who returned to England spread stories of New England's inhospitable winters — accounts that summoned images of the Sagadahoc colony and disrupted the claim that the region was or could become, by dint of industry, a second England.

Out of necessity Puritan writers of the first generation became prophets of meteorological moderation, explaining the human role in climatology and assuring prospective migrants, and themselves, that New England's comparatively harsh winters and short growing season did not subvert either the reality or the promise of the region as a *new* England. The cultural baggage that settlers transported to the New World included an attachment to an English diet and a desire to preserve customary foodways. Colonists experimented with English seeds while authorities publicized evidence that familiar plants grew in New England. Promoters also stressed that improving the land—clearing woods, planting fields, and organizing towns—would, over time, moderate the climate just as it had in England. In this commonly held view, New England's climate, like its fertile but unimproved terrain, was "as England hath been in quondam times." Would anyone, William Wood asked, "condemn that which is as England hath been," namely, "colder in winter and hotter in summer?"[40]

Wood and other promoters responded to common seventeenth-century fears that colonizing a new environment with a different climate would result in physical (and cultural) degeneration. Wood assured his readers that New England would not rob them of their English complexion; winter would always undo summer tanning, restoring natural color and preventing the kind of un-English swarthiness that branded seamen. Moreover, the cold climate of New England promised to revitalize an ancestral "inward constitution."[41] As early as 1630, Salem minister Francis Higginson praised New England's hearty climate. "Experience doth manifest that there is hardly a more healthful place to be found in the world that agreeth better with our English bodies," Higginson wrote in "New-Englands Plantation." "Many that have been weak and sickly in old England by coming hither have been thoroughly healed and grown healthful and strong."[42] Though Higginson died a year later of a fever, early New England proved to be an uncommonly healthy colonial society, especially in contrast to Virginia. New England's population grew significantly, the consequence of a low deathrate and not just a high birthrate. By the early 1640s, one Puritan publicist saw the hand of Providence in the effects of the New England climate. "God hath so prospered the climate to us," the anonymous author of *New England's First Fruits* (1643) reported, "that our bodies are hailer, and children born stronger, whereby our number is exceedingly increased."[43] The ostensible surge in the birth of twins in New England was held up as compelling evidence of the region's invigorating climate and environment. The decision of Richard Mather, patriarch of the famous Puritan clerical dynasty, to name a son Increase (b. 1639) suggests how the biblical command to multiply and subdue the earth was far more than publicists' propaganda in the 1630s.[44]

New England's promoters and early chroniclers thus attempted to dispel prevailing concerns over colonial degeneration with prospects of English physical as well as moral and social renewal in the New World. The New England landscape offered the promise that industry would produce competency, not an earthly paradise inimical to Puritan religious beliefs. So, too, the region's climate would reinforce Puritan religiosity; New Englanders would avoid the physically and morally enervating consequences of England's tropical and semitropical colonies. The colonists would be compelled to labor to improve the landscape, and thereby the climate, in order to secure a comfortable sufficiency. And as New Englanders swung their axes through the forested acres that lay beyond the fields cleared by Native Americans, Puritan industry produced a bounty of wood that, writers consistently pointed out, relieved winter's discomfort. Such an abundance, one promotional writer stressed, enabled settlers "to build warm houses and make good fires, which makes the winter less tedious." Another Puritan leader informed readers in the heavily deforested homeland that firewood in New England was "a great deal cheaper than [what] they sell billets and faggots [for] in London." Transported from a world of scarcity to a land of forested abundance, industrious Puritan families, it has been estimated, consumed an average of forty cords of wood a year.[45]

Over the course of the first generation, New England's weather changed in ways that supported the belief that improving the landscape moderated the climate. The 1630s and 1640s witnessed severe winters that abated beginning in the 1650s. In *Wonder-Working Providence of Sions Savior in New England, 1628–1651* (1654), the first published history of the founding of New England, Edward Johnson claimed that cleared forests and the spread of cultivated farmland had altered "the very nature of the seasons, moderating the Winters cold of late very much."[46] *Wonder-Working Providence,* the most important interpretation of early New England produced by the first generation, ignored the Native Americans' remaking of the regional landscape that had benefited the first migrants. For Johnson, as for so many Puritan writers of the second generation, New England had been just a "howling wilderness"—an image of the presettlement landscape that amplified the heroic, inspirational narrative of Anglicization that needed to be told. "[T]his remote rocky, barren, bushy, wild-woody wilderness," Johnson wrote, "a receptacle for Lions, Wolves, Bears, Foxes,

Rockoones, Bogs, Bevers, Otters, . . . a place that never afforded the Natives better than the flesh of a few wild creatures and parch't Indian corn . . . , now through the mercy of Christ [has] become a second England for fertileness in so short a space, that it is indeed the wonder of the world." [47]

Scholars who have examined the religious motives for New England's settlement have often located in the region's founding the birth of an *American* identity, not the reaffirmation of English origins. Though they were nonseparating Congregationalists who did not spurn the Church of England, the Puritans nevertheless abandoned the corrupt homeland before God visited His awful judgment on the depraved English nation. Such rejection of Old World corruption formed the prelude to the embrace of the New World promise, emboldening the Puritans to imagine the founding of New England in eschatological terms—as a milestone in history's progress toward the millennium. New England, indeed America, would transcend the vices, the poverty, and the historical burdens that remained the scourge of Europe until the inauguration of the millennium. In short, the founding of New England, with the Puritan's aggrandizing moral militancy, consuming self-consciousness, and rhetorical proficiency, launched the development of a self-righteous American identity. One scholar recently summarized this powerful line of argument: "With American Puritans, indeed, we find for the first time the beginnings of a coherent American ideology, an ideology, that is, based on the premises of the ultimate separation of America, the New World, from the corruption of the Old World. Seeing their migration as an apocalyptic revelatory event, American Puritans were the first to accord America a singular independent role as a sacred place in the history of salvation." [48] In this view, New England was not imagined as a "new" England but as a New Israel, the land of the new chosen people—an identity that, when later projected onto the nation as a whole, resulted in sanctimonious American words and deeds. In particular, beginning in the 1960s scholars suggested that the Puritans' self-righteous "errand" into the American wilderness, conceived as a moral example to the world, culminated in the Vietnam War. [49]

The founding image of New England as a "city upon a hill" (drawn from Matthew 5:14–15) became central to compelling narratives of the Puritan origins of national identity and its expansionist conception of American moral superiority and missionary responsibility to the world.

Governor John Winthrop's powerful sermon of 1630, "A Model of Christian Charity," emerged as the seminal text not only for understanding the founding of New England but also for comprehending the roots of American identity. "We shall find that the God of Israel is among us," Winthrop announced aboard the ship *Arbella,* "when ten of us shall be able to resist a thousand of our enemies; when he shall make us a praise and glory that men shall say of succeeding plantations, 'the Lord make it like that of New England.' For we must consider that we shall be as a city upon a hill. The eyes of all people are upon us."[50] Winthrop's text, which was not published until the middle of the nineteenth century, supplied historians with what became a controlling image of New England's, and America's, ideological origins.

Winthrop's evocative words found a prominent place in political rhetoric beginning in 1960. In a speech delivered to the Massachusetts General Court shortly after his election to the presidency, John F. Kennedy compared his "task of building a new government on a new and perilous frontier" to Winthrop's mission. Kennedy informed his audience that "we shall be as a city upon a hill — the eyes of all people are upon us." In his view, America needed to complete the experiment that Winthrop had initiated, namely, to furnish a moral example to the world. After Kennedy, Winthrop's words and New England's founding were regularly invoked by presidents and presidential candidates. Ronald Reagan, for example, repeatedly described America as a "shining city on a hill."[51] Winthrop's words have promoted *American* self-congratulation; they have been summoned to challenge citizens to fulfill his historic *American* mission; they have been presented as prima facie evidence of the early Puritan paternity of *American* moral arrogance. Such entrenched scholarly and popular political interpretations depict Winthrop and the founding generation of Puritans simply as self-assured proto-Americans, not as transplanted, even uprooted and bewildered, *English* migrants. This line of interpretation has typically characterized the voluminous scholarship that examines Puritan religion.

But much Puritan religious writing and recent revisionist historical work suggest that the Puritan founders of New England were far from proto-American nationalists enunciating the birth of American moral imperialism; rather, they were conflicted English colonists wrenched from their ancestral homeland and filled with doubts about their New World experiment. After the *Arbella* sermon, for example, Winthrop never again used the image of New England as a city on a hill. Moreover, as one historian of Puritanism has persuasively argued, "the imagery of the exemplary city, the beacon or mirror, and the watching eyes abounded in the period" of English Protestantism's emergence when the homeland was imagined as an elect nation and Matthew's text was widely invoked.[52] Of course, Winthrop and other Puritan migrants believed that providential judgment was about to descend on England. "The Lord hath admonished, threatened, corrected, and astonished us, yet we grow worse and worse," Winthrop wrote to his wife in 1629, "so as his spirit will not always strive with us, he must give way to his fury at last."[53] Yet, given their personal and cultural bonds to their native land, Winthrop and the Puritan founders of New England resisted the transference of elect nation status from the Old to the New World.

In fact, the pioneering generation of New England Puritans remained transatlantic religious reformers. Even Winthrop's "A Model of Christian Charity," which was delivered while the *Arbella* rested at anchor in England and not during or after a transforming ocean voyage as is often assumed, responded to an English audience. For the Puritan migrants to New England confronted critics who saw their departure as hindering the cause of religious reform at home. "It will be a great worry to our church to take away the good people," Winthrop reported of critics' complaints, "and we shall lay it [England] more open to the judgment feared." Thus, the "eyes of the world" that would be on New England would be primarily of English Puritan critics looking for signs that the American experiment was a failure, not a success.[54]

Furthermore, a transatlantic perspective rather than a proto-American national identity informed the Puritan founders' rhetoric about a New Israel, a New Jerusalem, and the "chosen people" of God. English preachers customarily compared Reformed Protestant England to ancient Israel, a historical identification that many migrants to New England continued to accept. But terms like the New Israelites also described a more spiritual identity, the *Godly* citizens of the English nation; it even referred to the elect—those chosen by God for salvation—who were part of a universal church. In short, the first-generation New England Puritan rhetorical invocation of the New Israelites did not signal the adoption of a geographically situated American identity. Instead, it more typically referred to a transatlantic community of English saints. As the distinguished Puritan divine John Cotton told Winthrop's departing party in 1630, "be not unmindful of our Jerusalem at home, whether you leave us or stay at home with us." Cotton, who did not journey to New England for three more years, urged both departing and nonmigrating Puritans to pray for the progress of Jerusalem. "As God continueth his presence with us . . . ," he observed, "so be ye present in spirit with us, though absent in body; forget not the womb that bare you and the breast that gave you suck."[55]

Rather than emerging from a desacralization of England and a consequent sacralization of America as a New Israel, New England loomed in the Puritan imagination more modestly as a religious refuge—which some saw as only temporary—for *one* remnant of God's chosen people. The Puritan founders' writings are filled not with prophetic language exalting New England as a city on a hill but with the rhetoric of refuge and exile befitting an uprooted English people. "New England," Reverend Francis Higginson speculated in 1629, "might be designed by Heaven as a *refuge* and *shelter* for the non-conformists against the storms that were coming upon [England]." Similarly, John Winthrop wrote to his wife in 1629, "If the Lord seeth it will be good for us, he will provide a shelter and a hiding place." In bidding farewell to English migrants in 1631, Thomas Hooker, who would later sail to America and help establish the colony of Connecticut, reinforced the common Puritan view that "New England shall be a refuge for his Noahs and his Lots, a rock and a shelter for his righteous ones to run unto."[56]

However appealing it has been for historians and politicians to trace the lineaments of an American civil religion to the founders of New England, these Puritans were first and foremost displaced English religious reformers. Rather than self-assured millennialists embarking on a historically redemptive world mission, the Puritan founders more commonly saw themselves as colonial exiles; they strove to reestablish in New England the rudiments of the familiar world they had left behind and thus to ease their sense of an exiled English people.[57] To be sure, a religious mission inspired the families, friends, and fellow church members who comprised the Puritan exodus to brave an ocean crossing and the rocky shoals of coastal New England. But the Puritan founders framed this religious mission within a reformist vision that embraced the homeland. "It hath been no small inducement to us to choose rather to remove hither than to stay there," John Cotton reflected after settling in New England, "that we might enjoy the liberty, not of some ordinances of God, but of all, and all in purity."[58] New England enticed the Puritans not only as a prospective second England for fertility where traditional local customs would be safeguarded. New England also arose in the founders' imagination as a purified English Protestant preserve where reformed, even primitive, Christian ordinances would be harbored in anticipation of their reexportation to ancestral shores.

The Puritan architects of New England, one revisionist historian perceptively observes, "did not claim to forge a revolutionary new order but to revive an earlier past." They were engaged in an "errand of recovery." [59] The Puritan religious mission to New England, then, appears as a component of a larger restorationist campaign associated with an idealized English past. The recovery of purified religious ordinances was of a piece with a longing to protect ancient local liberties and to regenerate the English social order by "restoring" industry, discipline, and competency. The founders conceived of New England as a religious and social refuge where transplanted English colonists would be able "to live ancient lives." [60]

Of course, not all English dissenters who crossed the Atlantic in the 1630s found refuge in Puritan New England. Some were forced to the geographic and cultural margins of an emerging orthodox New England. The Puritans offered critics of the "New England Way" the "free Liberty to keep away from us." [61] Rhode Island became an "Isle of Errors" that still served a useful—perhaps even providential—purpose to the Puritans; its straggling settlements supplied intelligence on and served as a buffer against the sizable concentrations of Native Americans in the interior. The banished Roger Williams, for instance, helped secure the English-Narragansett alliance that decimated the Pequots. Yet Rhode Island was not part of a "new" England; instead, the Puritan imagination located tiny "Rogues Island" somewhere "between the devil and the deep blue sea." [62]

England also was perceived as an isle of errors, but the outbreak of the English civil war in the 1640s underscored the founders' intellectual and personal bonds to the homeland and their hopes for national redemption. The triumph of Puritan and parliamentary forces over the royal and ecclesiastical authorities who had harassed the exiles suggested to many New Englanders that the providential moment for England's restoration and for repatriation had arrived. In "A Dialogue between Old England and New" (1642), Anne Bradstreet, America's first published poet, recorded both her emotional investment in her native land and her hopes for English reform. New England consoled the mother country:

Dear Mother cease complaints & wipe your eyes;
Shake off your dust, chear up, and now arise,

You are my Mother Nurse, and I your flesh,
Your sunken bowels gladly would refresh,
Your griefs I pity, but soon hope to see,
Out of your troubles much good fruit to be;
To see those latter dayes of hop'd for good,
Though now beclouded all with tears and blood:
After dark Popery the day did clear,
But now the Sun in's brightness shall appear.[63]

While Bradstreet penned these lines, New England churches regularly appointed days of fast and prayer in support of the "blessed worke of a publique Reformation" in England. In a published sermon, *New England's Tears for Old England's Fears* (1641), Massachusetts minister William Hooke declared: "There is no land that claims our name, but England; we are distinguished from all nations in the world by the name of *English*. . . . Brethren! Did we not there draw in our first breath? . . . Did not that land first bear us, even that pleasant island, but for sin, I would say, that garden of the Lord, that paradise?"[64] Hooke left Massachusetts to enlist in the Puritan cause in England. Other founding clerical patriarchs along with hundreds of New Englanders remigrated in the 1640s and 1650s. Still countless others, inspired by the epochal events in England and prodded by friends at home, barely resisted the pull to return. Repatriated Puritans reported back to America that it was "a matter of high account to have been a New English man" in revolutionary England.[65]

The abrupt end of Puritan migration into New England eroded the economic boom—a significant decline in the sale of land and foodstuffs ensued, for example—that had brought prosperity to the founding decade. New England suffered through the first recession in its history. Economic dislocation, the halt of migration, ongoing remigration, and continuing expressions of disillusionment with the New World environment and climate by repatriated settlers—all these developments fostered a sense of crisis concerning New England's meaning in the 1640s and 1650s.[66] Of course, the vast majority of New Englanders, who had invested money and toil in homes, fields, and herds of livestock and who had begun raising American-born children, chose to stay. It devolved upon the Puritan clerics to explain New England's abiding purpose and identity.

Puritan leaders remained hopeful but increasingly cautious as they learned of the tumult in England leading up to the beheading of the king in 1649. Far from fleeing the homeland, "like mice from a crumbling house," and "treacherously giving up the defense of the common cause of Reformation," John Cotton suggested in 1648, New England's Puritans had instituted Congregational self-government and established churches that required a saving test for admission, furnishing a restorationist model for English reformers. New England had fulfilled its religious mission—to purge English Protestantism and preserve a re-pristinated Christianity.[67] Cotton and other distinguished Puritan divines drafted the *Cambridge Platform* (1648), which codified and explained New England reform for English edification. Self-congratulation sometimes mingled with proscription in New England Puritan tracts of the 1640s and 1650s. Custodians of a purified Protestantism, New Englanders needed to persevere in their mission while the burden of advancing the Reformation shifted to England, where accelerating discord and bloodshed muddled the providential meaning of civil strife.

Beyond closely monitoring English events and reasserting the relationship of New England's religious mission to the homeland in the 1640s and 1650s, Puritan divines cultivated a heretofore recessive element in the colonies' reason for existence: the conversion of Native Americans. After all, the original seal of the Massachusetts Bay Company depicted a Native American with the words, "Come Over and Help Us." Promotional literature from the late sixteenth century through the Puritan founding of New England singled out missionary work as one of the primary purposes of colonization. Not until the 1640s, however, when unsettling change compelled reaffirmation of New England's purpose and countless Native Americans had died of disease and gunfire, did conversion of the aboriginal population emerge rhetorically as an important aspect of the Puritans' religious mission. As the anonymous author of *New England's First Fruits* put it in 1643, "Let the world know, that God led not so many thousands of his people into the Wilderness, to see a reed shaken with the wind, but amongst many other special ends, this was not the least, to spread the light of the blessed Gospel, to such as never heard the sound of it."[68] Presumably, the thousands of Native Americans who perished from providential plagues that gave God's saints elbow room were not fit subjects for conversion.

The renewed promotion of New England in the context of the changed circumstances of the 1640s and 1650s reveals a defensiveness and even a pride of place that betoken, perhaps, the beginnings of an *American* Puritan identity. The author of *New England's First Fruits* combatively dismissed remigrants' faultfinding with New England: "Did not some doe so of the Land of *Canaan* it selfe, yet *Canaan* was never the worse and themselves smarted for so doing."[69] *New England's First Fruits* and the disquieting alterations of the 1640s inspired what has been identified as America's first folk song. "New England's Annoyances" (1643) satirized the alleged deficiencies of the region — from climate to diet:

> Instead of pottage and puddings and custards and pies,
> Our pumpkins and parsnips are common supplies;
> We have pumpkin at morning and pumpkin at noon,
> If it was not for pumpkins we should be undone.

In the face of religious upheaval at home, remigration, and new questions about the Puritan colonies' abiding purpose, "New England's Annoyances" lauded the endurance of the region's founders. Moreover, the song concluded with an orthodox Puritan endorsement of New England's unbroken providential promise:

> But you who the Lord intends hither to bring,
> Forsake not the honey for fear of the sting;
> But bring both a quiet and contented mind,
> And all needful blessings you surely shall find.[70]

"New England's Annoyances" and tracts such as *New England's First Fruits* intimate the stirrings of an Americanized regional identity in the 1640s and 1650s. But culturally and emotionally, the members of New England's founding generation remained English colonial exiles. The passing of the founders, the emergence of a new generation that had never known the homeland, and the collapse of the Puritan revolution in England all promoted the development of an Americanized regional identity after 1660. Yet this process of Americanization proved to be only a prelude to a sweeping re-Anglicization of New England's self-image in the first half of the eighteenth century.

From the Americanization to the Re-Anglicization of Regional Identity, 1660–1760

The transplanted English Puritans who seized physical and imaginative possession of New England created a regional identity that did not meet the cultural needs of the second generation. These descendants of the founders had never known the homeland. Moreover, the demise of the Puritan movement in England after the civil war of the 1640s and 1650s and the restoration of the monarchy in 1660 contributed to the religious isolation of New England. This growing perception of New World isolation was reinforced by the absence of any significant English migration to New England in the second half of the seventeenth century. The Congregational ministry became filled with native-born graduates of Harvard College, not English products of Cambridge University. Second-generation Puritans Americanized New England identity. They located an idealized past not in an ancestral homeland but in the founding and early history of New England, fashioning an epic account of regional origins that encouraged a new sense of place and a local patriotism that was characteristic of evolving colonial identities.

Yet this process of Americanization was not the culmination of New England's identity in the colonial era. In fact, Americanization was short-lived. From the turn of the eighteenth century through the decades leading to revolution, New England underwent sweeping re-Anglicization. England, determined to have more than a paper empire, tightened political control of its colonies. At the same time, increasing transatlantic trade opened new routes that not only spurred commercial interaction between Old and New England but also established pathways for English cultural influence. In addition, the great Anglo-American victory over the French at midcentury, which secured English control of North America, excited New England pride in British identity. These and other developments compelled third- and fourth-generation Puritans to reimagine New England identity in ways that reconciled narratives of the region's heroic religious past with eighteenth-century British imperial realities.

The Americanization of Regional Identity, 1660–1690

An Americanized voice emerges from "New England's Annoyances" (1643) and *Wonder-Working Providence of Sions Saviour in New England* (1654). The first American folk song and the first history of Massachusetts were both the work of Edward Johnson. A migrant to New England in 1630, Johnson helped found Woburn, held town offices, became militia captain, and served in the Massachusetts General Court. He was one of the pioneering civilian patriarchs of Puritan New England. His *Wonder-Working Providence* extols a short but glorious history in which Johnson felt very much a participant.

Johnson summons the image of a "hideous," "howling desart wilderness," not the fertile *new* England of Puritan promotional literature. The middle-class migrants who typically journeyed to New England with the familiar faces of kin, neighbors, and fellow church members acquire a more heroic identity in Johnson's account. The "generality of these men were meane and poore," he observes. As pioneering Puritans, they "foresooke a fruitful Land, stately Buildings, a goodly Gardens, Orchards, yea, deare Friends and neere relations" and settled in "this howling wilderness desart." But like ancient "chosen Israel," New England benefited from an "Ocean" of providential "Mercies." The "miraculous" emergence of a new England seemed to coincide with the revolutionary upheaval in the homeland. Clearly, the founders comprised "an Army out of our English Nation," soldiers of Christ who established "a New England to muster up the first of his Forces in." Johnson and his fellow new English Puritans retreated to the safety of the New World awaiting "a fresh opportunity to engage with the main battell of Antichrist, so soon as the Lord shall be pleased to give a Word of Command."[1]

On the one hand, Johnson remained a transplanted Englishman, using the ancestral land as a kind of surveyor's mark from which he could measure New England's cultural progress and record its providential history. He embraced the promise of the Puritan revolution in England, hoping that it might lead to the historical redemption of the exiles' retreat into their American wilderness refuge. But Johnson was far from convinced that events at home represented the "main Battell" with the Antichrist. *Wonder-Working Providence* unfurls not only the history of God's benedictions on New England; it proclaims Johnson's pride in the founders' accomplishments—and thus in his own. As he revealed in "New England's Annoyances," Johnson grew impatient with migrants who hastily quit New England, even if it was to join the Puritan cause at home. The founders' purpose endured "to rebuild the most glorious Edifice of Mount Sion in a Wilderness."[2]

Both *Wonder-Working Providence* and "New England's Annoyances" reaffirm the Puritans' founding mission; but just as important, they register the pride of place that evolves in colonial settings, particularly among members of the second generation. Historians who study the development of colonial societies have noted the growth of "a local patriotism that was essential to the formation of a collective self-image" among a colonial people. Colonists came to recognize that their "newly adopted land, though initially strange, had distinctive beauties of its own."[3] Michael Wigglesworth, the Puritan minister-poet who had arrived in Massachusetts in 1638 at the age of seven, expressed this emergent pride of place in 1662, even as he warned the second generation of the moral infirmities that threatened the region:

> Ah dear New England! dearest land to me;
>   Which unto God hast hitherto been dear,
> And mayst still be more dear than formerlie,
>   If to his voice thou wilt incline thine ear.[4]

Both Wigglesworth's and Johnson's early local patriotism derived primarily from the purified religious ordinances that were planted in New England and the productive pastoral society that accompanied such reform. But even distinctive New World "annoyances" could be a source of pride. "[L]et no man make jest of Pumpkins," Johnson wrote in *Wonder-Working Providence* of what had already become a regional symbol, "for with this fruit the Lord was pleased to feed his people to their good content, till Corne and Cattell were increased."[5]

In his local patriotism and his incipient mythologizing of New England's founding—representing the landscape as nothing but a barren desert wilderness, for example — Johnson anticipated lines of interpretation that would constitute the second generation's redrawn collective self-image. Following Johnson, second-generation writers employed history to reconfigure regional identity. But for the second generation, even more than for Johnson, an idealized New England past replaced English history as the locus of the formative events shaping regional identity. Johnson worried that God's "multitude" of mercies was "being already forgotten"; New England's brief, glorious history needed to be recorded for the sake of the founders and "their children's children." After 1660, however, the preservation of historical memory became a ritualized preoccupation and served as the handmaiden of regional restoration — a cultural drive for renewal that held up the founding of New England as an epoch comparable to biblical times and that produced American types of Aaron, Moses, and Nehemiah.[6]

The second generation thus historicized and Americanized their parents' collective identity. The historical account, the jeremiad, and even the Native American captivity narrative replaced promotional writings as the primary textual sites where New England was reimagined. The founders' descendants fashioned an inspirational, heroic historical narrative of New England's settlement. The Puritans' exodus from their debauched homeland became a "Great Migration," an epic, redemptive "errand" into a "howling desert wilderness" that was unimproved by Native American inhabitants. Such a mythologized historical account altered the founders' sense of New England as one subdivision of a transatlantic *spiritual* New Israel. The founders' offspring increasingly described the region as a place-bound "New English Israel," a land geographically distinct from and even morally superior to Old England. Moreover, a sense of moral isolation in combination with widely propagated didactic narratives of New England's origins fostered the American-born generation's New World pride of place. Most important, for second-generation clerical and lay writers the mythologized history of the New English Israel's settlement offered a useable past — a past that would redefine and shore up regional identity in response to the changing landscape of Puritan life.

After 1660 the shifting circumstances of New England colonial life encouraged the Americanization of regional identity. The collapse of the Puritan revolution and the restoration in England of the monarchy, and thus of Anglicanism, dissolved any lingering hope that ongoing Protestant reform would succeed in the ancestral land the way it had in New England. Some Puritans who had remigrated to England went into hiding under the Restoration; others returned to New England. As "Sion's Outcast" New England appeared as a New Israel, morally isolated from the spiritual wilderness of the world and bound in a special covenant with God. The founders' progeny, like "the seed of Abraham" and "the children of Jacob his chosen," one clerical historian admonished his readers in 1669, risked divine retribution if they failed to recollect God's "marvellous works *in the beginning and progress of the planting of New-England.*"[7]

The second generation's new, even provincial sense of moral isolation in America was reinforced by the demographic realities of New England life. In the first place, death increasingly silenced the Puritan founders, who carried their attachment to England to their graves. New migrants did not arrive to replace the founding generation. The Puritan settlement of New England in the 1630s appeared to the second generation as a Great Migration in part because the region did not become a magnet for new colonists during the rest of the seventeenth century. In fact, in the 1680s and 1690s New England experienced more out- than in-migration.[8] The second generation was comprised overwhelmingly of a native-born population, descendants of the founders with slender personal and cultural ties to England.

New England's population swelled by natural increase to 93,000 by the turn of the eighteenth century. This demographic growth altered the texture of life precisely at the time restorationist historical narratives became such a shaping element in regional identity. Population growth fueled land hunger. In contrast to colonies such as Virginia, where primogeniture prevailed, New England fathers divided property among all or most sons. With large families and multiple sons to settle, land acquisition became one of the constants of New England life, threatening to destabilize traditional notions of competency and sufficiency. "Land! Land!" complained Increase Mather, "[It] hath been the idol of many in New England. Whereas the first planters . . . were satisfied with one acre for each person, and after that with twenty acres for a family, how have men since coveted the earth."[9]

Mather certainly oversimplified the competency of the first generation as part of his strategy to arrest what he and others saw as the religious declension of his era. But far more than the fevered imagination of a still culturally powerful clergy accounts for the social criticism and rhetoric of declension so characteristic of the historical-minded second generation. For in addition to a new sense of moral and cultural isolation from England, the second generation also confronted the reality of secular colonial development that posed a challenge to New England's religious origins and identity. Population growth, increased commercial trade, land hunger, and the surge of contention and litigiousness that accompanied such changes provoked concerns that Puritan New England was gradually succumbing to "Rhode Islandism."[10] Moreover, the emergence of what Puritan authorities labeled "the profane"—secular elements pursuing essentially economic ends—reinforced fears of a corrupting licentiousness commonly associated with the Isle of Errors, that "sewer of New England," as one prominent Puritan descendant of the founders characterized Rhode Island.[11] From the fishermen who established temporary settlements in coastal Maine and New Hampshire preceding permanent colonizers to servants who accompanied the Puritan migrants, New England had long sheltered the profane. But expanding trade and the growth of port towns during the seventeenth century produced highly visible concentrations of New Englanders who resided, often boastfully, outside the Puritan fold. One Marblehead fisherman mocked Puritan authorities by "vowing to have his dog baptized."[12] The profane substituted the tavern for the meetinghouse. By the late seventeenth century, taverns far outnumbered meetinghouses in some port towns. In 1681 Bostonians supported forty-five taverns. "New England" rum—a by-product of trade with the West Indies where molasses was produced—had already begun to replace beer and ale as the drink of choice, with a resulting increase in drunkenness in Boston and other port towns.[13]

Not surprisingly, drunkenness was added to acquisitiveness, contentiousness, and a perceived growth of religious indifference as evidence of Puritan New England's declension and nascent Rhode Islandism. The course of colonial development, combined with the second generation's cultural distance from England, intensified both regional self-consciousness and official apprehension that New England's distinctive moral identity was threatened by the corrosive forces of economic ambition. History was pressed into the service of filiopietism, cultural preservation, and social regeneration. The prolific writers of the second generation created a grand *American* narrative of New England's origins that mythologized the first generation and that continues to obscure the realities of early life in the region.

Consider, for instance, the second generation's historical account of the New England landscape that the founders encountered. Promotional goals no longer shaped representation of the New World environment, nor did the cultural need to imaginatively assimilate an alien land to the familiar pastoral England that migrants had left behind. The settlement landscape was now recalled as a barren tract, a "howling wilderness," an "American Desart." Of course, such symbolic rhetoric conveyed religious meaning; wilderness and desert described the moral and spiritual emptiness of the New World—underscoring the providential test that the New Israelites confronted in America. But, as Edward Johnson demonstrated, wilderness and desert also acquired a literal meaning. They portrayed a historic landscape as it was imagined in the second generation and beyond—a New World stage where the heroic drama of New England's settlement unfolded.

Early accounts of the openness of New England receded into obscurity. Only recently have we recovered the extensive Native American reworking of the land, including controlled burning that cleared fields for planting and hunting. Such Native American changes on the land, however, did not serve the didactic, filiopietistic historical narratives of the second generation the way they aided the promotional and survival needs of the founders. Even Plymouth, established at the site of a recently decimated Native American village, came to be described simply "as a place (they supposed) fitt for situation; at least it was the best they [the settlers] could find."[14] Only the heroic labor of the New Israelites, assisted by Providence, transformed the howling desert-wilderness of New England into a New Canaan within one generation.

The notion of the Great Migration to New England undergirded the second generation's didactic story of the region's founding. As historians have recently pointed out, the Puritan settlement of New England was overshadowed numerically by the tens of thousands of English migrants who forsook the homeland during the seventeenth century and resettled in Ireland or in a southern or Caribbean colony. More than one hundred thousand migrants, for example, journeyed to England's southern colonies and well over twice that number to its Caribbean island colonies.[15] Unlike other English colonies, New England did not experience sustained, sizable in-migration after the early 1640s, which encouraged the second generation to recall the pioneering settlement of the region as a great historical event.

But the colonization of New England evolved in the second generation's historical imagination as a Great Migration not primarily as a consequence of its size but because of the spiritual motives of the individual settlers and the overarching religious mission of their New Israel. The notion of the Great Migration served to remind an increasingly commercial age that New England, as a historical successor to ancient Israel, stood above other English colonies as a religious enterprise. "Let merchants and such as are increasing Cent per Cent" not lose sight of New England's lofty founding purpose, John Higginson urged in *The Cause of God and His People in New England* (1664). "It was not for worldly wealth, or a better livelyhood here for the outward man" that the founders journeyed into the American wilderness, Higginson insisted. "My Fathers and Brethren, this is never to be forgotten, that *New England is originally a plantation of Religion, not a plantation of Trade.*" Six years later, in *New-Englands True Interest,* William Stoughton commemorated the *"pious and religious Parents, the Lord's faithful Covenanting Servants"* who comprised the Great Migration. "They are a *holy Root* unto their Seed," he exhorted the pioneers' descendants, "and the Lord may well expect that the Branches should be answerable to the Root." Stoughton memorably summarized what the Great Migration had come to mean: "God sifted a whole Nation that he might send choice Grain over into the Wilderness." [16]

The exiled founders who had sought shelter, refuge, a hiding place in New England had never called their exodus from their homeland a great migration. Nor had they represented their measured religious purpose as an "errand into the wilderness." But after Samuel Danforth addressed the Massachusetts General Court in 1670 with the sermon, *A Brief Recognition of New-Englands Errand into the Wilderness,* the phrase joined the Great Migration as a widely employed historical shorthand for the official story of New England's founding. The Puritan errand into the wilderness signaled a new "theology of place" that buttressed the developing local patriotism of second-generation colonials. New England became, Danforth and other ministers reiterated, the biblical "Candlesticks" that represented the primitive Christian churches: the redeeming light of God's chosen people in the spiritual wilderness of the world that now even seemed to include England. In short, though the second generation did not abandon the understanding of New Israel as embracing a transatlantic and even universal church of believers that transcended geographic boundaries, the rhetorical power of the Great Migration and the errand into the wilderness meant that New England came increasingly to be imagined as a historically and theologically exceptional place. Founded for religious purposes, shaped by reformed religious ordinances, and peopled by a heroic generation with a disproportionate number of saints who carried God's "Candlesticks" to the New World, New England was a most favored nation with

1670 Errand into the Wilderness

an historical claim as a New Israel.[17] If the roots of national sanctimony and a civil religion that sacralized New World beginnings reside in Puritan New England, they may be located in the second generation's revisionist, Americanized account of regional origins, not in the historical consciousness and cultural baggage that first-generation English migrants transported into exile. (Eighteenth-century re-Anglicization, however, would disrupt linear historical progress toward an American identity; as we shall see, the homeland would be fully reincorporated into the New English Israel.)

The second generation's high-flown rhetoric of a Great Migration and an errand into the wilderness has encouraged scholars to read back into the first generation the new theology of place that revised New England's religious identity in the second half of the seventeenth century. John Winthrop's "city upon a hill" thus became the earliest proclamation of America's moral isolationism and historical exceptionalism. But such a reading diminishes the generational divide that separated Winthrop's and Danforth's sense of place. Winthrop led *English* migrants to a New World exile; Danforth spoke to their American sons and daughters increasingly self-conscious of their New England identity.

The second generation's regional identity was not rooted in what can be dismissed as a historical fiction of New England's origins and its exceptionalism. Literate middle-class families dominated the settlement of the region, setting New England apart from other New World colonial societies. The staying power — even down to the present — of the second generation's heroic historical narrative of regional identity arose not only from the prolific literary output of the founders' descendants and from inventive, redolent phrases like the Great Migration, the errand into the wilderness, and God's New English Israel. The persuasiveness of the second generation's didactic account of regional origins and distinctiveness also derived from its factual underpinnings. Terms such as the Great Migration were not historical fictions or propagandistic inventions of still ascendant Puritan cultural authorities. Rather, like the recollection of the New England landscape as a desert-wilderness, they were "partial truths," stories whose inclusions and exclusions were shaped by the second generation's need to understand and deploy its history to revise regional identity in the face of the new realities of colonial life.[18]

In many respects the peopling of New England and the accomplishments of the first generation did comprise a Great Migration. But the second generation invoked the term to mythologize early New England history. The Great Migration eliminated the pioneers' uncertainty, bewilderment, and disappointment as well as their record of remigration. The founders became legendary religious figures shorn of their mortal dimensions as English folk engaged in the quotidian tasks of building a life in exile and warding off the disillusionment with early New England that Puritan poet Anne Bradstreet acknowledged. Bradstreet's "heart rose" in silent rebellion against the "new world and new manners" that she encountered in a region that seemed to fall short of a second England.[19]

The second generation's notion of an "errand into the wilderness" bolstered the heroic mythology of the Great Migration and enlarged the Puritans' original religious mission. New England had offered the founders a shelter and a hiding place, where pure religious ordinances could be established and safeguarded in anticipation of renewed reform at home. The second generation reimagined this mission as an errand into an American wilderness to erect a place-bound New Israel, an isolated "Candlestick" that illumined a spiritually barren world. Moreover, by envisioning the errand as establishing a plantation for religion not for trade, the second generation oversimplified, even distorted, the early history of New England. (One result has been a running historical controversy about the relative importance of economics and religion in the original migrants' motives for coming to the New World.) The errand into the wilderness became a metaphor that seemed to separate religion and economics, the sacred and the secular. Although it served the restorationist aims of the second generation, the metaphor tended to misrepresent the founders' unwillingness to compartmentalize their colonial endeavor. Puritan promotional literature, for instance, stressed the potential productivity of a fertile *new* England, though economic aspirations were constrained by a religious culture that promoted competency.

Most important, the second generation's interpretation of New England's founding as a redemptive religious errand into the wilderness overlooked the economic reality of early life in the region. Land hunger and speculation certainly accelerated during the second generation, encouraging histories and sermons that idealized the founders' seemingly purer religious motives. But land hunger is inscribed in the earliest New England records as a kind of regional birthmark. As early as 1635 the Massachusetts General Court issued an order regulating the settlement of new towns in response to the dispersal of land-seeking migrants: "hereafter noe dwelling house shalbe builte above halfe a myle from the meeting house, in any newe plantation, graunted at this Court, or hereafter to be graunted, without leave from the Court, (except myll houses & fferme [farm] houses of such as have their dwelling houses in same towne)." A year later, after repeated complaints about the quality and limited size of land allotted to them, more than eight hundred Puritan migrants abandoned eastern Massachusetts and founded Connecticut. They were drawn to the Connecticut River Valley, where they established the towns of Wethersfield, Windsor, and Hartford, by reports of abundant fertile land that seemed to fulfill the promise of Puritan promotional literature.[20] The second generation's edifying narrative of a heroic religious errand into the wilderness elided this record of initial disappointment, land hunger, economic ambition, and population dispersal.

Similarly, the second generation's mythologized account of New England's founding erased evidence of first-generation avarice that had threatened to subvert Puritan competency. The case of Robert Keayne did not serve the second generation's sacred script of the Great Migration and the errand into the wilderness. For in 1639 Keayne, a devout Puritan and Boston import merchant, was heavily fined for price gouging and then censured by the First Church for "selling his wares at excessive Rates, to the Dishonor of Gods name, the Offence of the General Court, and the Publique scandall of the Country."[21] Keayne may have been a first-generation exception; after all, he was harshly criticized and punished. But John Winthrop thought otherwise, suggesting that Keayne may have been singled out as an example. Of the Boston merchant's celebrated case, Winthrop noted that "all men through the country [were] guilty of the like excess of prices."[22] Such a frank acknowledgment of early Puritan economic ambition, even by the man whom the second generation saw as an American Moses, failed to temper the high-flown, inspirational rhetoric that purged the founders' religious errand of any worldly taint.

The leaders of the second generation employed, and invented, new cultural means for transmitting their Americanized and historicized understanding of New England's collective identity. The Native American captivity narrative was one of their cultural inventions. The Puritan captivity narrative emerged in the aftermath of King Philip's War, in 1675–76, the Native American rebellion incited by the Wampanoag sachem known to his people as Metacomet. The war destroyed more than a dozen towns, took the lives of hundreds of white residents, and exacted an even higher price from southern New England's Native Americans. The devastating struggle came to be seen as providential chastisement, followed by deliverance, for a backsliding New English Israel (Figure 2). From King

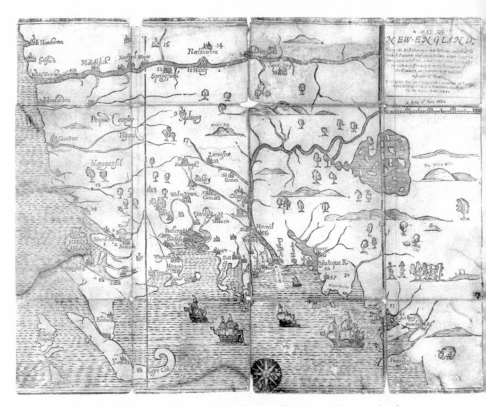

FIGURE 2. John Foster, "Map of New England" (1677). This was the first map printed in America. An illustration of Foster's woodcut, the map appeared in William Hubbard, *A Narrative and the Troubles with the Indians in New England* (Boston, 1677). Through numbers and fortresslike symbols it documents the widespread attacks of King Philip's War (1675–76), but it also offers a visual representation of New England's triumph over this "affliction." Courtesy of the Osher Map Library, University of Southern Maine.

Philip's War through subsequent conflicts with Native Americans and their French allies, Puritan ministers, who continued to dominate access to publication, seized on the captivity narrative, shaping its content and conventions to bolster orthodoxy and the Americanized narrative of New England identity. Not surprisingly, captivity narratives became one of the most popular forms of writing in late seventeenth- and early eighteenth-century New England.

Mary Rowlandson's *The Soveraignty and Goodness of God* (1682) stands as the archetype of the genre. The daughter of participants in the Great Migration, Rowlandson married a minister and settled in Lancaster, Massachusetts. In early 1676 King Philip's warriors attacked the town and captured Rowlandson and others. After eleven weeks during which she traveled and camped with the enemy, Rowlandson was ransomed in May. Apparently advised by her husband, and perhaps by other clerics, Rowlandson fashioned her ordeal into an enormously popular and inspirational frontier adventure tale that became a New England cultural epic.[23]

Much has been written about how Rowlandson's narrative is an allegory of the Puritan conversion process. Her capture becomes a journey into the spiritual wilderness of her own soul. Captivity awakens her to the moral deficiencies and spiritual complacency of her previous life. She comes to accept captivity as a deserved providential affliction—functioning as a stand-in for the larger Puritan community that needed to accept the war as an instrument of God's wrath. After initial acceptance of her moral predicament, Rowlandson confronts new crises that test her faith and finds herself in close combat with despair. Through constant policing of her emotions, she cultivates a Job-like patience, places her faith in God, and is finally saved from her captivity to sin and its specter of consignment to hell.

Though Rowlandson and her clerical sponsors shaped her ordeal and deliverance into a didactic spiritual pilgrimage, her account incorporated far more than the moral geography of Puritan conversion. It evoked the physical landscape of New England in a way that reenacted the founding Puritan errand into the wilderness. Rowlandson and her contemporaries were members of a postheroic generation. They had not abandoned home, braved a "vast and furious ocean," and faced a "howling desart wilderness." In short, the first generation's heroic New World deeds were magnified by the fact that its migrating members had a "geographical correlate" to their religious pilgrimage.[24] Their spiritual quest was bound up with a real journey to the New World.

Captivity became a way for members of the second generation such as Rowlandson to acquire heroic status through a physical journey–spiritual pilgrimage that rehearsed the cultural mythology of New England's founding. Consider Rowlandson's departure from Lancaster and its parallels to the forced exodus of her father's generation: "I must turn my back upon the town, and travel with them [the Native Americans] in the vast and desolate wilderness, I know not wither. . . . God was with me in a wonderful manner, carrying me along, and bearing up my spirit, that it did not quite fail." Leaving behind the bounded pastoral English order of Lancaster, she is thrust into the kind of primeval landscape that the second generation imagined its ancestors had encountered. Rowlandson evokes what she variously characterizes as a "desolate wilderness" and a "howling wilderness," the landscape associated with the legendary era of the Great Migration. The marauding Native Americans, skulking from encampment to encampment, leave no lasting improvement on the land. Rowlandson's epic journey reenacts an imagined founding errand into the wilderness even to the point where survival requires the temporary adoption of Native American ways; she is forced to eat such fare as boiled horse's feet and broth thickened with bark. As with the founding generation, Rowlandson's survival in a new colonial world raises the fear of cultural degeneration. Her "restoration," then, embraces not only religious salvation but cultural deliverance as well.[25]

Representing the Puritan community as a whole, Rowlandson, through her ordeal, reasserts the second generation's identity as God's New English Israel. "Oh, that my People had hearkened to Me," she quotes the Bible, "and Israel had walked in My ways, I should soon have subdued their enemies, and turned My hand against their adversaries."[26] Her restoration parallels the larger New English victory in King Philip's War. Both triumphs reaffirm New England as the home of a "peculiar people." Rowlandson's personal trial and the communal tribulation that precedes deliverance from the conflict with King Philip certify that God reserves His reforming rod for those from whom He expects so much.

Rowlandson's captivity narrative thus bears the imprint of the jeremiad —the most powerful second-generation medium for mythologizing regional history and reconfiguring regional identity. Unlike the captivity narrative, the jeremiad was not a New England Puritan cultural invention. A ritualized sermon of chastisement summoning a covenanted people to reform their ways and appease divine wrath, the jeremiad, as recent scholarship has stressed, was a staple of English Protestantism that underpinned the first generation's decision to abandon the homeland. For England had been originally conceived as a covenanted nation—God's chosen people—and the recipient of special divine judgments and mercies, a collective identity that animated the reforming impulse of English Protestantism. In large measure, the founders of New England forsook the ancestral homeland precisely because of the national covenant. The English Church and people, far from engaging in continuing Puritan reform, came to be seen as a corrupt, backsliding nation about to be visited with divine afflictions equal to its breaches of providential expectations. New England offered a hiding place from divine displeasure where a remnant of God's chosen nation—England—could prosecute reform and wait out the convulsions at home.[27]

The founding generation's indictment of England resembles the jeremiads of the second generation with their sweeping arraignment of a backsliding chosen people—the New English Israelites. But second-generation writers Americanized the jeremiad. First, their inspirational rhetoric encouraged the imaginative relocation of the covenanted nation —the New Israel—to the New World. But, as one scholar has persuasively argued, the second generation also transferred to America the "golden age of religion" against which decline was to be measured and the restoration of piety modeled. For the founding generation, England had backslid from the initial promise of the Protestant Reformation and from its efforts to restore purified, biblically based ordinances that recaptured the pristine piety of early Christianity. For second-generation American Puritans, New England's founding era emerged "as Protestantism's finest hour," a revival of reformed, "primitive" Christianity whose patriarchs acquired an identity comparable to the fathers of the early Christian church.[28] In short, the Americanization of the jeremiad involved the geographic relocation of the national covenant to the New World and the historical relocation of the idealized heroic era of primitive Christian piety to New England's settlement.

This Americanization of English religious tradition transformed the jeremiad into the second generation's most potent medium for mythologizing New England's creation. Rather than on Sunday, when theology and spiritual conversion preoccupied Puritan preachers, the jeremiad was reserved for ritualized occasions—fast and thanksgiving days, like those sparked by King Philip's War, and colonial election ceremonies, when members of the new governing body convened with ministers for moral instruction. Such "civic preaching" became institutionalized in the Puritan strongholds of Massachusetts and Connecticut, with addresses typically prepared for publication and directed at a wide audience.[29] Consequently, the jeremiad's interpretive conventions of a heroic settlement, followed by generational decline, and providential afflictions infiltrated poetry, the captivity narrative, and Puritan historical works.

The second generation relied on the jeremiad, more than any other Puritan form of expression, to perform the cultural work of negotiating and propagating New England's revised, historicized identity. The jeremiad spoke to the second generation's new cultural and religious isolation from England. It responded to the real and perceived growth in the worldliness of colonial life—helping ministers, for example, patrol the shifting borders of competency in an age of increased commercial activity and land speculation. Above all, the jeremiad ritualistically explained the crises of the second generation like King Philip's War as providential judgments on a backsliding covenanted people.

The numerous judgments on the sons and daughters only made New England's founding era seem like an unprecedented age of divine mercies and thus of religious piety. Weather problems, for instance, came to be seen as providential afflictions on the second generation. Diarists recorded how New England's weather turned sharply colder in the 1680s and 1690s. Puritans accepted that the "intemperature of the aire, yce, thunder, unseasonable raines, drouthe, hailes, and what soever is extraordinarie in the world, are the fruites of sinne." [30] One second-generation minister in Connecticut attributed a drought to New England's spiritual aridity: "If God rain not righteousness on you it may be expected that he will rain something else," he admonished the laity. "Seek this gentle rain that the storm of his wrath [will] fall not upon you." [31] Similarly, Puritan minister-poet Michael Wigglesworth composed a jeremiad in verse in 1662 in reaction to a severe drought. In the voice of God, Wigglesworth rehearsed the heroic epic of the Great Migration and questioned the diminished piety of his contemporaries:

> Are these the men that erst at my command
>   Forsook their ancient seats and native soile,
> To follow me into a desart land,
>   Condemning all the travell and toile,
> Whose love was such to purest ordinances
>   As made them set at nought fair inheritances?

As with the captivity narrative, the movement in Wigglesworth's jeremiad paralleled individual conversion, progressing from judgment to awakening, despair, acceptance, reformation, hope, and salvation. Wigglesworth, speaking with the authority of God, concludes with an assertion of New England's chosenness:

> Cheer on, sweet souls, my heart is with you all,
>   And shall be with you, maugre Sathan's might:
> And whereso'ere this body be a thrall,
>   Still in New-England shall be my delight.[32]

The rhetorical flogging of the second generation concludes in the reaffirmation of the region as God's New English Israel.

The Puritans' God employed other means, beyond Native American warfare, natural disasters, and a worsening climate, to smite a backsliding second generation. In November 1676, as New England still coped with the aftermath of King Philip's War, a devastating fire ravaged the center of Boston. Charred buildings, including the Second Church, seemed to proclaim continuing divine displeasure with the town's failure to restore the piety of its founders. Eight years later England thrust itself into colonial affairs, threatening to transform New England's political landscape and imposing the most serious "affliction" on the second generation since King Philip's War. In 1684 the home government dissolved the Massachusetts Charter. English authorities then proceeded to organize all the settlements from Maine to New Jersey under the Dominion of New England headed by a royally appointed governor, who clumsily sought to use Congregational meetinghouses for Church of England services and claimed the power to revoke land grants under the old charter (an appropriate menace for a generation's seeming absorption in land acquisition). Faced with an unprecedented assault on the founders' historical achievements, most Puritan ministers resisted direct political commentary—even election-day sermons ceased. Puritan preachers underscored the urgency of renewed personal piety and moral reform to preserve the region's spiritual identity as a New Israel, whatever final political arrangements emerged.[33]

In many respects, the clerical response to the Dominion extended the moral appeal enunciated by a synod of ministers several years earlier. In *The Necessity of Reformation* (1679), the ministers dispatched a blunt jeremiad that scattered incense on the founders as it cataloged the moral frailties of their sons and daughters. "What are the Evils that have provoked the Lord to bring his Judgements on New England?" the ministers asked. The second generation had forgotten "the errand upon which the Lord sent us hither . . . [and] is far short of those whom God saw meet to improve in laying the foundation of the Temple here." From Sabbath breaking to intemperance, the provoking transgressions could be traced to a corrupting worldliness: "There hath been in many professors an insatiable desire after Land, and worldly Accommodations. . . . Farms and merchandizing have been preferred before things of God."[34]

Reform would proceed from a collective acknowledgment of and rededication to New England's distinctive founding principles. For the region differed from other English colonial societies "in that it was not any worldly consideration that brought our fathers into this wilderness, but Religion."[35] The Reforming Synod seized on church covenant renewals as a principal instrument of reform. Such covenant renewals had been part of Puritan devotional life, but they acquired a new cultural currency with the second generation's Americanized jeremiad. Covenant renewals became ritualized restagings of New England's mythologized founding. The sons and daughters recited the original church covenants solemnized by their parents, signing their names to the sacred document just as heroic ancestors had done. These ceremonies, like the presentation of jeremiads during communal observances, added an element of performance to the second generation's creation of a historicized New England identity.

The campaign of covenant renewal promised to help arrest what the Reforming Synod deplored as the "degeneracy of the Rising Generation," the jeremiad's rhetorical foil for the mythologized founders. A discourse of descent, degeneration, even "Criolization" circulated through post-Restoration jeremiads, shaping the historicized collective identity of second-generation colonials. "Were our fathers as a *noble vine,* and shall we be as the degenerate plant of a strange vine?" William Stoughton challenged his audience in an election-day sermon in 1670. Stoughton imagined Judgment Day, when "There shall be brought forth a *Register of the Genealogies of New-Englands sons and daughters.* How shall we many of us hold up our faces then, when there shall be solemn rehearsal of our *descent* as well as our *degeneracies?*" Three years later Urian Oakes reiterated what was fast becoming the reigning biblically based trope of the jeremiad: New England's "Noble vine planted by the Lords own right hand is become degenerous." In *Pray for the Rising Generation* (1679), Increase Mather quoted Jeremiah and continued the incantation: "I planted thee a noble vine, wholly a right seed, how then art thou turned into the degenerate Plant of a strange vine unto me?"[36]

It remained for Increase Mather's son Cotton to incorporate "Criolian degeneracy"—cultural and racial crossbreeding—into the jeremiad's rhetorical arsenal. With the resumption of the election-day sermon in 1689, the twenty-six-year-old became the youngest minister to address the political and religious leaders of Massachusetts. In a sermon titled *The Way to Prosperity,* young Mather warned against the "want of education in the rising generation," a deficiency that threatened to "speedily dispose" New England to the "sort of Criolian degeneracy" that had corrupted other

New World colonial societies.[37] Mather apparently had in mind the colonies of New Spain, where cultural and racial interbreeding between Europeans and native people produced a "degenerate" colonial population that lived under the shadow of the imperial homeland. "Creolization" identified the geographic isolation, cultural inferiority, and racial threat posed by life on the colonial periphery. It spoke to common fears of colonization as a process of environmental-racial degeneration and cultural miscegenation that usually enabled home countries to view their colonies with considerable disdain. In short, Mather linked religious declension to a powerful discourse of colonial degeneration—creolization—that had more than a passing connection to the jeremiad's rhetoric of New England as a "degenerous" transplanted vine.

But the threat of creolization played out in an interesting way in Cotton Mather and perhaps in the jeremiad as a whole. In the first place, Mather referred only to a particular "sort" of creolean degeneracy, which had not yet engulfed New England. The founders' descendants, after all, did not interbreed with native people the way Spanish and French colonials did. Cultural crossbreeding, however, posed a more serious threat. The Americanized jeremiad of the second generation held up the founders as heroes precisely because they had resisted a corrupting creolization—especially in the form of cultural miscegenation, that is, "Indianization." The captivity narrative reenacted this triumphant resistance, and jeremiads continued to castigate Native American–like behavior. The 1679 Reforming Synod of ministers, for example, singled out the transgressions of land-hungry settlers in the New England outback who "forsake churches and ordinances, and [seem] to live like Heathen." Moreover, young Cotton Mather, who ascribed such "abominable things" as indolence and lax child rearing to Native Americans, used the jeremiad to put second-generation New Englanders on guard against a subversive colonial inclination to "Indianize."[38]

The New Englandized jeremiad, the Native American captivity narrative, the region's mythologized founding, the geographic relocation of the New Israel—all of these second-generation elements of a historicized regional identity amounted to a constructive creolization or Americanization of the founders' collective self-image. Not surprisingly, then, in his magisterial *Magnalia Christi Americana* (1702), a multivolume history of New England written in the decade after his election-day sermon, Cotton Mather, in a colonial American accent, spoke positively of a limited creolization. "I add hereunto, the Notables of the only Protestant University that ever *shone* in that hemisphere of the New World," Mather wrote of his volume on the history of Harvard College, "with particular instances of Criolians, in our biography, provoking the whole world with vertuous objects of emulation."[39] Harvard College reflected the safeguards that the first generation had established to thwart a corrupting creolization in New England: an educated ministry, government-supported local churches and schools, and a literate laity equipped to read the Bible and engage in moral self-improvement. Such traditions sustained Mather's local patriotism and American pride of place. "Indeed New England is not heaven, that we are sure of!" he granted. "But for my part, I do not ask to remove out of New England except for a removal into heaven."[40]

Preachers deployed the jeremiad's rhetoric of degeneration to revitalize traditional bulwarks against a corrosive process of colonial creolization. As long as the founders' civic-religious institutions and ordinances remained vital, New England would preserve its historical distinctiveness and moral advantage over both the imperial homeland and other colonies. New England's degeneration only loomed so large, jeremiads reassuringly stressed, because the region was held to a high moral standard—a standard that the mythologized founders had attained. "Our Lord Jesus Christ from Heaven may thus Argue with us," Cotton Mather pointed out, "*If other People do wound me by their Sins, 'tis not such a Wonderful and horrible Thing.*" But God used a different moral calculus for His "*People* of New England, *a People that . . . I have known above the Families of the Earth.*" Another Jeremiah prophesied that though the New Israel might "yet be more sinful & more miserable," once God asserted His sovereignty and afflicted a backsliding people, He "would again *restore, reform* and *bless* New England." As Increase Mather summarized the moral drama of the jeremiad, "the Lord may afflict us . . . but he will not destroy us."[41] The jeremiad swelled a rhetorical tide of declension that served primarily to buoy up the second generation's claim on the special destiny of New England. Thus, the jeremiad provided a civic medium for the second generation's historicizing and aggrandizing of New England's collective self-image—an identity that addressed the interpretive needs, and the apprehensions, of American or creole sons and daughters inhabiting a different colonial world from their parents.

Cotton Mather's *Magnalia Christi Americana* ("A History of the Wonderful Works of Christ in America") culminated the second generation's historical reinvention of New England—the remapping of regional identity that had been initiated by Edward Johnson's *Wonder-Working Providence* and that the jeremiad had expedited. The scope of Mather's work matched what had now become an epic, mythologized account of New England's origins and religious meaning. Four volumes examined the history of its settlements, the lives and accomplishments of its governors and distinguished ministers, and the history of Harvard College. Three additional books documented the work of church synods, the "wondrous" events, and the "Afflictive Disturbances" of regional history. Mather, who was born in 1663, straddled the second and third generations. In some respects the *Magnalia* responded to new imperial realities of the 1690s that would underwrite the eighteenth-century re-Anglicization of New England's collective self-image. But the *Magnalia* was overwhelmingly an extension of the second generation's historicizing work. Mather labored to preserve such private documents as journals and diaries, many of which he consulted in composing the *Magnalia,* that were choice specimens of the founders' illustrious piety.[42]

Sounding the familiar note of the jeremiad, Mather acknowledged being "smitten with a just fear of encroaching and ill-bodied *degeneracies*" in New England. The *Magnalia* may be read as a monumental memorial to a heroic past. "But whether New-England may *live* any where else, or no," Mather noted, "it must *live* in our History!" His biographies of magistrates and ministers are elegies that follow the conventions of Puritan funeral sermons. Indeed, as one scholar has accurately pointed out, death strides through the *Magnalia*'s pages "in references to interment, burial, graves, gravestones, epitaphs, sepulchers, ashes, urns, memorials, funerals, decay, and embalming."[43] Such imagery was not the product of a morbid psyche or even of a mind curdled by the diminution of clerical authority at the end of the century. Rather, the *Magnalia* elaborates on the rhetoric of the jeremiad with characteristic Matherian overkill.

Mather extends, for example, the analysis of Nathaniel Morton's *New Englands Memoriall* (1669), a major but neglected second-generation history-jeremiad that served as a standard account of the region's settlement well into the nineteenth century. "Oh poor *New England,* consider what thou now art!" Morton exhorted his readers. "*Repent, and do thy works, saith the Lord; so may thy peace yet be as a river, and thy righteousness as the waves of the sea.*"[44] *New Englands Memoriall,* building on early elegies in Johnson's *Wonder-Working Providence,* recorded the deaths of Puritan leaders year by year, even including funeral verse and gravestone epitaphs. The death of John Cotton, the distinguished Boston minister, summoned up the loss of other founding Puritan patriarchs:

And after Winthrop, Hooker's, Sheperd's [*sic*] Herse,
Doth Cotton's death call for a mourning Verse?

. . . .

In Bostons Orb, Winthrop and Cotton were;
These lights extinct, dark is our Hemisphere.

Morton and Mather document the late-seventeenth-century emergence of a new culture of memorialization. This commemoration of the deceased extended beyond the jeremiad and works of history and biography to the growth of New England gravestone iconography, the extensive printing of funeral sermons, and the expansion of mourning rites.[45]

Whatever anxieties Mather revealed about the New English Israel's future, the *Magnalia*'s memorialization was not intended as a literary mausoleum for the founders' expiring way of life. Rather, the *Magnalia,* like the jeremiad, represented a useable past; preservation, memory, and epic narrative were means of contemporary reformation and ways of influencing the future. Distressed by secular challenges to "*the true interest* of New-England*,*" Mather turned to history to reverse or at least forestall the demise of the founders' piety and accomplishments: "but certainly one good way to save that *loss,* would be to do something that the memory of the *great things done for us by our God,* may not be lost, and that the story of the circumstances attending the *foundation* and *formation* of this country, and of its *preservation* hitherto, may be impartially handed unto posterity." In his volume on the region's governors, Mather described his "hopes that there will yet be found among the sons of New-England, those young gentlemen by whom copies given in this History will be written after."[46]

Mather's voice is that of a second-generation local patriot fluent in the idiom of New England's mythologized history. He proudly identifies himself as a "native" of New England, referring to the region as "my country." The majestic Connecticut River becomes an American "Nilus." The venerable history of the founding generation sustains his pride of place. John Winthrop is sketched as "Nehemias Americanus," the *American* Nehemiah, who commanded the Puritans' redeeming "errand into the wilderness." The founders confronted a landscape that Mather variously depicts as an "American desart" and a "howling wilderness." He evokes the customary epic of the Great Migration, which was not propelled by "any worldly consideration." Instead, God inspired "thousands which never saw the *faces* of each other, with a most unanimous inclination to leave all the pleasant accommodations of their native country, and go over a terrible ocean into a more terrible *desart,* for the *pure enjoyment of all his ordinances.*" Providence rewarded the founders' piety with divine blessings for the "NEW-ENGLISH ISRAEL." Mather, like second-generation Jeremiahs, still invoked the image of a spiritual, universal Israel, arguing that "Geography must now find work for a Christiano-graphy." But the *Magnalia* consumates the second generation's shift to representations of New England as a place-bound, historical New Israel. "My New England," Mather boasted after completing the *Magnalia,* "has one thing that will weigh down more than forty of the best things that other countries can brag of; that is, religion, religion, religion!"[47]

The second generation's historicized collective identity, which the *Magnalia* offered in such a swollen version, bestowed on New England an early historical self-consciousness that distinguished it from other American colonial societies. Moreover, the Puritan religious and cultural investment in history would have lasting consequences for the region. It is not simply that the resonant historical phrases — the howling wilderness, the errand, the Great Migration — coined and propagated by the second generation have decidedly shaped popular and scholarly understanding of New England's early history. The second generation's historical work also established a tradition that would place New England in the forefront of efforts to study and preserve the American past. The region became the home of the first state historical societies founded in America, for instance, and New Englanders dominated the writing of American history in the early republic and throughout the nineteenth century.

But even as the second generation consolidated its historicized and Americanized revision of regional identity, colonial circumstances had begun to change. The third and fourth generations had to revise regional identity again, wedding their heroic past to a new appreciation of their membership in the British Empire.

The Re-Anglicization of Regional Identity in the Eighteenth Century

"Sarah Silsbe is my name[.] I belong to the English nation[.] Boston and Christ is my salvation."[48] These words, embroidered on a sampler by ten-year-old Sarah Silsbe, encapsulate the eighteenth-century revision of regional identity that reconciled New England's religious heritage with a new pride in the English nation. Third- and fourth-generation Puritans executed an imaginative reaffiliation with the mother country, an interpretive process that was propelled by the structural integration of New England and other American colonies into an emergent British Empire in the eighteenth century. By 1748, when young Sarah completed her sampler, the re-Anglicization of New England identity was far advanced, part of a larger cultural transformation in which English influences pervaded all the colonies as a newly aggressive imperial state took repossession of its American provinces.[49]

Politically, economically, and culturally, third- and fourth-generation Puritans resided in a colonial world far different from the New England of their parents and grandparents. Beginning in the late seventeenth century, English officials exercised unprecedented political vigilance over the New England colonies. A new determination to regulate trade within the empire paralleled the reassertion of English political authority. Far from hindering commerce, however, "navigation acts" provided a stable set of arrangements in which trade between New England and the mother country flourished. In particular, New England's expanding population became a major market for English manufactured goods, imports that moved through networks of credit and created a transatlantic community of merchants, brokers, and manufacturers. The integration of New England into an empire of commerce established the pathways for traffic in English books, periodicals, ideas, values, and aesthetic tastes. At the same time, a prosperous, expansive Protestant Britain found itself almost continually at war with its New World rival, Catholic France. In New England, a series of imperial conflicts that began in the 1690s ended with the British victory in the Seven Years' War (1756–63), which secured English control of North America. The confrontations with France and England's final victory infused New Englanders with a powerful sense of pride in their membership in the British Empire. Sarah Silsbe recorded this pride, even as she clung to Puritan religious tradition. At her tender age, she had already absorbed the eighteenth-century Puritan revision of regional identity.

The short-lived Dominion of New England (1685–89) proclaimed the growing English determination to exert tighter political control over the American colonies. The Dominion reorganized all of New England, and later New York and New Jersey, into one colony. In 1686 the royally appointed Edmund Andros assumed the governorship of the Dominion and promptly displayed his contempt for colonial rights and traditions. The Dominion was received in New England not only as another affliction on the second generation, but more important for the process of cultural re-Anglicization that would follow, Andros's regime was decried as an assault on the English liberties of loyal subjects. Such a defense of New Englanders' rights as Englishmen would soon be accelerated by the Glorious Revolution, the collapse of the Dominion, and new arrangements that altered the political landscape on both sides of the Atlantic and compelled a retelling of the Puritan errand into the wilderness.[50]

The events surrounding and following the Glorious or "Bloodless" Revolution of 1688–89 proved to be a constitutional turning point in England that shaped American colonial politics down to independence and promoted the political re-Anglicization of New England identity in the eighteenth century. The Glorious Revolution overthrew the Catholic, autocratically predisposed James II, who had ascended the throne in 1685 and strongly supported the Dominion of New England and the "royalization" of the American colonies. William of Orange, who had been invited by Protestant and parliamentary representatives to depose James, assumed the throne with his wife Mary, James's daughter. The Glorious Revolution not only restored Protestant succession; it also imposed new constitutional limits on the monarchy. William and Mary, as a condition of their assumption of the throne, were required to acknowledge the rights of Parliament. The revolutionary settlement continued with the passage of a religious toleration act in 1689 and a bill of rights in 1692. The Glorious Revolution thus became an Anglo-American constitutional landmark. There was no single written document that comprised an English constitution. Rather, the "constitution" referred to an accumulation of documents, precedents, and arrangements that stretched from the Magna Carta to the Glorious Revolution.[51] In the aftermath of the revolutionary settlement, the Puritan architects of regional identity had reason to defend New Englanders' constitutional rights as "Englishmen" and to divide seventeenth-century English history into pre– and post–Glorious Revolution eras. Such shifting political ground, and the larger cultural rapprochement between mother country and the New England colonies of which it was a part, required a revision of the second generation's heroic narrative of the region's founding.

The immediate impact of the Glorious Revolution in New England, however, involved the legitimization of the overthrow of the Dominion and a new set of colonial political arrangements that testified to English officials' continuing determination to secure colonial supervision. In 1689 Governor Andros was jailed and then shipped back to England. Two years later a post-Dominion settlement brought major political change. A new charter transformed Massachusetts into a royal colony with a Crown-appointed governor. A property requirement replaced church membership as the basis of voting rights. The charter extended England's religious toleration to New England, except for Catholics. Plymouth was incorporated into Massachusetts, and the land of the Pilgrims that would enter American mythology in the nineteenth century came to be known as the "Old Colony." The charter confirmed Massachusetts's jurisdiction over Maine, which the Bay Colony had extended to those settlements in the 1650s. New Hampshire, over which Massachusetts had also exerted its authority in the 1640s, was reestablished as a royal colony as it had been reorganized in 1679 when it separated from the Bay Colony.

More than two-thirds of New England's population—the residents of Massachusetts, New Hampshire, and Maine—now lived under royal government. Only Connecticut and Rhode Island retained independent charters, which would be repeatedly scrutinized and threatened in ensuing decades. Moreover, the independent colonies, like all of New England, fell under commercial regulations, such as those of the Navigation Act of 1696, that expanded to America both the British customs service and the admiralty court system to try violations of trade law. Political appointees and customs officials in major port towns stood out as the human faces of a newly assertive imperial state. By the early eighteenth century all the New England colonies recognized the need to appoint permanent agents in London, where political and economic decisions affecting lives and fortunes three thousand miles away were handed down. These paid agents were often joined in London by New England merchants and politicians on personal missions of self-interest. Colonial visitors frequently met on London's "New England Walk" or at establishments such as the "Sun of New England Coffee House," transporting back to the provinces the ways of the imperial metropolis.[52]

The rush of imperial policy and of English history thrust New England into a new colonial era. British officials imagined the Puritans' New English Israel as simply one subregion of an emergent empire; they pursued policies that promoted the region's political and economic integration into an imperial framework. Beginning with the political changes initiated by the Glorious Revolution, however, the guardians of New England's identity acknowledged the reality of re-Anglicization while they labored to preserve the region's distinctive historical self-image.

Historians have often depicted the dismantling of the Bible Common-wealth by the Massachusetts Charter of 1691 as the end of the Puritan era. Indeed, contemporary Puritan critics of the charter voiced a similar judgment, heaping scorn on the new document as a pale substitute for the charter that John Winthrop had transported to America at the start of the Great Migration. Clearly, the coercive and exclusive elements of the Puritan state vanished, never to reappear. Yet, as the second genera-tion's jeremiads attest, the official props of Puritan orthodoxy were already under duress in the decades leading up to the second charter. The horta-tory pleading of the jeremiad revealed a heavily voluntaristic campaign to preserve New England's Israel — a crusade of persuasion by histori-cal incantation that would continue after the second charter dissolved the theocratic elements of the Puritan state. From the first defenses of the charter in the 1690s through election-day sermons, jeremiads, and histori-cal works of the eighteenth century, Puritan leaders extolled both their rights as English citizens and their heritage as New English Israelites.[53]

The Mathers, the drum majors of New England tribalism, launched the interpretive process that incorporated the new circumstances of colo-nial life into a revised narrative of the region's heroic founding. After the overthrow of King James, Increase Mather spent two years in England working unsuccessfully for the restoration of the old Massachusetts Char-ter. He then reconciled himself to the new charter of 1691 and defended its promise. Reminding critics of the history of Puritan persecution in England, Mather insisted "that by this Charter great privlidges [*sic*] are granted to the People of New England, and in some particulars, greater than any they formerly enjoyed: For all English liberties are restored to them." New England Congregationalism would now exist not by English forbearance but by constitutional protection, "a Wall of Defence about the Lord's Vineyard in that part of the World."[54] The charter amounted to a fulfillment of the original errand into the wilderness, for the founders had journeyed to New England in pursuit of *English civil liberty* as well as the freedom to worship.

Increase's son Cotton picked up on this re-Anglicization of the errand. The *Magnalia* (1702), for all of its mythologizing of New England's historic identity, still registers the new presence of imperial England in regional life. It records the views of an often-conflicted provincial leader, proud of his native roots but ever mindful of how the imperial metropolitan world relegated him to a place at the empire's cultural margins. Mather embraced the Glorious Revolution and the English safeguards to New England religious freedom. Under the new charter, he insisted, the Massachusetts General Court possessed "as much Power in New-England as the King and parliament have in England. . . . All the liberties of their holy religion are for ever secured." The *Magnalia* recited the inspirational epic of the Great Migration and the heroic errand into the wilderness, but Mather sometimes carefully situated his grand narrative in the context of the Anglo-American identity politics of the post–Glorious Revolution era. He remained as strongly committed as any second-generation historian-Jeremiah to preserving the collective memory of New England's heroic founding, recounting how the fathers were "driven into the wilderness." But he disavowed "all intemperate expressions of our anger against our drivers." Such passion was unbecoming in a "historian" and a "Christian," Mather claimed.[55] It also did not speak to the emergent re-Anglicized identity formation of turn-of-the-century New England.

The *Magnalia* outlined elements of the interpretive process that eighteenth-century election speakers, Jeremiahs, and historians would employ for a revised, post–Glorious Revolution understanding of New England's founding. Mather stressed the nonseparating Congregationalism of the founders, evidence of their continuing loyalty to the English Church and nation. Though the heroic forefathers were victimized by official harassment and driven "into the horrid Thickets of *America*," this persecution "we consider not as possessing the Church of England, but as inspiring a *party* which have unjustly challenged the name of the Church of England." This faction exploited the "unbounded *prerogative*" of the Crown to oppress the Puritan founders, who accepted the "*fundamentals* of Christianity" in the Church of England, "only questioning and forbearing a few *disciplinary* points." With respect to these fundamentals of Reformed Christianity, Mather concluded, "the planters of New-England were *truer* sons to the Church of England than that part of the church which . . . banished them into this plantation." Mather refracted New England history through the prism of the Glorious Revolution and the new charter. The "factional" religious despotism, abetted by royal prerogative, that set the Great Migration in motion became identified with the threat of absolutism that incited the revolt against James II and the Dominion of New England. The errand into the wilderness and the Glorious Revolution were inspired by a common quest to secure English civil and religious liberty. Moreover, whatever sympathy they may have shown for the Puritan cause in the English civil war of the 1640s and 1650s, the founders of

New England did not see themselves, Mather stressed, as Separatists or sectarians, but as reformers within the national church.[56]

The *Magnalia* and Increase Mather's earlier defense of the new Massachusetts Charter suggested how the re-Anglicization of the errand into the wilderness and the Great Migration could imaginatively accommodate the new realities of colonial life and thereby sustain an updated heroic narrative of New England's founding. Eighteenth-century guardians of regional identity continued the re-Anglicizing of New England's history and collective self-image, a process that was particularly evident during the years that marked the centennial of the Great Migration. One election speaker who addressed Massachusetts officials in 1730 characteristically contrasted the England that emerged from the Glorious Revolution with the homeland that hounded the forefathers into exile. "Their native Country," Thomas Prince observed, "which ever since the Glorious Revolution, has been an happy land of Ease and Liberty, was in those former Times as the Land of Egypt to those Pious Men; and their Lives were made exceeding bitter with Religious Bondage." Yet the founders, who subscribed to the doctrinal orthodoxy of the Church of England and only sought to purify its forms of worship, renounced any intention to separate from the national church. From a post–Glorious Revolution perspective, persecution of the founders served a providential, even imperial, end. Religious persecution now became an artifact of English history that brought New England into existence — a region, Prince boasted, of "religion, good order, liberty, learning, and flourishing towns and churches, which have . . . reflected a singular honor to the persons and principles of its original settlers for this hundred years." [57]

New England's "flourishing towns" suggested how an industrious, prosperous, expanding eighteenth-century population both benefited from and contributed to the well-being of the empire. In another centennial account of New England's founding, Reverend Thomas Foxcroft attributed an imperial motive to the founders. "Here they hoped to enjoy the Freedoms and Privileges of *English* Government and to enlarge the British Dominions." The Puritan patriarchs were almost reimagined as agents of empire who held the welfare of the homeland, not just of their souls, at the center of their Great Migration. Foxcroft, of course, preserved religion as the inspiration of the errand into the wilderness, where the founders welcomed "*brown Bread and the Gospel [as] good Fair [sic]*." Still, his heroic story could be read as an imperial narrative, for the Puritan forefathers colonized "a great and terrible Wilderness, a Land of Deserts, and of Pits, and of the shadow of Death." Through a combination of providential oversight and the operation of English liberties, this wilderness became a prosperous land of "earthly Comforts."[58]

In an election-day sermon of 1734, four years after Foxcroft's centennial history, John Barnard referred to the privately sponsored early colonization of America as "the first founding [of] the British Empire in this distant part of the world," imposing on disparate and disconnected settlement efforts an eighteenth-century sense of imperial purpose and pride. Barnard celebrated the history of New England rights "which belong to Englishmen as the happy subjects of Great Britain," venerable privileges "confirmed to us by a royal Charter from the ever memorable King William." The Massachusetts Charter of 1691 came to be enshrined in the eighteenth century as New England's "Magna Carta." Barnard conceded that there was "no particular form of government appointed by God," but New England existed under the full protection of the British constitution, a divine blessing and the "best" possible civil arrangement for Puritan descendants. Barnard accounted himself "happy that I know not a single true New England man in the whole Province but what readily subscribes to these sentiments and hopes we shall continue to be the genuine members of that glorious Constitution."[59]

As comparisons of the Massachusetts charter to the Magna Carta suggest, eighteenth-century agents of the re-Anglicization of regional identity engaged in a process of politically homologizing colonies and imperial homeland—an interpretive strategy that recalled the founding generation's Anglicizing of the New England landscape. The Massachusetts House of Representatives seized on the new charter and the Glorious Revolution to assert possession of the same "powers & Privileges here as the house of commons in England."[60] Throughout the eighteenth century, ministers and magistrates lauded the "balanced constitution" of homeland and colonies that the Glorious Revolution institutionalized. English constitutional arrangements incorporated distinct social elements into a government that balanced monarchy (the king), aristocracy (the House of Lords), and democracy (the House of Commons). Such social and political equipoise furnished a constitutional safeguard against governmental encroachment on English liberty. The eighteenth-century enshrinement of England's balanced constitution not only provided a basis for colonial lower houses, like those of New England, to claim parliamentary rights against royally appointed governors and upper houses; it also encouraged election preachers, politicians, and citizens to conceive of their governments as scaled-down versions of England's balanced constitution.[61]

As confrontations with Catholic France for control of North America accelerated during the first half of the eighteenth century, New Englanders were increasingly instructed about the cherished privileges bestowed by their Anglo-Protestant civil-religious heritage. "The form of our government is justly the envy of most other nations," an election speaker enthused in 1754, "especially of those which have either no parliaments at all, or such as may be banished at the word and pleasure of a tyrant, which comes much to the same thing." New Englanders' prized eighteenth-century patrimony sprang from the founders' errand to secure their *civil* and religious freedom. "Our ancestors, tho' not perfect and infallible in all respects, were a religious, brave, and virtuous set of men, whose love of liberty, civil and religious, brought them from their native land into the American deserts."[62] This sermonizer, like the speakers and writers who preceded him, found it relatively easy to braid political re-Anglicization into the second generation's mythologized narrative of the Great Migration which carried the forefathers on a heroic errand into a howling desert-wilderness.

But the second generation's investment in the New English Israel proved more problematic for regional identity in an era of re-Anglicization. A strong identification with ancient Israel had originated in New England's sense of moral and cultural distance from the homeland in the aftermath of the collapse of the Puritan revolution in England. How could the conception of a "peculiar people" that New Israel conferred on New England survive the impact of empire and re-Anglicization? Should it survive? After all, the errand into the wilderness and the Great Migration had been revised to reconcile New England's distinctive history with the imperial political realities that resulted from the Glorious Revolution. Did those revisions not lend sufficient historical support for a new, re-Anglicized regional identity? In other words, the notion of a New English Israel threatened to disrupt what we can now see as the re-colonization of New Englanders' collective self-image — re-Anglicization functioning as a British cultural imperialism that invaded the intellectual precincts of late Puritanism.

Not surprisingly, some guardians of regional identity abandoned the New English Israel as the relic of an unenlightened Puritan age. As early as 1706, an election-day sermon of John Rogers challenged any facile association of New England and ancient Israel, even questioning the very notion of a chosen covenanted nation. All countries throughout history have been afflicted or blessed based on their behavior, Rogers argued. Unlike human beings, nations are not judged in an afterlife; they have to be rewarded or punished in this world to preserve God's moral order. Thus universal divine law rather than a special covenant requires "that a People should be prosperous or afflicted according to their general Obedience or Disobedience."[63]

Such a withdrawal from the idea of New England as a New Israel, however, did not subvert the epic narrative of the Great Migration or of the errand into the wilderness, as Benjamin Colman demonstrated in 1723. Colman ministered to Boston's Brattle Street Church, founded in 1699 and perhaps the most re-Anglicized Congregational society in all New England. After ancient Israel, the clergyman insisted, "God has *never . . .* assayed to go and take him a Nation from the midst of another nation, by temptations and signs and wonders, by a stretched out arm and great terrors." Still, while distancing himself from the typology of the New Israel, Colman preserved the defining historical elements of New England's mythologized founding. The founders were not the New Israelites, "yet the presence of God with our *Fathers . . .* was very remarkable in bringing them into this Land, making room before them, and drawing out the Nation that before possess'd it." Though not an Old Testament peculiar people, the Puritan founders were nevertheless providentially blessed, for "God it was that gave them the Wisdom and Courage and Strength, a heart to subdue a waste Wilderness, and to fill it with Towns and Villages."[64]

Some eighteenth-century interpreters of regional identity, particularly in moments of moral exhortation and historical commemoration, espoused a traditional interpretation of the New English Israel. In his election-day sermon of 1730, for example, Thomas Prince offered a familiar description of New Englanders as a covenanted people: "And here I cannot forbear observing, that there never was any People on Earth so parallel in their general History to that of the ancient ISRAELITES as this of NEW ENGLAND . . . : that excepting Miracles and changing Names, one would be ready to think, the greater Part of the Old Testament were written about *us;* or that *we,* tho' in a lower Degree were the particular Antitypes of that primitive People."[65] Similarly, Thomas Foxcroft invoked the customary imagery of a "chosen generation": "It was the God of *Israel,* who conducted his People over the wide and hazardous Ocean, and prepared a Sanctuary for them in a strange land." Foxcroft leaned heavily on the jeremiads of the second generation, which assertively advanced the identification of New England as a New Israel. He quoted famous lines from those jeremiads, such as William Stoughton's ringing pronouncement that "God *sifted* a whole Nation that he might send a *choice* Grain over into this wilderness." [66]

Despite the reservations or outright rejection displayed by some cultural leaders, New England's identification as a New Israel survived transit to the eighteenth century. Moreover, continuing threats from Catholic France encouraged the re-Anglicization of New Israel itself. "British Israel" would represent something of a return to the founding generation's sense of a transatlantic covenanted nation. In sum, British Israel would enable eighteenth-century New Englanders to reconcile historic, tribal elements of regional identity with the centripetal forces of empire and re-Anglicization.

Before the final midcentury triumph of British Israel in the Anglo-American imperial victory over the French, commerce exploded within an expanding empire. Trade not only created economic channels for the ongoing re-Anglicization of New England identity. Material consumption also provoked a new wave of jeremiads and a chorus of distress over spiritual decline. Once again, New England appeared to be in moral decay.

In 1721 Jeremiah Dummer, who served as the colonial agent for Massachusetts in London and had provided the same representation for Connecticut and Rhode Island, published *A Defense of the New England Charters.* Dummer was responding to renewed British efforts to abolish the region's charters, especially those of the two nonroyal colonies, Connecticut and Rhode Island. He reminded British authorities that the founders settled New England not just to seek freedom of worship but also "to increase the nation's wealth and enlarge her dominions." The New England colonies remained highly profitable to the homeland. "There is no sort of manufacture," Dummer observed, "but what the subjects there demand in a greater or less proportion, as they have ability to pay for it; everything for the use, convenience, ornament, and (I say it with great regret) the luxury and pride of life." [67] At the same time that he mounted his economic defense of the charters, Dummer acknowledged a moral unease over New England material consumption—an appetite for English goods that furthered the re-Anglicization of regional life and that aroused mid-eighteenth-century Jeremiahs like the leaders of the religious revival known as the Great Awakening.

Eighteenth-century New Englanders were drawn into an "empire of goods" fueled by what has been described as a "consumer revolution." A burgeoning population and increasing wealth transformed the American colonies into a major market for English manufactured goods. New England became a lucrative corner of this emergent empire of commerce, credit, and consumption. The region's population surged from 93,000 in 1700 to approximately 450,000 by 1760. New England merchants expanded their role as brokers between English manufacturers and colonial consumers, industriously plying trade routes and relying on a structure of credit to respond to market demands. The infamous slave trade, whose American phase was dominated by New England and particularly Rhode Island merchants in the eighteenth century, comprised only one, relatively minor, aspect of a so-called triangular trade. New England merchants pursued commercial exchange with the Middle Colonies, the West Indies, and even southern Europe, seeking goods or bills of credit that would enable them to acquire English manufactured items.[68]

The availability of these consumer goods stretched well beyond New England's port towns. Large merchants extended credit to customers, often inland shopkeepers who set up small stores sometimes in their homes. One rural Connecticut store in the 1730s and 1740s carried items ranging from "lace," "gloves," "mohair," "tiles," "earthenware," "pots," and "pans," to "tea," "buckles," "silk," "spectacles," and "looking glasses."[69] The empire of goods penetrated backcountry New England, the region's abundant waterways aiding a nascent commercial network that linked inland communities, port towns, and the metropolitan world.

Of course, it was in such ports as Boston, Salem, Portsmouth, Newport, and New Haven, where the wealthiest merchants resided, that the consumer revolution of the mid-eighteenth century and its attendant re-Anglicization of regional life registered its greatest impact. With the profits from trade, merchants burnished their self-image as colonial gentlemen. The political, economic, and imaginative integration of the colonies into a British empire encouraged New England merchants to emulate the English gentry. The profits from trade supplied the means to acquire the material trappings of a re-Anglicized, genteel way of life: carriages, wigs, portraits, and Georgian "mansions." Large, symmetrical, center hall, two- and three-story homes, based on designs from English architectural books, became the most visible markers of both a quest for gentility and the re-Anglicization of New England culture and material life. English publications such as architectural and courtesy books became commodities of trade themselves, suggesting how the empire of goods transmitted English styles, tastes, and values, not just consumer items. New Anglo-American social rituals like tea drinking required appropriate implements, such as imported Staffordshire china. Plates, which replaced the traditional bowl, led to the purchase of knives, forks, and wine glasses; these and other domestic artifacts proliferated along with teacups and saucers. Taverns like the Crown Coffee House in Boston acquired these accoutrements of domestic gentility as well as such comfortable furnishings as leather chairs. Imitating an English gentlemen's club, the Crown offered patrons an array of imported wines.[70]

Merchants in port towns were the most conspicuous consumers of imported goods and cultivators of a related English gentility. But other social elements in these towns participated in the mid-eighteenth-century consumer revolution. As one Boston observer wrote in 1748, "The furniture and expenses of every tradesman now equal those of the merchant formerly, those of the merchant surpass those of the first-rate gentleman; those of the gentleman, the old lords."[71] The empire of goods also spread geographically, from ports to inland river towns, and beyond to the hinterland. After examining regional material culture in the first half of the eighteenth century, a leading historical archaeologist suggested that New Englanders "were more English than they had been in the past since the first years of the colonies."[72]

The Puritan religious establishment responded in different ways to the commercial and cultural invasion that comprised the empire of goods, just as it had reacted to political re-Anglicization. Alterations in meetinghouse architecture, for example, signaled a process of ecclesiastical re-Anglicization that paralleled the rise of Georgian homes. The traditional plain New England meetinghouse began its century-long evolution into the fabled white-steepled church. Reflecting the Puritans' revulsion against the "Romanist" ecclesiastical architecture of the Church of England, the traditional New England meetinghouse was a plain, unpainted structure with a square or rectangular shape. Such buildings were steepleless; often a bell was mounted on the roof or, in some towns, simply located on the ground nearby. The interiors of New England meetinghouses were also plain, designed as "aural" buildings centered on the pulpit and the spoken word so crucial to Puritan worship, rather than on an altar and sacramental ceremonialism.[73]

Influenced by the eighteenth-century re-Anglicization of New England culture and material life, the traditional meetinghouse began its slow development into an esteemed regional icon, a process that was not complete until the early nineteenth century. In 1699 the Brattle Street Church in Boston built the first Congregational meetinghouse containing a bell tower and spire. The construction of Anglican churches in eighteenth-century New England encouraged some congregations to continue the modifications of the traditional meetinghouse that were launched by Brattle Street. Christ Church, a Georgian structure with a spire that soared nearly two hundred feet, was built in Boston in 1723; it became an impressive architectural model as well as a symbol of the power of the Church of England and its metropolitan culture. Two years later Newport Anglicans began construction of a new Trinity Church, a steepled wooden building that resembled Boston's Christ Church. Such eighteenth-century Anglican churches influenced the architecture of New England meetinghouses built in the ports and large inland towns. Boston's Old South Church (1729–30), for example, boasted a stately spire that was attached to a more conventional rectangular meetinghouse — a modification of Puritan tradition that served as a hybrid architectural analogue to the rhetorical re-Anglicization of regional identity in election-day sermons and historical accounts.[74]

Meetinghouse interiors also began to change in the eighteenth century in ways that suggested the ecclesiastical impact of new wealth, the domestic empire of goods, and the re-Anglicization of Puritan tradition. Pew cushions, expanded pulpits, and architectural alterations such as arched windows all documented an eighteenth-century desire for more comfort and style in primitively austere Puritan meetinghouses. Consider the First Church in Hingham, Massachusetts. At midcentury the members authorized major improvements, including the construction of a "wine glass" pulpit with carved panels that was set in front of arched windows. Carpenters also built new box pews that were sold to families. In Hingham and other New England towns, the construction and sale of family pews in the eighteenth century announced the emergence of new wealth — successful entrepreneurs, who, as part of a quest for English-like gentility, sought churchly recognition of their recently acquired status.[75] Of course, eighteenth-century New Englanders only gradually modified ecclesiastical tradition, continuing, for instance, to reject instrumental music or heat in their meetinghouses. Yet the re-Anglicization of New England culture and identity in the first half of the eighteenth century initiated the physical changes that would, over time, transform the region's primitive meetinghouses into widely recognized "churchly" markers of regional identity.

Re-Anglicization not only fostered physical alterations to the Puritan meetinghouse and revisions of New England's historicized identity; it also encouraged changes among the clergy as well as in religious practices. Ministers increasingly donned wigs, that eighteenth-century emblem of gentility. More important, they accepted a seemingly "Anglican conception of clerical legitimacy." New England's founders had practiced a system of clerical ordination in which the laity both elected and ordained ministers. By the eighteenth century the laity only chose the minister; ordination fell under the control of other clergymen, who preached sermons on these occasions that described the prerogatives and responsibilities of the clerical office. The products of a re-Anglicized understanding of ministerial authority, such quasi-professional ordination sermons were first published only in the eighteenth century.[76]

Unlike shifts in ordination, which broadly affected the Puritan ministry, changes to inherited religious worship were largely confined to a group of "catholick" and rationalist Congregational clergy who preached primarily in port towns and in substantial commercial communities like Hingham, locations where meetinghouse architecture first began to change. Serving in the vanguard of religious re-Anglicization, this new breed of Congregational ministers was heavily concentrated in eastern Massachusetts, often preaching to parishes filled with merchants engaged in the empire of goods. Influenced by the writings of Anglican clergy and shaped by the rationalism of the early Enlightenment, these catholick Congregational ministers increasingly adopted a stance of religious moderation. Although they continued to accept traditional Puritan piety, including the need for spiritual rebirth, they now displayed "a willingness to overlook differences of opinion about the 'smaller things' in religion" and adopted a tolerant, even ecumenical attitude toward other Protestant groups.[77] Most of these clerical representatives of reason and moderation spurned any easy identification between New England and ancient Israel.

The catholick clergy's re-Anglicization extended well beyond a rejection of the tribal elements of New England identity and an openness to "churchly" modifications to the Puritan meetinghouse. Re-Anglicization infiltrated eighteenth-century religious worship as well. Brattle Street Church, for example, instituted public recitation of formal prayers such as the Lord's Prayer, a practice that contradicted the traditional Puritan animus against Romanist "set forms" in either prayers or hymns. Brattle Street and other congregations under moderate ministers also abandoned the public relation of conversion that had been instituted by the founding generation. A candidate for admission to church was required to provide public testimony describing the experience of spiritual rebirth. But catholick clergy began to hear relations in private or to abandon them altogether as a condition of church membership.[78] Public relations of conversion, like the stark New England meetinghouse, seemed to strike re-Anglicized clergy as a vestige of a sectarian Puritan past.

From the mythologized founding errand to church architecture, clerical ordination, and worship practices, re-Anglicization made significant inroads into Puritan religious tradition—part of a larger reorientation of New England culture and regional identity. Yet religious accommodations to the forces of re-Anglicization did not satisfy some eighteenth-century Puritan descendants, who defected to the Church of England. The most stunning defections took place at Yale College in 1722. Yale itself had been founded in 1701 partly in response to the growing rationalism and latitudinarianism of Harvard. Thus Yale and much of the Congregational establishment reacted with shock when seven ministers and tutors announced at commencement in 1722 that they were converting to Anglicanism and would pursue ordination by a bishop in London. Despite this defection and the continuing growth of the Anglican Church in New England, the region would remain overwhelmingly Congregational.[79]

Moreover, shortly after the shocking Anglican betrayal in New Haven, Yale graduates provided leadership of the Great Awakening, a series of religious revivals that were, on one level, an orthodox response to the progress of re-Anglicization. The beginnings of the Great Awakening are usually located in the local revivals that Jonathan Edwards (Yale, 1720) led in his Northampton, Massachusetts, parish and in other towns of the Connecticut River Valley during the mid-1730s. By the early 1740s the local revivals entered a new phase, a more general awakening in New England that was emboldened by the masterly performances of the traveling English revivalist George Whitefield. The critical role of Whitefield suggests how the Awakening itself was enmeshed in the very process of re-Anglicization whose baneful effects revivalists like Edwards roundly criticized. Whitefield's involvement in the Awakening underscored the mid-eighteenth-century transatlantic traffic in ideas so characteristic of life in the emergent empire. Whitefield transformed revivalism into a commodity characteristic of the empire of goods. As one scholar has shown in detail, Whitefield borrowed advertising techniques from promoters of the consumer revolution, and he followed commercial trade routes blazed by merchants and peddlers who marketed English imports.

Even Jonathan Edwards's books describing and defending American revivalism became commodities in a transatlantic market of religious ideas and "goods." Edwards books were admired, widely read, and indeed published in Britain.[80]

Clearly, the Great Awakening was entangled in the imperial network that served as a conduit for re-Anglicization. But the Awakening's message remonstrated against the religious and social consequences of re-Anglicization—the growing rationalism of Congregationalism fostered by Anglican books and ideas and the expanding consumption of English imports. The necessity of a new spiritual birth served as an antidote to an advancing rationalism and gentility in religious life. Thus Edwards reasserted the importance of a public relation of conversion as a condition for church membership. Unlike the catholick Congregational clergy, he and other supporters of revivals looked not to contemporary Anglican writers for guidance but to classic works of American and English Puritanism. The Great Awakening stimulated the republication of works by New England's founders and by seventeenth-century English Puritans.[81]

The Great Awakening was a reaction to the empire of goods as much as it was a response to the growing rationalism, formalism, and gentility of New England Congregationalism. Edwards's critique of the "worldliness," "extravagance in fashions," and "covetousness" of the Connecticut River Valley's commercial way of life suggests how the consumer revolution revitalized the jeremiad tradition during the era of the Great Awakening.[82] The Connecticut River linked inland New England to the metropolitan world via a trail of English goods, tastes, and ideas. A group of so-called River Gods—a handful of families with interlocking control of land, trade, and political power—comprised the local gentry. Edwards's social criticism and the jeremiads of the Great Awakening as a whole seem to document a new level of commercial activity and consumption in New England life.

In contrast to most catholick Congregational clergy, Edwards often cast aside restraint in attacking the commercial order over which the River Gods presided. From the pulpit he reproached his congregation: "when neighbors meet, you shall hear but little talk about soul concerns. They'll be full of talk about their worldly business, about this and the other worldly design, about buying and selling." In 1742, with the Awakening at high tide, Edwards's church approved a new covenant. The signers vowed "to devote our whole lives to be laboriously spent in the business of religion: ever making it our greatest business." They promised to resist the "solicitations of our sloth and other corrupt inclinations, or the temptations of the world." Nevertheless, the progress of the empire of goods continued to incite Edwards's moral indignation. In a sermon to his Northampton parishioners, he assailed the advance of consumption. "The land is becoming exceeding extravagant," he fumed. "Common people show an affection to be like those of high rank; country towns . . . affect to be like the metropolis." For Edwards, the mid-eighteenth-century empire of goods "encourage[d] a general excess."[83]

Revivalism seemed only an interlude in New Englanders' continuing attachment to trade and consumption—a pause in the steady economic integration of the region into Britain's commercial empire. When religious ardor waned in the late 1730s and abruptly collapsed in the mid-1740s, Edwards invoked the city on a hill, but not to hold up Northampton and New England as moral exemplars. Rather, the backsliding from the high spiritual promise of revivalism and the notoriety that it conferred on town and region meant that, as a city on a hill, "we disgrace ourselves & expose ourselves to contempt."[84] Edwards knew that in the mid-eighteenth-century empire news traveled fast, moving from colony to colony and from America to England along imperial routes of trade, communication, and cultural interaction. Revivalism, like Northampton's reputation, became a "commodity" in a transatlantic traffic of religious information. At the end of the 1740s Edwards wrote a lengthy treatise endorsing a transatlantic "concert of prayer" to promote revivalism, a plan that had been proposed by Scottish Presbyterians who closely monitored the Great Awakening.[85] Edwards's preaching and writings, which, among other things, condemned the consequences of the empire of goods, transformed him into an international representative of New England's imperial outpost. His endorsement of an *imported,* transatlantic religious strategy—the concert of prayer—suggests how the Awakening contributed to the ongoing integration of New England into an imperial order, even as revivalists excoriated the corrupting consequences of the empire of goods.

Of course, though he resisted Anglican religious rationalism and criticized the expanding market for British goods, Edwards embraced political re-Anglicization—that is, the eighteenth-century pride in English constitutionalism and the understanding of New England's founding errand as a quest for *English* civil and religious liberty. English subjects did not have to fear "a papish king" or the "despotick power," he wrote, that ruled "the Turkish domains, Muscovy and France."[86] Edwards joined Puritan ministers of every stripe and New Englanders generally in Anglo-American patriotic efforts to combat French Catholic ambitions to impose religious and political "tyranny" on Britain's North American colonies.

The periodic imperial warfare between England and France in the eighteenth century, culminating in the Seven Years' War, markedly aided the eighteenth-century re-Anglicization of New England. Military spending pumped money into the regional economy, which stimulated trade and consumption. New England's proximity to New France underscored the region's dependence on the motherland for protection. Above all, the prospect of Catholic political and religious despotism swelled pride in New England's British heritage of Protestantism and constitutionalism.[87]

From the mid-1740s through the Seven Years' War, which began a decade later, conflict with France offered a crusade in which revivalistic moral fervor could be redeployed. The concert of prayer, for example, aimed to enlist transatlantic revivalism in the defeat of the "Scarlet Whore" and its political and religious threat to Anglo-American Protestantism and constitutionalism. New England Puritans drew on their rhetorical stockpile—jeremiads, fast day and thanksgiving sermons, and a historical identification with ancient Israel, all of which became religious weapons in the arsenal of imperial warfare. In 1745 a New England army captured Louisburg, the French fortification on Cape Breton and the so-called Gibraltar of the West. Thanksgiving sermons invoked the providential triumphs of ancient Israel: "Let the inspired language of *Moses,* and the *whole Body of the Jewish Nation,* be ours upon this memorable occasion." Military setbacks such as those in the opening stages of the Seven Years' War resulted from New Israel's moral backsliding. Prayer, fasting, repentance, and reform promised to placate God and remove the French threat to what Edwards described as "the civil & religious Liberties & privileges of the British Plantations in America & all that is dear to us."[88]

The midcentury imperial struggle with Catholic monarchical France revitalized New England's Protestant identity as a New Israel. But it tended to restrain the exclusive, sectarian aspects of that identity already rejected by catholick Congregational clergy and laity. The menace of French religious and political tyranny underscored the common British heritage of Protestantism and constitutionalism that colonies and homeland shared. The people of England and New England comprised a "peculiar" nation. The course of re-Anglicization during the midcentury conflict with France encouraged ministers to invoke God's British Israel, a covenanted identity that encompassed Protestants in Old and New England.

In 1754 Massachusetts election speaker Jonathan Mayhew outlined a portentous Gallic horror involving "motley armies of French and painted savages taking our fortresses, and erecting their own, even in our capital towns and cities!" He implored New Englanders to defend their British heritage against popery and tyranny, reminding descendants of the Puritan founders that we "have always distinguished ourselves by a jealousy of our rights, by our loyalty, and our zeal for the common interest of his Majesty's dominions on the continent." Six years later, when Canada fell, a Connecticut minister proclaimed the victory "of more Importance than has ever been made by the *English,* since *England* was a nation."[89] The thanksgiving sermons surrounding the capture of Canada celebrated the chosen status of the British people. "Divine Providence has seemed to point out *Britain* from the beginning as a favorite nation, to make it a pattern to other Kingdoms," Reverend Samuel Langdon observed in a thanksgiving sermon delivered in Portsmouth, New Hampshire, near the end of 1759. Shortly afterward Boston minister Thomas Foxcroft offered thanks for the "Remarkable Providences" bestowed on "British Israel," divine blessings that extended from the Reformation to the "Growth and Flourishing of the New England colonies," the Glorious Revolution, and the conquest of Canada. Among New England Puritans in particular, the imperial victory excited civil millennialism, the intoxicating hope that Protestantism and political liberty would begin a steady progress toward engulfing the world.[90]

To be sure, all of colonial America experienced the eighteenth-century process of re-Anglicization and the surge of pride that resulted from the British victory over the French. But New Englanders, as residents of the most English region of colonial America, and geographically over-exposed to the menace of French absolutism, emerged with a powerful sense of relief and Anglo-American pride. "Born and educated in this country, I glory in the Name of Briton," New Hampshire minister Jeremy Belknap confided to his diary in 1762. As "British Brothers," Americans could now live happily under the "glorious Throne of BRITANNIA," a New Hampshire newspaper editor enthused two years later.[91] Such British patriotism accounts for a new burst in the growth of Anglican churches in New England in the years leading up to independence. In Connecticut, for example, sixteen new churches were built between 1761 and 1774 and another twenty congregations were organized but without church buildings. Not surprisingly, in the 1760s New England almanacs began to list Christmas and saints' days recognized by the Church of England.[92] The new appeal of the national church represented only a small part of the re-Anglicization of New England identity that imperial triumph extended and solidified.

Despite the steady progress of the Anglican Church, New England remained staunchly Congregational on the eve of the Revolution. It also remained the most literate American region with the most highly developed origins narrative and collective identity. Eighteenth-century guardians of this historicized identity adjusted its imagined boundaries to accommodate the process of re-Anglicization that stretched from the aftermath of the Glorious Revolution to imperial victory over the French.

Notwithstanding the cultural homogeneity of its overwhelmingly white population, New England was neither conceptually nor rhetorically stable during the colonial era. It could not be because the region was not a static colonial world on the ground. Moreover, the changing course of New England identity from the 1630s to the 1760s reveals no steady, relentless growth in the Americanization of the region's collective self-image. Certainly, the founding generation adapted to the abundance of the New World physical setting, particularly the bounty of land. But these English migrants imagined and shaped their New World refuge in the image of the homeland. Compared to their parents and to the third and fourth generations, the sons and daughters of the founders inhabited a New England whose historicized identity recorded a sense of emotional and cultural distance from the mother country. Yet in the eighteenth century the Americanized rhetorical conventions of this historicized identity—the errand, the Great Migration, the New Israel—encountered and absorbed major elements of the re-Anglicization of New England colonial life.

Because of the need to explain the American Revolution, historians have tended to look back on the colonial era, especially the eighteenth century, to uncover the growth of nationalist sentiment. But until shortly before independence, colonials justified the revolution as a defense of their "British" rights.[93] Nationalism seems more a product than a cause of the American Revolution. Still, newly independent Americans did not easily slide from an imperial to a national identity. Indeed, through the nineteenth century—and beyond—"America" was an ongoing rhetorical and political project. In the immediate aftermath of political nation making, it became increasingly evident that America was little more than a collection of distinctive states coexisting under a distant and weak federal government. The influential New England founder of American geography recorded this reality, even as he tried to remediate it. In the process, he reimagined the region in ways that served a New England geopolitical agenda in the early republic.

Regionalism and Nationalism in the Early Republic

The American Geographies of Jedidiah Morse

The Anglo-American imperial victory over the French reinforced the colonists' collective sense that they were "British Brothers" with their transatlantic English compatriots. British policies initiated in the mid-1760s gradually dissolved colonial illusions. After a decade of defending their *British* rights, Revolutionary Americans confronted the brute facts of their imperial existence: the mother country viewed them, with undisguised metropolitan contempt, as subordinate subjects—coarsened inhabitants of a peripheral colonial world designed to serve the homeland's interests. Independence upended New England's re-Anglicized regional identity.

An emergent ideological script, "republicanism," helped the Revolutionaries negotiate their withdrawal from the empire; it also would profoundly shape political decisions that followed independence. Republicanism involved not just a rejection of monarchy but a reassessment of the fundamental premises of England's balanced constitution— the glorious model of colonial political experience. The policies that drove Americans from the empire originated with the king and his ministers. The concentrated power of the monarchy seemingly corrupted the other branches of the home government. Thus, England's vaunted balanced constitution furnished no safeguard for American liberty. Revolutionary republicanism involved a rejection of monarchy and a fear of the centralized political power that it represented. Aristocracy next fell victim to republicanism. The corrupting influence of the king and his minions encouraged a sweeping reevaluation of England's constitutional order. In particular, Revolutionary republicanism challenged the idea that liberty would be preserved against government encroachment by a political framework that balanced countervailing social elements of monarchy, aristocracy, and democracy. Revolutionary republicanism came to lodge political sovereignty in "the people." Though in reality "the people" meant white males, in republican thought it referred to the demos, the commonality of citizens not broken down into the discrete social groupings of English constitutionalism.

Revolutionary republicanism sought to reconcile power and liberty, order and freedom, in a government representative of "the people." Virtue supplied its ballast. The success of a republican government and society rested on a virtuous, informed, public-minded citizenry committed to industry, simplicity, competency, even frugality. Virtuous citizens, jealous of their liberty, would exercise vigilance over rulers' infringements on their rights; but republican virtue also promised an ordered liberty that would not degenerate into raw self-interest, material extravagance, and licentiousness. Sam Adams spoke of America as a "*Christian Sparta*," suggesting the ancient roots of republicanism.[1]

Yet the "classical" republicanism of the Revolutionary era was also imbued with Puritanism, the righteous rhetoric of the jeremiad, for example, audible in the morally charged vocabulary of virtue. New England's moralistic republicanism installed religious piety as the taproot of virtue. In short, New Englanders Puritanized republicanism, espousing an ideology that was morally accented by the pieties of their religious heritage. But New England's Revolutionary leaders also republicanized Puritan history. They reimagined the founders of the region as the new nation's preeminent proto-republicans who had resisted an earlier English assault on civil liberty. Moreover, Revolutionary New Englanders projected their region's sense of chosenness onto the new nation. Independence from the corrupt mother country confirmed *America's* covenanted relationship with God as a republican New Israel, a redoubt of liberty and virtue in a fallen world that now embraced England. "There is no one (I trust)," a Connecticut minister proclaimed in 1777, "whose mind is not at once struck with the description of Israel, as being a most perfect resemblance of these American Colonies: almost as much so, as if spoken with a primary reference to them."[2]

The Revolution thus not only launched the republicanization of regional identity; it also stirred an emergent sense of nationalism. Independence and union dramatically complicated the geopolitics of New England identity. Inhabitants of the most culturally homogeneous corner of the new nation, Revolutionary New Englanders, far more than the citizens of other regions, inherited a highly developed collective self-image derived from Puritanism's lush culture of print. The Revolution, nation making, and the politics of the early republic thrust New Englanders into a national arena that primarily served to augment their sense of regional difference, usually couched in terms of their republican superiority. Even before independence New England delegates to the Continental Congress complained of the popularity of dancing, the theater, and other worldly diversions in Philadelphia. From the Congress in 1775, John Adams reported on the differences he discerned among the delegates. "The characters of gentlemen in the four New England colonies, differ as much from those in others, as that of the common people differs; that is, as much as several distinct nations almost," he wrote to a fellow patriot at home. "Gentlemen, men of sense or any kind of education, in the other colonies, are much fewer in proportion than in New England."[3]

Long before the run-up to the Civil War, the cultural and political encounter between New England and the South heightened Yankee regional self-consciousness. Drawing on New England's historic invocation of the New Israel and on regional leadership of resistance and revolution, descendants of the Puritans in the early republic often trafficked in the politics of virtue as if they had cornered the market. New Englanders, Thomas Jefferson caustically observed, are "marked like the Jews with such a perversity of character."[4] Decades before a powerful, defensive southern regional identity emerged, it was New Englanders who inherited, republicanized, and asserted in the context of national politics the new nation's most well-defined sense of regional distinctiveness and cultural superiority. Furthermore, long before the South was evangelized and transformed into America's Bible Belt, New Englanders occupied the nation's most churched region. Shaped by Puritan tradition and the communalism of regional life, New England's moralistically inflected republicanism confronted a more secular Southern, Jeffersonian variant—a republicanism steeped in the rhetoric of individual rights and opportunity, rather than communal order, and suspicious of government intrusion in religion or "private" matters such as the ownership of slaves. Long before secession emerged as the rally cry for Southern grievances, New England harbored the strongest disunionist sentiment, a threat that was remonstrative and real and one that culminated in the Hartford Convention of 1814.[5] In short, far from tempering New England's historic self-image of regional distinctiveness and substituting an emergent generalized American identity, independence and union established a framework for an enhanced awareness of and a new political investment in regional difference.

Yet New Englanders shared with other Americans a nascent national identity in the early republic. Indeed, New England political and cultural leaders expressed a "national regionalism."[6] New England, many believed, would function as a republican "city upon a hill" for the rest of the nation. The region's superior ways and institutions offered a republican recipe for the New Englandization of the nation. Born of Puritan tradition and of New England's prominent role in the Revolution, such national regionalism foundered in the early republic, frustrated by a secular, individualistic, pluralistic, and expansive geopolitical order. For some aggrieved regional leaders, secession became, if not an alternative to New England's leadership of the nation, a political strategy that might restore its power in the Union.

Jedidiah Morse (1761–1826) was one of these aggrieved national regionalists. Morse has been justifiably dubbed "the father of American geography." He deserves another title as well—geopolitical patriarch of New England's republicanized collective identity in the young nation. As a minister, Morse represented continuity with earlier guardians of regional identity. He was schooled in the religious and historical writings of his Puritan predecessors. A latter-day Puritan, Morse has often served as a whipping boy for historians of the early republic—his sometimes crabbed, even conspiratorial clerical perspective symptomatic of a reactionary Congregational religious establishment desperately clinging to its hoary moral and civil prerogatives.

Not surprisingly, preoccupation with Morse's prominent clerical career has precluded an examination of his even more important, innovative role as the author of the most successful geography texts in the early republic. Morse assumed the task of revising New England's colonial identity to address the new circumstances of geographic and political union. His numerous and widely read texts advanced a geocultural interpretation of New England's distinctiveness that endeavored to reconcile regionalism and an incipient nationalism. Morse was the first writer to conceive of New England as a cultural region, the early republic's only cultural region. A nation within a nation, New England's cultural coherence derived from the homogeneity of its people, a sacred history, and shared habits, customs, and institutions broadly diffused across the region from their original hearths in Connecticut and Massachusetts. Morse's texts exalted New England as the republic's republic, a model for the rest of the Union.[7]

Morse's highly successful career as a geographer paralleled the rise of New England's Federalist establishment—the political movement that rallied support for the ratification of the Constitution and that coalesced into a party by the mid-1790s. Morse's textbook amalgam of republicanized Puritan moralism and regional cultural imperialism permeated Federalist politics. "Rule, New England! New England Rules and Saves," Federalist sloganeering exhorted.[8] But though Morse commanded the field of American geography and his texts propagated the region's claim to republican preeminence, the Federalist vision of New Englandizing the new nation faltered. The father of American geography, whose richly textured interpretation of New England as a cultural region found such resonance in Federalist circles, then positioned himself at the center of the party's secessionist politics.

Union, Region, Nation, and the Republican Culture of Print

Mid-eighteenth-century colonial Americans regarded themselves as members of the British Empire; independence did not mean that they automatically reimagined themselves as Americans. Indeed, the Revolutionaries' shift from defending their British rights to invoking universal natural rights in the Declaration of Independence, one historian has recently argued, reflected "the political language of a colonial people who had not yet invented a nation and, therefore, who had not yet constituted a common history."[9] Imagining America into existence proved to be a long-range, continuous process that stretched to the Civil War and beyond. Well before the United States became a continental nation, it was already a far-flung republic characterized by ethnic, racial, and religious diversity, a union of states that had been founded at different times and for different reasons.

Independence initiated a decades-long "search for an American identity" among the disparate citizens of a decentralized republic. Union established the political context for the first, often halting steps toward the creation of a national consciousness. In particular, national rituals such as celebrations of the Fourth of July, the Constitution, and Washington's Birthday encouraged a dawning sense of American identity. The emergence of national political parties with different regional bases made the early republic's fledgling "American" patriotism a contested field.[10]

Morse's "American" geography texts were products of the politics of regional and national identity in the early republic. Like his Puritan ancestors, he wielded the printed word as a tool of moral improvement. His texts were civic interventions designed to steer the progress of an inchoate national identity and an American republican culture along New England lines of development.

In *The American Geography*—published in 1789, the same year George Washington was inaugurated—Morse called citizens of the new republic "Federo-Americans." Political union amounted to only the first step in nation making. "America" resided in the future, in an anticipated time, Morse wrote, "when the language, manners, customs, political and religious sentiments of the mixed mass of people . . . shall become so assimilated, as that all nominal distinctions shall be lost in the general and honourable name AMERICANS." [11] Morse gave early voice to what would become the official assimilationist model of American identity. But his assimilationist nationalism was not simply a forward-looking vision; it was rooted in regional chauvinism, in an abiding pride in New England's comparative cultural homogeneity. Morse's putative "American" geography, then, inscribes a tension between regionalism and nationalism, between the reality of a seemingly brittle political union and the prospect of an American nation, a prospect that appeared to require the "New Englandizing" of the republic. Even as he labored to advance geographic knowledge of the new union as a building block in the creation of an American identity, Morse displayed his fierce attachment to New England, and he documented how the early republic was a mosaic of local and regional histories, loyalties, and lived experiences. His textbooks were primers of nationhood that revealed the emergent but fragile location of "America" in the early republic's geopolitical imagination.

Morse grew into adulthood in tandem with the birth of the republic. But he remained a steadfast son of Connecticut, like other stalwart Federalist cultural representatives and regional jingoists such as lexicographer Noah Webster and Yale president Timothy Dwight. Morse was born in 1761 in Woodstock, Connecticut, a small farming town in the northeastern corner of the colony. Woodstock belonged to the so-called land of steady habits, the homogeneous village world of Connecticut where an entrenched religious orthodoxy and venerable local institutions—the church, the town meeting, schools, the militia—established safeguards for ordered liberty. "As well attempt to revolutionize the Kingdom of Heaven as the state of Connecticut," Noah Webster observed. The land of steady habits would prove to be a bastion of the Federalist Party and a hot-house of secessionist politics. Connecticut would also persist at the core of Morse's personal identity and as the moral axis of his republican geography. His texts offered a "Connecticut-centered" view of New England. The state loomed in his imagination and in the moral landscape of his books as "New England's New England," the locale where the distinctive republican features of regional life achieved their fullest realization.[12]

Morse's pious father, who served as a deacon of the Woodstock church and town representative to the Connecticut General Assembly, sent young Jedidiah to Yale College in 1779. Founded in 1701, Yale prized its religious orthodoxy, especially as Harvard acquired a more "catholick" cast. A devout and dutiful son, Morse professed hope that he had experienced conversion during his sophomore year and was admitted to communion in the college chapel. Because of poor health he had been spared military service. As the tumult of revolution continued, he proceeded on what appeared to be a conventional path into the Congregational ministry.[13]

Morse graduated from Yale in 1783, and soon geography seemed to excite his ambition more than theology. He remained in New Haven, studying for the ministry while teaching at a school for young girls. In 1784 he published his first text, *Geography Made Easy*. He later described the work as a "Juvenile Essay"; the text was written "to accommodate a school of young ladies I was then teaching at New Haven, and my ideas scarcely extended beyond the limits of my native State, Connecticut."[14] Like a seasoned scholar looking back on the initial results of his creative awakening, Morse passed judgment on his modest text after he had published such works as *The American Geography* (1789) and *The American Universal Geography* (1793), volumes that reached national and international audiences. Yet his later works displayed striking continuity with his "Juvenile Essay." *Geography Made Easy* presented the Mid-Atlantic and Southern states as individual geographic units, but New England took on the characteristics of a highly republican cultural region. "[In] the four flourishing New England states," Morse warmed to his subject, "the inhabitants . . . are noted for the simplicity of their manners, the purity of their morals, their noble independence, the equal distribution of their property, the industrious cultivation of their lands and for the enjoyment of all the necessaries and conveniences of life." Connecticut, in the form of an idealized Woodstock writ large, occupied the imaginative center of Morse's New England. "The people in this state," he enthused, "are generally industrious, sagacious husbandmen; generous and hospital to strangers, and good neighbors."[15] Provincial patriotism and a hybrid ideology of Puritanism and republicanism stalk the pages of Morse's texts beginning with *Geography Made Easy*.

The volume proved to be a surprising commercial success. "My geographies sell beyond my most sanguine Expectations," he wrote to his father in early 1785. "I have sold between 3 & 400 within 3 weeks."[16] His New Haven publisher struggled to respond to the demand. Morse had stumbled on a potentially wide audience: citizens of the new republic, or "Federo-Americans," groping their way in the 1780s toward the establishment of a comprehensive national political framework and seeking information about the diverse and recently confederated states as the first step in imagining themselves as a nation, not simply a union. Morse carried all his provincial baggage into what unfolded as a highly successful career that enlisted geography in the service of guiding a political work in progress—the American republic.

Morse was licensed to preach in 1785, but he resisted permanent installment as a pastor. Instead, he returned to Yale as a tutor in 1786 and continued to prepare for the ministry. He also began compiling information for an ambitious book, the first comprehensive American geography text. He envisioned a work that would "grow and improve as the nation advances toward maturity."[17] Like the Puritan patriarchs on whose shoulders he stood, Morse sought to shape history, not just live it. He laced his texts with the moralism, didacticism, attachment to order, and pride of place that constituted his New England heritage. The regional sensibility that informed his moral geography reflected larger conflicts vexing New Englanders during the early republic—tensions between liberty and order, growth and stability, opportunity and virtue. Morse embraced the prospect of the newly confederated states as an expansive republican empire, but he venerated the order, the institutionalism, the piety, the ethnic homogeneity, and the middle-class steadiness of town-centered New England.[18] In his hands, geography became a surrogate for the Puritan jeremiad—a way of stabilizing a dynamic republic and of ordering an ever-changing New England as the nation and the region contended with both the promise and the unsettling consequences of the American Revolution.

Morse's texts emerged from a world that was in geographic flux. People were on the move; boundaries were being penetrated and redrawn; new geographic categories were evolving. Victory over the British opened the trans-Appalachian West. Migrants moved into Western territories that were often claimed by more than one state. Disputes arose over the extension of the Mason-Dixon line westward. The Revolution brought about shifts in state capitals, from older, coastal communities to newer, more centrally located towns. The center of the federal government moved from New York to Philadelphia, while plans proceeded for a new "Federal City" located neither in the North nor the South.[19] Such changes made the republic a shifting geographic world, symptomatic of a larger opening of American society that resulted from the expulsion of British authority.

New England was not isolated from the geographic change that swept through the early republic. New Englanders flocked westward and northward. What had been often called "New Connecticut," the province of Vermont peopled with thousands of migrants from the land of steady habits, struggled for autonomy against the authority of New York. Similarly, land-hungry migrants from southern New England swelled the District of Maine's population; by the 1780s there were already serious calls for Maine independence from Massachusetts. New England also witnessed resistance to old state capitols and even changes such as the transfer of New Hampshire's seat of government from Portsmouth to Concord. Morse seemed to accept the geographic openness and possibilities of America when his texts shifted the prime meridian from Greenwich, England, to Philadelphia, an act of geographic patriotism.[20] But given his New England values and sensibility, he could never uncritically accept the fluid geopolitical order that seemed aborning in the early republic. His first extended trip outside of New England provoked his unease about the state of the Union; it also confirmed that New England was a comparative land of steady habits whose republican way of life needed to be preserved as a model for the nation.

Morse continued to gather information for *The American Geography,* his ambitious new text. In 1786 he arranged to fill the pulpit of a Congregational church in Midway, Georgia, on a temporary basis. The appointment enabled him to organize a research and promotional trip for *The American Geography.* He intended take the measure of the republican world outside New England, talk to prominent leaders and Revolutionary luminaries, and drum up interest in his geographic work. Morse received encouragement from Benjamin Franklin and George Washington. During his visit with Washington in Virginia, Morse discussed Shays' Rebellion.[21] This farmer protest in western Massachusetts in 1786 challenged the political and economic dominance of the state by eastern interests. The unrest was transformed into a "rebellion" by supporters of a strong national government who pressed for what became the Constitutional Convention. Shays' Rebellion represented precisely the post-Revolutionary change that Morse and others feared would destabilize even New England.

Still, Morse's travels only confirmed the relative steadiness and republican promise of New England. He was shocked to discover how few people attended church, particularly in the South. "How different from New England," he recorded privately. "Thrice happy is Connecticut in this respect." He confided to his father that the trip offered him a "great opportunity to learn human Nature. I am extremely sorry to find it so extremely depraved." In the South he found more than the moral landscape wanting; the Southern countryside lacked the order and compactness of the New England town, what for Morse was both an emblem of communalism and an aesthetic object. "I cannot but give preference to my own country," he concluded.[22] Morse's encounter with the South paralleled the disquieting experience of another Connecticut cultural "nationalist." Lexicographer Noah Webster, who served as an adviser on *The American Geography,* observed the South contemporaneously with Morse. Webster deplored an alien landscape in which residents "fix their churches as far as possible from town & their play houses in the center." Out of "50 planters in [Alexandria,] Virginia, who sold Tobacco, [only] 4 or 5 could write their names," he claimed. "O New England! How superior are thy inhabitants in morals, literature, civility and industry," Webster brooded.[23] Already in the 1780s, in the flush of independence and military victory, Morse and Webster were anxious nationalists wedded to Connecticut standards and clinging to hope for the future of the republic but increasingly repelled by the seemingly vulgar, disarrayed world they found beyond New England.

Morse returned from the South in the summer of 1787, as the Constitutional Convention pursued its work in Philadelphia. He continued to compile information for *The American Geography* while he resisted accepting a permanent pastorate. To capitalize on the interest generated by the creation of a new national government, he delayed publication of his work until 1789 and included a copy of the Constitution in his text. With his detailed geography book completed, Morse accepted a call to the Congregational church in Charlestown, Massachusetts, where he would serve his entire ministry (1789–1819) and, often to the neglect of his clerical duties, carry on the work that secured his reputation as the father of American geography.

In 1793, fours years after the publication of *The American Geography,* Morse released a revised and expanded two-volume work, *The American*

Universal Geography. He reported in 1794 that he had already sold well over twenty thousand copies of his texts.[24] For thirty years he revised and updated his works while creating abridged editions for schools. Morse's texts tutored a generation of American youth, from grammar school to college, in the rudiments of American geography and of New England republican superiority. Probate records of home libraries also reveal the enormous popularity of his texts in the early republic. His geographies, along with Noah Webster's *Speller,* competed with the Bible and hymn books as the staple volumes of home libraries in New England and beyond.[25]

Morse produced new works that capitalized on a burgeoning reading audience in the early republic and that incorporated the moral geography of his texts. In 1797 he published *The American Gazetteer,* a geographic dictionary that repackaged his New England–centered view of the Union. Seven years later he and fellow minister Elijah Parish coauthored *A Compendious History of New England.* A school text that nicely complemented Morse's geography books, *A Compendious History* extended the traditional Puritan heroic narrative of New England's founding: "A body of men more remarkable for their piety and morality, and more respectable for their wisdom, never commenced the settlement of any country." But traditional providential history served as the backdrop to the cultural geography of New England, that is, to an exposition of the region's republican "Population; Character; Amusement; Learning; [and] Religion."[26] Both the *Compendious History* and *American Gazetteer* went through multiple editions and enlarged the corpus of Morse's work available to a broad reading public.

Morse wrote, continually revised, and regularly abridged his texts, commanding the field of geography in the early republic with a printed output that daunted prospective competitors. The prolific author and his ever-widening audience signaled the emergence of a new, republican economy of cultural production and consumption. According to republican ideology, the survival of the republic rested on an informed and virtuous citizenry. By elevating the sovereignty of the people, Revolutionary republicanism encouraged another kind of democratization: the diffusion of useful knowledge that would transform individuals into responsible citizens. The Revolution altered the cultural terrain of the early republic. Newspapers, print shops, and especially libraries spread across New England, for example. A new print culture of self- and civic improvement, encompassing works from the *Autobiography of Benjamin Franklin* to the *Farmer's Almanack,* burst into post-Revolutionary life. This new world of print was often tied to the need to improve citizens' knowledge of and ties to the republic. As Morse announced in the preface to *The American Geography,* his text was "calculated early to impress the minds of American youth with an idea of the superior importance of their own country, as well as to attach them to its interests." [27]

Morse's texts belong to the new republic's Franklinian print culture of self-improvement and to the kindred post-Revolutionary search for an American identity. His dominance of the field of geography, moreover, suggests the preeminent place of New Englanders in the early republic's burgeoning "American" print culture. In the 1780s and 1790s, for instance, Noah Webster emerged as the "father of American grammar." In the *American Speller Book* or "the Blue-Back Speller" (1783), Webster, Morse's Connecticut cultural ally, championed an American way of spelling, writing, and speaking. The numerous editions of Webster's *Speller* sold in the hundreds of thousands. While he reaped the financial rewards, Webster labored on his *American Dictionary,* whose moral-laden and politically charged definitions of words such as "liberty," "equality," or "republican" propagated New England standards. Other New Englanders, in addition to Webster and Morse, contributed significantly to the rise of a new American print culture: Nicholas Pike, *American Arithmetic* (1788); Robert Thomas, *The Farmer's Almanack* (1792); Caleb Bingham, *The American Preceptor,* a reading and speaking text (1794).[28]

Morse, Webster, and other regional leaders of the new republic's print culture were the heirs of Puritan tradition. They sprang from a literate society long invested in the printed word, education, and personal and civic improvement; they were from a region with an exalted self-image as a moral exemplar. New Englanders in the early republic extended the Puritans' esteem for historical study. In 1791 Massachusetts established the first state historical society, intended as a national institution with corresponding members throughout the republic. Two of the next three historical societies were founded in New England, including the American Antiquarian Society (1812).[29]

Moreover, in the 1790s New Englanders led the republic in the production of state histories. These texts comprised yet another aspect of the republican print culture linked to the need for an informed citizenry and to civic improvement; they also served as a prologue to regional domination of the writing of "American" history in the nineteenth century. With the exception of Rhode Island, all the New England states—including Vermont, which was only admitted to the Union in 1790, and the District of Maine—boasted freshly minted histories in the 1790s. No other section of the republic approached this achievement. The New England histories paralleled the state-by-state accounts in Morse's geographies. Morse's works and the state histories, even as they privileged New England, endeavored to build a sense of nationhood inductively by disseminating knowledge about the varied local cultures that made up the republic. As one state historian put it, "Without accounts of the individual states, the true condition of the federal union could not be adequately assessed."[30]

Jeremy Belknap's three-volume *History of New Hampshire* (1792) stands out as the most distinguished of the early state histories of New England. Belknap was a founder of the Massachusetts Historical Society and an adviser to Morse; in the latter capacity he gave the "New England" section of *The American Geography* a prepublication review. Belknap concluded the third volume of his *History of New Hampshire* with an idealized republican vision of the New England social order as a national model. His apostrophe to the reader elevated regional, even local design into a national ideal for a republic still discovering and making itself:

> Were I to form a picture of happy society, it would be a town constituting of a due mixture of hills, valleys and streams of water: The land well fenced and cultivated; the roads and bridges in good repair; a decent inn for the refreshment of travelers. . . . The inhabitants mostly husbandmen; their wives and daughters domestic manufacturers; a suitable proportion of handicraft workmen, and two or three traders, a physician and lawyer, each of whom should have a farm for his support. A clergyman of any denomination, which should be agreeable to the majority. . . . A school master who should understand his business and teach his pupils to govern themselves. A social library, annually increasing, and under good regulation. A club of sensible men, seeking mutual improvement. . . . No intriguing politician, horse jockey, gambler or sot; but all such characters treated with contempt. Such a situation may be considered as the most favorable to social happiness of any which this world can afford.[31]

Morse filled out this paean to the New England's village social order. In his hands, New England emerged as the new republic's only cultural region. His moralistic geographies sought to codify and stabilize the region's cultural distinctiveness while conveying his hope for the "New Englandization" of the republic. Morse appointed himself geography schoolmaster to the new nation.

New England as a Cultural Region

Morse's texts introduced readers to the physical geography of the newly
federated states; he drew "The face of the Country," detailing the rivers,
the topography, the soil, the climate, and the minerals that comprised
the varied landscape of the republic.[32] But Morse was more interested in
human behavior. His books offered a historically informed cultural geography of republicanism in the new nation. He broadly sketched the physi-
ognomy of the early republic, but his regional loyalties and Puritan heritage concentrated his angle of vision.

In the first place, Morse privileged the New England states by can-
vassing them from two geographic perspectives. He began by presenting
the states as part of a coherent cultural unit, outlining their shared history and their defining "customs" and "habits." He also examined each
New England state on its own terms, situating it on a continuum of "New
Englandness." For Morse, Connecticut resided at the imaginative center
of New England; Rhode Island, as it had for the Puritans, existed beyond
the region's cultural borders.

Morse introduced the non–New England states individually; they were
political jurisdictions lacking internal cultural coherence and were uncon-
nected by custom, habit, and history to their neighbors. To be sure, he
conceded that slavery established its imprint on the South. But understandably, he was more struck by the rawness and diversity of the South.
It lacked the mature social institutions of New England; an expansive
region, the South had yet to acquire the entrenched collective consciousness that New England already possessed. A comparable creation of a
Southern identity would have to await the sectional conflict over slavery.
In *The American Universal Geography,* Morse tried for the first time to define
the "three grand divisions" of the republic: "*Eastern, Middle,* and *Southern*
States." He included his detailed description of New England under the
Eastern states. For the Mid-Atlantic states, the second grand division, he
managed only one and a half pages of largely physical description. And
for the South, the "Third and *much the largest* Grand Division," *The American Universal Geography* offered the reader half a page! Morse ultimately
abandoned his general description of the other grand divisions, even as
he updated his interpretation of New England as a cultural region.[33]

As Morse's inconsistent use of grand divisions suggests, he was struggling for a geographic vocabulary that would enable him to impose conceptual order on the new republic. He did not have a ready-made geo-

graphic lexicon on which to draw. Yet terms such as "cultural region," "cultural hearth," and "sectionalism" fit the geography of the early republic that is inscribed in his texts. New England was a relatively compact, homogeneous region with a collective memory; its people displayed distinctive character traits and inhabited a world of well-developed civic institutions. For Morse, the states outside of New England lacked such essential cultural characteristics and, therefore, any sense of collective identity. The non–New England states could only be linked through sectionalism—alliances that shifted from issue to issue as states pursued their political and economic interests under a federal union.[34] But Morse's New England sensibility could never enable him to embrace a pluralistic republic loosely sutured by political and economic interests. Morse envisioned the future America as one extended cultural region with New England as its republican hearth.

Morse represented New England as a nation within a nation, but the region itself was in the throes of change. New Englanders, like their contemporaries in the early republic, were a people in motion, with migrants on the move within and from the region. "New England may, with propriety, be called a nursery of men," Morse observed, "whence are annually transplanted, into other parts of the United States, thousands of its natives." Such mobility roused his hopes for the New Englandizing of the Union as republican-bred natives transported their values and institutions to settlements beyond the region. Other changes disquieted Morse. *The American Geography* lamented the "extravagant importations" of post-Revolutionary New England. An unfavorable balance of trade resulted from "luxuries, or at best the dispensable conveniences of life," that flooded into the region.[35]

Importations did not pose the only threat to New England republicanism. Morse discerned the menace of licentiousness in post-Revolutionary New Englanders' litigiousness and prickly "jealousy" of their liberty. "Where a people have a great share of freedom, an equal share of virtue is necessary to the peaceable enjoyment of it," he intoned. "Freedom, without virtue or honor, is licentiousness." For the geographer as Jeremiah, a "restless, litigious, complaining spirit" betokened "a dark shade in the character of New Englandmen."[36] Like the Jeremiahs who preceded him and examined New England's identity in more purely religious terms, Morse's geographies endeavored to delimit change, to fix the boundaries of a region in transition. He translated earlier understandings of New England's distinctiveness into the language of republicanism. He thereby updated the region's collective identity, and he deployed his moralistic geography to stabilize the customs, habits, and institutions that, he insisted, defined New England's republican culture.

Morse's encounter with the pluralistic society outside of New England, especially in the Mid-Atlantic states, provoked a new awareness of his region's cultural homogeneity and the republican benefits that accrued from this condition. Though he eschewed use of the Yankee label, Morse conceived of New Englanders as an ethnic group whose common history and heritage underwrote the region's republican stability. "The inhabitants of New England are almost universally of English descent," he seemed to exult. "There are no Dutch, French, or Germans, and very few Scotch or Irish people in any part of New England." The population shared a common linguistic, cultural, and religious heritage and even displayed a physical resemblance. "The New Englanders are generally tall, stout, and well built," Morse observed, and women "generally have fair, fresh and healthful countenances."[37] His geography signaled an ethnicization of New Englanders that would have been inconceivable to his Puritan ancestors, however much they paraded their British ancestry. A growing "ethnic" New England consciousness in the early republic was generated by increasing knowledge of and contact with the society beyond the region's borders. The formation of New England Societies by transplanted Yankees was one indication of this development. The first New England Society was established in New York City in 1805; its charter described it as a voluntary association "of individuals, allied to each other by a similarity of habits and education" as well as of regional origins. Members were required to be a "New England man by birth, or the son of a member," though non–New Englanders could be admitted to this "ethnic" society by a two-thirds vote of the members.[38] These societies, which spread to the South and West, gathered to commemorate their members' regional cultural heritage and served as institutional expressions of mobile New Englanders' group consciousness and historical-mindedness. The ethnic identity proclaimed by Morse's geographies and the New England Societies differed from the "national prejudices" that the geographer observed particularly in the Mid-Atlantic states. Morse held up republican New England as the "real" America. "New Englandness" became an ethnic identity to supplant other ethnic identities—a normalizing, assimilationist, even nativist regionalism that would be frustrated by the refractory social order of the young republic.[39]

New England's common ethnic and cultural heritage yielded "a hardy race of free, independent republicans." It also begat stabilizing social institutions that nurtured virtuous citizens and the ordered liberty that Morse cherished. Though he was often disquieted by what he saw as New Englanders' excessive mobility, consumption, and attachment to liberty, he extolled the civic culture of the region and its restraining effect on licentiousness. Local government, churches, schools, and the militia constituted New England's town-centered civic institutions. Like other travelers in the early republic who journeyed outside the region, Morse discovered not only the exceptionalism of New England's cultural homogeneity but also the distinctiveness of its civic landscape. New England could legitimately boast of possessing the new nation's most developed social order, a legacy, he pointed out, of "venerable ancestors."[40] Morse's geographies advanced a religious-political agenda: defining and celebrating New England's civic distinctiveness as a way of solidifying a region of steady habits.

Moreover, an established civic culture encouraged Morse and other leaders to imagine the region as the most republican, and therefore the most "American," corner of the Union. John Adams, for example, recorded in his diary in 1786 a conversation he had in London concerning the regrettable differences between Virginia and New England. Adams offered "a Receipt for making a New England in Virginia." He presented a town-centered view of the "Scaenes where New England men are formed": "In all Countries, and in all Companies for several Years, I have in Conversation and in Writing enumerated the Town, Militia, Schools and Churches as the four causes of the Growth and Defence of N. England. The Virtues and Talents of the People are there formed. Their Temperance, Patience, Fortitude, Prudence, and Justice, as well as their Sagacity, Knowledge, Judgment, Taste, Skill, Ingenuity, Dexterity, and Industry."[41] Such tributes to New England's town-based civic institutions enabled Morse and cultural leaders to reconcile regionalism and nationalism, to advance New England as a civic model for the early republic.

In "Greenfield Hill" (1794), for instance, Timothy Dwight penned a poetic hymn to New England's republican village culture, where the region's "sires" established the "noblest institutions":

Beneath their eye,
And forming hand, in every hamlet, rose
The nurturing school; in every village, smil'd
The heav'n-inviting church, and every town

A World within itself, with order, peace,
And harmony, adjusted all its weal.

Dwight ended his epic poem with the prospect of New Englanders fashioning a republican "America," at least among the Northern states. Westward migration from the region that Morse described as a "nursery of men" fired Dwight's imagination with a continental vision of a "Greater" New England:

Soon shall thy sons across the mainland roam;
And claim, on far Pacific shores, their home;
Their rule, religion, manners, arts convey,
And spread their freedom to the Asian sea.[42]

Morse's geographies participated in a larger post-Revolutionary New England discourse that sought to harmonize a new, republicanized awareness of regional distinctiveness with an emergent sense of American nationhood. Ironically, the region's *distinctive* civic culture and its *exceptional* ethnic homogeneity encouraged New England to be imagined as "America's America."

Such national regionalism, furthermore, was reinforced in the early republic by New England's claim on leadership of resistance and revolution. As John Adams saw it, New England's unique civic culture and republican character propelled the region to the forefront of the Revolutionary "Defence" of liberty. Suppressing evidence of loyalism and neutrality, Morse asserted in his geographies that in states like Connecticut there were "but few citizens who did not join in opposing the oppressive measures of Great Britain." Connecticut and New England spawned a united, republican population that was "active and influential . . . in bringing about the Revolution."[43] As we shall see, when Morse and other frustrated Federalists flirted with secession, they framed it as a patriotic act that harked back to the American Revolution.

In his texts, however, Morse avoided secessionist politics; he remained content to present the texture of life in town-centered New England—a cultural analysis that explained the region's leadership of the Revolution and established it as a republican exemplum for the nation. Among New England townspeople, for example, religion restrained the profane behavior that Morse observed or heard about in other parts of the republic: "The odious and inhuman practices of dueling, gouging, cock-fighting and horse-racing, are scarcely known here." Pious Puritan customs endured as part of civic life, curbing the spread of licentiousness. Fast and thanksgiving days as well as election sermons, which persisted well into the nineteenth century, comprised a "distinguishing" regional heritage that descended from noble ancestors. Morse republicanized older Puritan historical narratives that shaped New England's collective memory. Conferring a revised, republican interpretive order on regional identity, the geographer-Jeremiah sought to stabilize the inherited social order — an arrangement grounded in deference to clerical authority. Morse hoped that New England's "ancient" pious "habits," which had secured the region's republican character, "will ever be sacredly preserved."[44]

Beyond the moral tone of civic life in New England, Morse celebrated the public school as a pillar of the region's distinctive republican ways. A system of town-supported schools, which dated from the midseventeenth century, fostered literacy not only for a laity bent on religious improvement but for an informed republican citizenry as well. Struck by the contrast with the South in particular, Morse claimed that "a person of mature age, who cannot read and write, is rarely to be found" in New England. He even lauded the democratization of knowledge that such literacy encouraged and to which his geographies contributed. "In New England, learning is more generally diffused among all ranks of people," he enthused, "than in any other part of the globe; arising from the excellent establishment of schools in every township."[45]

The thousands of copies of newspapers that "circulated in almost every town and village" impressed Morse as a striking example of how literacy bestowed a superior republican civic culture on the region. Of course, New England had long been in the forefront of American newspaper publishing. The *Boston Weekly News-Letter* (1704) and the *New England Courant* (1721) were the first papers established in colonial America. At midcentury, New England continued to have more newspapers than any other region. By the mid-1790s, Timothy Dwight reported, the number of American newspapers had swelled to well over one hundred, nearly half of which were published in New England.[46]

While Morse applauded New England's tradition of literacy and the diffusion of information in the early republic, he also recorded and cautioned against the seemingly baneful social effects of these developments. The democratization of knowledge disrupted customary channels of information and authority. Morse described a New England "where every man thinks himself at least as good as his neighbour, and believes that all mankind are, or ought to be equal." In a world that proclaimed the sovereignty of the people, widespread literacy and an expansive print culture tended to erode traditional lines of authority. Morse warned against an "impertinence" and *"impertinent inquisitiveness"* that threatened to leach into the New England character.[47]

Morse's observations on New England literacy, and his geographies themselves, emerged out of what has been called the "village enlightenment"—the expansive republican print culture of personal and civic improvement that swept over the region in the post-Revolutionary decades.[48] His texts were artifacts of this explosion of print and knowledge. But they were also jeremiadlike throwbacks, works devised to contain and shape change. For all of its republican resonance, the geographer's voice remains that of a Puritan patriarch negotiating the preservation of his own authority and propagating a familiar version of traditional New England values.

"Mediocrity," "industry," "frugality"—these and related words recur like an incantation in the "New England" section of his texts when Morse turns to the social character of regional life. Except for a brief discussion of trade and some admonishing references to extravagance and luxury, the geographies convey little sense of the dynamic commercial order of early republican New England. Though Morse barely observed this economic world, he became one of its many agents. First, his geographies were part of a commercialization of knowledge—the new, profit-making culture of print that was tied to the civic aspirations of the early republic. More important, Morse invested the healthy profits from the sale of his books in banks, land, canals, and turnpikes.[49] In fact, as shown in the next chapter, one reason Morse could lavish praise on New England's town-centered republican life was because, after decades of population dispersal, town centers were renucleating in the early republic as economic nodes of the region's growing commercial agriculture. The result was the white New England village—the orderly cluster of Federal-style homes and businesses in a town center, the geographic marker of an economic order that presented Morse and other New Englanders with new investment opportunities.

But in the geographies, Morse imagined the socioeconomic order of the New England village more in relationship to his native Woodstock than to the rising commercial town of the early republic. Competency and equality prevailed in his republican towns. In New England, a family's sons shared in the generational transfer of land. Over time, of course, family estates shrank through constant subdivision, placing in motion the land-hungry migrants who set out for northern New England or the West. But the region's traditional land division perpetuated "that happy mediocrity among the people," Morse insisted, "which by inducing economy, and industry, removes from them temptations to luxury, and forms them to habits of sobriety and temperance." The New England town springs from the pages of Morse's text as a society of middle-class republicans still wedded to competency. Morse raises the issue of a lower class only to question whether "such a class may be said to exist in New England."[50] Though grounded in real traditions and social patterns that enabled him to present New England as a distinct cultural region, Morse's books still embroider the economic circumstances of town life. Morse submits a hortatory still portrait of the moral economy of the New England town as if to arrest its development.

Indeed, he appears to urge contentment on New Englanders, for in "no part of the world are the people happier, better furnished with the necessaries and conveniences of life, or more independent than the farmers of New England." Such a "hardy" breed of freeholders wore their "plain, simple, and unpolished" manners as a badge of their republican character. Recalling New Englanders' early, stout defense of their liberty against the British, Morse enshrined the town-based militia as the sentry of the region's republican, landholding order. "Few countries on earth, of equal extent and population," he boasted, "can furnish a more formidable army than this part of the union."[51]

Morse transmutes New England from New Israel to Christian Sparta. As mini-Christian republics, New England towns record a seamless historical development from Puritan past to republican present. Morse's narrative both described and delimited New England. By repeating the same geographic account in edition after edition — that is, by textualizing New England's essential cultural differences from the rest of America — Morse attempted to fix the region's moral coordinates. Moreover, his textual efforts to stabilize New England as an institutionally ordered, Christian republic served a nationalist goal. Morse and many of his contemporary descendants of the Puritans continued to imagine New England as the moral and civic tutor to others.

After presenting a detailed analysis of New England as a "Grand Division," Morse's works compassed the individual states. Although he did not possess the regional geographer's terminology of core and periphery, his mapping of New England as a cultural region imposed precisely that spatial order on the states. Morse imagined Connecticut as New England's heartland; much of newly settled northern New England remained part of a land of steady habits still in the making; Rhode Island, in contrast, was a borderland that Morse, following Puritan tradition, all but evicted from New England.

Rhode Island acquired notoriety as the anti-image of the orderly Christian republic that Morse's geographies venerated. Rhode Island only ratified the Constitution, under duress, in 1790. It was perceived in other corners of New England as a licentious republic where feeble or nonexistent institutions allowed liberty to degenerate into unbridled individualism and disorder. Rhode Island distressed Morse as an "unhappy state," where "all religious institutions have been more neglected . . . than [in] any other of the New England States." Outside of Providence and Newport, Morse complained, "The bulk of the inhabitants . . . are involved in greater ignorance perhaps than in any other part of New England." Rife with religious sects and "*Nothingarians*,"[52] the "Isle of Errors" persisted as an irritating regional eyesore; Rhode Islanders inhabited a world beyond the cultural borders of New England's republic of steady habits. In its religious pluralism, secularism, individualism, and faction-based politics, the state remained a scandal to New England. It seemed to be culturally aligned not with its neighbors but with the social order and ethos that Morse observed in the Mid-Atlantic states. Rhode Island's "un–New Englandness" was imprinted on its landscape, though Morse does not explicitly record this physical difference. Symptomatic of its historically attenuated communalism, Rhode Island largely failed to develop the white nucleated towns and villages that created a distinctive regional landscape from Connecticut to Maine.

The emergence of nucleated towns in the newly settled North encouraged Morse's hopes for the ongoing "New Englandization" of the regional periphery. The Connecticut River Valley of Vermont and New Hampshire and the District of Maine continued to be settled by migrants from Connecticut and Massachusetts—New England's cultural hearth of Puritan tradition and "ancient," integrated institutions. "There is no characteristical difference between the inhabitants of this and the other New England States," Morse wrote of New Hampshire. "As to the character, the manners, the customs, the laws, the policy and the religion of the people of Vermont," he observed of the first new state admitted to the Union, which was filled with Connecticut migrants, "it is sufficient to say they are New England men." Morse was more tentative about rapidly developing Maine. In 1789 he noted the District's "ardent desire" for independence from Massachusetts, a separation that would not be achieved until 1820. He praised the "hardy" and "robust" people of Maine and anticipated that Massachusetts civic culture would shape the orderly development of the District. Morse was encouraged by plans, initiated as early as 1788, for a Maine college. Bowdoin, a Congregational institution founded in 1794, embodied the moral-civic vision that inspired his hope for Maine's full social and cultural integration into Federalist New England.[53]

The traditional Puritan strongholds of Massachusetts and Connecticut dominate Morse's analysis of the individual New England states. But whereas he fixed Boston as the capital "not only of Massachusetts, but of New England," Morse located Connecticut as the imaginative center of republican New England. Connecticut did not have the stain of a witchcraft hysteria on its past, a blot that, well into the nineteenth century, complicated Massachusetts efforts to claim a republican past—to retell the story of its religious origins in a way that served a republican collective identity. Moreover, Connecticut had not been rocked by the agrarian unrest that incited Shays' Rebellion. The land of steady habits loomed in Morse's imagination as the cultural heartland of New England republicanism. He devoted over thirty pages, more than to any other New England state, to explaining how "Connecticut has ever been a republic, and perhaps as perfect and as happy a republic as has ever existed."[54] Both in his general discussion of New England and in his separate description of Connecticut, Morse compiled and configured regional geographic facts in the service of a national moral vision.

The "New England" section of *The American Geography* and *The American Universal Geography* illustrated his Connecticut-centered perspective on the region. Seizing on the physical centrality of the Connecticut River Valley, Morse imaginatively transformed it into a kind of New England Nile— a majestic artery that linked distant towns and diffused cultural values. "On this beautiful river, whose banks are settled almost to its source," he rejoiced, "are many pleasant, neat, well-built towns."[55] He proceeded to march the reader through four states, up the western bank of the Connecticut and down its eastern shore. The intrepid geographer led a moral excursion into the heart of republican country, mapping an inland empire of virtue and ordered liberty. When Morse turned to his separate, detailed examination of Connecticut, the state fully emerged as the seat of New England republicanism.

Connecticut, of course, laid claim to being the land of steady habits in part because independence had not necessitated a new state constitution. Colonial Connecticut had staved off royalization. In the early republic, the old charter, under which freeholders elected the governor, continued to serve as a constitution. "Connecticut has uninterruptedly proceeded in her old track, both as to government and manners," Morse explained, "and, by these means, has avoided those convulsions which have rent other states into violent parties." Connecticut was New England's "ancient" republic.[56]

Having republicanized Connecticut's political heritage, Morse tackled its religious tradition. "The best in the world, perhaps, for a republican government," he declared of the state's religious institutions. "As to the mode of exercising church government and discipline, it might not improperly be called a republican religion."[57] Connecticut's religious establishment operated under a modified Congregational plan that attempted to balance liberty and order, the elements so central to Morse's republicanism. Each church chose its own minister, admitted and disciplined members, and generally governed local ecclesiastical affairs. But local churches formed county associations that licensed ministers, recommended policies, and provided clergy to settle disputes between congregations and pastors. The county associations met annually as a general association.

Such ecclesiastical arrangements, Morse seemed to suggest, made religion a common school that instilled republican habits—habits transferable to the civic sphere of local and state government. But the ecclesiastical structure of Connecticut also preserved deference to clerical authority, as ministers exerted influence through the county and general associations. Not surprisingly, Connecticut boasted New England's strongest religious establishment, which was buttressed by orthodox Yale College and the phalanx of evangelical ministers such as Morse who numbered among its graduates. Connecticut ministers had been part of the "black regiment," the rank-and-file patriotic Congregational clergy who supplied moral leadership to the American Revolution. Their political activism continued during the early republic. A Yale student from the South described his stupefaction over the Connecticut clergy's political engagement: "The clergy so far from being the meek and lowly followers of Christ . . . are the most violent partizans, the most busy electioneers . . . ," he bemoaned. "Their situation and importance here give them an influence and importance but little thought of in the states southwardly of this."[58]

Morse's panegyric to Connecticut's republican religion described the clergy's status in revealing terms. *The American Geography* lauded the ministry for representing "a kind of aristocratical balance" in the state, which served as a "check upon the overbearing spirit of republicanism." An entrenched religious establishment, with the clergy as civic leaders, shaped Connecticut as a land of steady habits. Of course, the Christian republicanism that Morse saw enshrined in the state elevated deference to a sign of virtue. For Morse, as for Timothy Dwight, Noah Webster, and their fellow Christian republicans who would fill the ranks of New England's Federalist Party, resistance to established authority by religious dissenters and political insurgents clamoring for a widened suffrage would only be received as a symptom of regional moral decay.[59]

Morse's Connecticut offered a tutorial on the workings of a virtuous republic. Beyond its cultural homogeneity and its stable political and religious institutions, Connecticut claimed a citizenry with a "thirst for learning" and improvement. "More of the young men in Connecticut, in proportion to their numbers, receive a public education, than in any of the states," Morse contended. Not Boston, not Philadelphia, but Connecticut deserved recognition as the *"Athens of America."* [60] Thus did Morse's classical republicanism become attached to geographic boosterism.

Morse imaged Connecticut as a pastoral republic—a town-centered middle landscape where "mediocrity" prevailed. But he lacked an aesthetic sense; didactic geography became his calling card. He was either unable or unwilling to evoke the beauty of New England's heartland the way Connecticut artist Ralph Earl or poet Timothy Dwight did. "The whole state resembles a well cultivated garden," Morse reported in bloodless prose, "which, with that degree of industry that is necessary to happiness, produces the necessaries and conveniences of life in great plenty." Dwight aestheticized Morse's vision of Connecticut as the "real" New England. In "Greenfield Hill," he poeticized the land of steady habits, infusing "painterly" beauty into Morse's didactic subject:

> Fair is the landscape; but fairer still
> Shall soon inchant the soul—when harvest full
> Waves wide its bending wealth. Delightful task!
> To trace along the rich, enamell'd ground,
> The sweetly varied hues; from India's corn
> Whose black'ning verdure bodes a bounteous crop,
> Through lighter grass, and lighter still the flax,

The paler oats, the yellowish barley, wheat
In golden glow, and rye in brighter gold.
These soon the sight shall bless. Now other scenes
The heart dilate, where round, in rural pride
The village spreads its tidy, snug retreats,
That speak the industry of every hand.[61]

Here is the layered, balanced landscape of Morse's Connecticut summoned poetically as a "finished" republican scene. Morse was content with
textual persuasion, mobilizing geography to stay change in Connecticut,
to advance New England as a region of steady habits, and to project his
moral vision onto the rest of the republic.

Not So Grand Divisions:
The Mid-Atlantic and Southern States

"To be a true Geographer, it is necessary to be a Traveler," Jeremy Belknap advised Morse as he planned *The American Geography.* The provincial Morse resisted Belknap's counsel. When he published the first editions of *The American Geography* and *The American Universal Geography* in
1789 and 1793, a trip to Georgia to fill a temporary pastorate constituted
Morse's principal firsthand experience of the world beyond New England. Throughout his career, the sedentary geographer relied heavily on
information supplied by others. In the preparation of *The American Geography,* for instance, Morse sent questionnaires to prominent individuals and
solicited assistance through notices placed in newspapers.[62] He created a
translocal community of informants—"Americans" who participated in
his geographic construction of the nation.

Morse's limited travels and the geographic knowledge he acquired
from his sources only enhanced his sense of New England's difference
from the rest of America. His geographies remind us how regional identity is relational. In the colonial era New England continually defined
and redefined itself with reference to England. Independence established
a national republic in which regional identities would be increasingly
forged through a reciprocal process of collective differentiation. Morse's
texts, for all their attention to nationhood, actually announce this new,
"national" phase of region making in American history. His confron-
tation with the world beyond New England both sharpened his understanding of the region's distinctiveness and stiffened his bonds to his

home "country" of steady habits. In turn, the dialectic of his new regional patriotism informed his mapping of the Mid-Atlantic and Southern states.

Morse could not discern regions outside of culturally homogeneous New England. He examined the Mid-Atlantic and Southern states individually, failing to see regional patterns in the very information he reported because he peered through a New England lens. The ethnic diversity of New York State unhinged him. Albany was inhabited not by steady republicans but by "a heterogeneous collection of people, invested with all their national prejudices, eager in the pursuit of gain, and jealous of a rivalship." Though Morse noted that the Revolution had brought change to Dutch descendants of New York's founders, he still reported that their "unacquaintedness with the English language, and their national pride" remained obstacles in the way of republican improvement.[63]

New York could not claim New England's heroic origins. "The design of the Dutch in coming to this country was not to improve their minds, nor to erect public seminaries of science, but to increase their fortunes." In other words, New York lacked a republican past. In New York City, Morse discovered "the gayest place in America," but its civic life seemed frail. As for libraries, "societies for the encouragement of sciences, arts, manufactures," and "well regulated academies," one might inquire "but could not, at present, be answered satisfactorily."[64]

As with New York, Morse found New Jersey's ethnic and religious diversity disorienting. He surrendered his powers of observation and his New England predilection for creating, not simply recording, geographic order: "it cannot be expected that many general observations will apply." Morse responded similarly to Pennsylvania's pluralistic social order. "A proportionate assemblage of the national prejudices [of its people]," he wrote of the state's cultural diversity, "the manners, customs, religions and political sentiments of all these, will form the Pennsylvania character."[65] New Englanders possessed a discernible character grounded in their cultural homogeneity and shared history. But the Mid-Atlantic states, considered individually or collectively, did not comprise a comparable cultural region.

Yet Morse's New England standards and his elevation of cultural homogeneity as a republican model shielded him from the implications of his own geographic evidence. The Mid-Atlantic states did not possess New England's collective consciousness as a region. But in their religious and ethnic diversity, their worldly individualism, their interest-based political factionalism, their detachment from deference and historical tradition, the Middle States shared patterns of development. They did not conform to Morse's New England–imbued model of classical republicanism; rather, the geopolitical world of the Mid-Atlantic states pointed toward the "American" future—to the more secular, pluralistic, even Jeffersonian republican society of the nineteenth century in which opportunity and individualism trumped moralistic, deferential notions of virtue and order.

In the South, too, Morse's search for a New England–style cultural coherence produced a state-by-state account that led him to ignore his own evidence of a shared folk culture in the region. His depiction of Virginia drew heavily on Jefferson's *Notes on the State of Virginia,* but he also relied on his own experience and the less-than-flattering accounts of other travelers. Morse dismissed Virginia's designation as the *"ancient dominion,"* which promoted the state's claim on leadership of the Union. He quoted Jefferson for support. "It is certain, however, that her [Virginia's] northern sisters, though willing to yield to her in point of age, believe, not only that she is not superior, but that she is far from being equal to some of them, in point of literacy, mechanical, nautical, agricultural, and manufactural improvements," Jefferson wrote. "A few singular instances excepted, the Virginians have made very little progress in the arts and sciences." Recalling his visit to Williamsburg, the colonial capital of Virginia before the transfer of government to Richmond, Morse reported that he found "no trade—no amusements, but the infamous one of gaming—no industry, and very little appearance of religion." [66]

The real and imagined South of Morse's geographies functioned as the anti-image of sober, republican New England. The Southern states were impaired by the primitive state of organized religion and a resultant "profane" public culture. In Virginia, the collapse of the Anglican religious establishment during the Revolution and the recent rise of the Baptists and Methodists had begun to establish evangelical Christianity, though it was a Southern variant, Morse grumbled, "composed of the mingled effusions of piety, enthusiasm, and superstition" characteristic of an "ignorant," "poorer sort of people." Virginia was part of the least churched region in the early republic. In 1790, we now know, only 14 percent of whites and less than 4 percent of blacks belonged to the Baptist, Methodist, and Presbyterian Churches, the major denominations that would secure the South as the center of America's Bible Belt. Even as late as 1815, just 17 percent of the Southern white population had joined these churches. The evangelical South emerged during the generation before the Civil War, the generation that also created a powerful sense of Southern identity.[67]

Morse thus observed and read accounts of a largely secular and expansive South that had not yet acquired the collective regional identity possessed by compact New England. Beyond coastal towns such as Charleston, South Carolina, he described a backcountry Southern landscape of dispersed settlements devoid of the familiar markers of his republican world. In North Carolina, for example, he deplored the absence of a New England–like Sabbatarianism, "which considered merely in a civil view, is an excellent establishment for the promotion of cleanliness, friendship, harmony and all the social virtues." Instead, he found the Sabbath in North Carolina "generally disregarded, or distinguished by the convivial visitings of the white inhabitants, and the noisy diversions of the negroes." The religious life of Georgia appeared no better: "the greater part of the state," he reported ruefully, "is not supplied by ministers of any denomination."[68]

Morse acknowledged that slavery and climate shaped the way of life throughout the Southern states. But he argued that these factors eroded republicanism, not that they created a cultural region. "There is no peculiarity in the manners of the inhabitants of this state," he proclaimed of South Carolina, "except what arises from the mischievous influence of slavery; and in this, indeed, they do not differ from the inhabitants of other southern states." Slavery undermined the development of a republican moral economy in the South by encouraging "indulgence," "ease," "luxury, dissipation and extravagance." The climate conspired in the erosion of Southern industry. As Morse described Carolinians, they "sooner arrive at maturity, both in their bodies and minds, than the natives of colder climates. They possess a natural quickness and vivacity of genius superior to the inhabitants of the north; but too generally want that enterprise and perseverance, which are necessary for the highest attainments in the arts and sciences."[69]

On the one hand, the South emerges from Morse's texts as a raw domain lacking the cultural coherence, geographic order, and stable civic landscape of republican New England. On the other hand, however, Morse compiled information, albeit tendentiously, that documented grounded cultural patterns in Southern life. To his comments about slavery, climate, dispersed settlements, and irreligion, we may add his observations on the profane public culture that he discovered and read about in the South. From Virginia to Georgia, he reported, horse racing, cock-fighting, gambling, and other "manly" diversions were part of Southern life. Too many North Carolinians, Morse complained, "spend their time in drinking, or gaming at cards or dice, in cock-fighting or horse racing." Boxing matches that ended in gouging were also common. "In a country that pretends to any degree of civilization," Morse wrote sarcastically, "one would hardly expect to find a prevailing custom of putting out the eyes of each." The sober New Englander stared down what we now recognize as some of the conspicuous aspects of the South's male-centered folk culture—a secular world rooted in individualism, honor, rituals of manhood, and loyalty to kin. Even the Christianization of the South in the nineteenth century would have to proceed by accommodating the ingrained ways of the folk, the uneducated "lower sort" who overrun Morse's pages on the region.[70]

Nineteenth-century New England abolitionists such as Harriet Beecher Stowe would come to imagine the South as "America's Latin America"—an exotic, semitropical land of moral laxity and indulgence.[71] In many ways, Morse anticipates the South of *Uncle Tom's Cabin*. His geographies serve up an alien, un-American territory. By conflating his moralistic republicanism with Americanism, Morse fashioned homogeneous New England into America's America. His texts republicanized and nationalized long-standing Puritan notions of New England's moral and cultural superiority; they also situated much of the rest of the republic, especially the South, in a disarrayed, seemingly foreign "country" distant from the land of steady habits.

Morse provoked criticism. One prominent Virginian objected to his depiction of Williamsburg in *The American Universal Geography*: "A few more touches of the reverend Geographer's pen would have exhibited to us Sodom, or Gomorrah, on the eve of eternal wrath." Even New England produced critics. A religious opponent of Morse protested that the geographer had done "everything in his power to raise the character of the eastern states, Rhode Island excepted, and to depress that of the southern states." This detractor found Morse's declamations "against drunkenness, gaming, and even heresy," inappropriate for "a system of geography." Yet most critics, even as they offered corrections and suggested improvements, welcomed his works as highly "useful and instructive."[72] Morse texts, which bound valuable information for citizens of the early republic with New England preachifying, dominated the field of American geography through the second decade of the nineteenth century.

From Morse's Geographies to Dwight's *Travels*

Timothy Dwight (1752–1817) stands out as one influential New England cultural leader who learned from and promoted Morse's geography texts. A native of the Connecticut River Valley, Dwight shared Morse's perspective on New England as the authentic republican nation within the nation as well as the geographer's "ethnic" consciousness. Dwight helped organize the first New England Society and participated in its initial meeting in New York City in 1805.[73] Dwight and Morse became Federalist allies, politicized guardians of regional identity in the cultural wars of the early republic.

A graduate of Yale, Dwight assumed the presidency of the college in 1795, after service as a Revolutionary chaplain and a twelve-year pastorate over the Congregational church in Greenfield, Connecticut. Under his leadership Yale persevered as a bulwark of orthodoxy, joining smaller institutions such as Dartmouth, Williams, and Middlebury in educating tradition-minded clerical and lay leaders for the New England heartland. Predictably, Morse's geographies became fixtures in the curriculum of Yale and its sister institutions. One of Dwight's sons, Sereno, helped Morse prepare an edition of *The American Universal Geography*. In turn, Morse's son Richard, a Yale student, assisted President Dwight on a geography project of his own.[74]

Beginning in 1796 and continuing for nearly two decades, Dwight annually set out by horseback to explore New England and later New York. Each fall, when Yale students returned home for harvest, he mounted his horse for a lengthy trip; typically, a shorter jaunt followed in winter or spring. He claimed to have traveled twelve thousand miles in two decades. Dwight's horseback excursions offered healthy exercise and an opportunity to examine the progress of the republic. Dwight compiled extensive notes, which were often transcribed by Yale students, including young Richard Morse.[75]

By 1808 Dwight had accumulated and revised detailed notebooks on his travels that had passed through revision; doubtless Jedidiah Morse, his intimate friend and associate, urged publication. That year Dwight chose Morse to announce plans to issue his travel accounts. "Dr. D. of N[ew] H[aven] is preparing for the press Observations on a Series of Journeys through the States of N.E. & New York," Morse wrote, "intended to illustrate the Topography, Agriculture, Commerce, Government, Literature,

Manners, Morals and Religion of those countries. This Work, as understood, is considerably advanced."[76] But Dwight continued to travel and to revise his accounts. His *Travels in New England and New York* (1821–22) was not published until after his death in 1817.

Dwight's work crowds the shelf of New England travel writing as the bulkiest ever produced on the region. The modern edition runs to four volumes comprising more than fifteen hundred pages—"Letters" teeming with historical facts, topographical descriptions, cultural observations, and moral pronouncements. Unlike Jedidiah Morse, Dwight brought to his writing about New England a poetic sensibility. His plain prose sometimes springs to life in the *Travels,* especially when he expounds on the "undulating" landscape of the Connecticut River Valley. Dwight also differs from Morse in other ways. Repeated travels across the region, over two decades, encouraged him to record a more dynamic and constantly changing New England than the relatively stable cultural region of Morse's geographies.

Yet these and other differences do not obscure a compelling fact: Dwight's travel volumes—in their Connecticut centeredness, their ethnic consciousness, their moralistic republicanism, their regional patriotism and imperialism, and their mapping of the progress of steady habits—add up to an amplification of Morse's cultural geography of New England. Dwight sprinkled his *Travels* with references to the work of his close friend.[77] Through conversations the two political allies reinforced their common geocultural vision of New England. Moreover, their shared moral geography derived from a similar background. Sons of the New England interior, the two graduates of Yale were steeped in regional history, attached to a Puritanized republicanism, and determined to protect clerical authority as part of a larger deferential praxis that reconciled order and liberty. Morse and Dwight embodied the aspirations of the Federalist Party's Congregational mullahs. Their Christian republicanism and regional patriotism permeated the geopolitical outlook of New England's powerful Federalist Party in the early republic.

Dwight's *Travels,* like Morse's geographies, locate the Connecticut River Valley as the republican hub of New England. The physical movement in the *Travels* consolidated the valley's position at the center of the author's moral universe. Setting out from New Haven, Dwight crisscrossed the valley or followed its river banks into the New England heartland and then back to Yale. He lavished praise on the little republics of the valley, "An undulating country ornamented with farms, groves, and well-appearing houses." Mount Holyoke, in Massachusetts, offered "the richest prospect in New England and not improbably in the United States": the procession of white villages that graced the northern and southern reaches of the Connecticut River Valley. America did not possess Europe's "melancholy grandeur," its "decayed castles and ruined abbeys." But the Connecticut Valley afforded a sublime republican vista. Thus, for Dwight, as for Morse, the valley was not simply an object of regional pride; it traced a republican topography for the nation.[78]

Following Morse and John Adams, Dwight extolled the local civic landscape of New England. In the preface to the *Travels* he established his moral bearings. Dwight, the pilgrim as moral topographer, recorded the progress of a New England landscape "composed of neat houses, surrounding neat schoolhouses and churches, adorned with gardens, meadows and orchards," and inhabited by self-sufficient freeholders in "universally easy circumstances." In other words, all of New England is measured against the familiar and idealized world of the Connecticut River Valley. The land of steady habits — imagined as New England's middle empire of sober republicanism — regulates the moral geography of Dwight's *Travels*. A town-centered, institutionally ordered, pastoral landscape enabled the republic of Connecticut in particular to shine politically as a city on a hill. "Connecticut is a singular phenomenon in the political hemisphere," Dwight observed, almost parroting Morse. "Such a degree of freedom was never before united with such a degree of stability."[79]

Dwight plotted the Connecticut River Valley as a sanctuary of New England republicanism, the site where civic-minded village settlement was "realized in its fullest extent." But Dwight, embellishing Morse's geography with richly textured local detail, still rendered New England as a cultural whole. He observed steady habits and institutions throughout his travels. And when corners of the region failed to meet his moralistic republican standards, he remained hopeful for the ongoing social and cultural integration of New England as a land of steady habits. Indeed, *Travels* takes on the qualities of a promotional tract. Dwight labors to persuade his readers, and himself, that New England will extend its republican ways and abide, as he announces at the beginning of the book, as "that part of the American republic in which its strength is principally found."[80]

Rhode Island, to be sure, defined the limits of his optimism. Following Morse, Dwight used the state to draw the cultural boundaries of his New England. Most of Rhode Island appeared beyond republican redemption, undeserving of his time or commentary. Dwight dispatched the state in several pages. If he was unable to erase it from the map of New England, he could at least imaginatively diminish what was already the smallest state. As his horse trotted through the countryside west of Providence, Dwight strained to locate familiar New England cultural markers. Instead, he found an alien landscape. "The whole tract is a collection of thinly scattered settlements," he groused, "without a village or even a hamlet." Rhode Island's moral and civic deficiencies were legible on the ground. The border crossing into Connecticut altered not only the landscape but also Dwight's mood and expectation. "At Sterling," he recorded with relief, "we were pleasantly advertised that we had entered the state of Connecticut by the sight of a village with a decent church and schoolhouse in its center, and by the appearance of comfortable dwellings and better agriculture."[81]

When Dwight encountered a Rhode Island–like landscape in newly settled tracts of Vermont and Maine, he developed a kind of "frontier thesis" that foresaw the diffusion of the New England way over time. In Vermont, the "*foresters*" or "*pioneers*" cleared the forests, built log cabins, and "prepare[d] the way for those who come after them." Sober, industrious farmers succeeded the often restless foresters and characteristically transformed "the desert into a fruitful field." The second wave of hearty freeholders became the culture bearers of New England's republican ways. In Vermont, Dwight held out the hope that the press of migrants from the lower valley, that "nursery" of steady habits, would continue to shape the state as a "New Connecticut."[82]

Even his early visits to Maine did not shake Dwight's confidence in the diffusion of the New England way. He journeyed to Maine three times during an eleven-year period beginning in the mid-1790s. The District's landscape of scattered townships and plantations struck him as "like that of other recent New England settlements," though the "dissolute character" of lumbermen and fishermen seemed to be too much on display. By his last visit in 1807, Dwight reported, the tide of immigrants from Massachusetts had brought republican progress to the state. "The sober, industrious husbandmen of southern New England are now emigrating in shoals to this country," he noted. "The interior is settling in the New England manner. Schools are established in great numbers. Churches, always decent and not unfrequently handsome, are built." Of course, he failed to record the acrimonious land war of early republican Maine that pitted migrants who were sometimes squatters against absentee landholders. However, he did worry that independence from the stabilizing influence of

Massachusetts might retard Maine's republican progress.[83] Through a process of observation and projection Dwight incorporated Maine into his republican New England. But at the geographic margins his New England was still a landscape under moral cultivation rather than the "finished scene" of the land of steady habits.

Nevertheless, a new appreciation of New England's relative ethnic homogeneity infused Dwight's musings on the region's cultural cohesiveness. Dwight extended Morse's ethnicization of New Englanders. Moreover, like Morse, he spurned the Yankee label; Dwight used "Yankee" only once in his notebooks and then crossed it out. Yet he translated the old Puritan notion of a "peculiar people" into an ethnic identity. Following Morse, Dwight portrayed New Englanders as a people exhibiting "national characteristics."[84] A distinctive culture of descent sustained his hopes for the continuing integration of the region and for the New Englandization of republican America.

Dwight boasted of New England's common history and ancestry, which distinguished the region from other parts of the Union, promoted group consciousness, and upheld the promise of republican stability. But neither Dwight nor Morse saw themselves as mere recorders of the new awareness of New England's cultural difference provoked by the political reality of nationhood. For decades Puritan historians had drafted and revised heroic narratives to fashion and uphold the collective identity of a literate people. Dwight and Morse continued this interventionist tradition of toiling on behalf of group consciousness, not just assuming that it would emerge from shared circumstances. Dwight and Morse incorporated into a republican narrative familiar notions of New Englanders' chosenness—their sense of moral superiority and providential destiny as a "peculiar people." In the process, the authors anchored New England's claim to unrivaled republican virtue not only in the homogeneity of its people but also in their ethnic character.

Early in the first volume of *Travels* Dwight sketched the ethnic elements that underpinned his regional pride. Invoking the work of Thomas Prince, Jeremy Belknap, and Morse, among others, he proclaimed that "no sober New Englander can read the history of his country without rejoicing that God has caused him to spring from the loins of such ancestors." Dwight also reveled in the fact that New Englanders and other Americans comprised a "race" descended from England, not France. Yet his nationalism compelled him to portray New Englanders as far more than transplanted Englishmen and Englishwomen. As Morse suggested in his geographies, New Englanders were physically recognizable; they were even "discernible without much difficulty" from English people, Dwight claimed. In contrast to the "frequently fleshy" English, "Our countrymen are taller, more agile, have frequently dark hair and black eyes, and the muscles are more strongly marked both in the limbs and in the face."[85] On one level, Dwight was defending New Englanders, and Americans, against continuing theories of New World degeneration that harked back to earlier anxieties about colonial life. But Dwight's and Morse's comments about New Englanders' appearance also suggest something new: an attention to physical distinctiveness that was not central to earlier interpretations of regional identity and that signaled a growing ethnic awareness in the republic's most homogeneous region. Writers and artists would soon shape selective physical attributes of New Englanders into the image of the Yankee, a figure who became an ethnic stereotype in the hands of outsiders.

Dwight's and Morse's disavowal of the Yankee label suggests less a resistance to a complete ethnicization of New Englanders than an objection to this colloquial identifier. Still, they ultimately located the region's distinctiveness in the character of its people—a hearty republican character forged from ancestry, history, piety, and even climate. For Dwight, the New England character was etched into the regional landscape. Republican New England, "the numerous, cheerful, and beautiful towns and villages," derived from the enterprise and diligence of an "extraordinary people."[86]

In one of the "Letters" in *Travels,* titled "Characteristics of the Men and Women in New England," Dwight extended the generalized account of "authentic" New Englanders presented in Morse's geography texts. Dwight applauded the "energy and activity of mind" that New Englanders displayed. A "resourceful," "ingenious" people, their "energy is evinced by the spirit with which they have subdued an immeasurable wilderness, and with which they visited every part of the ocean for fishing, and every town on its shore for commerce." Repeated images of motion and improvement—enterprise, energy, ingenuity, industry—pointed toward the mobile Yankee on-the-make of nineteenth-century lore. But Dwight domesticated his New Englander. The "peculiarity" of the New England character did not reside wholly in an "active spirit." Rather, to their energetic ways, New Englanders "unite a general disposition to a quiet, orderly, and obliging deportment, to treat strangers and each other with civility, to submit to lawful authority, and to obey even the recommendations of their rulers."[87] Dwight's interpretation of New England-ers as a uniquely republican people was rooted in the real world observed in his travels. But he encountered a place and a people in motion. He created an idealized, stable image of the New England character that con-veyed his own republican hopes for a region that reconciled liberty and order, enterprise and competency, individualism and deference.

Dwight's travels in upstate New York, like his encouragement to the members of the New England Society in New York City, confirmed his sense of ethnic identity with his "countrymen." Between 1799 and 1815 Dwight made five trips to central and western New York. He observed the New Englandization of the area, which Morse, unable to stay abreast of the rapid geographic changes of the early republic, did not adequately record. Thousands of New Englanders, constituting a "Yankee exodus," had migrated to central and western New York. These "immigrants," Dwight enthused, transported New England ways and character traits. Dwight's pen glided through a catalog of New England attributes on dis-play. Settlers of New England stock exhibited an "intelligent, ingenious, acute, versatile" character; they were also "sober, orderly, [and] moral" as well as "ardent, enterprising, resolute, patient, active, industrious, and persevering." Where the migrants failed to rise to the standards of their regional heritage and ethnic identity, Dwight blamed "restless foresters," who, as in northern New England, preceded the arrival of more steady re-publican farmers. The surge of migrants and the imprint of their inherited habits, he predicted, meant that New York would increasingly develop "as a colony from New England."[88]

The final paragraphs of *Travels* address the threat of disunion. If heated talk of secession ever became a reality, Dwight was confident that "New England and New York will, almost of course, be united in the same political body."[89] Unlike Morse, he did not become a vocal advocate of secession politics, but neither did he shrink in despair from its potential consequences. Both Dwight and Morse expressed and promoted a geog-raphy of New England tribalism, a geocultural perspective that informed the Federalist Party and that combined with regional political grievances against the national government to foment secessionist sentiment.

The Politics of Regional Identity

In 1801 the two clerical geographers established a newspaper in Bos-ton, the *New England Palladium,* to preserve "the government, morals, religion, &. state of Society in New England."[90] Dwight and Morse used the *Palladium* to propagate their republican ideology and to prosecute their campaign against enemies of the Federalist Party. Dwight has come to be known as the "Pope of New England Federalism" for the influence he wielded, as Yale president, in Connecticut—the conservative citadel of regional politics in the early republic. Morse, though he did not have Dwight's institutional base, emerged as one of the leaders of the Federalist Party's Congregational College of Cardinals. His widely read texts distilled and disseminated a collective identity for the region and a geopolitical view of the nation that became entrenched in New England's powerful Federalist Party. As Morse's texts suggested and as the Federalist descendants of the Puritans believed, New England held a privileged claim on leadership of the republic—a claim bolstered by history as well as by the region's recent role in the Revolution. But such Morse-Federalist national regionalism became increasingly frustrated by the political ascendance of Virginia. Moreover, New England's moralistic republicanism—with its emphasis on ordered liberty, virtue, and deference to authority—increasingly confronted a secular world, and a Jeffersonian ideology, not only preoccupied with opportunity, mobility, and individualism but also distrustful of government and of established churches. By 1804, when he published his *Compendious History of New England,* the discontented father of American geography had been reborn as the region's most prominent clerical supporter of secessionist politics.

Strong regionalist sentiment in New England found political expression in three decades of secessionist discussion that culminated in the convention of 1814 held at Hartford, in the imagined center of Morse's culture region. As early as the 1780s, under the Articles of Confederation, serious New Englanders raised the prospect of separatism. "It is . . . now time to form a new and stronger union," a Boston paper observed in early 1787, advocating the formation of "a new Congress, as the Representative of the nation of New England."[91] Such secessionist appeals originated in the growing sense of New England's distinctiveness generated by continuing political involvement with other parts of the Union and by the failure of the weak government of the Articles to protect regional interests. The ratification of the Constitution in 1788 forestalled any movement toward secession. The Federalist supporters of ratification saw the new, stronger government as a bulwark of ordered liberty—as a restraint on the republican excesses of the Revolution. As Morse complained in *The American Geography,* the struggle for independence "introduced into New England a flood of corruptions," by which he meant an overzealous attachment to individual liberty and a concomitant distrust of traditional authority. The new, expanded federal government would help secure the Revolution and establish an orderly republic. Equally important, the new political framework offered populous New England both the opportunity to defend its interests and the prospect of leading the Union.[92]

Morse's geographies, with their aggrandizing of New England as a cultural region and their national regionalism, were politically situated. His volumes inscribed the geopolitics of Federalist New England: the promise of the Constitution as an alternative to secession; a heightened sense not only of New England's cultural distinctiveness from other states but also of its separate political and economic interests; a self-righteous claim, indeed, a moral duty born of history, to lead the republic. Morse's texts performed political work; they helped consolidate Federalist ideology—the party's national regionalism and moralistic republicanism—in the early republic.

When the geopolitical project of Morse and his fellow New England Federalists, so promising in the early 1790s, began to founder, secessionist sentiment resurfaced. The geographic expansion of the republic undermined New England's aspirations for political dominance of the Union. New England exported people to New York and then to the West; in the absence of significant immigration, the New England birthrate did not produce the demographic swell experienced by other sections of the country. Population growth outside New England, particularly in the South, and the admission of new states to the Union diminished New England's political influence. The election of 1800 inaugurated a period of disillusionment for Morse and New England Federalists—a disaffection from the national government that fostered a regional sense of grievance and rekindled secessionist discussion.[93]

The election to the presidency of Thomas Jefferson, of course, thwarted John Adams's plans for a second term. Jefferson initiated an unbroken twenty-four-year reign of Virginia presidents. Virginian control of the national government seems to have slowed the development of an exclusive Southern regional identity as the Jeffersonians built an intersectional political party. The opposite occurred in New England, where seeming political marginalization dashed the hopes of the Federalists, including cultural overseers like Morse, Dwight, and Noah Webster, for regional leadership of the nation. The frustrations of national politics after 1800 intensified Federalist New England's sense of both separateness and besiegement. Morse resorted to concluding his letters with the appeal, "GOD save our New England."[94]

The land of the Puritans now existed under the political thumb of the region that Morse's geographies constructed as an exotic territory. The Southern states were merely "fiefs" of Virginia. "There is a spirit of domination engrafted on the character of the southern people," one Federalist argued in 1801 echoing Morse's geography. "Of all the inhabitants of this continent they are the most imperious in their manners." What is democracy, another Federalist asked, but "an indian word signifying *'a great tobacco planter, who had herds of black slaves.'*"[95]

In this regional war of words, slavery took on new political significance. Morse's geography texts ignored the history of slavery and the presence of African Americans in New England. To be sure, at its height in the middle of the eighteenth century, the predominately enslaved black population of New England was perhaps never more than 3 percent. But in Boston blacks comprised 10 percent and in Newport they represented nearly 25 percent of the population in the 1750s. Estate inventories from Morse's Connecticut document the possessions of mid-eighteenth-century families, one-quarter of whom owned slaves. Such evidence suggests that, though their overall numbers in New England were modest, slaves comprised significant segments of the late colonial population in particular locales and that the ownership of one or two bond servants was more widespread than is commonly believed. By the time Morse composed his geographies, the Revolution had put slavery on the road to extinction in New England. But in the 1780s gradual emancipation was the strategy of choice. As a result, there were still legally held slaves in New England after the turn of the nineteenth century. In addition, emancipation provoked the racism of whites who feared competition for jobs as well as miscegenation.[96] Morse's texts offer no commentary either on race relations in republican New England or on the history of slavery in the region. They depict New England as a historic place inhabited solely by white freeholders.

Slavery emerges from Morse's geographies as a corruption of republicanism that has shaped the "imperious" Southern character. For Morse and his Federalist allies, Southern slavery acquired a new political urgency after 1800 that sometimes revealed the contour of New England racism. Slaves counted as three-fifths of a white person for the purpose of apportioning representation. An expanding Southern slave population added to New England's political disadvantages in the Union and elicited not so much the moral outrage that we associate with the abolitionist era but racist rhetoric fueled by disgruntlement. The South appeared as a collection of "rotten . . . Negro boroughs." As a Boston paper asked, "Why should *their* slaves be represented if denied the rights of suffrage, in preference to *our* horses and oxen." [97]

The Louisiana Purchase of 1803 visited new anxieties on New England leaders—concerns about a burgeoning federal union that was politically, ethnically, and physically the antithesis of a compact, homogeneous land of steady republican habits. In their optimistic moments, Federalists such as Morse and Dwight continued to embrace the prospect of a "Greater New England," the would-be creation of migrants to New York and the Northwest Territory. But this regional expansion was overwhelmed by the expected geopolitical consequences of the Louisiana Purchase. "The relative strength which this admission gives to a Southern and Western interest," one Connecticut Federalist grumbled, "is contradictory to the principles of our original union." In 1804 a Federalist leader in Massachusetts complained: "The people of the East cannot reconcile their habits, views, and interests, with those of the South and West. The latter are beginning to rule with a rod of iron." The father of American geography shared this dismay. The dramatic physical expansion of the Union not only undermined the regional cultural imperialism that was stitched into the fabric of Morse's geography texts; the Louisiana Purchase bound New England to a far-flung, diverse republic that threatened to erode the region's steady habits. As Morse confided to a correspondent, "Connected as we now are with—I will not say what—I fear we shall be by degrees drawn into a vortex in which our [New England] Institutions and the principles and habits which are their fruits and which are our glory and happiness will be engulfed and lost." [98]

The Louisiana Purchase aggravated New England nativism. Morse's texts and Federalist politics were the products of the Union's most homogeneous region. His geographic hymns to New England as a cultural region offered an assimilationist republican model for the nation. But the Louisiana Purchase added new "alien" elements to the already unsettling ethnic mix that Morse encountered beyond New England. As one Federalist put it, Jefferson's territorial acquisition invited into the republic a "*Gallo-Hispano-Indian omnium gatherum* of savages and adventurers." "Let us no longer pray," another Federalist argued as he contemplated the new French and Spanish inhabitants of the republic, "that America may become an asylum to all nations." As Morse did in his geographies, many

Federalists increasingly took refuge in their descent "from the best English stock."[99]

By 1804 Morse was a leader of a small group of Federalists who seriously discussed secession. Disunion, however, made little headway as the Federalist Party began to lose its political grip on New England. A highly politicized and sometimes strident regionalism alarmed moderates, who allied with the Federalists' traditional enemies—religious dissenters who resented the Congregational establishment that prevailed in Connecticut and Massachusetts and insurgent "republicans" who rejected a politics of deference. Jefferson's Democratic-Republican Party won even Massachusetts in 1804.[100]

Yet the Federalist politics of disunion, with Morse at its epicenter, persisted and actually gained support in the decade after 1804. Federalists labored, as Morse had in his geographies, to reconcile regionalism and nationalism and thereby to keep the prospect of secession alive. Virginia's dominance of an expanded republic altered the original plan of union. The threat of secession did not amount to disloyalty; rather, it was resistance to the real sectionalists, "the perfidious Virginians," and their "abhorrent domination" of the Union. Federalists urged New Englanders to "resist the encroachment of Southern despotism" and to vow "never [to] be governed by Southern Slaves." Federalists wrapped secessionist politics in the flag of Revolutionary patriotism—a maneuver that was simultaneously regional and national. New England had been in the forefront of the struggle for independence, whereas Virginia had betrayed the original plan of union; it remained for the descendants of the Puritans to redeploy their resistance to British tyranny. Patriotic New Englanders would beat back Virginia's attempts to enslave them.[101]

Jefferson's trade embargo of 1807–9, intended to coerce warring England and France to respect American rights at sea, and the declaration of war against England in 1812 helped revive the Federalist Party, reanimate secessionist politics, and reinforce a sense of New England's distinctive place in the Union. The embargo and then the war disrupted regional trade, underscoring the economic difference between commercial-maritime New England and the agrarian South. Especially in coastal New England, always a wellspring of Federalist support, a renewed sense of political and economic grievance fortified regional identity and inflamed secessionist sentiment. In Salem, the daughter of a sailor proclaimed her identity on a sampler:

Amy Kittredge is my name
Salem is my dwelling place
New England is my nashun
And Christ is my Salvation.

Kittredge's more prominent townsman, Federalist grandee Timothy Pickering, described how his affections for place extended "in what you deem
their natural order—toward Salem, Massachusetts, New England, the
Union at large." A few Federalists took to flying flags with five stars and
stripes, the banner of a New England confederacy.[102]

By 1814 some Federalists aggressively pressed for a convention that
would air regional complaints and perhaps consider secession. Morse
urged individual members of the Massachusetts General Court to call for
such a meeting. If Massachusetts exercised "bold & lofty" leadership,
he argued, "the other states will follow us." Morse's cultural ally and the
"nation's schoolmaster," Noah Webster, was one of the drafters of the first
circular calling for a convention. In October, the Massachusetts legisla-
ture endorsed the plan for a convention. A heartened Morse wrote to his
father: "[The convention] is, under Providence, the source of my hope
of salvation to our country. I hope all the N. Engd. states will unite in
sending Delegates & that wisdom, firmness, & energy will mark all their
deliberations."[103]

In December twenty-six delegates assembled in Hartford. The legisla-
tures of Connecticut, Massachusetts, and Rhode Island sent representatives, but in New Hampshire and Vermont only three counties along the
Connecticut River elected delegates. Rather than embracing secession,
the convention proposed amendments to the Constitution that addressed
festering Federalist grievances and New England's diminished place in
the Union. These amendments were intended to rein in the power of the
South and its expanding frontier. Representation in the federal government would be based only on the free white population. The admission
of new states, embargoes on trade, and declarations of war would require a two-thirds majority of Congress; presidents would be restricted
to one term; the same state would be prohibited from providing successive presidents; and naturalized citizens would be barred from serving in
Congress.[104]

The delegates endorsed a plan for another meeting in the following
summer, but before then the convention was discredited. By early 1815

news of a peace treaty and of Andrew Jackson's glorious New Year's Day victory over the British in the Battle of New Orleans stimulated national pride. The New England Federalists' opposition to the war and their dalliance with secession in Hartford now acquired the odium of treason. New England opponents of the Federalist Party exploited the Hartford Convention, billing it as "the foulest stain on our escutcheon."[105] The party was never able to mount a comeback.

Jedidiah Morse, whose geography texts were so intertwined with the rise of the party and its national regionalism, went the way of New England federalism. He revised *The American Universal Geography* for the last time in 1819 and then retired to New Haven. But the Morse-Federalist aspiration to judge and shape the world outside of New England according to regional standards did not dissipate.

Morse was long removed from the life of the republic and tattered Federalist remnants were far distant from the party's heyday in 1831, when Alexis de Tocqueville arrived in America to begin his famous journey. In *Democracy in America* Tocqueville reported that thirty-six members of the U.S. Congress were natives of Connecticut. "The population of Connecticut, which constitutes only one forty-third part of that of the United States," Tocqueville observed, "thus furnished one eighth of the whole body of representatives." Led by Connecticut, migrants from the region had created what came to be known as the "Second New England" (New York) and what would be called the "Third New England," which stretched to Michigan. The proliferation of familiar regional town names in the states of the Old Northwest Territory recorded the progress of a New England diaspora.[106]

The creation of a Greater New England in the North during the antebellum decades coincided with new efforts of stay-at-home New Englanders to revise regional identity in ways less overtly political than their Federalist predecessors. In the years leading up to the Civil War, New England continued to differentiate itself from the South and to pursue a regional aspiration to shape the culture of the North. The white village, the Yankee figure, and the mythological Pilgrims helped new guardians of regional identity to demarcate their states from the South and to advance New England as the cultural hearth of the North.

Greater New England
Antebellum Regional Identity
and the Yankee North

Jedidiah Morse and his Federalist allies politically overplayed their imaginative and ideological investment in New England as the nation's republican city on a hill. But the region's political and cultural agenda of national regionalism persisted through the decades from the bicentennial of Plymouth's founding in 1820 to the Civil War. The ongoing growth of a Greater New England, the extension of the region's tradition of literacy and cultural production, and heightened interregional strife over slavery—such developments encouraged antebellum New Englanders to continue revising collective identity at home while broadening the region's influence on a developing "Yankee North."

The fabled Yankee character did not become central to New England, and increasingly Northern, identity until after 1820. In fact, the antebellum decades witnessed the emergence of new icons that encoded a revised regional identity and that have powerfully shaped the imaginative construction of New England down to the present. If the Yankee bestowed a distinct and enduring post-Puritan identity on the region's people, the compact white village, anchored by a steepled church, came to define the "real" New England on the ground. Moreover, a newly invented Pilgrim past supplied an updated historical narrative that linked the Yankee character and the white village to New England's religious and republican origins. In sum, antebellum regional identity cohered around new markers and revised narratives that redefined New England as a distinctive place with a "peculiar" people and a sacred past.

New England's acclaimed antebellum literary and cultural renaissance compelled clergymen to relinquish their role as the primary guardians of regional identity. Writers, artists, reformers, and politicians, as well as ministers, became the agents of New England's antebellum national regionalism. The Northern military victory over the Confederacy advanced a cultural triumph as well: the ascendancy of a Greater New England of the imagination. Between 1820 and the Civil War, the white village, the Yankee character, and the Pilgrims were transformed from New England to American icons.

Place: The New England Village from John Barber to Harriet Beecher Stowe

Jedidiah Morse and Timothy Dwight labored both as recorders and as promoters of New England's cultural distinctiveness in the early republic. Their writings signaled the rise of the most recognizable visual marker of New England regional identity: the central village, comprised of a cluster of houses and businesses encircling a white-steepled church. The region's fabled central villages experienced a delayed birth; they were the offspring of Morse and Dwight's generation. Yet the stately homes, the neat town commons, the orderly landscape of stone walls and picket fences, the churchly edifices that replaced primitive Puritan meetinghouses—these familiar elements of village iconography only coalesced over time. It was the generation after Morse and Dwight that witnessed the continuing and dramatic physical transformation of New England's central villages.

Furthermore, writers and artists of the antebellum generation extended both the cultural geography of Morse and Dwight and the geopolitics of regional identity. From the 1820s to the Civil War and beyond, visual and literary representations of an idealized New England village elevated a real, emergent landscape into a national icon. The white village became "a model setting for the American community" that announced continuing regional ambitions to New Englandize the West and to assert republican superiority over the South.[1] But as an artistic and literary icon, the white village also contributed to political work at home. It reassuringly imaged the region as a pastoral, stable Yankee world precisely at a time when factories and mills were propelling New England to the forefront of the industrial revolution and when Irish immigrants were initiating changes that would, in less than two generations, bring about the ethnic transformation of the region. Artists and writers exploited the newly groomed white village as a synecdoche for the regional landscape and way of life as a whole. In addition, they selectively represented the New England village itself, muting conflict and change and conferring a seemingly timeless stability on a landscape born of nineteenth-century commercial development.

John Barber (1798–1885) and Harriet Beecher Stowe (1811–96) offer visual and literary perspectives on the place of the New England village in the regional and Northern imagination. In the 1830s Barber produced more than four hundred engravings of New England town centers, the largest and most important visual documentary of the white village before the rise of photography. In the same decade Stowe launched her writing career with a story set in a quaint New England village, the location of so much of her prolific literary output. The work of Barber and Stowe suggests how the New England village became a regional icon through a process of nineteenth-century historical development and cultural invention.

The Puritan founders transferred to New England not only English town names and a familiar geographic lexicon; they also transplanted customary English settlement patterns. Social historians and geographers have examined how New England towns were established on a continuum of open field and enclosed field principles that reflected the dominant practices of the English subregions where members of the founding generation originated. Puritans from areas of England where the manor system remained strong were inclined to adopt an open field town plan in the New World. In open field towns, settlers were given small house lots in a central village. Farmland and pasturage, held by the town "in common," was parceled out in strips, where neighbors owned land next to each other in a series of open fields. Farmers walked from the central village to their outlying acreage scattered in the open fields surrounding their house lots. In open field towns authorities tightly controlled the distribution of common land, allocating modest amounts of acreage gradually over decades. Enclosed field towns established a more dispersed pattern of settlement. In these towns Puritan settlers were able to consolidate house lots, planting fields, and pasturage on enclosed farmsteads.[2] One consequence was that, unlike open field towns, enclosed field settlements had attenuated village centers, with little more than plain, unpainted, steepleless meetinghouses occupying the landscape.

Some towns, reflecting the mix of Puritans from different parts of England, appear to have combined elements of both settlement patterns.

What seems clear, however, is that the enclosed field system and a dispersed pattern of settlement became the prevailing social arrangement, especially among interior towns planted away from New England's major rivers. Even in the Connecticut River Valley, where compact settlement persisted, the availability of land and the growth of the population eroded the open field system. Across the region, an abundance of land and large families with sons who needed farm acreage to achieve economic independence and competency undermined the open field system and fostered population dispersal. Indeed, by the early 1640s even the little commonwealth of Plymouth had been so altered by the scattering of its colonists that leaders debated whether the original settlement by the harbor should be abandoned. "Many having left this place," William Bradford reported, ". . . the church begane seriously to thinke whether it were not better joyntly to remove to some other place, then to be thus weakened, and as it were insensibly dissolved."[3]

The enclosed field system, with its dispersed farmsteads and thinly populated village centers, emerged as the dominant settlement pattern of colonial New England towns. In many towns, farmers quickly began exchanging and purchasing adjacent lots in open fields, converting their scattered holdings into contiguous farms. They then moved their village center homes to their new, outlying farmsteads. The proprietors of new towns found it easier to attract settlers with land policies that encouraged enclosed fields and therefore a dispersed pattern of settlement. Even in eighteenth-century northern New England, plans for compact towns foundered in spite of frontier conditions. In Maine and New Hampshire, town maps often inscribed a nucleated settlement ideal, dictated at least in part by the need for defense against the French and Native Americans. But in a now familiar New England pattern, land-hungry farmers redesigned the town plan on the ground. They integrated their lots, formed independent farmsteads, and created a decentralized rural landscape. As Joseph Wood has convincingly documented, the colonial town typically evolved as an ensemble of villages and hamlets.[4]

New England's rotating school system developed as one creative response to the dispersed sociogeography of most colonial towns. A schoolteacher spent several weeks or months moving from school to school in the hamlets or villages that comprised most New England towns. One New Hampshire community, for instance, voted in 1731 to build schoolhouses in its "Severall Quarters." The town then required the schoolmaster "to be Remov'd to Each of the said houses and to continue there by Keeping Schoole according to the Equall proportion of Rates that said Quarter of the town pays."[5]

In most New England towns, central villages or "Quarters" did not function as the socioeconomic nucleus of community life. Daily life revolved around dispersed farmsteads and local villages — the usual sites of economic exchange and social interaction between townspeople engaged largely in subsistence agriculture. Thus, throughout the colonial era central villages remained thinly populated, neglected, and often unsightly. The plain meetinghouse presided over the central village. Steepleless and unpainted for much of the colonial era, meetinghouses began to change in the eighteenth century. In many cases improvement simply amounted to adding a coat of paint, with brown, blue, yellow, and red far more common than white.[6]

Besides the meetinghouse, central villages often boasted a tavern to refresh travelers and a few houses, but little else. Town commons or greens were far from the cultivated emblems of civic pride and republican order that they would become in the nineteenth century. Townspeople mustered neither the time nor the will to clear boulders, remove stumps, drain swamp water, and grade the land fronting a meetinghouse. In fact, as common town property — a remnant of a much more expansive "commons" tradition that Puritan settlers brought with them from England — the public land surrounding the meetinghouse was vulnerable to abuse by townspeople. As late as 1803, a traveler in Litchfield, Connecticut, described the inhabitants' disregard for the meetinghouse lot that eventually developed into one of the region's glistening town centers. The site was littered with "fragments of old fences, boards, woodpiles, heaps of chips, old sleds bottom upward, carts, casks, weeds and loose stones, lying along in wild confusion." The main road in front of the meetinghouse was "scandalously bad," marred with "ruts and gutters" and "deep gullies" along its path.[7]

Throughout colonial New England meetinghouse lots, which would form the nucleus of handsome commons and greens in the nineteenth century, were disfigured by the crisscross of oxcart ruts and horse wagon tracks left by outlying villagers as they approached the tavern or meetinghouse. The erection of sheds to protect the horses of "outlivers" who came to the meetinghouse for Sunday services added to the unsightly appearance of village centers. Ministers railed against "horseshed Christians" who did not behave properly between Sunday morning and afternoon services. Some towns such as Litchfield built "Sabbath day" or "nooning" houses, yet another addition to the ragged vernacular landscape. These small, unfinished structures provided shelter between Sunday services for townspeople who traveled from outlying hamlets.[8]

The absence of civic pride in village centers and the triumph of a dispersed pattern of town settlement might be read as a geographic narrative of the breakdown of Puritan communalism. Certainly, the American adaptation of English enclosed field settlement patterns and the demise of open field practices suggests how New World conditions accented Puritan individualism. Yet the central village meetinghouse endured as more than a reminder of communalism; it persisted as the site for the ritualized practice of community. Moreover, the rotating school suggested how New England's local civic culture could adjust to a decentralized spatial order. As scholars from a variety of disciplines have argued, community is not necessarily grounded in particular physical arrangements. Communalism involves real and imagined relationships between people that are not always disclosed by physical geography. Ironically, a new commercialism and economic individualism transformed New England's dispersed towns into compact white central villages that artists and writers then constructed as emblems of the region's venerable communalism.

Across the region the white village sprang to life as an actual and emblematic New England landscape between the late eighteenth and the first half of the nineteenth centuries. Morse and Dwight recorded the beginnings of this geographic transformation, but they failed to situate it in the context of dynamic commercial activity. The enterprise and mobility of early republican New England struck the clerical geographers as both praiseworthy and unsettling. They did not describe how the colonial landscape was rearranged by the winds of economic change or how the white village became a commercial center in the early republic.

In the decade after independence was achieved, population growth, the rise of urban centers, and the spread of mills and factories across the New England countryside created new economic opportunities for farmers. Improvements in transportation facilitated the exchange of goods and the integration of rural New England into a commercial agricultural economy. In response to the need for better roads, corporations laid out turnpikes and levied toll charges on travelers. Canals also advanced the economic integration of the region. "No country on the globe is better watered than New England," Morse had claimed in *The American Geography.*[9] But nineteenth-century canals, by linking lakes, lesser rivers, and major waterways and by establishing navigation routes around obstacles such as waterfalls, significantly improved commercial transportation and exploited geography to shape New England into an economic region. Closer to midcentury, the rise of the railroad, whose piercing whistle and belching smoke so disturbed Henry David Thoreau and whose arrival altered the rhythm of life in Concord, Massachusetts, culminated the antebellum improvements in transportation that expedited the spread of a new commercial world.

Again, the important work of geographer Joseph Wood documents how the compact white village emerged as both an economic node in and a prosperous symbol of this new order. The old central village became a commercial focal point that linked farmers to extralocal exchange. Merchants, bankers, lawyers, and tradesmen (coopers, blacksmiths, and wheelwrights) began to build homes, offices, and shops in central villages to provide services to farmers who were increasingly engaged in a market economy. Central villages acquired a new purpose and physical appearance; they became commercial hubs with a compact arrangement of houses and businesses owned by professionals and artisans.

A neoclassical and republican ethic, which enshrined order, balance, and simplicity, informed the architectural and landscape aesthetic of the commercial village.[10] The neoclassicism of the white village encoded the post-Revolutionary summons to install republican values in public life that would secure the future of the new nation. White paint, for example, was associated with the color of stable, enduring classical buildings; white spoke the language of virtue and simplicity. But the color white, like the new physical layout of the central village as a whole, also proclaimed the prosperity and even class consciousness that the new commercial order bestowed on New England villages. White paint was more expensive to produce than colored paint; it was recognized as the tint of wealth.

The new commercial prosperity of central villages called attention to the numerous unsightly meetinghouse lots, which were gradually refashioned into orderly town commons or greens. What often became the central village green had been too small to function as a common pasture in the colonial era. Common pastures, such as the large Boston Common, were located outside of central villages. But in most New England towns, common, open field arrangements declined in favor of enclosed farmsteads. It was usually the meetinghouse lot, not communal pasture land, that evolved into the nineteenth-century common or green.[11]

With Federal and later Greek Revival homes, churches, and businesses fashioning a new cultural aesthetic for the central village, meetinghouse lots became a site of civic improvement and pride—though not without resistance. Throughout the first half of the nineteenth century, village improvement societies moved to impose aesthetic order on these neglected places. With the removal of trash, boulders, and stumps, the grading of land, laying out of paths, planting of trees, and erection of fences, the meetinghouse lot was transformed from a relic of the vernacular colonial townscape into a picturesque arrangement that came to be perceived as an enduring marker of New England's historic communalism.[12] Such improvements were part of a larger reordering of the New England townscape that included the straightening of roads and the erection of fences as well as the construction of many stone walls. In its architecture and landscape design, the white central village seemed to embody New England's classical republican and communal ways and to mask the dynamic commercialism that was its lifeblood.

In the 1830s, after three decades had conferred prosperity and a new spatial order on the regional landscape, foreign visitors from Alexis De Tocqueville to Charles Dickens recorded favorable impressions of village-centered New England. Dickens, for instance, was struck by the "aspect of newness on every object" in New England villages. "Every little colony of houses has its church and schoolhouse peeping from among the white roofs and shady trees," he wrote, "every house is the whitest of white; every venetian blind the greenest of the green." To Dickens, the structures that created the idyllic beauty of New England central villages "looked as if they had been built and painted that morning, and could be taken down on Monday with very little trouble."[13] From a European perspective everything in America appeared new to Dickens, but he was certainly unaware, in 1839, of the recency of New England's white villages.

While prominent foreign travelers like Dickens and Tocqueville observed town life, John Warner Barber was busily creating a visual record of the central villages. Born in East Windsor, Connecticut, in 1798, Barber apprenticed with a local engraver in his youth and established his own business in New Haven in 1823. A devout Congregationalist, he soon applied his considerable skills as an engraver to the publication of illustrated historical and religious books. *Historical Scenes in the United States* (1827) was his first major book and *The Bible Looking Glass* (1866), which sold 175,000 copies, his most successful. Barber's output of illustrated volumes rivaled the literary enterprise of Harriet Beecher Stowe, his contemporary interpreter of New England history and local life.[14]

In the 1830s, perhaps inspired by Timothy Dwight's example, Barber's

FIGURE 3. John Barber engraving of Farmington, Connecticut. Barber, *Historical Collections of Connecticut* (1836). Courtesy of the Maine Historical Society.

horse-drawn wagon made a circuit of towns and villages throughout Connecticut and Massachusetts. Both in notes and sketches Barber recorded what he observed. His sketches became engravings for his books. One engraving is of Barber himself, busily drawing a New England village from an elevated site that reveals a compact configuration in all of its reassuring orderliness (Figure 3). His *Historical Collections of Connecticut* (1836) and *Historical Collections of Massachusetts* (1839) each bulged to six hundred pages of text. Offering both histories and up-to-date descriptions of towns, the volumes contained a total of four hundred engravings. The success of these collections, which were reissued through the 1840s, led to the publication of six additional histories of states beyond New England. Part of the appeal of Barber's works derived from the accuracy of his engravings. The village scenes, he insisted, "have been rendered with care [so] that anyone with this book in hand can place himself within a yard or two of the precise spot from whence the drawing was made." [15] Barber informed his readers when he occasionally eliminated a structure from an engraved scene so that he could more fully depict an important building or location.

Yet the self-imposed requirements of accuracy did not obscure the moralism he conveyed in words and images. Barber sought to engrave virtue, local pride, and Yankee pastoralism on the hearts and minds of his readers. The principle that informed his illustrated religious volumes shaped his town histories of New England: "the eye sends impressions home to the soul more readily, more forcibly, and more permanently, than any other of the senses." [16] The *Historical Collections* of Connecticut and Massachusetts uphold New England as the "Garden of the United States," not the "cold and sterile soil" of outsiders' imaginations. [17] In Barber's images New England is invariably in full bloom. Moreover, although his narratives describe the proliferation of mills, factories, and canals, which often penetrated to the doorstep of the commercial village, nevertheless it is the white central townscape in all of its pastoral and middle-class Yankee splendor that dominates the visual representation of place and people in his volumes. Barber, an industrious, successful, self-made artist-artisan who pulled up stakes and moved to New Haven, typified precisely those social elements and economic forces that created the white commercial village. He accurately depicted a real landscape, but he imagined and visually stylized the white village in ways that appealed to and validated the accomplishments of New England townspeople like himself.

Steepled churches reside as the center of Barber's village engravings, imaging New England as an ongoing religion-imbued region. But here, as in nineteenth-century town life, the Congregational Church had to compete with other denominations, principally the Methodists and the Baptists. The disestablishment of the Congregational Church freed up meetinghouse lots to become commons or greens for the town as a whole. The spire of a white church became the emblematic architectural detail of the nineteenth-century central village assemblage. Even Methodist and Baptist societies gradually adopted the new churchly architecture that transformed the Congregational meetinghouse of colonial times.

Barber's engravings capture the evolution of New England church architecture into the iconic structures that graced the emergent white commercial village. Consider, for example, his image of Durham, Connecticut, which was completed in 1835 (Figure 4). A new white Greek Revival Congregational Church built that year appears next to the old, seemingly unpainted meetinghouse only days before it was torn down. The rectangular meetinghouse with a side entrance exemplifies colonial tradition. The cupola on top of the exterior stairwell may have been a late addition to the plain meetinghouse, typical of the modest architectural changes made in many eighteenth-century towns. The churchly edifice of 1835 embodies a dramatic break with the past. The plain meetinghouse with a side-to-

FIGURE 4. John Barber engraving of the Durham, Connecticut, central village with an old, plain colonial-style meetinghouse and a new churchly structure. Barber, *Historical Collections of Connecticut* (1836). Courtesy of the Maine Historical Society.

side layout has been altered into a white church with stately pillars and windows, a front-to-back arrangement of space, and an expanded cupola, if not one of the soaring spires that increasingly hovered over compact villages.

Barber's images also chronicle changes in domestic architecture that made two-story neoclassical and Greek Revival homes part of the new central village order. Most New England houses throughout the colonial period were small single-story "cape" style dwellings. Surviving, well-preserved Georgian colonial homes constructed in the mid-eighteenth century largely by merchants in coastal ports and river towns were not representative of the much more common, modest structures scattered across the regional landscape.[18] Barber's engravings of nineteenth-century villages such as Northampton, Massachusetts, document the spread of impressive Federal and Greek Revival homes, churches, and civic buildings (Figure 5). Barber devoted full-page illustrations to many towns like Northampton, where domestic architecture in particular announced the accomplishments of entrepreneurs like himself, prosperous townspeople

FIGURE 5. John Barber engraving of the Northampton, Massachusetts, central village. Barber, *Historical Collections of Massachusetts* (1839). Courtesy of the Maine Historical Society.

who undoubtedly comprised a major audience for his books. His large engravings of major New England town centers, then, not only popularized the principal marker of regional identity; they also visually consolidated the class identity of the makers of the white village. In addition, Barber's concentration on village centers excluded the far more modest homes of less successful New Englanders who resided beyond the borders of his focus. One often has to turn to his small engravings of outlying rural towns and villages to see the mixed architecture of nineteenth-century New England. His image of Orange, Massachusetts, for instance, reveals a more vernacular townscape, including one-story homes, than the neoclassical architecture of the white village (Figure 6).

The engraving of Orange also exhibits two common types of New England fencing, the rail and the worm fence. A neoclassical and republican cultural imperative to infuse the world of politics and everyday life with order accelerated the bounding of the New England landscape in the nineteenth century. Fences may have made good neighbors, but like neoclassical architecture, neat town commons, and straight roads, they inscribed a commitment to republican order and virtue. The bounding of the village landscape exuded a faith in improvement and evidence of republican progress. Fenced house lots and fields signaled the presence of the private virtue and order on which the success of public life depended.[19]

FIGURE 6. John Barber engraving of Orange, Massachusetts. This clustered village is composed of more modest structures than those found in large, bustling towns. Rail and movable worm fencing, rather than stone walls, helps order the landscape. Barber, *Historical Collections of Massachusetts* (1839). Courtesy of the Maine Historical Society.

Barber's engravings not only record the extensive fencing of the New England landscape; they also document the spread of stone walls and white picket fences, two improvements that came increasingly to define the regional townscape. For much of the colonial period, the abundance of wood encouraged a New England preference for rail and worm fences. Erecting stone walls involved intensive labor that many farmers rejected. While some farmers invested time and effort in stone walls, others simply piled up stones by the sides of their fields. Still others settled on a compromise—low stone walls topped by rails. By the late eighteenth and early nineteenth centuries, deforestation of the countryside combined with a neoclassical landscape aesthetic to launch a new phase of stone wall construction in New England. "For the last few years," a Connecticut resident observed in 1812, "there has been an increased attention to the building of stone fences; till which time chestnut rails were mostly used and the timber was fast decreasing."[20] In his *Travels,* Timothy Dwight also noted the surge in the construction of stone walls. Moreover, Dwight may have been the first person to represent stone walls as Barber visually rendered them—as an emblem of New England's distinctive republican way of life. "A farm well surrounded and divided by good stone walls," Dwight observed, "presents to my mind, irresistibly, the image of tidy, skillful, profitable agriculture, and promises to me within doors the still more agreeable prospect of plenty and prosperity."[21]

Dwight praised a particular type of stone wall, not the hasty constructions of colonial farmers but the artful enclosures depicted by Barber that were "skillfully laid in an exact line with a true front."[22] Thus, it was both the style and the spread of stone walls in the nineteenth century that transformed them into icons of Yankee industry and virtue (Figures 7 and 8). No wonder Thoreau punned on the name of Walden Pond, complaining that the landscape of Concord and New England was too "walled-in." Many of the new stone walls that disturbed him were the fruits of Yankee labor. In the mid-nineteenth century, one Connecticut resident recalled the "stone bees" of his youth "when all the men of a village or hamlet came together with their draft of cattle and united to clear some patch of earth which had been stigmatized by nature with an undue visitation of stones and rocks."[23] But the enclosing of the nineteenth-century landscape with stone walls involved more than the calloused hands and sturdy backs of fabled Yankees coming together in communal stone bees. It also depended on the hired or indentured labor of blacks, Native Americans, and Irish immigrants. A skillfully built stone wall in a white village often proclaimed the financial success and social standing of a professional and only indirectly signaled the person's Yankee industry. A stone wall was often a monument to the worldly achievement that enabled the local person of wealth and rank to pay for its construction.

The white picket fences that Barber depicted in village centers such as Monroe, Connecticut, also functioned as a marker of both neoclassical-republican aesthetics and social status (Figure 9). Like stone walls, white picket fences proliferated on the New England townscape in the nineteenth century. They extended the balance, order, and simplicity of neoclassical architecture to the landscape, the front yard that served as the transitional zone between the home and the public space of the compact village. But white picket fences, even more than neat stone walls, betokened the worldly success and status of village leaders. White picket fences required costly sawn wood, expensive paint, and often skilled hired labor.[24] Among other things, the white picket fence protected social distinctions within the compact commercial village.

Fencing the town common also originated as part of nineteenth-century efforts to reorder and improve public space. Barber's engravings

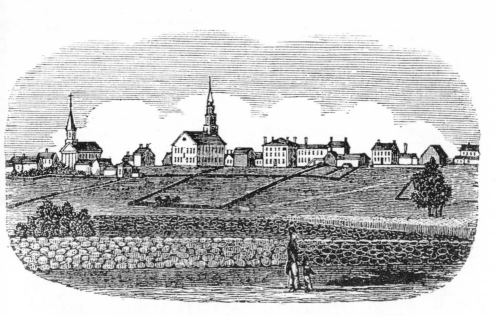

FIGURE 7. John Barber engraving of Charlton, Massachusetts, a village with large, neat stone walls. Barber, *Historical Collections of Massachusetts* (1839). Courtesy of the Maine Historical Society.

FIGURE 8. John Barber engraving of Marlboro, Massachusetts. This is another of Barber's many representations of stone walls and their role in establishing physical order on the regional landscape. Barber, *Historical Collections of Massachusetts* (1839). Courtesy of the Maine Historical Society.

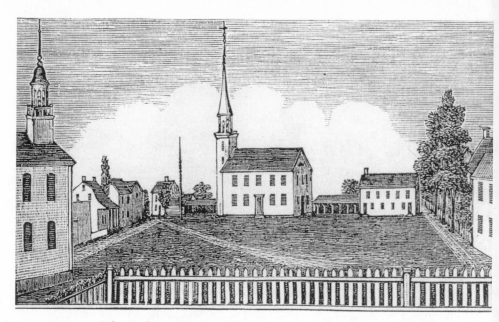

FIGURE 9. John Barber engraving of Monroe, Connecticut. White picket fences became a marker of wealth and status as well as a commitment to physical order. Barber, *Historical Collections of Connecticut* (1836). Courtesy of the Maine Historical Society.

depict many fenced town commons, such as in Framingham, Massachusetts, where improvement efforts included planting trees in deforested village centers (Figure 10). But engravings of other towns suggest that central village improvements sometimes lagged even as commerce and compact settlement advanced. In New Canaan, Connecticut, the common land has not been graded, the cemetery appears forlorn, and refuse litters the roadside (Figure 11). Erecting a fence was often the first step in upgrading the common. A fence blocked the random crisscrossing of the common by oxcarts and wagons that defaced the landscape with ruts and wheel tracks. But farmers outside the central village often resisted the fencing of the common for the inconvenience it imposed on them.

Indeed, outlying townspeople frequently opposed efforts to improve the common and refused to appropriate public money. Central village improvement societies, often without town money and in the face of out-livers' protests, spearheaded efforts to reorder the common or green and to align it with the neoclassical aesthetic that was increasingly shaping private property in the compact village. But even in central villages there were often conflicts surrounding proposed improvements to the com-

FIGURE 10. John Barber engraving of Framingham, Massachusetts. The first nineteenth-century public improvements to neglected and deforested town centers often involved planting trees and fencing the common or green. Barber, *Historical Collections of Massachusetts* (1839). Courtesy of the Maine Historical Society.

mon. In Keene, New Hampshire, for example, merchants opposed both the fencing of the common and the planting of trees in 1844.[25] The fence, they complained, would disrupt convenient access to their shops and the growth of trees would interfere with the easy sighting of the establishments. In towns such as Woburn, Massachusetts, trees planted on unfenced commons had to be "boxed" to protect them from oxcarts and wagons (Figure 12). On the whole, Barber's engravings and the text that accompanies them represent the white central villages as the outcome of a communalism and consensualism that went back to the Puritans. But the architecture of the central village registered social distinctions within town life that were the results of commercial transformation. Moreover, the town common emerged as a site of nineteenth-century conflict over change. Improvements succeeded gradually, despite the resistance and parsimony of many townspeople. Harmony and communalism dominate Barber's visual representation of town life, obscuring the market forces, mobility, and social tensions that thrived in unison with the growth of the white village.

Consider the human figures in Barber's engravings. His central villages

FIGURE 11. John Barber engraving of New Canaan, Connecticut. A central white village has begun to emerge, but the common remains unimproved. In some towns "outlivers" opposed improvements to central villages. Barber, *Historical Collections of Connecticut* (1836). Courtesy of the Maine Historical Society.

are almost uniformly populated by respectable middle-class Yankees, not earthy farmers or factory hands. Dressed in Sunday finery, they stroll as families to and from the pastoral, orderly central village (Figure 13). These engravings capture the popularity of walking, New Englanders' principal form of recreational exercise in the nineteenth century. The graded paths of improved town commons provided a public place for such activity. Some towns built "promenades." In 1826, for example, the leaders of Brunswick, Maine, filled in a swamp and created a walking "mall" in the central village.[26] In his essay on "Walking," Thoreau would critique the vogue of the reputable promenading that Barber depicts, because the bounded pastoral village cut people off from a more vital romantic experience with undomesticated nature. Townspeople might begin "by burning the fences" which along with other improvements had, in Thoreau's view, made the landscape "tame and Cheap."[27] But Barber's engravings draw the boundaries of respectable, controlled public behavior. His human figures link private virtue to public accomplishment. In their dress and com-

FIGURE 12. John Barber engraving of Woburn, Massachusetts. The common in this beautiful central village is unfenced, but the town has resorted to "boxing" young trees to protect them from the wheels of wagons and oxcarts. Barber, *Historical Collections of Massachusetts* (1839). Courtesy of the Maine Historical Society.

FIGURE 13. John Barber engraving of the village green in Taunton, Massachusetts. Barber repeatedly images New England as a pastoral, noncommercial world in which respectable middle-class Yankee families promenade in their best clothes. Barber, *Historical Collections of Massachusetts* (1839). Courtesy of the Maine Historical Society.

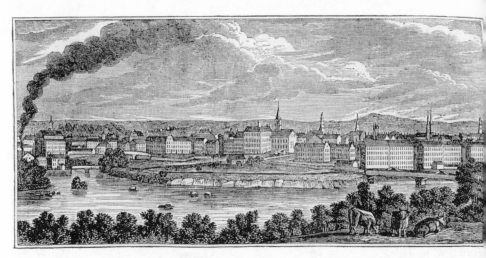

FIGURE 14. John Barber engraving of Lowell, Massachusetts. Barber depicts the manufacturing center from across the Merrimack River with a pastoral foreground. The engraving perpetuates the familiar, orderly visual conventions of his village scenes. Barber, *Historical Collections of Massachusetts* (1839). Courtesy of the Maine Historical Society.

portment the families who inhabit his engravings embody the order and balance of the white village itself.

Of course, in addition to outlivers who often opposed central village improvements, laborers and factory hands were important elements of the new social order of the commercial town. Barber's written text describes the rise of factories and mills throughout Connecticut and Massachusetts.[28] Small-scale mills, not Lowell-like communities, dominated the early stages of manufacturing in New England, firing hopes that the region would create a "non-urban" industrial order distinct from what was developing in England. Barber's *Historical Collections* seem to underscore this promise. They provide detailed information, drawn from state "Statistical Tables," of the industrialization of New England and include a few images of predominately factory towns. But the engravings in his books overwhelmingly represent New England as a middle-class pastoral world. Even in the image of Lowell, the industrial landscape is compatible with village tradition (Figure 14). Lowell is depicted from the northern bank of the Merrimack River with a pastoral setting in the foreground. In spite of the ominous black smoke that disrupts the scene, numerous church spires establish visual and moral continuity with the white village and regional

FIGURE 15. Frederic E. Church, *New England Scenery* (1851). Only the tip of the church spire is visible, framed by the tree in the foreground and the mountain in the background. By midcentury the white village had become such a familiar artistic and literary icon that only a church spire was needed to evoke a larger landscape assemblage. Courtesy of the George Walter Vincent Smith Collection, George Walter Vincent Smith Art Museum, Springfield, Massachusetts.

tradition, and a compact orderly architecture suggests New Englanders' ability to control industrial development.[29]

In the decades after he published *Historical Collections* of Connecticut and Massachusetts, Barber's New England became increasingly urban and ethnic, peopled by growing numbers of Irish immigrants. Yet visual representations of the "real" New England continued to invest the regional landscape with pastoral conventions similar to Barber's. Even painters of the romantic sublime employed the white-steepled church to establish the man-made and natural distinctiveness of the regional landscape. From Thomas Cole's *New England Scenery* (1839) to Frederic Church's identically titled painting of 1851 a white church resides near the center of an otherwise romantically wild setting. Indeed, in Church's *New England Scenery* (Figure 15), only the tip of the church spire is needed to remind the viewer of the iconography of the white village that Barber and artists who followed in his train had made popular. John Barber's work contributed to a larger cultural triumph in antebellum New England: the imaginative victory of the idealized pastoral white village over industrialism and romantic sublime nature as the reigning visual image of the regional landscape.

More than any other mid-nineteenth-century writer, Harriet Beecher Stowe elevated the emergent compact New England village into a literary icon that paralleled the visual representation of the regional landscape that descended from Barber's engravings. Stowe limned the pastoral world of the New England village, slighting its incubating commercialism to create a region of the literary imagination that erased urbanism, industry, and the Irish from a changing landscape. Like Jedidiah Morse's Woodstock and Timothy Dwight's Greenfield, Stowe's Litchfield, Connecticut, the town of her youth, functioned as a real and imagined place that offered literary entrée to the indigenous sociocultural terrain of village-centered New England.

In 1834, while John Barber traveled through Connecticut compiling drawings for his *Historical Collections,* the twenty-three-year-old Stowe published her first significant short story. "A New England Sketch" holds up the pastoral village of Newbury as representative of regional life. "Did you ever see the little village of Newbury, in New England?" she asks. "I dare say you never did; for it was just one of those out-of-the-way places where nobody came unless they came on purpose: a green little hollow, wedged like a bird's nest between half a dozen high hills, that kept off the wind and kept out foreigners." Stowe wrote "A New England Sketch" after she and her family had moved to Cincinnati, a bustling city teeming with transplanted New Englanders whose memories of youthful lives often embellished the stability of the village world they had left behind. "You don't know how coming away from New England has sentimentalized us all!" Stowe confided to a sister who remained in Connecticut. "A New England Sketch" portrays Newbury as an unchanging, tradition-bound, archetypal New England town, not the vital commercial node that more commonly characterized nineteenth-century compact villages. Newbury's "inhabitants were all of that respectable old steadfast family who make it a point to be born, bred, married, to die, and be buried all in the selfsame spot."[30]

Like the fixed engraved scenes that persisted through new editions of Barber's *Historical Collections,* Stowe's fiction repeatedly returned to the same village landscape. As Lawrence Buell has argued, from "A New England Sketch" through her fictional autobiography, *Poganuc People,* published more than forty years later, Stowe's "imaginative sociology" of regional life rested on a selective and nostalgic representation of a pastoral, ethnically homogeneous village landscape that was actually undergoing dramatic alteration.[31] Her fictional sentimentalization of village-centered New England resonated with a wide national audience, especially the scores of transplanted Yankees in New York and the West, such as those in Cincinnati who established a New England Society in 1846.

The village as literary icon acquired a moral standing in Stowe's fiction, just as it did in Barber's *Historical Collections.* Consider Stowe's most popular work, *Uncle Tom's Cabin* (1851), a book about the South (which she never visited) whose moral compass, nevertheless, is fixed on the white New England village. Miss Ophelia, the middle-aged Vermont cousin of slavemaster Augustus St. Clare, journeys to New Orleans (after consulting Morse's *Geography*) to join the plantation household. Stowe introduces Ophelia with a familiar description of her village origins:

> Whoever has travelled in the New England states will remember, in some cool village, the large farm-house, with its clean swept grassy yard, shaded by the dense and massive foliage of the sugar maple; and remember the air of order and stillness, of perpetuity and unchanging repose, that seemed to breathe over the whole place. Nothing lost, or out of order; not a picket loose in the fence, not a particle of litter in the turfy yard, with its clumps of lilac bushes growing up under the windows.[32]

This New England scene is readily familiar to consumers of stylized images of the village landscape like the scores produced by John Barber.

The iconography of the orderly, compact New England village serves as the backdrop for Stowe's literary invention of the exotic, un-American South. Her particularization of the physical and moral landscape of Miss Ophelia's place of origin is followed by a description of the disorienting New Orleans plantation of her cousin. Ophelia's carriage halts before a mansion "built in the Moorish fashion." Entering an interior courtyard, the bewildered Vermonter encounters a setting "arranged to gratify a picturesque and voluptuous ideality." She peers up at a gallery "whose Moorish arches, slender pillars, and arabesque ornaments, carried the mind back, as in a dream, to the reign of oriental romance in Spain." No church with a stately spire disturbs the worldly plantation society. The "heathenish" surroundings establish the moral distance Ophelia has traveled from the simplicity, order, and virtue of the white New England village.[33]

The plantation's flora confirm that she has entered an alien, sensual land far removed from John Barber's townscape of maples and elms planted in orderly rows. Ophelia begins to feel the lurid influence of "huge pomegranate-trees, with their glossy leaves and flame-colored flowers, dark-leaved Arabian jessamines, with their silvery stars . . . , lemon-scented verbenas . . . [and] mystic old aloe." The "bloom and fragrance" of her seemingly tropical surroundings reinforce the corrupting extravagance of St. Clare's mansion.[34] Landscape and architecture reveal the moral indulgence that sustains the slave system and that sanctions Ophelia's assertion of the superiority of New England's village ways.

Aunt Ophelia is a cultural emissary of village New England, whose order, pastoral simplicity, and virtue are ennobled by Stowe's construction of a regional foil in the exotic plantation South. Simon Legree, the other major New England character in *Uncle Tom's Cabin,* is also a Vermonter, but one whose life adds up to a renunciation of inherited village ways. Stowe appears to imagine Vermont as the heartland of village-centered New England — and for good reason. Vermont, of course, was an extension of her native Connecticut, but at midcentury it had not been altered by industrialization and "foreigners" as much as southern New England had. Moreover, the absence of the mountainous sublime romantic landscape that New Hampshire boasted led to the consistent imaging of Vermont as the most pastoral subregion of New England.[35] The state seemed to reside in the mid-nineteenth-century regional imagination, and Stowe's, as one large John Barber engraving. In addition, Vermont had been the first New England state to abolish slavery. While still a territory and little more than a cluster of fledgling villages, Vermont outlawed slavery in 1777.

Simon Legree repudiates the village-centered republican culture of New England by abandoning Vermont first in pursuit of wealth and adventure at sea and then for life as a slavemaster on a run-down plantation in the Deep South. In Vermont, Legree's pious mother had regularly taken him to worship "at the sound of the Sabbath bell." On his plantation Legree announces to the ill-fated Uncle Tom, "I'm your church now! You understand, — you've got to be as I say."[36] Stowe evokes the contrasting physical and moral landscape of village New England and the plantation South. Legree's world lacks the restraining communal institutions of New

England—its republican ecology—captured by Barber's engravings of civic and religious buildings in the central village.

Stowe's description of Legree's plantation, like her account of the setting of the St. Clare mansion, maps the moral distance that the brutal master has traveled in forsaking New England's ordered pastoral world for his chosen life in the slave South. The road leading to Legree's plantation winds "through dreary pine barrens . . . and now over log causeways, through long cypress swamps, the doleful trees rising out of the slimy, spongy ground, hung with long wreaths of funereal black moss." The lawn of the plantation house is "covered with frowsy tangled grass, with horse-posts set up, here and there, in it, where the turf was stamped away, and the ground littered with broken pails, cobs of corn, and other slovenly remains." The plantation house also testifies to Legree's moral dereliction: "some windows stopped up with boards, some with shattered panes, and shutters hanging by a single hinge,—all telling of coarse neglect and discomfort." [37] A ruthless, hardscrabble slaveholder, Legree inhabits a world socially distant from the indulgent, aristocratic St. Clare. But for Stowe they embody the class-bound world of the slave South, encouraging her to enshrine the middle-class industry and equality of the New England village.

The sketches collected in *Oldtown Folks* (1869) constitute Stowe's most important contribution to the mid-nineteenth-century emergence of the New England village as a literary icon. Oldtown is a composite village, though it is based in part on her husband's experience growing up in Natick, Massachusetts. As if to avoid having to deal with industrialization and "foreigners," that is, with a changing regional landscape, Stowe locates her representative New England village not in the hinterland of Vermont but back in time. Her sketches recall "ante-railroad times," serving up "New England in its *seed-bed,* before the hot suns of modern progress had developed its sprouting germs into the great trees of today." [38] In other words, *Oldtown Folks* is an exercise in fictional nostalgia for a pastoral, homogeneous village world that had already undergone significant alteration when John Barber completed his engravings three decades earlier.

Oldtown Folks imaginatively halts the progress of commerce in the nineteenth-century village—ongoing economic change and even urbanization in Stowe's lifetime that was accelerated by the railroad. (Thoreau complained that the railroad had infected rural New England with a pervasive busyness and with city ways and appetites.) Instead, the social order represented by Oldtown has hardly changed from the tranquil engravings of Barber, which also concealed the commercial underpinnings and class divisions of the compact New England village. Stowe's imaginative rendering of Oldtown is of a piece with her youthful sketch of Newbury penned for nostalgic Yankees transplanted in the Midwest. The opening pages of *Oldtown Folks* ground the reader in a familiar tableau: "Hither and thither, in the fertile tracts of meadow or upland, . . . were some two-dozen farmhouses, hid in green hollows, or perched on breezy hill-tops; while close alongside of the river, at its widest and deepest part, ran one rustic street, thickly carpeted with short velvet green grass, where stood the presiding buildings of the village." Oldtown's meetinghouse, "with its tall white spire," dominates the central village.[39]

Though on one occasion Stowe refers to Oldtown as "a brisk Yankee village," her pastoral idyll follows "A New England Sketch" in depicting a de-commercialized, static order "so innocent in the general tone of its society that . . . no one ever locked the house doors of a night."[40] Yet, like John Barber's career, Stowe's life was shaped by the mobility and economic opportunity of a dynamic nineteenth-century Yankee social order that undergirded the placid, pastoral white village imagined by artists and writers. By the time Stowe composed her novelistic paean to the stable life of village-centered New England, she had moved from Litchfield, to Hartford, to Boston, to Cincinnati, to Brunswick, Maine, to Andover, Massachusetts, and finally back to Hartford. Moreover, like Barber, her prolific output and pursuit of the main chance in the nineteenth-century literary marketplace produced handsome profits. She shrewdly published sketches in periodicals and then collected them into books like *Oldtown Folks* where they yielded more royalties. These profits enabled her to build an impressive home in Hartford, a Victorian version of the two-story "mansions" of successful professionals and entrepreneurs that crowd Barber's central village engravings.[41]

If commerce and mobility do not intrude on Stowe's pastoral village, neither do "foreigners" like the Irish laborer James Collins, whose shanty supplied the lumber for Thoreau's legendary hut at Walden Pond. Stowe adds diversity to the New England village by trotting out Oldtown's "few Negroes" and its remnant Native Americans. But representatives of these groups are treated as safe objects that contribute a dash of local color to the village scene. Primus King, for example, is introduced as "a gigantic, retired whaleman, black as coal, with enormous hands and feet, universally in demand in all the region as assistant in butchering operations." Native Americans serve as objects of village charity, if not sympathy, especially at Thanksgiving, when "all the poor, loafing tribes, Indian and half-Indian, who at other times wandered, selling baskets and other light wares, were sure to come back to Oldtown." [42]

Stowe's "well-regulated village" shines as a tolerant, communal, post-Puritan pastoral world, defaced neither by industrialism nor religious zealotry. The balance of nature and civilization that establishes Oldtown's physical beauty coincides with the equilibrium of its social and political order. The devout people of Oldtown, even its mossback Calvinists, resemble the newly mythologized Pilgrims — simple republican pietists — rather than firebrand Puritans. Oldtown's religious landscape recalls the competing church spires that anchor Barber's central village scenes. Tolerance among thriving denominations, not lingering theocratic ambitions, defines New England's religion-centered civic stability. Oldtown's Congregational Parson Lothrop is a gentle, open-minded soul "formed in the cooling-down of society, after it has been melted and purified by a great enthusiasm." [43]

Oldtown Folks represents a culmination of the mid-nineteenth-century "cult of the New England village," the transformation of a new townscape into a visual and literary icon that selectively portrays the region as a pastoral, homogeneous, and stable world. This cultural invention not only excludes industrialization and its attendant alterations of the region; it also obscures the energetic commercialism of the white village itself. Across the decades that stretched from "A New England Sketch" to *Oldtown Folks,* Stowe dwelled on the "smallness, isolation, cohesiveness, innocence, and unchangingness" of village-centered New England. [44]

Such sentimental pastoralism, which was propagated in visual and literary texts, appealed to a wide audience, especially transplanted New Englanders. In 1867 Henry Ward Beecher, Stowe's brother and pastor of the Plymouth Congregational Church in Brooklyn, filled with New York Yankees, published a New England novel of his own, for which he received an impressive $30,000 advance. *Norwood, or Village Life in New England* suggests that the region's towns are like "the scriptural city upon a hill—some Jerusalem, lifted up, and seen from afar, in all its beauty." Beecher's sister similarly exuded a Civil War–era triumphalism—a confidence in the superiority and progress of New England social ideals. "New

England has been to these United States what the Dorian hive was to Greece," Stowe observed in *Oldtown Folks*. "It has always been a capital country to emigrate from, and North, South, East, and West have been populated largely from New England, so that the seed-bed of New England was the seed-bed of this great American republic, and of all that is likely to come of it."[45]

Stowe voiced New England's abiding national regionalism, a perspective that embraced the village as an *American* social ideal. Migrating New Englanders on the "Yankee runway" that extended through the Old Northwest Territory helped transform the village into far more than a regional icon. Mobile Yankees like the Beechers not only planted New England town names on the northwestern landscape; they also laid out communities with greens, commons, and white-steepled churches and institutions such as schools and lyceums that reproduced elements of the New England village.[46] These migrants, like the ones who clustered around the Stowe family in Cincinnati and for whom Harriet composed "A New England Sketch," may have been the major consumers of the pastoral literary and visual images that secured the iconic status of the white village. Such transplanted New Englanders also participated in the evolution of other regional cultural inventions into national icons: the Yankee and the Pilgrim.

People: The Invention of the Yankee

Jedidiah Morse and Timothy Dwight recorded the growing ethnic identity of New England folk in the early republic. Yet they both refused to employ the label "Yankee" to designate the regional character. From the 1830s through the 1860s, in contrast, Harriet Beecher Stowe's writings are filled with Yankee dramatis personae. Stowe created a diverse, complex cast of regional characters, women and men, who testified to her literary efforts to negotiate the complicated and controversial subject of "Yankeeness," of a distinctive regional character. The Yankee as a New England and American type fully emerged only in the decades after 1820, paralleling the rise of the compact white village as a regional and national symbolic landscape.

Moreover, like the white village, the Yankee was both a real regional type and a culturally invented figure. Yankee characters in fiction, art, and political oratory as well as on stage embodied behavioral traits rooted, for example, in the mobility, restlessness, and pursuit of commercial opportunities that comprised the economic order underpinning the compact white village. The famous Yankee peddler served as an agent of this new commercial world. But Yankeeness was also a constructed identity, as critics, defenders, and entertainers deployed the regional character in selective and scripted ways. In the 1830s, for instance, one noted stage Yankee and his producer visited Massachusetts towns searching for dramatic "folk" material, with an ear tuned to the comic excesses of the New England dialect that could be embellished for urban audiences.[47]

To many non–New Englanders, particularly in the South, the Yankee was far from simply a comic figure. Rather, Yankee traits transported by a mobile people threatened to swamp the nation. The New England Yankee contended with the Southern cavalier and the Western frontiersman in nineteenth-century interregional conflict over whose traits and traditions would prevail in the shaping of the national character.[48] New Englanders such as Stowe attempted to redeem the Yankee from the cultural assaults of outside critics.

But the Yankee character was contested within New England itself. Yankeeness became an important cultural location where the changing nature of New England republicanism was debated. Perhaps the two main characteristics of the Yankee were a commercial shrewdness and a restless mobility. The Yankee, typically, was on the move and on the make. The Yankee signaled a real and imagined decline in classical republicanism whose emphasis on order, restraint, deference, and the public good was increasingly supplanted by the ethos of a dynamic market economy that redefined virtue in more individualistic and opportunistic terms as the commoner's natural ability (a native shrewdness) to seize the main chance, get ahead, and outdo one's competitors and social superiors. Was New England in danger of becoming a region of peddlers and horse traders? Yankees needed not only to be defended from Southern assaults; they also had to be redeemed from their own antirepublican excesses. Writers like Stowe and Lydia Maria Child would summon women both to reform the regional character and to enrich cultural representations of Yankeeness.

The Yankee, who came to life in the mid-eighteenth century with the comic figure of Yankee-Doodle, thus developed by the middle decades of the nineteenth century into a complex regional type. The antebellum Yankee donned a variety of guises that embodied conflicting traits that seemed to compete for dominance of the New England character. Furthermore, migrating New Englanders fashioned a real and imagined "Yankee North," a terrain on which the region's continuing national ambitions advanced. The Northern victory in the Civil War secured the Yankee's status as the preeminent American character type, symptomatic of New England's long-standing cultural aspiration to imprint its regional values on the nation.

It is fruitless to search for New England use of the Yankee label in the vast outpouring of Puritan-inspired seventeenth- and eighteenth-century writing about regional identity. "Yankee" originated in the seventeenth century as an epithet hurled against the English inhabitants of the region by their foes. As the term gained cultural currency in the late eighteenth and early nineteenth centuries, writers from Noah Webster to Washington Irving speculated on its derivation. Both authors attributed it to Native Americans. Irving, for example, suggested that Yankee derived from "Yankoo," a Native American word that described the English as "silent men." A more plausible explanation is that Yankee is of Dutch origin. The word may have developed from "Jan Kees," literally John Cheese, a Dutch term of derision that was used by the inhabitants of New York to ridicule the English, especially the residents of Connecticut who constantly clashed with New Yorkers over boundaries between the two colonies.[49] For most of the colonial period, then, New Englanders shunned "Yankee" as an identifier of regional character.

"Yankee-Doodle," the Revolutionary marching tune, signaled a new, positive appropriation of a heretofore opprobrious locution. Both the British and the Patriots marched to competing versions of "Yankee-Doodle." The British strain perpetuated the old, derisive use of the Yankee label. Perhaps the earliest printed English version of "Yankee-Doodle" dates from 1777. It locates the origins of the song and the figure of Yankee-Doodle in the era of the French and Indian War, when New England's army of unprofessional soldiers fought side by side with British regulars. The English rendition ridicules the Yankee soldier, whose frontier, "Indian style" of fighting against the French and in the opening skirmishes of the Revolutionary War struck the British as cowardly:

> Brother Ephraim sold his cow and bought him a commission,
> And then he went to Canada to Fight for the Nation,
> But when Ephraim he came home he proved an arrant Coward,
> He wou'd'n't fight the Frenchmen there for fear of being devoured.

This English version recommends that the song "be sung thro' the Nose, & in the West Country drawl & dialect."[50] The New England nasal accent, attributed here to the English geographic origins of many of the region's inhabitants, functioned as a grating reminder to outsiders of New England's distinctiveness in the colonial era; it remained at the center of humorous and critical characterizations of the Yankee in the nineteenth century.

The British "Yankee-Doodle" of 1777 announces sarcastically that the tune has been "Christened by the Saints of New England" as "The Lexington March." Beginning with the Battle of Lexington-Concord two years earlier, New Englanders marched to their own rendition of "Yankee-Doodle," which celebrated the courage and military ingenuity of the Revolutionary fighting folk. In "M' Fingal," his patriotic poem begun in 1776, Connecticut's John Trumbull captured the native pride that shaped American versions of "Yankee-Doodle":

When Yankies, skill'd in martial rule,
First put the British troops to school;
Instructed them in warlike trade,
And new manoeuvres of parade;
The true war dance of Yanky-reels,
And *manual exercise* of heels;
Made them give up, like saints complete,
The arms of flesh and trust the feet.[51]

A year later an English observer conceded that "*Yankee Doodle* is now their [the Patriots'] favorite paean, a favorite of favorites, played in the army, esteemed as warlike as the Grenadier's March—it is the lover's spell, the nurse's lullaby."[52] The popular song encouraged the Revolutionary political rebirth of the Yankee figure. As Jonathan or "Brother Jonathan," the Yankee came to represent the native virtue and ingenuity of embattled American rustics resisting the corrupt metropolitan world of John Bull (Figure 16).

But the cultural redemption of the Yankee during the Revolutionary war was circumscribed; it did not lead to a national identity for the newly independent states. The British and their Loyalist American supporters continued to invoke the older associations of the Yankee, apparently exploiting the term as a regional epithet to divide the Revolutionaries. In 1784 one English visitor remarked that "the New Englanders are disliked by the inhabitants of all the other provinces, by whom they are called Yankeys."[53] From the 1780s through the early nineteenth century the regional political conflicts of the early republic repatriated the Yankee to

BROTHER JONATHAN *Administering a Salutary Cordial to* JOHN BULL.

FIGURE 16. Amos Doolittle, "Brother Jonathan Administering a Salutary Cordial to John Bull" (1813). This political cartoon repeats the Revolutionary image of the virtuous Yankee as the rustic Brother Jonathan resisting corpulent, corrupt John Bull. Courtesy of the American Antiquarian Society.

New England soil, where outsiders perceived the character, as originally beheld by the Dutch, as the embodiment of despised provincial traits that posed a threat to other regions.

Even in post-Revolutionary New England, Yankees occupied conflicted cultural ground. On the one hand, as Yankee-Doodles, they represented the republican virtue and attachment to liberty of New England common folk. On the other hand, the Yankee label persisted, especially in Federalist circles, as an epithet now encumbered with new, troublesome Revolutionary associations: the New England commoners' increasingly bold assertions of their rights, native ability, and distrust of deference and hierarchy. It is not surprising, then, that Jedidiah Morse and Timothy Dwight refused to invoke "Yankee" in their detailed delineations of the New England character. To such Federalists, the term not only continued to carry the infection of its origins as a disparagement of New Englanders; it had also acquired the political contagion of Yankee-Doodle. "Yankee" resonated as a verbal sign of the empowerment of commoners who rose up against the august authority of John Bull and who had now become restless Jonathans on the regional political landscape. Morse and Dwight, by expunging Yankee from their accounts of the regional character and by attributing political and commercial excesses of New Englanders—the "Knavish, artful, and dishonest" trickery of peddlers, for example—to a small minority, endeavored to reform, not just report on, regional behavior.[54] They represented New Englanders as John Barber would exhibit them, as orderly, middle-class communalists, not restive Yankee Jonathans.

The Federalists' reservations about the real and symbolic Yankeefication of the New England character are revealed in the first major literary representation of the Yankee, which appeared in *The Contrast,* Royall Tyler's play of 1787. The son of a wealthy Boston family, Tyler graduated from Harvard in 1776, studied law, was admitted to the bar in 1780, served in the militia, and in 1786–87 assumed the rank of major in the suppression of Shays' Rebellion, the agricultural protests of Yankees and Yankee-Doodles, that is, New England rustics and war veterans. Tyler reveals his patriotism through the play's contrast between the foppish, effeminate Dimple who exudes a pretentious English gentility and an honest, virtuous American, appropriately named Colonel Manly. Both characters have contrasting servants in the fawning Jessamy and the naive Jonathan. Tyler's Jonathan, a subordinate character in *The Contrast,* stands as the first American dramatic representation of the Yankee, a comic figure who would move to center stage in the numerous Yankee plays of the 1830s and 1840s. But Tyler's Jonathan is not just a politically innocent dramatic creation trotted out for comic relief. Jonathan becomes burdened by Tyler's proto-Federalist anxieties about the corruption of the New England character and the impertinence of common Yankee folk. Predictably, Shays' Rebellion intrudes into Tyler's patriotic play.

Jonathan is served up as a country bumpkin, a rustic Yankee-Doodle who has gone to town, in this case bewildering New York City. Though he serves as Colonel Manly's valet, he is quick to vow that "no man shall master me." Jonathan's bold assertions of his love of liberty and belief in equality ("My father has as good a farm as the colonel") as well as his naive inquisitiveness register the attitudinal and behavioral changes brought about by the Revolution that so troubled Federalists like Tyler, Morse, and Dwight. The servant grudgingly admits his sympathy for Daniel Shays and his followers: "I vow I did think the sturgeons [insurgents] were right." [55] Jonathan repeatedly butchers the English language, revealing his ignorance and calling into question the empowerment of ordinary

Yankee folk encouraged by the Revolution. *The Contrast* thus challenges the Revolutionary ennoblement of Yankee-Doodle and demonstrates the emerging Federalist distress over the Revolution's destabilization of the New England character. Tyler not only launched the career of the stage Yankee; he also positioned the New England Jonathan at the center of politicized debate over the nature of the regional (and later the American) character and how its corruptions might be counteracted.

In the early republic the mobility of New Englanders and their pursuit of commercial opportunities provoked additional concerns about the Yankeefication of the regional character and the betrayal of republicanism. Of course, such activity could be incorporated into a republican discourse of Yankee industry and enterprise that underwrote an ideology of regional cultural imperialism as the North became New Englandized. Timothy Dwight and other influential Federalists harbored such a vision. Dwight's discourse of New England ethnic traits in his *Travels,* with its refusal to employ the Yankee image and its celebration of enterprise, industry, and order, sought to establish a standard of "authentic" republican New Englandness shorn of its Yankee excesses. These excesses came to reside in a legendary figure, kin to the Yankee-Doodle rustic, namely, the notorious Yankee peddler, who carried mobility and commercial "enterprise" to extreme lengths. "The consequences of this employment, and of all others like it, are generally malignant," Dwight lamented. "Men who begin life with bargaining for small wares will almost invariably become sharpers." [56] Yet the peddlers whom Dwight deplored were products of the post-Revolutionary commercial order that brought the compact white village, which he poeticized, into existence. In fact, peddlers were often the relatives and neighbors of merchants and manufacturers in New England village centers. The Yankee peddler, like the rustic republican Jonathan, was both a real figure grounded in the post-Revolutionary commercial world and a culturally invented one deployed in cautionary and frequently humorous tales about the corruption of the New England and American republican character by "sharpers'" values.

New England peddlers had been common before the American Revolution as brokers in the colonial empire of goods. But their importance and numbers grew in the early republic, particularly during the decades that preceded the expansion of railroads, which speeded the transportation of goods to geographically extended markets. In New England, the changes that propelled the growth of the compact white village—the advance of the commercial order, the increase in shops and factories, the laying out of turnpikes and canals—all created new opportunities for peddlers, who became ubiquitous figures throughout the region, among transplanted Yankees in New York and the West, and even in the South.

For many young New England males, peddling became, like school teaching, a temporary livelihood pursued on the journey toward another occupation. Some peddlers purchased goods from merchant suppliers, whereas others functioned as salesmen on monthly salary or commission. Family members of merchants and manufacturers sometimes peddled goods, though trusted neighbors seem to have been more common. The typical peddler stocked a horse-drawn wagon with an array of items increasingly produced in New England's commercial villages: tinware, spoons, clocks, combs, and a whole array of "Yankee notions," small items that could be easily transported. Personally tied to New England's white villages, peddlers were important agents of its commercial order. John Barber, who so effectively celebrated the New England village, was himself a kind of itinerant peddler who produced and marketed engravings in a geographic circuit that matched the range of the most mobile Yankee drummer.[57]

The peddler's reputation as a Yankee "sharper" was based on the realities of his trade. First, bartering was a central element in his salesmanship. In exchange for his wares, a Yankee peddler often had to take another item, which could be swapped or sold along his travels or brought back to New England. The financial success of a trip usually depended on the peddler's shrewdness in calculating the value and marketability of a bartered item. The peddler's notoriety as a sharper was also promoted by local merchants who were his competitors. Even in New England, the peddler often intruded on local markets, provoking his rivals to malign his character. By the 1830s the legendary story of Yankee peddlers duping customers with wooden nutmegs was in circulation. In that decade Thomas Haliburton popularized the image of the cunning Yankee trader in a series of books featuring the homely wisdom of Sam Slick, a clockmaker and peddler from "Slicksville, Connecticut." In Haliburton's hands, the New Englander as Sam Slick became a cross between Yankee-Doodle and the Yankee peddler, a sly, opinionated, and material-minded representative of the region's common folk.[58]

Haliburton, a Nova Scotian, transmuted the "land of steady habits" into "Slicksville, U.S.A.," but the Yankee was an object of concern within New England as well. Whether in his political manifestation as the upstart, liberty-loving commoner or the sharp trader, the Yankee raised concerns about the unrepublican temper of post-Revolutionary New England life. As early as 1799 "A Real Patriot" complained in the *Connecticut Courant* that peddling "has injured, if not ruined, the morals of a large portion of young men in many of our towns."[59] As a cultural figure the Yankee embodied an ambivalent regional legacy as well as a split personality. The execrable Yankee of Dutch imagination persisted, only partially redeemed by the virtuous, ingenious rustic Yankee-Doodle pitted against John Bull who was so central to Revolutionary republican ideology. In the post-Revolutionary era the Yankee commoner's jealousy of his liberty often seemed to degenerate into an unrepublican "impertinence" toward social and political authorities, with laudable enterprise and industry metamorphosing, within a new market order, into the locomotive of crass commercialism exemplified by the peddler.

In an 1815 essay, "Sketches of the American Character," one interpreter attempted to define how the Yankee was riddled with contradictory traits, his constitution a shifting cultural compound: "simplicity and cunning, inquisitiveness from natural and excessive curiosity, confirmed by habit; credulous, from inexperience and want of knowledge of the world; believing himself to be perfectly acquainted with what he partially knows; tenacious of prejudices; docile, when rightly managed; when otherwise treated, independent to obstinacy; easily betrayed into ridiculous mistakes; incapable of being overawed by external circumstances."[60] The Yankee's behavior seemed changeable, fluid, even unstable, like the texture of the post-Revolutionary world in which the New England and American commoner began to emerge. "Yankeeness" became a shorthand for tensions within New England republicanism. By the antebellum decades, the discourse of New England Yankeeness evolved a reformist agenda to domesticate, even feminize, the regional character. Cultural resources would be deployed to contain the Yankee character, to stabilize it along more classically republican lines, to frame it, as John Barber did, in the image of respectable middle-class enterprise, industry, and order.

But "Yankee" resisted cultural containment not just because nineteenth-century New England proved to be such a dynamic world. Rather, Yankee also remained a floating and contested identity because the character became a location of interregional as well as intraregional conflict. In the decades after the War of 1812, the so-called second war for independence from John Bull, the Yankee Jonathan became the major figure in an American debate over the lineaments of the national character, contention that stiffened resistance to New England's national regionalism and cultural imperialism. The South, of course, repeatedly invoked the Yankee as an embodiment of the acquisitive, predatory values associated with the commercial-industrial North. The mobile Yankee, often outfitted in self-righteous, hypocritical attire and linked to the treachery of the Hartford Convention, served as a foil for the mythology of the Southern cavalier who presided over the benevolently paternal labor system and genteel social order of the South.[61] But even in the North, the Yankee persisted as an object of controversy. As New England migrants poured into the states west of the region, they acquired not only a new group consciousness but also a heightened and not always welcomed visibility in the eyes of non-Yankees.

Consider, for example, Washington Irving's "Rip Van Winkle" and "The Legend of Sleepy Hollow," both published in 1820. Literary scholars have commented on anti-Yankee elements in these tales, but Irving's animus against New Englanders must be related to the historical development of the Yankee figure. In addition, his two classic stories are better understood as responses to regional change and conflict, particularly the nineteenth-century rise of a commercial, mobile, expansive New England. "Rip Van Winkle" is not a parable about the general pace of change in America; it focuses on a particular period and a historically specific source of change—the New England Yankee. Rip, a descendant of the original Dutch settlers of New York, is a decidedly unenterprising villager steeped in the lore and reposeful traditions of his Dutch heritage. He seems to embody Jedidiah Morse's view of New Yorkers, though Irving is not endorsing the New England geographer's moral perspective on Dutch "deficiencies." Rip's symbolic twenty-year slumber causes him to miss the Revolution, the upheaval Irving blames for unleashing New England Yankees on America.

Rip returns to the post-Revolutionary village and encounters a new order, with the Yankee excesses that even New England Federalists cautioned against: "There was a busy, bustling, disputatious tone about it, instead of the accustomed phlegm and drowsy tranquility." Rip's complacent neighbors have been overrun by Yankees like the "lean, bilious-looking fellow, with his pockets full of handbills, [who] was haranguing vehemently about rights of citizens—elections—members of congress—liberty—Bunker's Hill—heroes of seventy-six—and other words, which were a perfect Babylonish jargon to the bewildered Van Winkle." A parsimonious New England Yankee—the exploitative and aptly named Jonathan Doolittle—has taken over the village inn, cleverly altered its image of King George, and relabeled it "General Washington." During Rip's absence his wife succumbs to another exemplar of New England's marauding Yankee ethos. Dame Van Winkle, Rip learns, perished when "she broke a blood-vessel in a fit of passion at a New England peddler."[62] "Rip Van Winkle" records Irving's despair over the uncontested triumph of Yankeeism, offering a counternarrative to Timothy Dwight's contemporaneous celebration of the enterprising, industrious ethnic customs of migrants who were fashioning an ever-expanding Greater New England.

In "The Legend of Sleepy Hollow," New England Yankeeism is dealt an imaginary, though temporary, setback, as if Irving conceded that there was no halting the Yankee juggernaut on the ground. Ichabod Crane is a gangly upstart Connecticut bumpkin, a self-important, moralizing schoolmaster with a peddler's soul. In short, Ichabod is not only a descendant of Yankee-Doodle and a progenitor of Sam Slick; he is a multilayered literary figure who suggests the increasingly protean cultural representation of the Yankee in the nineteenth century.

The restless Crane invades Sleepy Hollow, planning only to "tarry" in the placid Dutch village on his sojourn toward the accumulation of wealth. His physical appearance inscribes the lack of proportion and balance in the New England character. He is an entertaining but frightening ethnic stereotype, Irving's response to Jedidiah Morse's physically proportioned and "generally tall, stout and well built" New Englander. A "scarecrow" of New England culture, Crane "was tall, but exceedingly lank, with narrow shoulders, long arms and legs, hands that dangled a mile out of his sleeves, feet that might have served for shovels, and his whole frame most loosely hung together." His head resembled a "weathercock," his protruding ears and spindly neck helping him determine "which way the wind blew." His "long snipe nose," a convention that traced back to early representations of Yankee-Doodle and Brother Jonathan, underscores New Englanders' distinctive nasal accent. Crane is proud of his skill at psalmody, a cultural achievement that proclaims the aesthetic impoverishment of Yankee New England. His singing voice, with its "peculiar quavers," rises above the congregation on Sunday mornings. Even after he is driven from the village, irritating strains, "which are said to be legitimately descended from the nose of Ichabod Crane," continue to reverberate in the church.[63]

Crane's calculating shrewdness is done in by his even more powerful Yankee superstition and bumpkinlike gullibility. The offspring of New England's Puritan past, the Yankee Crane is still immersed in the works of Cotton Mather. He is proud of his New England "learning." An avatar of the region's sense of superiority rooted in Puritan tradition, Crane exhibits a dimension of Yankeeness that would grow in importance with interregional conflict in the nineteenth century: he arrogates to himself the role as intellectual and moral tutor to others.

The Connecticut pedagogue carries his putative Yankee advantages into the contest with the quasi-frontiersman Brom Bones for the hand of Katrina Van Tassel, the coquettish American maiden. Crane views a prospective union with Katrina through the eyes of the ambitious Yankee peddler that he is, rather than from the bonds of affection and sensuality, alien emotions to the cold, materialistic New England character. Crane covets the land Katrina will inherit and calculates how it "might be readily turned into cash, and the money invested in immense tracts of wild land, and shingle palaces in the wilderness." He dreams of joining restless Connecticut migrants in advancing the frontier of the New England diaspora. With Katrina safely mounted in a wagon, "he beheld himself bestriding a pacing mare, . . . setting out for Kentucky, Tennessee, or the Lord knows where."[64]

Crane's Yankee version of the American dream is frustrated by the ingenuity of Brom Bones, who, in the guise of the headless horseman, terrorizes the credulous Crane, drives him from Sleepy Hollow, and gains Katrina. But Irving was too astute an observer to transform Brom Bone's triumph into a larger nineteenth-century defeat of New England Yankeeism. In a postscript to the story Crane resurfaces as a member of the Corporation of New York City. Ichabod, like so many mobile, calculating Yankees, has found a place in the world.[65]

Though a comic figure and the butt of Irving's ridicule, Ichabod Crane represents the most richly textured Yankee in early nineteenth-century American culture. Irving incorporates into Crane's character not only Yankee-Doodle and the peddler, but also the Yankee as the deformed scion of Puritanism and the Yankee as embodiment of New England's patronizing intellectual and moral arrogance, real and perceived attributes that would be increasingly problematic in nineteenth-century interregional political strife. Despite the imaginative expulsion of the Yankee from the garden of Sleepy Hollow, Irving was certainly aware in 1820 that Ichabodism had corrupted republicanism, that the consequences of the Revolution could not be reversed, and that New England would continue, in Morse's words, as a "nursery" of the nation. Indeed, as a resident of England when he wrote "The Legend of Sleepy Hollow" and "Rip Van

Winkle," Irving knew that in English eyes the New England Yankee was already the archetypal American. As a Virginian abroad was informed by an English lady in 1817, "To us you are all Yankees, rascals who cheat the whole world."[66]

In the decades after the War of 1812, the Yankee began to appear in Northern plays, magazines, and art as a national character. Indeed, the Yankee, even more than the Western frontiersman with whom he shared many traits and who was often a transplanted New Englander, reemerged as the most popular folk representative of a distinctive, indigenous American republican culture. In other words, the Revolutionary Yankee-Doodle experienced a cultural rebirth. Though the South continued in its steadfast resistance to the Yankee, the character performed increasingly important cultural work in the North, from the so-called Jacksonian age of commoners through the rise of romantic celebrations of rustic life and ordinary folk. In his essay on "Self-Reliance" (1839–40), for example, Ralph Waldo Emerson, the Transcendental Yankee, lauded the versatility and moral mettle of New England Jonathans and their superiority over educated urbanites. "A sturdy lad from New Hampshire or Vermont," Emerson wrote in a new take on Ichabod Crane, "who in turn tries all the professions, who *teams it, farms it, peddles,* keeps a school, preaches, edits a newspaper, goes to Congress, buys a township, and so forth, in successive years, and always, like a cat, falls on his feet, is worth a hundred of these city dolls."[67]

Emerson's early essays such as "Self-Reliance" were manifestos of American cultural nationalism. They also coincided with a new phase in the cultural production of the Yankee: the character's participation in Northern efforts to fashion an American identity. In magazines like *Yankee Doodle* and *Yankee Blade* and in popular stage characters like Jonathan Ploughboy and Jedidiah Homebred, the Yankee's virtue and excesses, his speech and humor, were offered as representative, if embellished, qualities of American life and manners. Beginning in the 1830s, the enormous popularity of Seba Smith's "letters" of Captain Jack Downing, the rustic philosopher from Down East Maine, testified to the rebirth of the Yankee as an American type. A short while later, James Russell Lowell created his own rustic philosopher and critic of Southern slavery, Hosea Biglow, and railed against the "open maligners" of the Yankee character "who have given it that hardness, angularity, and want of proper perspective, which, in truth, belonged, not to their subject, but to their own niggard and unskillful pencil." As the editor of *The Yankee,* a periodical founded in 1828,

FIGURE 17. William Sidney Mount, *Farmers Bargaining* (1835). Restless Yankee rustics whittle as they match wits and traders' skills negotiating the sale of a horse. Courtesy of the New York Historical Society.

claimed with a mixture of exaggeration and accuracy, "The word *Yankee* is no longer a term of reproach. It is getting to be a title of distinction."[68]

The patriotic, nationalist image of the Yankee circulated from the printed word, to the stage, to the painter's canvass. In the 1830s New York artist William Sidney Mount, using his neighbors on rural Long Island (which had been part of New England) as subjects, completed a series of rustic Yankee scenes. *Farmers Bargaining* was received, like other contemporary representations of American Jonathans, as "an image of pure Yankeeism and full of wholesome humor" (Figure 17).[69] The farmers, busily engaged in the folk practice of whittling, carefully eye one another as they match wits in negotiating the sale of a horse. The painting seems to celebrate an unencumbered market order where a horse trader's values and native skill carry the day—a democratic image of Yankeeism imbued with the spirit of a commercial meritocracy. In short, the mid-nineteenth-century Yankee reemerged not only as a patriotic figure but also as a cultural purveyor—an ideological peddler—of a newly legitimate, individualistic market order. Emerson's Yankee self-reliance, however abstract and intellectual, still urged compatriots to "detach themselves" and to embrace the revitalizing prospect of "living property," property acquired by individual exertion and therefore rooted in life experience.[70]

As a peddler of ideological freight participating in mid-nineteenth-century nationalist and capitalist discourses, the New England Yankee was not a seamless character. He persisted as a product of a checkered cultural history and as an object of Southern scorn. Moreover, the character continued to be a cultural location—particularly in the Yankee heartland of New England—where conflicts within nineteenth-century republicanism were confronted. Though a Jonathan's ingenuity, enterprise, self-reliance, and simplicity could be played off against the leisured self-indulgence of the wealthy Southern slaveowner, the Yankee nevertheless posed a threat to classical republicanism. The self-reliant values of the market threatened to transform New Englanders into a race of unrestrained horse traders and peddlers, hardly a fulfillment of the classical notion of republican virtue. Yankee women were summoned to stabilize the regional character along more acceptable republican lines.

From Yankee-Doodle to Ichabod Crane and Jonathan Ploughboy, the New England character was consistently represented by masculine figures. Beginning in the 1820s, however, Yankee women enriched and became republican custodians of the regional character. With the growing separation of home and work, mothers were increasingly recognized as the principal shapers of character. They typically resided outside the marketplace and its peddler's calculus. The domestic sphere could abide as a realm where classical republican virtues such as self-denial, restraint, and order were preserved. Furthermore, women, as the guardians of republican tradition, could instill in children, and even in husbands, the values that would regulate Yankee excesses in public life.[71]

Such was the notion of Yankee womanhood and Yankee domesticity that writer-reformer Lydia Maria Child offered the public in her enormously successful *The American Frugal Housewife*, "Dedicated to Those Who are Not Ashamed of Economy." A combination domestic manual, advice book, and collection of recipes, *The American Frugal Housewife* was published in 1829 and reprinted twenty-eight times by 1842. Like Morse's *American Geography*, Child's text was suffused with a New England per-

spective that reached a wide national audience. The author did not invoke the Yankee by name, but she quoted Ben Franklin on the cover, associating her work with his popular "Yankee" writing and persona. More important, she confronted the issues of mobility, acquisitiveness, and republicanism that dominated the cultural dialogue over Yankeeness and its shaping of the regional and national character.[72]

The American Frugal Housewife, for instance, responded to the restless mobility identified with the Yankee that created a Greater New England, where Child's book undoubtedly sold well. The text transmitted information that suggested how mobility had disrupted intergenerational oral tradition. It systematized in print folk remedies and practical household advice for a population on the move to the West and to cities. A small, portable, inexpensive, and practical (though moralistic) volume, *The American Frugal Housewife* was itself a "Yankee notion," an indigenous cultural artifact brimming with down-home wisdom, yet shrewdly aimed, like the stage Yankee of the period, at a dawning "national" patriotism. Imported recipe books and manuals, Child notified her readers, did not suit the republican character of America. Her work, as the title indicated, was "adapted to the wants of this country." Child was not above speaking in Yankeeisms or in the genuine rustic earthiness of the stage character. She offered plenty of advice for storing food "down cellar" and was not squeamish about offending genteel sensibilities: she recommended ear wax as a curative, especially for "those who are troubled with cracked lips."[73] Clearly, the Yankee on stage, as a rustic philosopher and as a Franklian virtuous republican, shaped the creation and the reception of *The American Frugal Housewife.*

Child domesticated Yankee character traits; she transported Yankeeness into the household, where it now became the ideological companion and, indeed, rival of Yankeeness in the marketplace. She formalized and popularized the image of the matriarchal Yankee, who assumed the burden of safeguarding the American character from its antirepublican excesses. She insisted that "the situation and prospects of a country may be justly estimated by the character of its women."[74] The national character would be formed in the home, not simply by Yankees peddlers and Jonathans in the marketplace.

Women could redeem their men from the kind of avarice associated with the Yankee peddler. "Let women do their share towards reformation—Let their fathers and husbands see them happy without finery," Child urged, "and if their husbands and fathers have a foolish pride in seeing them decorated, let them gently and gradually check this feeling, by showing that they have better and surer means of commanding respect." Women were to practice Yankee "ingenuity"—domestic shrewdness—to enshrine industry, economy, frugality, simplicity, and self-discipline in the home. Such historically resonant words, which harkened back to classical republicanism and Puritan notions of competency with their moral reservations about an unbridled market economy, formed the ideological spine of Child's book. "A luxurious and idle *republic!*" she warned. "Look at that phrase!—The words were never made to be married together; everybody sees it would be death to one of them." Women could create a Yankee-republican moral economy at home to counteract the acquisitiveness and "sharper's" values of the market. The frugal American housewife would safeguard the republic by influencing the behavior of men and molding the values of children. Instruct children "to save everything,—not for their *own* use," Child continued, "for that would make them selfish—but for *some* use." Women's work became part of "republican motherhood," the female responsibility to shape the character of family members, especially children, so they would move into public life as productive, virtuous citizens. As Child put it, for the patriotic frugal housewife the home stood "as the gathering place of the deepest and purest affections; as the sphere of woman's *enjoyments* as well as her *duties.*"[75]

The American Frugal Housewife suggests a Yankeefication of the cult of domesticity and republican motherhood. At precisely the time the Yankee reappeared in the North as a cultural representative of the nation's indigenous folk, Child published her popular patriotic text that assigned women the role of reforming and stabilizing the contested Yankee character. Moreover, she employed a Yankee vernacular to impart her reformist agenda. " '[M]any a little makes a mickle,' " she informed her readers, sounding like a cracker-barrel Yankee philosopher. "Look frequently to the pail, to see that nothing is thrown to the pigs which should have been in the grease-pot," she exhorts in the manner of an unsophisticated stage Jonathan. "Look to the grease-pot, and see that nothing is there which might have served to nourish your own family, or a poorer one."[76]

The American Frugal Housewife signaled a new development in the cultural production of the Yankee: the increasing participation of women in the representation of the region's character. From the 1830s forward, writers such as Harriet Beecher Stowe created a gallery of literary figures—frugal and pious domestic types who were unmistakable Yankees. Stowe's women softened or feminized the Yankee character, an imaginative fulfillment of the cultural prescriptions of republican womanhood in which females were to bring the "male" sharper's market predilections more in line with traditional republicanism.

Stowe's first important story, which drips with nostalgia for the New England village she had left behind, explores the Yankee character in gendered terms. In fact, "A New England Sketch" (1834) unveils prescriptive literary representatives of frugal, Yankee domesticity. The story takes place in the home of Uncle Lot Griswold, a cantankerous rustic Yankee with a character "that a painter would sketch for its lights and contrasts rather than its symmetry." Uncle Lot is a variation on the familiar, conflicted nineteenth-century Jonathan whose virtues and foibles are simultaneously praiseworthy and disconcerting. "He had the strong-grained practical sense, the calculating worldly wisdom of his class of people in New England; he had too, a kindly heart; but all the strata of his character were crossed by a vein of surly petulance that, halfway between joke and earnest, colored everything that he said and did."[77] Uncle Lot is a cranky Yankee, a born contrarian, an amusing stage character who adds local color to the village scene.

Lot's wife Sally, on the other hand, is a shrewd Yankee housewife who knows how to cultivate her husband's virtues. She brings "symmetry" to the household, suggesting how women can temper the masculine excesses of the Yankee character. "Aunt Sally was precisely as clever, as easy to be entreated, and kindly in externals, as her helpmate was the reverse," Stowe continues her literary excavation of the strata that formed the regional character. "She was as cheerful and domestic as the teakettle that sung by her kitchen fire, and slipped along among Uncle Lot's angles and peculiarities as if there never was anything the matter in the world." Daughter Grace, rather than son George who dies, unites in her balanced character the Yankee virtues of her parents. Grace seems to combine male and female Yankee traits, as her intellectual alertness suggests. "Like most Yankee damsels, she had a longing after the tree of knowledge, and, having exhausted the literary fountains of a district school, she fell to reading whatsoever came in her way."[78] Stowe's Yankee women are often strong, assertive, even masculine, their mission to domesticate the character and behavior of their men requiring a New England androgyny. Stowe herself, while fulfilling the responsibilities of domesticity and motherhood, became through her writing the principal breadwinner for her family. A republican mother who peddled domesticity in the literary marketplace, she found in the mirror of her own life elements of

7, the bluestocking

the cross-gender model of the Yankee character that she examined in her fiction.

Just as Stowe's novels and stories repeatedly revisited the village setting of "A New England Sketch," so too they returned to the gendered profile of the Yankee character traced in that early short story. Consider again the two major New England characters in *Uncle Tom's Cabin,* the Vermonters Miss Ophelia St. Clare and Simon Legree. Slaveowner Augustus St. Clare's Yankee cousin is a portrait of industry and frugal domesticity; she is unable to restrain her "clear, strong, active mind" or her steadfast "conscientiousness," the "granite formation" of Yankee womanhood. Miss Ophelia quickly takes command of the plantation household. She rises at four o'clock on the "first morning of her regency" and launches her "onslaught on the cupboards and closets of the establishment of which she had the keys." As Lydia Maria Child contended, the moral order of the household—and of the nation—originates in the kitchen. Miss Ophelia injects into the St. Clare plantation house the discipline that its mistress is unable to muster. The indulgent, self-centered Marie St. Clare, Stowe's imagined Southern belle, serves to underscore the sturdiness and republican primacy of Yankee womanhood. "Indolent and childish, unsystematic and improvident," Marie has been debauched by the slave system; the disorder of her household and the languor of her domestic slaves are casualties of her moral infirmity.[79]

Miss Ophelia's pursuit of domestic reformation within the St. Clare family is a harbinger of the Yankee crusade to put the national household in order. But Ophelia, a representative of the reformist potential of Yankee womanhood, must also confront her own moral blindspots. Her horror of slavery stops short of embracing blacks as human equals. Still, her Yankee "conscientiousness" prevails. Out of a sense of "duty," she takes Topsy, the mischievous young household slave, back to Vermont to educate her in Yankee ways. Topsy grows up to be a Christian missionary in Africa.

Miss Ophelia exudes the kind of Yankee domesticity that Child lauded. But Stowe's character is a Yankee spinster, a figure who would grow in importance in New England life and in the regional literary imagination. Yankee mobility skewed sex ratios in many New England communities as women often stayed behind, a demographic trend continued by the deadly consequences of the Civil War. Like Miss Ophelia, the spinster often became a motherly domestic presence in a relative's household or joined the ranks of the legendary Yankee schoolmarms, the "New England nuns" who feminized the teaching profession in the nineteenth century.[80]

In *Uncle Tom's Cabin,* Stowe offers Simon Legree as one morally debilitated mobile Yankee who leaves women and domesticity behind him. Her demonic slavemaster conveys her anxieties for the male, market-driven Yankee character unleavened by republican motherhood and domesticity. Legree becomes a brutal Southern slaveowner, but Stowe suggests that his behavior is a corruption of his Yankeeness. Legree is a rootless, unattached, mobile Vermonter. "Far in New England," Legree's mother "had trained her only son, with long unwearied love, and patient prayers." But Legree "despised her counsel" and left home "to seek his fortunes."[81] His Yankee journey in pursuit of worldly reward carries him to the South, where his sharper's values are unchecked. In Stowe's moral universe, Legree's exploitation of his slaves—his treatment of them as commodities to be bought, sold, and used—is the ultimate consequence of a calculating, materialistic, *male* Yankee preoccupation. Simon Legree is Ichabod Crane armed with absolute power, the Yankee schoolmaster who liberally dispensed corporal punishment now a lord of the lash.

Stowe consistently associates Legree's inhumanity with his rejection of his Yankee mother. He returned home to Vermont only once, and his mother "knelt at his feet" and beseeched him to reform. He "threw her senseless on the floor, and, with brutal curses, fled to his ship." Legree next receives a letter from home with a lock of his mother's hair and learns that she has died, but not before blessing and forgiving him. He burns the letter and its memento of his mother. Legree, who views everything and everybody "merely as an implement for money-making," is Stowe's Yankee incubus: the rapacious, mobile, "detached" male unredeemed by a republican mother or a pious, frugal wife.[82] In Simon Legree, the Yankee peddler as petty sharper has mutated into an avaricious demon who exploits humans as commodities. But Legree is Stowe's portent, her peddler in extremis issued as a summons to Yankee womanhood. For Stowe, like Child, sustained her confidence in the moral and cultural power of wives and mothers to domesticate the regional and national character.

Oldtown Folks continues Stowe's gendered literary representation of the Yankee character just as it extends her imaginative invention of the New England village. Oldtown is a Yankee matriarchy in which a cast of women characters complements the Uncle Lots. Grandma Badger, for instance, is the lengthened shadow of Miss Ophelia dignified by the wisdom of age.

Grandma Badger, who reads "manly" theology texts, radiates the acumen, stout piety, and sedulous domesticity that Stowe attributes to authentic Yankee womanhood. This matriarch of Oldtown "belonged to that tribe of strong-backed, energetic, martial mothers in Israel, who brought to our life in America the vigorous bone of muscle and hearty blood of the yeomanry of Old England," Stowe enthuses in language that both ethnicizes and masculinizes this flower of Yankee womanhood. "She was a valiant old soul, who fearlessly took any bull in life by the horns, and was ready to shake him into decorum."[83] Presumably even Simon Legree would have succumbed to such a magisterial Yankee matriarch.

Aunt Lois is another representative of Yankee moral rectitude and domesticity in Oldtown. The tap of her "imperative" heels at four o'clock in the morning serves as the "reveille" of the Badger household. Stowe humorously suggests how Aunt Lois's investment in domestic order resembles military regimentation. But her martial spirit, like Grandma Badger's, is harnessed to redeeming Yankee virtues. Aunt Lois, "[a] woman of business, who always knew what she was about," never fails "to finish meritoriously her household tasks and to supplement Uncle Fliakim's forgetful benevolence."[84] Aunt Lois and Grandma Badger embody the equipoise — the domesticating and stabilizing influence — that Stowe's women contribute to the Yankee character.

Such gendered literary representations of New England Yankeeness were not confined to women writers, moreover. In *The House of the Seven Gables* (1851), for example, Nathaniel Hawthorne created his own morality play about the Yankee character, pitting the patriarchal, acquisitive Colonel Pyncheon against his country cousin Phoebe. The young Yankee maiden not only transforms the decayed house into a home; she tames the Yankee commoner Holgrave, who is bent on avenging the Pyncheon family's victimization of his ancestor, Matthew Maule, the rightful owner of the property.

Still, the imaginative rise of female Yankeeness at midcentury did not crowd out the older male types. Men continued to dominate representations of the New England character just as the cavalier, the frontiersman, and later the cowboy were the totemic figures of other regional cultures. Furthermore, at midcentury the discourse of Yankeeness, in which gender had been employed to negotiate the complexity of regional character, remained conflicted. The Yankee, with a history that stretched back to the colonial era, persisted as a multilayered cultural production of critics, apologists, entertainers, and reformers from within and outside of New England.

New Englanders themselves continued to grapple with the cultural richness and complexity of the Yankee character. In his brilliant address, "A Plea for Capt. John Brown" (1860), Henry David Thoreau defended the radical abolitionist by manipulating the entrenched discursive conventions of Yankeeness. Invoking the image of Revolutionary Jonathans, Thoreau presented Brown as "a New England farmer, a man of great common sense, deliberate and practical as that class is," an unlettered but virtuous commoner who "would have left a Greek accent slanting the wrong way, and righted up a fallen man." He pursued his reconstruction of Brown's regional genealogy by also identifying the abolitionist as a "transcendentalist" Yankee who inherited a sense of moral purpose that linked him to the Revolution and to the religious founders of New England. But then Thoreau turned on his audience, evoking the specter of its peddler's code. Of Brown's raid on the federal arsenal in Harper's Ferry, Virginia, he heard critics ask, "Yankee-like, 'what will he gain by it?' as if he expected to fill his pockets by the enterprise." "No doubt," Thoreau continued his rhetorical assault on Brown's Yankee detractors, "You can get more in your market for a quart of milk than for a quart of blood, but that is not the market that heroes carry their blood to."[85]

Brown, a native of Connecticut who had shifted about Ohio, Pennsylvania, New York, and Kansas, suggested the physical and cultural expansion of New England in the nineteenth century that advanced the creation of a "Yankee" North. The Civil War, which Brown helped provoke, consolidated the nationalist triumph of the Yankee. From a regional epithet disdained by colonial New Englanders, "Yankee" became, by the mid-nineteenth century, the ascendant signifier of the American character.

Past: The Invention of the Pilgrims

The rise of the Pilgrims in the Northern imagination paralleled the emergence of the Yankee. In fact, like the Yankee label, the term "Pilgrim Forefathers" was not used by colonial New Englanders to describe Plymouth's settlers. The founding of Plymouth itself remained an uncommemorated, even obscure, local event overshadowed for most of the colonial era by the "Great," expansive Puritan migration into New England. By the middle decades of the nineteenth century, however, the story of the Pilgrims had been transformed into an epic account of the religious and republican origins of New England and America.

The Pilgrims sprouted alongside the Yankee and the white village as historically grounded and culturally invented components of a revised nineteenth-century regional identity. Indeed, the mythologized story of the Pilgrims furnished a historical narrative that bolstered the republican ideology undergirding representations of the virtuous Yankee character and of the orderly white village. The nineteenth-century "rediscovery" of the Pilgrims conferred on New England a religious and proto-republican past seemingly unburdened by the record of intolerance and persecution that disfigured Puritan history. The Pilgrims' communalism, for example, appeared to establish the historical origins of the republican values that guardians of regional identity such as Harriet Beecher Stowe imputed to the idealized white village. Similarly, the Pilgrims' colonial ordeal evoked a plain, humble republicanism that seemed to locate the historical antecedents of the Yankee virtue and simplicity that nineteenth-century writers like Stowe extolled.

The "invention" of the Pilgrims encouraged nineteenth-century New Englanders to republicanize regional religious history. Moreover, a powerful discourse of the Pilgrim Forefathers gradually reshaped the image of the Puritans. In a word, the Puritans were "Pilgrimized." They were reimagined in ways that acknowledged but often mitigated their intolerance and that stressed their republican kinship with the virtuous, unvarnished founders of Plymouth. Just as the Plymouth colonists had eased Puritan hardships in the 1630s by supplying food, the mythologized Pilgrims interceded in the nineteenth century to help rescue their neighbors' historical reputation and proto-republicanism. A triumphalist Pilgrim-Puritan narrative of *America's* religious and republican origins would advance as a crucial element in New England's national regionalism during the Civil War.

The settlers of Plymouth were both too small in number and too divided between religious believers and worldly "strangers" to engender intolerance or attract the notice of the world beyond their plantation in any significant way. When the *Mayflower* anchored off Cape Cod in November 1620, less than half of its 103 passengers numbered among the "saints," the religious dissenters who wished to separate completely from the Church of England. Hired hands, servants, and strangers, not devout religious Separatists, comprised the bulk of the *Mayflower's* human cargo. Between

1621 and 1623 three more ships transported small groups of settlers to Plymouth in which strangers outnumbered saints. By the end of Plymouth's first decade less than four hundred people had journeyed to the plantation, with strangers and servants comprising a solid majority of the colonists.[86] Clearly, in its scale and character, the peopling of Plymouth in the 1620s constituted no "Great Migration."

The Separatist leaders of Plymouth had received a patent from the Virginia Company to establish a "plantation" in Northern Virginia. But the *Mayflower*'s voyage carried the colonists to Cape Cod, beyond the territory specified in their patent. Strangers on board, bent on pursuing economic ends in the New World, now questioned the legal authority of Plymouth's leaders and threatened to strike out on their own. On November 11, 1620, forty-one men signed a covenant in the cabin of the *Mayflower* that Governor-historian William Bradford described as a response to the "discontented & mutinous speeches . . . of the strangers amongst them." The signers agreed that

> Haveing undertaken, for the glorie of God, and advancemente of the Christian faith, and honor of our King & country, a voyage to plant the first colonie in the Northerne parts of Virginia, doe by these presents solemnly & mutually in the presence of God, and one of another, covenant & combine ourselves togeather into a civill body politick, for our better ordering & preservation & furtherance of the ends aforesaid; and by virtue hearof to enacte, constitute, and frame such just & equall lawes, ordinances, acts, constitutions, & offices, from time to time, as shall be thought most meete & convenient for the generall good of the Colonie, unto which we promise all due submission and obedience.[87]

The nineteenth century would rename and enshrine this covenant as the "*Mayflower* Compact." The sacred document would be held up as America's first "republican" constitution, invoked to mythologize Plymouth's communal ethos and to establish the New England political origins of the American republic. But the firsthand accounts of Plymouth leaders make no apologies about the need to quell "discontents & murmurings" and "mutinous speeches & carriages." Born of exigency, the *Mayflower* covenant fell far short of a primitive republican constitution. Moreover, the subsequent dispersal of Plymouth's slender population, which provoked fears that the mother town by the harbor would have to be abandoned, undermined the communalism implied in the agreement. Not surprisingly, the *Mayflower* covenant occupies a modest place in colonial accounts of New England history. Puritan historians, for example, tended to see the "combination" in the context of how they viewed Plymouth as a whole, namely, as a historical curtain-raiser for their own providential drama and its far more consequential religious and political achievements.[88]

Later generations not only reimagined the *Mayflower* Compact as part of a New England and American republican genealogy; they also invented Plymouth Rock and the notion of the "Pilgrim Forefathers." The Plymouth colonists explored the Cape Cod area by land and sea during the month after their arrival. On December 10, they steered a shallop into Plymouth Harbor. Six days later the *Mayflower* anchored at the site of the first permanent settlement, its passengers gradually going ashore as crude shelters were erected. The Separatists' own accounts of these activities offer no mention of Plymouth Rock. It is highly unlikely, especially in the face of blustery December weather, that the Plymouth settlers would have guided their shallop toward a menacing boulder. Plymouth Rock does not appear in the colony's annals until more than a century after the first settlers landed. Furthermore, once historically unearthed, "Forefathers' Rock," as it was called, remained largely a local icon through the end of the eighteenth century.[89]

So, too, the rechristening of the Separatists *and* strangers as "Pilgrims" proved to be a late addition to a mythologized rendering of Plymouth's founding. The Separatists, like the Puritans of Massachusetts Bay, conceived of life as a pilgrimage—the kind of spiritual journey toward the celestial city that John Bunyan eloquently formulated in his seventeenth-century classic of Protestant piety, *Pilgrim's Progress*. The Separatists' wandering from England to Holland and then to the New World furnished a geographic correlate to their spiritual pilgrimage. But the founders of Plymouth described themselves as pilgrims in the generic, spiritual Protestant sense; they were, like all humans, "pilgrims and strangers" in this world, confronting hardship and temptation on their sojourn toward eternity.[90]

For seventeenth- and eighteenth-century historians who described Plymouth's founding, the designation "pilgrims" was far from the resonantly republican evocation that it would become in the nineteenth century. Colonial historians made passing reference to the Pilgrims of Plymouth in the common Protestant spiritual sense. Nathaniel Morton, who had arrived in Plymouth as a young boy in 1623 and who served as a secretary of the colony, published *New Englands Memoriall* (1669), which remained the standard history of the settlement through the first half of the nineteenth-century. Morton invoked the Separatists' description of themselves: "They knew that they were *Pilgrims and Strangers* here below, and . . . lifted up their eyes to Heaven, their dearest Country, where *God hath prepared for them a City,* and therein quieted their spirits." Similarly, in his magisterial *Magnalia Christi Americana,* Cotton Mather made only one reference to the Plymouth Pilgrims, describing how the hardships and deaths of the first winter served to remind them that they were simply sojourners in this life.[91]

From the Puritan histories of the late seventeenth century through Mather's *Magnalia* and Thomas Prince's commemorative *Chronological History of New England* (1730), Plymouth's settlement resided in the regional imagination as little more than a prologue to the Great Migration and the Puritan errand into the wilderness. Plymouth did not simply fall victim to Massachusetts Bay's consuming collective consciousness and its sovereign print culture. Rather, Plymouth's own history recorded only modest achievements. By the late seventeenth century the colony consisted of thinly populated settlements that stretched from Cape Cod to Narragansett Bay. Its small population continued to bear the mixed legacy of the saints and strangers who comprised its founding generation. Plymouth lagged well behind Puritan New England in the establishment of public schools.[92] It boasted neither the literacy nor the clerical leadership and historical consciousness that enabled Massachusetts Bay to fashion a collective identity.

After 1691 Plymouth ceased to exist as a distinct colony. Its towns were incorporated into Massachusetts under the new charter arrangements that followed the Glorious Revolution. This political development would enable nineteenth-century custodians of regional identity to underscore the affinities between Massachusetts Bay and Plymouth Plantation, to argue that "the spirit of the Pilgrims" infused the Puritan colony. But in the eighteenth century a politically diminished Plymouth was recalled merely as the "Old Colony." Plymouth's founders were typically identified not as Pilgrims but as the "first comers," the "old comers," or simply the "first planters." Even as late as 1799 Hannah Adams, in *A Summary History of New England, from the First Settlement at Plymouth to the Acceptance of the Federal Constitution,* struggled for an appropriate name for the founders of Plymouth. She avoided calling them Pilgrims and referred to them as "Plymoutheans."[93]

Still, Adams seized on the Plymoutheans' record of tolerance and recast them as republican progenitors. A pious "yet rational" people, the settlers of Plymouth were a "plain, industrious, [and] conscientious" breed, civic-minded adherents of "moral and social duties."[94] As she suggests, it was historians, politicians, ministers, and others during the Revolutionary era who began to retrieve from Plymouth's uneventful and obscure history an inspirational narrative of the civil and religious origins of the American republic.

As John Seelye has recently recounted in detail, the early stages of the American Revolution launched the process through which a large boulder on the beach of Plymouth Harbor would, over ideologically charged decades, come to be imagined as the "cornerstone" of America.[95] At the same time, Revolutionary Plymoutheans invented Forefathers' Day to commemorate the founding of the Old Colony. Forefathers' Day stirred the historical consciousness of the Old Colony in the Revolutionary era. By the nineteenth century it became a ritualized celebration enunciating a heroic narrative of republican origins that was deployed to revamp older Puritan accounts of New England's distinctive genesis.

Until the American Revolution, Forefathers' Rock endured in Plymouth as an obstacle to economic progress, not as a lodestone of local, let alone regional, identity. In 1741 commercial interests in Plymouth attempted to remove the boulder to build a new wharf. The rock refused to budge. The developers proceeded to erect their structure around the boulder, leaving part of it protruding from the wharf as an annoyance to people conveying goods. The construction of the wharf provoked the filiopietism of a ninety-four-year-old resident of Plymouth who traced his ancestry back to the first planters. Thomas Faunce's age and infirmities did not deter him from being transported to Plymouth Harbor, where he bid farewell to the rock that supposedly welcomed the forefathers as they strode ashore.[96] Faunce could not halt economic progress in Plymouth, but his dramatic valediction kept alive what was apparently a lightly regarded local legend. Within a few decades Forefathers' Rock would be repositioned as a Revolutionary touchstone, an imaginative relocation that was accompanied by the physical removal of the boulder to the center of the town. Forefathers' Day commemoration and Revolutionary politics dislodged the rock from decades of silent repose.

Forefathers' Day was established in 1769 to commemorate the landing of the first planters on December 22, 1620. (The new calendar added six days to the old calendar; the *Mayflower* had actually arrived in Plymouth Harbor on December 16.) Forefather's Day was the invention of the newly formed Old Colony Club, a group of wealthy Plymouth men who, like Thomas Faunce, claimed descent from the old comers. Organized as a fraternity of a handful of Plymouth's elite sons, the Old Colony Club met weekly, its members eschewing, as their records note, "intermixing with the company at the taverns in this town." In the first year of the club's existence, the members launched Forefathers' Day with a public ceremony and private banquet. Clams, oysters, codfish, and other seafood filled the menu as reminders of the deprivation and struggle for survival of Plymouth's founders. Indeed, the banquet fare was a precursor to what would become in the nineteenth century the New England clambake with its related evocation of a mythologized regional past. But the cuisine of the first forefathers' commemoration also resonated with the emergent republicanism of the Revolution. The Old Colony Club vowed to avoid "all appearance of luxury and extravagance" in its celebration. Forefathers' Day announced not only the beginnings of Plymouth's historical rebirth; it also signaled how the colony's uncelebrated, indistinct, even obscure history could serve a republican political cause. As one of the toasts at the first forefathers' commemoration informed club members, "May every person be possessed of the same noble sentiments against arbitrary power that our worthy ancestors were endowed with." Another toast linked American resistance to British policies with the persecution by Church of England authorities that had given birth to New England: "May every enemy to civil and religious liberty meet the same or a worse fate [execution] than Archbishop Laud."[97]

Beginning in 1769, then, the mythologizing and the politicizing of Plymouth's history advanced in ideological alliance. The members of the Old Colony Club, however, were unable to contain the politicized invocation of Plymouth's history that they had set in motion. The club continued to celebrate Forefathers' Day between 1769 and 1773 but under increasing pressure from Boston's Revolutionary Sons of Liberty to subordinate the commemoration to the needs of the Revolutionary resistance movement. Forefathers' Day, after all, did not memorialize a history that was only the inheritance of a handful of private club members; it honored a heritage of civil and religious liberty that the Revolutionary resistance movement claimed for all New Englanders. As American opposition to British policies stiffened in the 1770s, the Plymouth forefathers' early defiance of the "iron jaws of English civil and prelatical tyranny" connected the founding of New England to the Patriot movement. Revolutionary-era recollections of the first comers inspired political resistance, as a Boston newspaper revealed in its report on the Forefathers' Day celebration in 1774: "it may be safely affirmed, that all the potent thunders of Britain, cannot reduce us to more tremendous sufferings, than those distinguished patrons of religion and freedom, animated by sacred ardour, patiently endured."[98]

By 1774 the Old Colony Club had dissolved, most of its members finding refuge from Revolutionary fervor in the Loyalist cause. The Patriot movement took custody of Forefathers' Day and of what was now referred to in Boston as Plymouth Rock. In 1774 the Patriots led a team of oxen to Plymouth Harbor, intending to transport the boulder to the center of town where it would be stationed, next to the liberty pole, as a sacred artifact of New England's venerable quest for freedom. As it was being lifted from its resting place, the rock split in two. One part remained at Plymouth Harbor, and the other was moved to Liberty Pole Square and deposited in front of the meetinghouse where it would remain for two generations. Forefathers' Day continued to be celebrated in Plymouth between 1774 and 1780. Though Boston took notice of the ceremony, it remained primarily a Plymouth observance with the rock a local icon. As Revolutionary patriotism and military threats to New England subsided, even Plymoutheans failed to observe Forefathers' Day for more than a decade after 1781.[99]

The celebration was not revived until the 1790s. By then influential guardians of regional identity had begun to invoke Plymouth's history in support of new political ends. In the early republic Federalist leaders asserted ideological proprietorship of Plymouth's history, amplified its republican significance, and propagated a politicized narrative as part of their national regionalism—the campaign to establish New England antecedents and traditions as the basis of an American identity. But although the Federalists transformed the story of the Old Colony into far more than inspirational local history, Plymouth, the rock, the Pilgrims, and the *Mayflower* Compact did not become lodged in the Northern imagination until after the great bicentennial celebration of 1820.

Jedidiah Morse advanced the story of the Pilgrims in politically charged ways, just as he promoted so much of the Federalist agenda. His seminal geographies first issued in 1789 and 1793 as well as *The American Gazetteer* (1797) and *A Compendious History of New England* (1804) popularized a Plymouth origins interpretation of New England's republican distinctiveness. In the New England section of his geographies, for example, Morse highlighted the story of Plymouth to establish the historical primacy of the region's republican ways. "However rigid the New Plymouth colonists may have been at their first separation from the church of England," he reminded his readers, "yet they never discovered that persecuting spirit which we have seen in Massachusetts." Though Plymouth had in fact banished Quakers, the colony did not brandish state power against religious dissenters, and it compiled no record of witchcraft prosecution. Such a benign history enabled Morse to obscure how "strangers" had shaped Plymouth's development and to depict its people as "pious, solitary, Christians" who were virtual republicans from the start. In their first act in the New World, the Plymoutheans, anticipating the constitution making of the Revolutionary era, "formed themselves into a body politic, by a *Solemn Contract*," which served as "the basis of their government" and of the colony's tradition of ordered liberty. Morse's historical narrative of regional origins identified the little-known John Robinson, the Separatists' minister in Holland who died before ever setting foot in America, as the "Father of New England." [100]

Jeremy Belknap, the influential historian and adviser to Morse, extended the Federalist retrieval and deployment of Plymouth's history in the 1790s. As part of his campaign to mobilize history in the cultivation of a national identity for the young republic, Belknap published the two-volume *American Biography, or An Historical Account of Those Persons who Have Been Distinguished in America* (1794, 1798). In this patriotic work, the heretofore obscure patriarchs of Plymouth crowd out other historical figures. Belknap penned admiring biographies of seven Plymouth leaders, from John Robinson to Miles Standish, but included only two Puritans — John Winthrop and his son, who served as a governor of Connecticut. Standish's life occupies more pages than Winthrop's. Belknap, following Morse, also bestowed his historical blessing on what was fast emerging as a regional republican boast in political conflict with the South. The covenant signed in the cabin of the *Mayflower,* he claimed, represented the first American government "established on a truly republican principle." [101]

The observance of Forefathers' Day was reinstituted in Plymouth and Boston in the 1790s amid the Federalists' "rediscovery" of New England's "ancient" republicanism. Into the nineteenth century commemorators toasted Belknap for the "exalted merit, which his masterly pages, have done to our illustrious ancestors." [102] Belknap and Morse, responding to the interregional political strife of the early republic, reimagined Plymouth's past and furnished rich historical detail for Forefathers' Day celebrants and Federalist politicians. The familiar elements of a great regional saga — the Pilgrims, the rock, the compact — would begin to cohere and be diffused as part of a politicized renewal of Federalist interest in and recognition of the Old Colony's founding.

Consider the transformation and popularization of the term "Pilgrim," which does not appear in Forefathers' Day celebrations until 1793. Once introduced, however, the Pilgrim identity of the old comers crystallized Plymouth's meaning. By 1800 the commemoration of the forefathers at Plymouth was described as the "Feast of the SONS of the PILGRIMS," and toasts were offered to "illustrious Pilgrims." Ensuing celebrations summoned the heroic figure of the Pilgrims. In 1807 some Plymoutheans proposed the establishment of a Pilgrim Society to coordinate the Forefathers' Day celebration, collect artifacts that had descended from the founders, and build a monument to the "memory of the Pilgrims." [103] The society was not established until the approach of the 1820 bicentennial of Plymouth's founding. But the proposal of 1807 suggests how the Pilgrim identity was beginning to dominate the image of New England's first planters, even if most of them were strangers. The term "Pilgrim" acquired a new, politicized meaning distinct from its traditional Protestant religious use. It indicated that the founders of Plymouth were not so much engaged in a spiritual pilgrimage as in a historical sojourn that gave birth to republican America. "Pilgrim" connoted the pioneering status of New England's founders; the old comers were now imagined as the pioneers of civil and religious liberty in America.

The *Mayflower* Compact, like the Pilgrim identity, emerged as a revered artifact in this heavily Federalist narrative of New England republican origins. Plymouth's Separatist founders described their emergency agreement as a covenant or a "combination," the term used by Nathaniel Morton in *New Englands Memoriall* (1669). The Old Colony Club largely ignored the *Mayflower* combination, as did the Patriot celebrants of Forefathers' Day. The Sons of Liberty, who appropriated the commemoration for their own political purposes, viewed the first planters as rudimentary republicans but were far less enthusiastic about the *Mayflower* covenant. After all, in the cabin of the *Mayflower* the signers of the agreement proclaimed themselves "Loyal Subjects" and submitted to the authority of "our dread Soveraign Lord King." [104]

For more than a decade after 1776, the Revolutionaries embarked on republican constitution making at the state and federal levels. By the 1790s this experience began to reshape the perception of the *Mayflower* covenant as an "antient" constitution, a document that secured New England's claim on American republican primacy. Thus, the Reverend Chandler

Robbins, in a 1793 sermon marking the reestablishment of Forefathers' Day in Plymouth, hailed the founders' *Mayflower* combination as a "solemn contract" that, like the federal Constitution, provided the "foundation of their *civil* government." A year later, in his influential *American Biography,* Jeremy Belknap referred to the *Mayflower* agreement as a "written instrument," that is, a constitution that established America's first "republican" government. For John Quincy Adams, addressing a Forefathers' Day gathering in 1802, Belknap's instrument became a "compact" that won the "unanimous and personal assent by all individuals of the community to the association by which they became a nation." Adams's oration was immediately published and appears to have brought a rhetorical culmination to the evolution of the Pilgrims' agreement from exigent combination to a hoary republican compact. Nineteenth-century orators, historians, and politicians would increasingly hallow the *Mayflower* Compact as a sacred script in which the Pilgrims "subscribed [to] the first republican constitution of the New World."[105]

By reimagining the Old Colony as an ancient repository of New England and American republicanism, Federalists assembled from Plymouth's history an origins narrative that underwrote their politics of national regionalism. They also elevated Forefathers' Rock from its cultural emplacement as little more than a local icon. To be sure, Boston Revolutionaries had become aware of and politically invested in "Plymouth" Rock when the Sons of Liberty appropriated Forefathers' Day from the Old Colony Club in the 1770s. But the subsequent decline of Forefathers' Day halted the rock's development into a sacred regional icon. Beginning with the renewed Forefathers' Day commemorations of the 1790s, the rock — still residing in two different locations — became an object of growing regional veneration as an emblem of New England's granitelike republican foundation. "May the Empire which has sprung from their labours," participants in Plymouth's celebration of 1797 toasted the Pilgrims, "be permanent as the *rock of their landing.*"[106] Prominent Federalist politicians, who ardently participated in Plymouth's and Boston's Forefathers' Day observances, transformed Plymouth Rock into a talisman of New England's Pilgrim-republican tradition.

By the time Timothy Dwight visited Plymouth in 1800, his Federalist allies had adroitly incorporated the history of the Old Colony into their agenda of national regionalism. For him, Plymouth abided as "the cradle of New England." Dwight summoned the regional pride of place that he often reserved for his native Connecticut River Valley. "No New Englander who is willing to indulge his native feelings," he warmed to his subject, "can stand upon the rock where our ancestors set the first foot after their arrival on the American shore without experiencing emotions entirely different from those which are excited by any common object of the same nature." From John Carver to Miles Standish, Dwight lauded the Pilgrim fathers whose lives had only recently been chronicled in Belknap's *American Biography.* As founders of the republic, the Plymouth colonists were free "from all those stains which elsewhere spotted the character even of their companions [the Puritans] in affliction."[107]

As Dwight suggested, the story of the Pilgrims conferred on New England a narrative of republican beginnings unencumbered by the Puritans' record of intolerance. Plymouth furnished him and his fellow Federalists with a useable past—a history that could be deployed against Virginia's claims to American primacy in the politicized interregional strife of the early republic. Leaders of the so-called Old Dominion took advantage of the bicentennial of Jamestown's founding in 1807 to launch a commemorative counteroffensive against New England. "Shall Virginians surrender the palm to their brethren of the N. England states, who have instituted the feast of the Pilgrims," a Richmond citizen chided Southerners. Virginians established their own Forefathers' Day, which consecrated Jamestown as "chosen ground," the site where divine providence "first lay the sure foundations of political happiness."[108]

The Old Dominion, not the Old Colony, stood as America's first permanent settlement, New Englanders conceded. But the nation's republican roots resided in free Plymouth rather than in the slave South that originated with Virginia. As a toast at Plymouth's Forefathers' Day celebration in 1802 put it, "Our Sister Virginia:—When she changes three-fifths of her Ethiopian Skin, we will respect her as the head of our *white* family."[109] The Old Dominion could not boast of a Jamestown Compact. In commemorations, published addresses, and historical works Federalists enlisted the Pilgrims' record of tolerance, the *Mayflower* Compact, and the rock in their ideological tug-of-war with Virginia and Jeffersonianism for political and regional advantage.

Federalists also seized on Plymouth's story to shore up their deferential Christian republicanism at home. In commemorative toasts they reminded New Englanders that the *"liberty of the people is inseparable from the authority of the magistrate."* They positioned leading Federalist politicians in a republican tradition that derived from the *Mayflower* Compact, and they warned against a pernicious French influence on Jeffersonianism. "Timothy Pickering.—The Rock of State, firm while Frenchmen froth around its base," Forefathers' Day celebrants toasted John Adams's cabinet secretary in 1797. For Federalists, the Pilgrims embodied an indigenous Anglo-American republican tradition of ordered liberty, not an alien, Frenchified Jeffersonianism. Yet the Federalists' appropriation of the Pilgrims' story did not proceed uncontested in New England. Local Jeffersonians, who also traced their political bloodlines to Plymouth's humble founders, reminded the Federalists that there had been no parties among the Pilgrims or "offensive and abusive toasts." The anti-Federalist press suggested that Forefathers' Day commemorators behaved like *"Bacchanalian Pilgrims,"* who "polluted the anniversary with the principles of monarchy" and betrayed the republicanism of New England's founders.[110]

From the contested political terrain of the early republic, then, the Pilgrims, Plymouth Rock, and the *Mayflower* Compact embarked on a cultural journey that would install them as American icons. In 1811 Samuel F. B. Morse, a twenty-year-old graduate of Yale and the son of Jedidiah, completed one of the earliest paintings of the Pilgrims, titled *Landing of the Forefathers.* Four years later Henry Sargent exhibited *The Landing of the Fathers,* a grand canvass that portrayed the emergent heroic narrative of Plymouth's founding (Figure 18). Sargent put human faces on the Pilgrim leaders whom Jeremy Belknap had introduced individually to the reading public in *American Biography.* From Boston, the painting (later renamed *The Landing of the Pilgrims*) went on tour, perhaps even traveling into the South.[111] Clearly, by 1815 the epic saga of Plymouth had acquired notoriety both within and beyond New England. But it was only in the decades after 1820, the bicentennial of the Old Colony's founding, that Plymouth's story became embedded in New Englanders' historical understanding of their region. At the same time, the migration of Yankees, the establishment of New England Societies, and interregional strife over slavery secured the Pilgrims' place in the Northern imagination as the progenitors of America's republican traditions of civil and religious liberty.

Daniel Webster's overwrought oration at the public celebration of Plymouth's bicentennial in 1820 suggests the commencement of a new antebellum phase in the invention of the Pilgrims. Webster's grand address took several hours to deliver; in published form it runs to nearly fifty closely printed pages. Unlike Federalist commemorators who had preceded him, Webster did not tether Plymouth's history to a baldly partisan agenda. Yet he pursued a political project born of New England's national

FIGURE 18. Henry Sargent, *The Landing of the Fathers* (ca. 1815). Sargent's dramatic painting of armed pilgrims confronting a submissive Samoset depicted Miles Standish, Governor John Carver, and Elder William Brewster, all of whom were just beginning to appear in historical narratives of Plymouth's founding. Courtesy of the Pilgrim Society, Plymouth, Massachusetts.

regionalism. His rhetoric swelled as he traced how Plymouth gave birth to New England and how the region's superior republican ways were being transported by modern "Pilgrims" who would only be halted by Pacific shores.

Early in his address Webster joined in the developing consecration of Plymouth as a shrine in New England's civil religion—the republicanization of its religious past and the sacralization of its political heritage. In rhetorical flourishes that went well beyond Timothy Dwight's recorded encounter with Plymouth Rock twenty years earlier, Webster spoke of the *"genius of the place"* and its capacity to inspire awe. "We feel that we are on the spot where the first scene of our history was laid; where the hearths and altars of New England were first placed; where Christianity and civilization, and letters made their first lodgement." Plymouth's "republican" birth puffed up Webster's rhetoric, not just his regional pride. For the Pilgrims were "republicans in principle," the *Mayflower* Compact securing "the elements of a social system" before the colonists stepped on shore. "We have come to this Rock," Webster proclaimed, "to record here our homage for our Pilgrim Fathers; . . . our admiration of their virtues; our veneration for their piety; and our attachment to those principles of civil and religious liberty which they . . . establish[ed]." [112]

Webster imagined the Pilgrims as both simple republicans and progenitors of Yankee enterprise and improvement. In other words, his narrative linked humble colonial origins to a nineteenth-century ethos of energetic expansion, his rhetorical performance itself an imperial display of the vitality and moral presumption of his Yankee world. Plymouth begat New England, endowing the region with its "peculiar original character" that continued to elevate it above other parts of the Union: a cherished tradition of civil and religious liberty sustained by local institutions; a population of industrious, virtuous Yankees; and a social stability derived from wide distribution of and respect for private property. Relying on imaginative flights of rhetoric to carry his audience through a survey of colonial history, Webster delineated Plymouth's regional primacy and representativeness; the colony's founding principles exerted "a strong and decided influence" on ensuing New England history, "and especially on the great event of the Revolution." [113]

Webster not only advanced a narrative of Pilgrim republican origins; he also suggested that Plymouth gave birth to the property-based, institutionally ordered communalism of the white village as well as to the virtue and enterprise of the Yankee character. The ancestral spirit of New England's founders infused the region and the republic with traditions of stability and energy, order and restless improvement. From the exalted height of Plymouth Rock Webster discerned a Pilgrim-Yankee empire arising. "Two thousand miles westward from the rock where their fathers landed," he assured his local audience, "may now be found the sons of the Pilgrims, cultivating smiling fields, rearing towns and villages, and cherishing, we trust, the patrimonial blessings of wise institutions, of liberty and religion." Migrating Yankees were atavistic Pilgrims, demonstrating that not "rivers, or mountains or seas [can] resist the progress of industry and enterprise." Webster wove Plymouth's history into the political fabric of New England's ongoing national regionalism, which would soon be transferred from the Federalist to the Whig Party. [114]

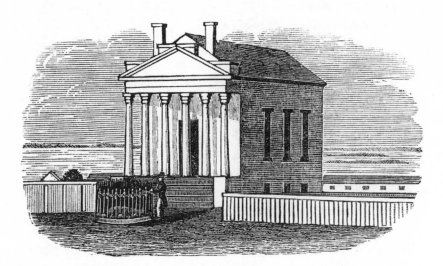

FIGURE 19. John Barber engraving of Plymouth Rock and Pilgrim Hall, shrines to New England's and America's origins. Barber, *Historical Collections of Massachusetts* (1839). Courtesy of the Maine Historical Society.

In the decades after Plymouth's bicentennial, the Pilgrims made a rapid rise to their lofty place in Northern cultural mythology. Pilgrim Hall, which opened in Plymouth in 1824, provided a permanent home for Henry Sargent's painting and a repository for extant artifacts of New England's founders. Ten years later the portion of the rock that had been deposited in the center of Plymouth in 1774 was removed to the front of Pilgrim Hall and placed behind an iron fence. John Barber offered an engraving of the scene, observing that "no true-born son of New England can visit this place, consecrated by the 'Pilgrim Fathers,' without emotion" (Figure 19).[115]

Barber depicted the physical enshrinement that preserved the rock against the recent assaults both of filiopietists and of Yankee sharpers who trafficked in souvenir chips. In *Democracy in America,* Alexis De Tocqueville recalled the reverence for Plymouth Rock encountered on his travels in the early 1830s. "This rock has become an object of veneration in the United States. I have seen fragments carefully preserved in several American cities." He reported that "fragments are venerated, and tiny pieces distributed far and wide." By the next decade the Pilgrims' heroic story conquered the sacred halls of the federal government in Washington. Artist Robert Weir received a ten-thousand-dollar commission for an impressive painting, *The Embarkation of the Pilgrims,* which he completed for the rotunda of the capitol in 1843.[116]

The rise of the historically minded Whig Party from the ashes of federalism provided a political medium for the dissemination of the Pilgrims' story to regional and national audiences. Arrayed against Jacksonian Democrats in the "second party system" that succeeded the Federalist-Jeffersonian Republican divisions, the Whigs attracted strong support within New England and among New England–born migrants outside the region. New England Societies, for example, which by midcentury were organized in cities from New York to Cincinnati to St. Louis, appealed to scores of Whig businessmen and professionals who were proud of their regional heritage and who saw themselves as industrious, republican legatees of the Pilgrim past. Whig political culture reinscribed an older Federalist commitment both to an expansive capitalist order and to social and political deference; Whigs recoiled from the leveling rhetoric of Jacksonian democracy. Imbued with a respect for religious and historical tradition, Whigs espoused "a vision of national progress that would be both moral and material."[117] Webster's Plymouth bicentennial address displayed such a Whiggish notion of historical progress. He offered a paean not only to the growth of American political and religious enlightenment but also to material "internal improvements," the chant of nineteenth-century economic and cultural nationalists. Webster saw the spirit of the Pilgrims in the proliferation of "roads, canals, and other public works," yet he also summoned the moral legacy of the Pilgrims, as when his address turned to the slave trade: "let us pledge ourselves, here upon this rock of Plymouth, to extirpate and destroy it. It is not fit that the land of the Pilgrims should bear the shame longer."[118]

Webster, of course, emerged in the 1830s as a leader of the newly formed Whig Party. The national regionalism of the New England Whigs welcomed an expansive economic order and the commercial, cultural, and geographic integration of the Union that it promised. Yet these same tribunes of economic progress invoked the moralistic rhetoric of classical republicanism when entrepreneurial individualism threatened to degenerate into raw self-interest and to erode civic virtue and social deference. In sum, whether it was the battleground of the Yankee character or the white commercial village and its imaginative overlay of order and stability or the moral-political legacy of the Pilgrim past, New England identity served as a cultural location where the tensions within Whig ideology were negotiated.

In fact, the Pilgrims represented a past that was invoked to shore up virtuous Yankeeness and to historicize the ordered liberty and idealized communal stability of the white village. As early as 1802, Yankee-Doodle was part of Plymouth Forefathers' Day celebrations. By midcentury Whig orators found much to praise in New Englanders' Pilgrim-Yankee ancestry. A descendant of John Winthrop concluded his Forefathers' Day address to the New England Society of New York in 1839 by linking Yankee virtue and Plymouth republicanism. The Pilgrims demonstrated how New England had been built "by Yankee arms," which laid a "Republican edifice" for the Union. Two years later a speaker before the same body saw the Pilgrims as the wellspring of Yankee virtue. He lauded "the cheerful industry, the hardy enterprise, the ingenuity, the calculation, the self-reliance, the thrift" of the New England character that "have, beyond dispute, their seat and source, chiefly, in the land of the Pilgrims." Such traits, "by which we are most known abroad, and most clearly discriminated, as a peculiar people, are Yankee traits." [119] A Yankee character wedded to and tempered by Pilgrim-republican tradition inspired Whig confidence in New England's and America's economic and moral progress.

So, too, the story of the Pilgrims reinforced Whig investment in a private property–based communalism as the safeguard of the ordered liberty and industry symbolized by the white village. The *Mayflower* Compact emerged as the holy writ of New England communalism. With the agreement, mid-nineteenth-century Forefathers' Day speakers repeatedly stressed, *"the Pilgrims formed themselves into a perfect community,* social, civil, religious." But nineteenth-century Whigs imagined the Pilgrims as industrious capitalists, not social and economic levelers. The Pilgrims quickly abandoned communal sharing of property; Plymouth flourished through industry and enterprise. In 1829 one admirer of the Pilgrims described their first governor, John Carver, as "a man of enterprise, intelligence, and great benevolence, and quite a businessman." [120] Whig hymns to Plymouth's communalism acquired the self-congratulatory lilt of nineteenth-century enterprise, transforming the Pilgrims into entrepreneurial republicans who pursued economic opportunities within the "constitutional" framework that derived from the *Mayflower* Compact. The Pilgrims came to resemble the prosperous denizens of the commercial white village and the successful, civic-minded Yankee businessmen who filled New England Society registers from New York City to St. Louis.

In the North, a Plymouth origins narrative of New England and American republican distinctiveness, propelled by the growing rift over slavery, increasingly gained rhetorical and cultural ascendancy over the story of the Old Dominion—a triumph that would be consummated by the Civil War. As one Forefathers' Day speaker put it in 1839, the "disappointment, discord, [and] wretchedness" of early Jamestown only magnified the precedent-setting accomplishments of Plymouth Colony. As the Pilgrims launched their republican experiment, Virginia had already initiated the South's "traffic in human flesh." [121] Nineteenth-century New England abolitionists represented escaped slaves as "Pilgrims" reenacting the heroic journey in search of liberty that gave birth to the region. An antislavery song of 1845 capitalized on the recently published *Narrative of the Life of Frederick Douglass,* the autobiography of the region's most famous ex-slave:

New England! New England! thrice-blessed and free,
The poor hunted slave finds shelter in thee. . . .
And the Sons of the Pilgrims my deep scars shall see,
Till they cry with one voice "Let the Bondmen go free." [122]

Of course, to Southerners Yankee abolitionists were the menacing offspring of New England's fanatical Roundhead past, not of its humble Pilgrim origins. And Hawthorne's widely read fictional accounts of New England's religious history propagated a less-than-heroic view of the region's religious underpinnings. Hawthorne was haunted by his own ancestral ties to the Salem witchcraft hysteria. Yet most nineteenth-century descendants of the Puritans and guardians of regional identity hardly displayed Hawthornean anguish in coming to terms with their religious heritage. The "invention of the Pilgrims" helped nineteenth-century New Englanders define how their Puritan past would be imaginatively retrieved. That is, a powerful discourse of Plymouth-republican origins encouraged antebellum New Englanders to Pilgrimize the Puritans—to disentangle from Puritanism's complex history those patterns and accomplishments that were of a piece with the Pilgrims' republican record.

It is understandable that nineteenth-century interpreters of New England's past increasingly conflated the Pilgrims and the Puritans. In 1828, for example, Lyman Beecher, a conservative orthodox admirer of the Puritans, established a journal, *Spirit of the Pilgrims,* to prosecute what he saw as a neo-Puritan campaign of religious revivalism. The elemental republican "spirit of the Pilgrims" permeates his daughter's fictional accounts of late Puritan-Yankee life. In 1843, capitalizing on the soaring interest in the history of Plymouth, Harriet Beecher Stowe collected some of her early stories examining the social texture of traditional New England life and published these nostalgic vignettes under the title *The Mayflower, or Sketches of Scenes and Characters among the Descendants of the Pilgrims*. The nineteenth-century discourse of the Pilgrims runs through Stowe's *Oldtown Folks*. In the first few pages of her detailed portrait of a typical Puritan town of the early republic, Stowe summons both the Pilgrims and Cotton Mather. Oldtown is even imagined as a sister town to the "historic" Plymouth that the nineteenth century created. The venerable village represents the Pilgrim-Puritan past that formed "the seed-bed of this great American Republic," Stowe observes. Oldtown, like Plymouth, suggests how New England civic-religious tradition was an ideological amalgam, the legacy of a "half Hebrew theocracy" and a "half ultra-democratic republic of little villages." [123]

Such a Pilgrim-Puritan narrative heralded a New England republican heritage that took its bearings from the "magnetic rock." [124] But for mid-nineteenth-century interpreters of the region's past, New England's ancient republicanism was not confined to the Town of Plymouth and its Old Colony satellites. Pilgrims and Puritans embarked on a common "errand into the wilderness" in pursuit of civil and religious liberty. Local self-government, lay control of churches, wide distribution of property—these and other shared republican elements of early New England seemed to overshadow religious differences between Pilgrims and Puritans, especially for orthodox Congregationalists like the Beechers. New England's founders as a whole came to be imagined as Pilgrims, that is, as courageous, virtuous republican pioneers—a common identity that Forefathers' Day speakers forged by way of contrast with the South. An orator in 1841, for example, detailed the educational accomplishments of the Puritans, including the founding of Harvard, to establish both New England's superiority over the South and its collective Pilgrim past. The Puritans' "conversation, their preaching, their writings were all imbued with the Pilgrim spirit" that made early New England "a golden age." [125]

The Pilgrim-Puritan narrative of regional origins advanced at midcentury in the face of the well-known history of early New England religious zealotry that Hawthorne exploited brilliantly in his tales exploring the catacombs of the human psyche. The nineteenth-century Pilgrimization of New England's religious past involved not only a reassessment of the republican achievements that united the Puritans with the founders of Plymouth; it sometimes also included an explanation of the Puritans' record of intolerance. Mid-nineteenth-century Forefathers' Day speakers stressed how the Puritans were far from unique in their belief in witch-craft; they accepted the "then universal opinion of the reality of commerce between human beings and the invisible powers of darkness." So, too, the persecution of Quakers arose from a now forgotten historical context. Far from the irenic religious group that the Society of Friends had become, the original Quakers reminded one Forefathers' Day orator of a despised mid-nineteenth-century religious sect — the Mormons. They behaved like "fanatics, disturbers of public peace and decency . . . uttering their wild exhortations, and foaming forth their mad opinions." Another speaker insisted that self-preservation, not intolerance, compelled Puritan sanc-tions against the Quakers: "In their manner of proceeding they outraged peace and order, openly cursing and reviling the faith and worship which New Englanders had come to the world's end to enjoy in quietness." [126]

New England's religious liberals, particularly the influential Unitarians of the antebellum decades, were less inclined than orthodox Congrega-tional writers such as the Beechers simply to conflate Puritans and Pil-grims and to historicize and thereby abate early New England intolerance. Rather, they drew on the discourse of the Pilgrims to redeem a useable religious-republican past from the mixed historical record. In *Hobomok: A Tale of Early Times* (1824), the first major fictional treatment of New En-gland's founding, Unitarian Lydia Maria Child criticized the patriarchal-ism of the region's forefathers but resisted a presentism that undermined a justifiable filiopietism. "In this enlightened and liberal age, it is per-haps too fashionable to look back upon those early sufferers in the cause of the Reformation, as a band of dark, discontented bigots," Child cau-tioned. "Without doubt, there were many broad, deep shadows in their characters, but there was likewise bold and powerful light." *Hobomok* ex-amines the founding of Salem, the first Puritan town in Massachusetts. But Child suggests that the seat of New England witchcraft was also the cradle of American republican ways: "Whatever might have been their [the founders'] defects, they certainly possessed excellencies, which peculiarly fitted them for a van-guard in the proud and rapid march of freedom." [127]

Three years after the publication of *Hobomok,* Unitarian Catharine Sedg-wick produced another major work of historical fiction that examined the region's founding decades. *Hope Leslie, or Early Times in Massachusetts* (1827), like *Hobomok,* records the liberal ambivalence over New England's reli-gious past at the same time that it reflects the commemorative rhetoric inspired by Plymouth's bicentennial. "Never was a name more befitting the condition of a people, than 'Pilgrim' that of our forefathers," Sedgwick observes. "It should be redeemed from puritanical and ludicrous associations which have degraded it, in most men's minds."[128] In the liberal historical script, Plymouth did not define the boundaries of the Pilgrim spirit, though the Old Colony's tolerance earned it high praise. Rather, for Unitarians like Child and Sedgwick the Pilgrim past was imagined as a regional religious heritage that coexisted with an oppressive Calvinist theology and the intolerance that it bred.

Of course, for New England liberals the widespread and recurring revivals of the Second Great Awakening, which crested in the early 1830s, complicated the discourse of the Pilgrims and historical assessments of the region's religious heritage. Revivals seemed to reanimate the spirit of the Puritans, provoking liberal anxiety about a new eruption of intolerance. But another, countervailing antebellum ritual provided both religious liberals and conservatives with occasions to appropriate New England's Pilgrim-Puritan past. Perhaps even more than revivals, historical commemorations prospered during the decades after the bicentennial of Plymouth's founding, ritualized Protestant feasts that, like Forefathers' Day, served a New England civil religion and the politics of regional identity. The numerous towns and churches established by the founding generation celebrated bicentennials during the three decades that preceded the Civil War. Antebellum New England became awash in historical commemoration, observances whose rituals and rhetoric, publications and pieties promoted the Pilgrimization of the Puritans.

Consider Ralph Waldo Emerson's 1835 bicentennial oration at Concord, Massachusetts, the first inland town settled by the Puritans. Emerson applauds its citizens for joining with "the people of New England, [who,] for a few years past, as the second centennial of its early settlements arrived, have seen fit to observe the day." He describes the Puritan founders of Concord as "pilgrims," who, like Plymouth's forefathers, "consumed many days in exploring the country, to select the best place for the town." Emerson draws on Edward Johnson's heroic early history of Massachusetts, *Wonder-Working Providence,* to extend the parallel between the Pilgrims of Concord and of Plymouth. Both groups made peace with the Native Americans. Moreover, like the settlers of Plymouth, Concord's pioneers consisted of "pilgrims [who] had the preparation of an armed mind, better than any hardihood of body" to sustain them through the ordeal of founding New England.[129]

In the tradition of Webster's bicentennial address of 1820, Emerson recounts Concord's colonial and Revolutionary experience, passing the historical mileposts that emblazon the town's (and New England's) Pilgrim-like virtue. His inspection of the town's annals discloses a history that closely resembles Plymouth's. "I find no ridiculous laws," he boasts, "no eavesdropping legislators, no hanging witches, no ghosts, no whipping of Quakers, no unnatural crimes." Concord's pilgrims raised a community on the bedrock of religion and self-government; their descendants' prominence in the Revolution proclaimed the town's constancy with the founders' principles. Emerson links Concord's surviving Revolutionary veterans to New England's forefathers. "The Pilgrims are gone; but we see what manner of persons they were who stood in the worst perils of the Revolution." [130]

Emerson salutes John Winthrop, establishing the congruence between Puritan and Pilgrim, Massachusetts Bay and Plymouth, New England's "republican" founders and the Revolutionaries. Winthrop cherished "much more their [the people's] love than his chartered authority." [131] From the 1820s through the Civil War and beyond, Winthrop assumed a crucial role as a cultural mediator between the Puritan and Pilgrim past. A strong but popular magistrate, he came to be appreciated as a virtuous leader who discharged his duties with moderation and pragmatism. Though a pious Puritan and a creature of his times, he came to embody, for nineteenth-century religious liberals and conservatives alike, "the character of a good ruler." [132] Indeed, Winthrop's historical figure and his political reign were assimilated to the accomplishments of William Bradford, the popular, long-serving governor of Plymouth who increasingly secured the recognition and admiration of nineteenth-century New Englanders.

The selective publication of major Puritan and Pilgrim historical texts between the 1820s and 1850s advanced a narrative of regional origins that incorporated both groups and that interlaced the political patriarchies of Winthrop and Bradford. In his monumental text, *Magnalia Christi Americana,* reprinted in 1820, Cotton Mather offered hagiographic biographies of Winthrop and Bradford as virtuous rulers, along with rich detail on the Puritan forefathers as a group. Six years later Nathaniel Morton's *New Englands Memoriall* was reissued, standing as a Plymouth companion volume to Mather's tome. In between the reprinting of these two works, Winthrop's private journal appeared for the first time in 1825. Titled *A History of New England,* it recorded the progress of the Massachusetts Bay Colony in the first two decades of settlement. [133]

Shortly after the publication of Winthrop's journal, one of the most famous Puritan texts, with its summons to a spiritual and physical pilgrimage and reference to a city on a hill, was issued for the first time. Winthrop's Arbella sermon, *A Model of Christian Charity,* was rescued from obscurity and published by the Massachusetts Historical Society in 1838.[134] The sermon circulated as a sacred writ in the discourse of New England origins, associated with the *Mayflower* Compact as regional scripture. The publication of such seventeenth-century texts continued for the next two decades. In the 1840s, for instance, Unitarian historian Alexander Young compiled two bulky volumes of primary documents on the founding of Plymouth and Massachusetts Bay. *Chronicles of the Pilgrim Fathers* (1841) and *Chronicles of the First Planters of Massachusetts Bay* (1846) furnished new evidence for the development of Forefathers' Day speeches on New England's Pilgrim-Puritan origins. Young's volumes were part of an antebellum campaign to preserve the writings of New England's proto-republican pioneers, an effort that led to the first complete edition of Bradford's history of the Pilgrims, *Of Plymouth Plantation* (1856). Lost for decades, the Bradford manuscript was discovered in England and returned to the United States for publication in 1856.[135] The midcentury appearance of such seventeenth-century texts, like the rituals and rhetoric of commemorative celebrations, flourished as a cultural practice that mythologized the story of New England's Pilgrim-Puritan origins.

Orators, editors, and writers invoked Winthrop as the representative Puritan, the Bradford of Massachusetts Bay who revealed that colony's civil and religious continuity with Plymouth. In 1820 Forefathers' Day celebrants in Plymouth offered a toast to "The memory of Gov. Winthrop; the friend and protector of the Plymouth Pilgrims." In his magisterial *History of the United States,* George Bancroft, the great antebellum historian, established Winthrop's kindred with his simple Pilgrim-republican neighbors. "In him," Bancroft wrote, "a yielding gentleness of temper and a never failing desire for unity and harmony were secured against weakness by deep but tranquil enthusiasm." In the unmistakable rhetoric of Forefathers' Day effusions, Bancroft held up Winthrop's public character as announcing "the transition of the reformation into virtual republicanism."[136] Winthrop's midcentury biographer pursued a similar tack, using the governor's life to align Puritan and Pilgrim history. A close study of Winthrop served "to mitigate, if not dispel," the facile association of Puritanism "with an austerity of disposition, a sternness of character, and a severity of conduct." Winthrop's life "exhibit[ed] at least one of the foremost of the Massachusetts Fathers as abounding in tenderness and love." Not surprisingly, "The most cordial relations always existed between Winthrop and the Plymouth colonists." [137]

To be sure, cordiality did not always mark Winthrop's dealings with critics of the Puritan state. But even this record of seeming intolerance acquired a new political tenor in the years before the outbreak of civil war. Especially after the enactment of the Fugitive Slave Law in 1851, a small minority of outraged abolitionists resuscitated the moral radicalism and "come-outer" spirit of the Pilgrim-Puritan past as a way of emboldening citizens to stand against slavery whatever the risk to the Union. In this politically inflamed context Winthrop's commitment to preserving the Puritan state took on a new meaning for moderates unwilling to allow abolitionism to threaten the Union. In a Forefathers' Day address in 1860, for example, poet William Cullen Bryant spoke at length about Winthrop, continuing the Pilgrimization of Puritan tradition and warning against disunion. Winthrop embodied "all the virtues of the grand old Puritan stock to which he belonged, with few of their faults." The governor's "enlightened" policies were only modified in response to disturbers of civil peace, "a sort of frenzy of which there are not wanting examples even in our own day." For Bryant, Winthrop's cooperation with Plymouth established "the seminal principle of our American Union — the embryo which afterward grew into our great league of states, . . . on pillars of which rash hands are now laid." [138]

On the eve of the Civil War, then, Pilgrim-Puritan tradition enlivened New England political life as a useable but contested past. The region's founding remained a sacred repository of high-minded, proto-republican precedent. But abolitionists and Unionists, like the religious liberals and conservatives before them, accented their heroic narratives of New England origins with the politics of the moment.

The Civil War reduced this ideological gap between abolitionist and Unionist readings of New England's heroic past. The war encouraged the moral rearmament of Pilgrim-Puritan history — the forefathers' crusading spirit now consonant with the righteousness of the Union cause. The war also marked the "national" triumph of the Pilgrim-Puritan narrative of American origins, just as it advanced the victory of the Yankee identity and of the white village as an iconic republican landscape. In 1863 President Abraham Lincoln declared Thanksgiving a national holiday. [139] What had been a regional celebration that gained a foothold in the Yankee North in the antebellum decades now became, in spite of continuing Southern resistance, an American ritual that expedited the course of New England's

FIGURE 20. George H. Boughton, *Pilgrims Going to Church* (1867). A visual
representation of the narrative of America's New England origins that
triumphed with the Civil War. Courtesy of the New York Historical Society.

national regionalism. Thanksgiving would replace the now obscure Forefathers' Day as the high feast day of New England and American civil
religion.

In 1867 George H. Boughton completed one of the most powerful and
familiar paintings of early New England history—a visual consummation of the region's military and cultural triumph in the Civil War. *Pilgrims
Going to Church* narrates the heroic errand into the wilderness that gave
birth to New England and the American republic (Figure 20). A Bible-
toting Elder Brewster is followed by women and children as they march
through Plymouth's stark wilderness. These pioneers of piety and domesticity are protected by vigilant armed guards, including the soldierly Miles
Standish in the center of the painting. Piety, domesticity, and community
are secured by the barrel of a gun—a visual rendering of New England's
origins that seemed to unite the founding errand with the militant crusade
and the moral combativeness of the Grand Army of the Republic.

Conclusion: Resistance and Triumphalism

Antebellum New England identity was riven with contradictions. The
white village emerged as the product of a dynamic commercial order, yet

it was imaged as an emblem of New England's venerable communal and republican past. The Yankee arose from New England soil as both an acquisitive sharpy and a virtuous rustic republican. The New England past recorded religious excesses and republic origins. Creating New England engaged antebellum guardians of regional identity in the cultural and rhetorical negotiation of these contradictions.

Critics from the region's margins proved to be particularly skillful exploiters of the tensions at the core of antebellum New England. Consider Henry David Thoreau, who marginalizes himself, albeit contrivingly, to the woods outside Concord to gain a moral surveyor's perspective on the town and New England life. Thoreau depicts Concord not as a steady little republic but as an urbanized, commercial world with growing numbers of hired farmhands and Irish laborers. Moreover, donning the pose of the virtuous, simple republican Yankee, he proceeds to castigate the parsimony and trader's ethos that pervades Concord. So, too, *Walden* summons New England's heroic past, only to highlight the contradictions at the core of its antebellum filiopietism. Thoreau, like Emerson, cites *Wonder-Working Providence,* Edward Johnson's pioneering history.[140] Thoreau's experiment at Walden Pond is framed as a kind of reenactment of New England's founding, as if to get regional history back on the virtuous course that Johnson applauded. For *Walden* is a jeremiad about New England's moral declension—a counternarrative to the celebratory rhetoric of Forefathers' Day. Though Thoreau remained deeply attached to Concord and to the region generally, his strictures threatened to subvert antebellum New England, which may partly explain the critical and commercial failure of *Walden.*

Other "Yankee" voices from the margins resisted major elements of the antebellum reinvention of New England. Contrarian Rhode Island, for instance, continued to trace its beginnings to Puritan persecution in ways that undermined the new Pilgrim narrative of the New England origins of American civil and religious liberty. As Rhode Island historian Samuel Greene Arnold put it in 1853, "The cause of the Pilgrim emigration was . . . the desire, not of religious freedom, but of freedom to enjoy their own religion." The American "spirit of liberty" was born in Rhode Island, Arnold insisted. "The influence of our example has extended far beyond our narrow borders and has already made the American Union one vast Rhode Island in principle and feeling." Plymouth Rock abided as primarily a gravestone of the Puritan past, whereas Rhode Island served as the New England reliquary of authentic republican origins.[141]

In addition to dissident cranky Yankees like Thoreau and Arnold, two powerful non-Anglo voices from New England's cultural margins labored to expose the exclusions from the commemorative narratives that underwrote antebellum regional identity. William Apess (1798–?), a Pequot descendant of the first New England tribe devastated by a Puritan-Pilgrim coalition in 1637, defiantly retold the region's colonial history from a Native American perspective. African American Harriet Wilson (1808–ca. 1870) laid bare the racial limits of New England identity, radically reducing the perceived moral distance between the region and the South that was so vital to Yankee national regionalism.

In his autobiography, *A Son of the Forest* (1829), Apess recounts the servitude, indebtedness, wanderings in search of employment, and alcohol abuse that ensnared him and that fashioned the dependent status of so many surviving Native Americans in republican New England. He also implicates cultural amnesia in his victimization, the history of his people distorted by and subordinated to the didactic, filiopietistic narratives of Pilgrim-Puritan descendants. Indentured to white families in early nineteenth-century Connecticut, the youthful Apess absorbs the dominant culture's view of Native Americans' propensity for treachery and violence—the representation of his people that undergirded triumphalist antebellum accounts of early New England. The celebratory historical writing and oratory about the past, Apess comes to realize, fails to record that whites "were in a great majority of instances the aggressors—that they had imbrued their hands in the lifeblood of my brethren, driven them from their once peaceful and happy homes—that they introduced among them the fatal and exterminating diseases of civilized life." [142]

Apess exposes Puritan-Yankee New England's dual historical displacement of Native Americans: the physical assault on tribal people and pillaging of their land followed by commemorative narratives that victimized "Indians" and their descendants again. Apess reclaims Native American history in his *Eulogy on King Philip* (1836), a fascinating address that subverts the celebratory rhetoric of Forefathers' Day by substituting an older medium for historicizing New England identity. The *Eulogy* recasts antebellum historical self-congratulation into a Native American jeremiad, one example of Apess's appropriation of the dominant culture for his own subversive purposes. Exploiting commemorative rhetoric and ideology, Apess mythologizes King Philip as a New England forefather in his own right and an authentic republican leader, the Native American George Washington, whose retreat across the Connecticut River, as

Pilgrim-Puritan invaders advanced, matched "that of Washington crossing the Delaware."[143]

Apess delivered his *Eulogy* twice in Boston on the 160th anniversary of King Philip's death in 1676, his performance serving as a counter-commemoration to Forefathers' Day and the run of regional observances in the 1830s. "Let the children of the Pilgrims blush," he exhorts his audience, "while the son of the forest drops a tear and groans over the fate of his murdered and departed fathers." Following the custom of antebellum commemorative addresses such as Webster's grand oration at the Plymouth bicentennial of 1820, Apess's gaze sweeps across the expanse of colonial history. Boldly striding into the thicket of celebratory narratives, he compiles the elisions from the official stories of regional origins, "the most daring robberies and barbarous deeds of death that were ever committed by the American Pilgrims."[144] He confronts his audience with a powerful narrative that links the colonial past not to New England's antebellum self-image of republican superiority but to the bloody "Trail of Tears" of the 1830s, the forced relocation of Native Americans in the South to Oklahoma.

Apess thus creates his own useable Native American past. The landing of the Pilgrims on December 22 ought to be recalled as a "dark" day of "mourning," not an occasion illuminated by commemoration; "let it be forgotten in your celebration, in your speeches, and by the burying of the rock that your fathers first put their foot upon."[145] Beyond casting rhetorical sand on Plymouth Rock, Apess appears to have had a hand in the dedication of a Native American countericon—Mount Hope Rock—at the site in Rhode Island where King Philip lived and was killed.[146] Mount Hope Rock represented another subversive appropriation of New England's commemorative ethos that Apess exploited so effectively in the *Eulogy*. But Mount Hope Rock, like William Apess and his writings, quickly receded into obscurity under the cultural onslaught of New England triumphalism. Apess's works, for all their literary skill and cultural audacity, were apparently shunned by the architects of antebellum regional identity. His writings fell out of print, not to be republished until 1992.

A similar fate met African American writer Harriet Wilson, though she authored an important work of fiction that, like Apess's writings, defied the pieties of the antebellum reinvention of New England. *Our Nig, or Sketches from the Life of a Free Black* (1859) appears to be the first novel published in the United States by an African American. A thinly disguised autobiography, it depicts domestic life in a "Two-Story White House, North" and documents that "Slavery's Shadows Fall Even There."[147] *Our Nig* also calls attention to the racial exclusions that underlay Yankee national regionalism, especially the abolitionist campaign to remake the South in the image of free white republican New England.

The white village, so central to antebellum regional identity, inscribed far more than a neoclassical aesthetic and a Whig republican ideology; it encoded the racial landscape of New England, which excluded slavery and blacks from the narratives of regional distinctiveness and republican ascendancy. From Jedidiah Morse's geographies, to the cultural invention of the pastoral village, to Forefathers' Day addresses, to the militant abolitionism of the 1850s, New England was consistently imagined as America's preeminent republic of free white industrious Yankees, a regional perception that rested on the counterimage of an indulgent, enslaved, Africanized South.

But New England had its own history of slavery and slave trading. When antebellum guardians of regional identity acknowledged this reality, they invoked Southern plantation bondage as a foil to diminish the size and significance of slavery in the Yankee past. By nineteenth-century Cotton Kingdom standards, colonial New England slavery appeared modest in scope and "mild" in its operation. The Revolutionary emancipation movement shattered the *legal* foundation of African American dependency in the region. With no legal legacy of dependency and with a historically "insubstantial" black population in comparison to the antebellum South, the guardians of regional identity represented New England as a free republic of white Yankees.[148]

Our Nig disrupted this narrative of regional identity and New England abolitionists' moral posturing over the slave South. Wilson, like Apess, proclaims the enduring presence of people of color and of racism in antebellum New England. Remapping the region's republican landscape, Wilson foregrounds the enduring dependency and marginalization of blacks that derives from prejudice, servitude, and indebtedness. She disavows any intention to "palliate slavery at the South, by disclosures of its appurtenances North." She even claims to have "omitted what would most provoke shame in our good anti-slavery friends at home." But *Our Nig* was sufficiently threatening to the antislavery movement and subversive of antebellum regional identity that Wilson had to forgo the kind of white sponsorship that led to the publication of slave narratives such as Frederick Douglass's. She published and sold the book herself, appealing to "my colored brethren universally for patronage."[149]

Wilson's background remains obscure. What seems clear is that she resided in New Hampshire in the middle of the nineteenth century and that she was living in Massachusetts when *Our Nig* appeared in 1859. Through the character "Frado," Wilson offers a fictionalized account of her own life—a story of racism, exploitation, and miscegenation. The offspring of a "fallen" white mother and a black father, Frado is abandoned by her economically hard-pressed family at the age of six and forced into indentured servitude to a white family. Far from being a virtuous Yankee housewife, Mrs. Bellmont, the tyrannical matriarch, is a "mistress [who] was wholly imbued with *southern* principles."[150] She is Wilson's female version of Simon Legree, a stay-at-home Yankee who brutally wields her power over Frado. Wilson mounts a devastating assault on frugal Yankee housewifery, the cult of domesticity, and republican motherhood—ideological conventions so central to the works of writers like Child and Stowe. Through admonition and guile Mrs. Bellmont attempts to marry off her children to individuals of wealth. Most of the Bellmont children scatter to different parts of the country, mobile Yankees rebelling against matriarchal tyranny.

With irony and defiance, the title of Wilson's fictional autobiography announces that Harriet-Frado is at once a "free black" and somebody's "nigger." Taking the measure of New England from its racialized margins, *Our Nig* drastically shrinks the moral distance between the "free" Yankee North and the slave South. Indeed, the landscape of Frado's New England suggests the region's moral and physical resemblance to the South, not its distinctiveness as a collection of steady republican villages. The Bellmont's two-story white dwelling is transformed from an icon of New England village republicanism into a Yankee plantation house. It is isolated from a village setting and from communal controls on Mrs. Bellmont's brutality. Free from the moral surveillance of the village, the mistress runs her household like a slave plantation, burdening Frado with ever-increasing responsibility and thrashing her for imagined provocations.

At the age of eighteen Frado completes her indenture, physically and emotionally depleted by her servitude. She is compelled at times to turn to the poorhouse, the official response to the poverty that she, and her mother before her, endures and that was not part of idealized representations of the white village. Yet the poorhouse seemingly becomes the most important civic institution in Frado's life of survival.

Frado later learns to weave straw hats, and she travels from New Hampshire to Massachusetts struggling to support herself. "Strange were some of her adventures," Wilson writes of Frado at the end of *Our Nig*. "Watched by kidnappers, maltreated by professed abolitionists, who didn't want slaves at the South, nor niggers in their own houses, North. Faugh! to lodge one; to eat with one; to admit one through the front door to sit next one; awful." [151] Wilson's publication of *Our Nig* received neither the assistance nor the acknowledgment of the New England antislavery or literary establishment. *Our Nig*, like the writings of William Apess, was hustled off the historical stage, only to be retrieved in the late twentieth century.

New England's celebratory antebellum national regionalism muffled voices from the margins and consolidated its narratives of regional distinctiveness in the triumphalism of the Civil War. The "white" village, the Yankee character, and the Pilgrims advanced New England's identity as the American homeland.

Old New England

Nostalgia, Reaction, and Reform in the Colonial Revival, 1870–1910

"The New England that has grown up with the last fifty years is not at all the New England that our fathers knew," Lucy Larcom lamented in her autobiography of 1889. A writer, teacher, and former Lowell mill girl, Larcom offered readers of the Gilded Age an elegiac account of life in the antebellum New England of her youth. With *A New England Girlhood,* she joined other writers of her generation who turned to autobiography to mourn not only the loss of youthful innocence but also the decline of a region from its moral zenith in the Civil War.[1]

One of the chapters, "Old New England," recalled a stable, communal, small-town Yankee world undisturbed by the advance of the very industrial order that the author had toiled for in Lowell. "Our republicanism was fresh and wide-awake," she recollected. Though a resident of the coastal town of Beverly, Massachusetts, Larcom stressed that she grew up in the village called "The Farms," a pastoral retreat of "courts," "lanes," and "zigzag picturesqueness." Beverly's connection to the sea meant that a few foreign "wanderers" with "swarthy complexions" and "un-Caucasian features" took up residence in the town. But old-time Beverly, unlike New England's seaports in the late 1880s, abided as a Yankee haven. "[W]e children felt at once that we belonged to the town," Larcom wrote, suggesting also that Old Beverly was a kind of ancestral heirloom, a possession of families like hers. Old New England recorded Larcom's sense of regional decline, a perception of historical displacement that encompassed feelings of her own cultural dispossession.[2]

Larcom and numerous other post–Civil War interpreters of regional life were the architects of "Old New England," a new geography of the imagination that dominated representations of regional identity into the twentieth century. On the one hand, nostalgia for Old New England registered Yankee reaction to disquieting alterations in the texture of life: the acceleration of ethnic, urban, industrial, and technological change that a generation experienced across the great divide of civil war. But, as Larcom suggests, Old New England was a cultural refuge—an embroidered, oversimplified ancestral past. The post–Civil War generation's imaginative and emotional investment in that era dramatically reoriented regional identity.

Antebellum regional identity had been rooted in retrospection, in a historically grounded understanding of New England's distinctiveness. But the historical narratives that had shaped its identity in the mid-nineteenth century were progressive. The Whig notion of history as a record of moral and material progress linked New England's past to a glorious American future. The white village represented venerable but progressive forces astir in New England life. The Yankee arose as a new, indigenous American type whose industry and ingenuity, redeemed of excesses, blazed the advance of a Greater New England. The Pilgrim-Puritan founders' quest for civil and religious liberty established New England as the seedbed for the rising glory of republican America. Antebellum New England seemed to embody the republican promise of an energetic "Young America." For all of its historical-mindedness, antebellum New England reaped the benefits of progress. It enjoyed the highest levels of schooling, literacy, lyceum participation, and newspaper readership, far surpassing the South, for example. It attracted visitors like Charles Dickens and Alexis De Tocqueville who observed its newly painted villages, progressive civic institutions, industrial experiments, and reform movements. In numerous ways, antebellum New England seemed to be enacting a Whiggish historical script that envisioned continual cultural and material improvement.[3]

Such a Websterian sense of progress, born of history and nineteenth-century development, did not long survive the New England triumphalism of the Civil War. The quickened pace of industrialization, urbanization, and, above all, ethnic transformation chipped away at Yankee confidence in New England's and America's future. The nation's most culturally homogeneous region confronted rising Irish politicians and expanding tenement districts crowded with immigrants who did not speak English. Old New England increasingly evolved into an object of nostalgia and veneration; it became the Yankee historical analogue to the Old South of the defeated Confederacy—that is, the imagined cultural apogee of regional life. A Southern-like sense of regional loss and even defeat came to haunt the victors. From the vital center of a young, republican, and Yankee America, postbellum New England seemed to decay into a Europeanized region: a society of urban squalor, industrial strife, class conflict, and the human offscourings of undemocratic governments. Indeed, progress, vitality, a village-centered order—these and other elements of antebellum regional identity appeared to migrate from New England to the emergent Midwest. This rising, young national heartland loomed as a pastoral "middle kingdom" between the industrialized East and the untamed West.

The political and imaginative rise of the Midwest did not vanquish decades of New England cultural imperialism. Postbellum native-born New Englanders continued to conceive of their region as an American cultural homeland—a notion that underpinned the memorialization of Old New England. The colonial revival supplied a medium for the cultural creation and political deployment of Old New England, yet another adaptation of regional identity. Sparked by historical anniversaries that were inaugurated with the centennial of 1876, the colonial revival inspired national historical commemoration and a new interest in the American past. In many respects, the celebration of Old New England constituted a regional expression of a larger colonial revival impulse in American culture. But New England clearly resided at the imaginative center of the colonial revival. In commemorations, historical writings, museum foundings, preservation, and antique collecting, New England people and their past dominated the cultural practices that comprised so much of the colonial revival. No wonder one scholar of American art concluded, quoting Emily Dickinson, that to "'see New Englandly' . . . was the essence of the colonial revival vision."[4]

If historical-minded and rapidly changing New England proved to be fertile ground for the colonial revival, Yankee women were largely responsible for cultivating the movement. One of them, Alice Morse Earle, compiled a remarkable record as the most popular, productive, and influential interpreter of the "old-times." As a prolific custodian of regional identity, Earle was a worthy successor to Harriet Beecher Stowe. She and her colonial revival collaborators expanded Stowe's work of placing women, domesticity, moral character, and daily life at the center of New England's historic distinctiveness.

In many ways, the colonial revival and commemoration of Old New England provided an imaginative escape from the dislocations of the present—a historical refuge where the native-born could indulge their nostalgia for simpler times. In its most insidious expression, the celebration of Old New England encouraged cultural retaliation against "swarthy" foreigners such as racialized characterizations of "ideal" New Englanders and ancestor worship. But for many colonial revivalists, Old New England represented a repository of traditions that needed to be preserved and invoked to revitalize Anglo-Puritan descendants, assimilate immigrants, and redress the perceived excesses of modern America. The creation of a summer haven for urbanites in historic Old York, Maine, and the restoration of Salem's House of Seven Gables as part of a settlement mission in a crowded immigrant neighborhood reveal two sides of the colonial revival cultural engagement with Old New England.

From Triumph to Descent

The most famous song to emerge from the crucible of civil war expressed a mid-nineteenth-century New England millennial faith in historical progress. "The Battle Hymn of the Republic" hailed "the watch-fires of a hundred circling camps" that illuminated the moral mission of the Grand Army of the Republic to redeem America as God's chosen nation. The war awakened the moral combativeness of New England's national regionalism. "[S]ix hundred thousand men have armed," minister Edward Everett Hale declared, "that they might carry good manners, honorable behavior, and a Christian civilization, to the South."[5]

Such Yankee triumphalism and imperialism would ultimately founder on the treacherous political terrain of Reconstruction. Yet, in the immediate aftermath of the war an optimistic nationalism prevailed in many corners of New England. The *Atlantic Monthly,* for example, the influential genteel organ of regional culture that had been founded in 1857 and had first published "The Battle Hymn of the Republic," espoused visions of national progress that radiated out from New England and the Northern victory in the war. As historian George Bancroft described the future in the pages of the *Atlantic,* in rhetoric that recalled the visions of Timothy Dwight and Daniel Webster, "With one wing touching the waters of the

Atlantic and the other on the Pacific, [the country] will grow to a greatness of which the past has no parallel."[6]

But signs of disillusionment soon appeared in bold print in the *Atlantic*. The ethical lapses of the Grant administration, which prompted Henry Adams to remark that the "evolution from President Washington to Grant was alone evidence enough to upset Darwin," seemed to signal the moral and political exhaustion of the Republican Party. The petering out of Reconstruction meant that the South would not be remade in New England's image. The *Atlantic* found pressing problems closer to home. In what would become a familiar grievance, a writer in 1873 decried the growing political power of "large gangs of ignorant foreigners superintended by a few skilled agents employed . . . by capitalists at a distance."[7] The postwar depression, sparked by the financial crash of 1873, plunged people into poverty and aggravated labor strife. Far from triumphing over the defeated South, many high-minded New Englanders began to feel that they were being deprived of the spoils of victory in their homeland. In *Poganuc People* (1878), the fictional autobiography of her early years, Harriet Beecher Stowe, the mother superior of Civil War–era New England, shrank from the changes that were altering the remembered idyllic New England of her youth. Poganuc, the quaint crossroads with the Native American name, summoned for Stowe "our New England villages in the days when its people were of our own blood and race, and the pauper population of Europe had not yet been landed upon our shores."[8]

Colonial revival commemorations of the 1870s not only encouraged patriotic and nativist nostalgia for earlier times that led to the imaginative birth of Old New England. They also provided a vehicle for New England leaders to pursue what Reconstruction had failed to accomplish: the cultural consolidation of the military victory over the South. Consider the work of Moses Coit Tyler, "the father of American literature," who, like so many prominent nineteenth-century New Englanders, used three names to declare his genealogical bona fides. Tyler, a native of Connecticut who traced his ancestry to Plymouth Colony, dominated the new field of American literature the way Jedidiah Morse had commanded American geography for a generation. A former minister, Tyler published the first American literature textbook. In 1875 he proposed that his New York publisher, George Putnam, underwrite the cost of a colonial literature survey that would take advantage of the new interest in the past stimulated by the approach of the centennial of American independence. Such a text would also fill a need created by the emergence of college and high school courses on American literature.[9]

Tyler's two-volume *History of American Literature* supplied colonial revivalists such as Alice Morse Earle with a preachy, morally uplifting, New England–centered account of the origins of American culture. After an opening chapter on the English background, Tyler devoted seventeen chapters to American literature, twelve of which focused on New England. "Since the year 1640," he boasted of the effects of the Great Migration, "the New England race has not received any notable addition to its original stock, and today their Anglican blood is as genuine and as unmixed as that of any county in England." Tyler, like other students of New England's founders, acknowledged the "dark side" of his ancestry. But in pious pronouncements, he extolled the mental discipline, moral stamina, and earnestness of the New England pioneers: "They were not acquainted with indolence; they forgot fatigue; they were stopped by no difficulties; they knew they could do all things that could be done."[10]

Tyler's text, as the colonial revival itself, represented a new phase of New England's national regionalism that had been grounded on the shoals of Reconstruction. New England–based or New England–bred writers dominated the study of American literature and American history in the postwar decades, producing the texts that were used across the country, even in the South. Writers like Tyler served as agents of a postwar New England–centered nationalism. Their books represented cultural consummations of the victory over the South. Texts such as Tyler's also defined an "American" heritage for growing numbers of immigrants, offering New England origins narratives of the nation's political and intellectual traditions.[11]

As Tyler's highly influential book suggests, the commemorations of the early colonial revival provided forums for the assertion of New England triumphalism in the face of the alterations of regional life that so unsettled people like Harriet Beecher Stowe and Lucy Larcom. At the local level, town and church anniversaries linked the Civil War victory to earlier New England glories. "A foreigner might think," Oliver Wendell Holmes observed in 1880, "that the patron saint of America was Saint Anniversary."[12] The Fourth of July and Memorial Day, established in 1868, became occasions for celebrating local anniversaries with the placement of Civil War canons or Union soldier monuments on town commons. Stationed at the center of civic life, such memorials signaled how the war was tied to town founding and to Revolutionary victory in a grand narrative of New England historical development.

But the 1880s sorely tested the self-congratulation of the early colonial revival in New England, provoking the nostalgia, nativism, and moral urgency that supplied the cultural currency for an imaginative investment in Old New England. The quickened tempo of ethnic transformation began to stir the crude nativism that had flashed in the antebellum decades with the Know-Nothing reaction to Irish Catholics. By this time the Irish had launched their political rise in southern New England, capturing the mayor's office in Boston in 1884. It would not be long before a succeeding Irish mayor would boast that "New England is more Irish today than any part of the world outside Ireland."[13]

During the 1870s and 1880s thousands of French Canadians flocked to industrializing cities and mill towns from Maine to Rhode Island. Dubbed the "Chinese of the Eastern States," the French Canadians were often recruited as strikebreakers. More than 500,000 "habitants" would cross the border into New England over the decades of mass migration. Welcomed as workers, the French, like the Irish, were Catholic hordes who failed to pass the cultural test of Yankee citizenship.[14]

After 1890 thousands of Italians, Poles, and Russian Jews boarded steamers destined for New England. Soon even small cities like Northampton, Massachusetts, claimed populations with a majority comprised of immigrants and their American-born children. A New Englander, Oliver Wendell Holmes plaintively conceded as immigration accelerated in the mid-1880s, would soon "feel more as if he were among his own people in London than in one of our seaboard cities." A short while later popular historical writer Samuel Adams Drake complained, in a book appropriately titled *Our Colonial Homes,* that the Paul Revere House and its environs in Boston's North End were overrun with unwashed aliens: "the atmosphere is actually thick with the vile odors of garlic and onions—of maccaroni and lazzaroni. The dirty tenements swarm with greasy voluble Italians. One can scarce hear the sound of his own English mother-tongue from one end of the square to the other."[15] The Immigration Restriction League, founded in Boston in 1894, would clear the air of arguments about the economic and cultural contributions of foreigners.

The mass immigration of the 1880s and 1890s aroused the feelings of cultural dispossession voiced by Lucy Larcom and provoked jeremiads bemoaning the demise of New England's Anglo-Puritan colonial heritage.

"We Yankees," grumbled Barrett Wendell, the Harvard professor whose identity was secured by the use of two last names, "are as much things of the past as any race can be. America has swept from our grasp. The future is beyond us." [16] Wendell, who found summer solace in the ancestral home in Portsmouth, New Hampshire, expressed a particularly strong inversion of the regional triumphalism of the post–Civil War years. Still, the face of the new New England taking shape disquieted Yankees who were far less nativist than the Harvard professor.

From the arrival of Irish masses in the 1840s, to the French-Canadian influx of the 1870s and 1880s, to the new immigration from southern and eastern Europe that so disturbed restrictionists, New Englanders were often conflicted about the arrival of foreigners. Immigrants supplied brawn to an economically expanding region, but the human "flotsam and jetsam . . . swept upon our shores," as one native described the newcomers, also posed a cultural threat to a Pilgrim-Puritan homeland whose ethnically homogeneous white population had swelled largely by natural increase over two centuries. Some Yankees blamed the foreign inrush of the 1880s and 1890s on greedy manufacturers and steamship companies, allies in the business of "Pipe Line Immigration." Tenement districts, filled with illiterate, unassimilated immigrants who seemed to be easy prey for political bosses, betokened the radically changed physical and civic landscape of Old New England.[17]

In fact, more than the brick factory or the granite mill, triple-decker housing was the preeminent marker of industrial-immigrant New England—an uncanonized icon of regional identity more common in many places than colonial houses and white-steepled churches. The triple-decker appears to have originated in Worcester, Massachusetts. New England developed the largest stock of triple-deckers in America; most of them were constructed during the heavy immigration that stretched from the 1870s to World War I. Though triple-deckers served as small middle-class apartment houses in the first streetcar suburbs inhabited by people trying to escape the changing inner city, the inexpensive multi-family structures were overwhelmingly built for the working class. In his autobiography, notorious politician James Michael Curley of Boston recalled the house where he was born in 1874 as a "cold-water walkup" in a wooden "three-story tenement" with an outhouse in the backyard. Huddled together along the waterfront, these dwellings formed a "corned-beef-and-cabbage riviera," he sarcastically noted.[18] In large cities such as Boston and Worcester, triple-deckers sheltered high percentages of the region's growing immigrant population. But even in the smaller mill centers and quarrying towns that extended from Connecticut to Maine, the triple-decker became New England's contribution to what is now called affordable housing, giving birth to "Corky Rows," "Petit Canadas," "Little Italys," and "Polish towns" (Figure 21).

The swarthy visage of the urban landscape was not the only source of anxiety over the demise of Old New England. Rural life, though largely untouched by immigrants, also seemed to be on the skids, buffeted by depopulation and an agricultural economy struggling to compete with Midwestern farmers. Some towns never fully recovered from the casualties and the mobility that resulted from native sons' participation in the Civil War. Other economically declining towns literally moved downhill. As railroads gradually penetrated the valleys of rural New England, hill towns were bypassed; residents migrated downhill or sought opportunities in cities or in the West.[19]

In *The New England Country* (1893) Clifton Johnson, a writer and photographer whose books trafficked in nostalgia for the rural life of olden times, described the consequences of population shifts in agricultural communities. The migration of the young and the death of their parents left behind farmsteads that were stark reminders of change in rural New England. "The shingles and clapboards loosen and the roof sags," Johnson reported, "and within, damp mossy decay has fastened itself to the walls, floor and ceiling of every room." Collapsing stone walls and overgrown bushes added to the desolate setting. "As time goes on, the house falls, piece by piece, and at last only the shattered frame stands, a grim memorial of the dead past."[20]

Such conditions in parts of rural New England sparked a series of articles in the *Atlantic Monthly* in the 1890s, with one writer worried about inbreeding among the mentally and morally infirm folk who stayed behind.[21] At the same time, the *Atlantic* provided a forum for Sarah Orne Jewett's elegiac fiction documenting the diminished prospect of backwater Maine. Jewett's fictional world is dominated not by enfeebled Yankees but by quaint, aged folk—especially women—noble survivors of communities drained of their youth and coping with straitened economic circumstances.

The decline of rural communities and the advance of a new urban, industrial, ethnic order became linked in the tourist economy of colonial revival New England. The narrator of Jewett's *The Country of the Pointed Firs* (1896) is a summer visitor seeking release from modern life in the city who

FIGURE 21. Triple-decker houses. New England had the highest concentration of triple-deckers. Most were built between 1890 and 1920. The structures varied in style and quality but preserved basic elements that often included porches. Photograph by the author.

is rejuvenated by immersion among the simple folk and local customs of small-town Maine, antiquities of Old New England. Recoiling from the hurried pace, squalor, and ethnic din of urban life, summer visitors, assisted by tourist promoters, imaginatively transformed graying backwater villages and Yankee country folk into embodiments of the "unmodernized picturesque."[22]

As Dona Brown, historian of nineteenth-century tourism, has shown, in the 1890s state economic development officials tutored New England farmers in the art and economics of catering to summer boarders from the city, an early version of the down-home practices that would comprise the bed-and-breakfast industry. States also advertised farmhouses that were for sale to city dwellers searching for the pastoral simplicity of old-time New England. Nostalgia and economic uplift inspired New Hampshire governor Frank Rollins to propose the creation of Old Home Week, when Yankee migrants would return to their native soil. "Sons and daughters of New Hampshire, wherever you are listen to the call of the old Granite State!" Rollins enthused in 1897. "Come back, come back! Do you not hear the call? What has become of the old home where you were born? Is it still in your family? If not, why not? Why do you not go and buy it this summer."[23] Old Home Week, with its expectation that returning natives would infuse new pride and money into rural communities, was officially established in New Hampshire in 1899, and the other New England states quickly followed suit. The creation of Old Home Week and the related popularity of family association meetings, like the Bowden family gathering in *The Country of the Pointed Firs*, suggests how antebellum national regionalism, institutionalized in the continental spread of New England Societies, reversed course. The cultural and economic resources of a Greater New England, it was now hoped, would be reexported to invigorate life in the old sod.

The problems of rural New England, the appeals of Old Home Week sponsors, and the Europeanized social order of Eastern cities all suggested how the heartland of a rising republic — America's America — had migrated away from New England in the postbellum decades. The states of the Old Northwest Territory now began imaginatively to coalesce into the "Midwest," a regional identity increasingly fashioned in opposition to the aged East and the Wild West so prominently on display in Buffalo Bill's traveling reenactment of frontier life. The Midwest, a middle cultural border whose states were not yet old enough to celebrate centennials, seemed to inherit the mantle of Young America — a vital, pastoral, small-town republican heartland whose sons dominated the presidency in the postwar decades. "One finds . . . in the Middle West today," an editorial writer observed early in the new century, "a larger proportion of men and women whose ideas, habits, and institutions are essentially those of Colonial America, and of England, than can be found now in the East." [24] Here was a powerful claim on colonial heritage by a spokesman for a region that had not even been part of colonial America.

The rhetoric and reality of Midwestern ascendancy, from agriculture to politics, seemed to suggest that New England as a region and its national vision had traveled downhill. The expansive region of antebellum pride and progress—the republican city on a hill—was now awash with nostalgia for the stable, homogeneous, simple world of Old New England. For some, Old New England offered an imaginative withdrawal from the present, the cultural equivalent of the Yankee retreat to country estates and private schools. But for other colonial revivalists, the values, customs, and material artifacts—the mortise and tenon—of Old New England comprised a living history that could be deployed to redeem the civic life of modern America. The most prominent and prolific interpreter of Old New England allied with this more progressive wing of the colonial revival.

Alice Morse Earle and Old New England

Alice Morse Earle (1851–1911) was the John Barber of Old New England, the industrious producer of textual and visual images of colonial life who, though often mentioned, has never been studied or appreciated as an architect of regional identity. Between 1891 and 1904 Earle produced eighteen books and more than three dozen articles on early America, perhaps the most impressive interpretive monument of the entire colonial revival and a pioneering body of work still useful to scholars and general readers. *Home Life in Colonial Days* (1898), one of her most important volumes, remains in print. Earle reached a wide and influential audience, popularizing colonial revival history and the texture of life in Old New England. *The Sabbath in Puritan New England* (1891), her first and most successful book, sold nearly twelve thousand copies during its first year and went through twelve editions in a little more than a decade.[25]

Earle's exhaustive reconstruction of Old New England responded to and shaped the historical tastes and cultural needs of such groups as the Colonial Dames and the Daughters of the American Revolution (DAR), hereditary organizations formed in the 1890s that mustered officers and foot soldiers for the colonial revival front. A member of both organizations, Earle dedicated *Colonial Dames and Good Wives* (1895)

TO

The Memory of the Colonial Dames
Whose blood runs in my veins
Whose spirit lives in my work.[26]

Colonial revival nostalgia for a simple ancestral world permeated Earle's books. She rhapsodized over the sight of lilac bushes in a farmhouse dooryard or the smell of bayberry candles — "the pure, spicy perfume of this New England incense"—which excited her "hereditary memory."[27] But the prolific author's output purveyed far more than indulgent wistfulness for an irretrievable past. Nor were her volumes simply antiquarian tomes, pots-and-pans history that responded to the burgeoning colonial revival antique market that Earle participated in and whose needs she acknowledged, most significantly in *China Collecting in America* (1892). Rather, her work re-created the social and material life of Old New England to spur her contemporaries to embrace preservation of the past and amelioration of the ills of the present. Through her books Earle labored to reaffirm Old New England as a moral and civic resource for life in the Gilded Age, not just to preserve it as a sentimental historical artifact of hereditary memory.

Long before the rise of social history, women's history, and the study of material culture, Earle retold the story of colonial America from the perspective of ordinary life, domesticity, and mothers and their homespun artifacts. In the face of changes to the family life of middle-class, native-born Americans—declining birthrates and an expanding female clerical workforce, for example—Earle deployed Old New England to shore up domesticity. At the same time, as her publishing and lecturing suggests, "heritage" served as a public domain that was not yet professionalized or male-dominated and that enabled women to assert their civic influence beyond the household.

Earle purported to be an interpreter of all colonial America. But even her inclusively titled volumes such as *Stage Coach and Tavern Days* (1900) displayed the interpretive dominance of Old New England that characterized the colonial revival. In *Costume of Colonial Times* (1894), she defended how New England "predominated" in her rendering of early American life. Earle adapted the techniques and the sensibility—the "romantic realism"—of local color writers like Sarah Orne Jewett to produce richly textured, evocative studies that lauded the virtue and stability of Old New England and encouraged colonial revival preservation activities, museum displays, and Americanization efforts.[28]

Earle traced her ancestry to the Great Migration, locating her roots in a genealogy that descended from Jonathan Fairbanks, of Dedham, who built New England's oldest existing timber frame house (ca. 1636), a photograph of which served as the frontispiece of *Home Life in Colonial Days*. Unlike her parents and her venerable forebears, Earle grew up with no direct social experience of the homogeneous village world of Old New England. Her father had migrated from Andover, Vermont, seeking economic opportunity in the industrializing world of central Massachusetts. He prospered in Worcester as a machinist, eventually becoming a partner in his own manufacturing company. Earle's mother was a native of small-town Maine.[29]

The Worcester where Earle was born in 1851 was far removed from the village life that her parents had left behind. At the time of her birth, for example, half the population of the industrializing city was of Irish descent. Worcester would soon become a magnet for French-Canadians and would develop into the triple-decker capital of inland New England. Earle observed these changes as a young adult and during visits to her parents after she left Worcester. The American Antiquarian Society, where she conducted research for her books, stood as an archival shrine—a point of entry into her ancestral past. With her books Earle erected her own historical edifice to a noble and useable past.[30]

In 1874 Alice Morse married Henry Earle and moved to fashionable Brooklyn Heights, New York. A native of Providence, Henry came from an established family whose lineage reached back to Rhode Island's beginnings. He worked as a Wall Street banker and broker while Alice, with the assistance of servants, cared for their four children born between 1876 and 1881. Brooklyn Heights was filled with mobile Yankees like the Earles, a presence announced by Henry Ward Beecher's Church of the Pilgrims, which, like so many Congregational societies established at midcentury, devised names to identify with New England's religious past. Earle joined the National Society of New England Women, a Brooklyn association for transplanted natives. Her writings would shape the colonial revival heritage activities of the National Society.[31]

From her comfortable, elevated Brooklyn world, Earle observed the changing social topography of modern America. In the 1880s five million immigrants made their way to the United States. Lower Manhattan, across

New York Bay from Brooklyn Heights, received a huge share of these new-comers. Throughout her career as a writer and lecturer, Earle refrained from nativist outbursts, but she did occasionally lash out at the "igno-rance and indifference which has made the political boss and his hench-men so powerful a promoter and controller in our present afflicted and afflictive city."[32] She doubtless observed the construction of Ellis Island, which opened in 1892, a symbol of alterations that threatened to consign the heritage of Old New England to the archives of institutions like the American Antiquarian Society. Earle's summer trips to Worcester con-firmed the perils that confronted New England tradition. Her antique-collecting forays into rural areas and her vacations at the Earle family's summer residence in backwater Wickford, Rhode Island, stirred a nostal-gic affection for the graying small-town world of Old New England.

Earle launched her writing career in 1891, when she was thirty-nine years old and the mother of four children, the oldest only fourteen. Ser-vants helped free up time for writing. Earle's record of accomplishment over the next fourteen years was unmatched during the colonial revival. Though it excludes the African Americans and Native Americans of Old New England, her work constitutes perhaps the most detailed reconstruc-tion of the region's Anglo-colonial world ever attempted. Her eighteen books typically run from three hundred to five hundred pages. Nor can they be dismissed as the antiquarian compost of genealogically obsessed Yankee New England. The products of original research, especially in probate records, Earle's volumes display broad knowledge of the colo-nial past. The best of them, such as *The Sabbath in Puritan New England* (1891) and *Customs and Fashions in Old New England* (1893), constitute a hybrid form that might be called local color history—an evocative re-creation of the past that incorporates the aesthetic sensibility of the regional lit-erary realism that descended from Harriet Beecher Stowe to writers like Sarah Orne Jewett. "A new and interesting method of studying history," Earle observed in a speech to the DAR, "is to begin with the history of the immediate surrounding of the individual, the town or village, local gov-ernment, etc., . . . making the individual observe for himself."[33] But her most important books were not simply nostalgic exercises in local and re-gional historical exactitude; they evinced the moral urgency of her quest to revitalize a useable past.

Earle published historical essays in journals like the *Atlantic Monthly* that featured local color fiction. These pieces reappeared as chapters in books. She then developed chapters into new books. For example, writing more as an ethnographer than an antiquarian in *Customs and Fashions in Old New England*, she examined the social and cultural life of the colonists from birth to death. Chapters on childhood, domestic life, travel, and taverns were then expanded into separate books. Earle continually recycled and broadened her material, arguing with her New York publishers— Scribner's and MacMillan—over design, paper quality, and illustrations. Her impressive output reflected industry and pride of craftsmanship, a reenactment of the Yankee artisanry that she celebrated in her writing. Indeed, through her book covers she visually allied her work with handmade colonial artifacts. The covers of *Home Life in Colonial Days* and *Colonial Dames and Good Wives*, for instance, were designed as samplers (Figure 22). Earle both reaffirmed and peddled tradition; the colonial revival boosted heritage into a growth industry. She negotiated her own contracts, capitalizing on her success to bargain for favorable financial terms and investing her considerable royalties in the stock market.[34]

Earle's audience consisted of people like herself: middle- to upper-middle-class New England offspring, residents of cities within and beyond the region coping with the dislocations of Gilded Age America and the growing sense of cultural dispossession that these dislocations engendered. She increasingly tailored her writings to women, the standard-bearers of the colonial revival. Her highly successful first book, *The Sabbath in Puritan New England*, was far less gender-specific than most of her subsequent volumes. Earle published her sympathetic study of the Puritans in 1891, on the eve of the bicentennial of the Salem witchcraft hysteria, the most embarrassing episode in New England's colonial past.

The Sabbath in Puritan New England displayed Earle at her local color best. She had tested her literary skills in an essay, "The New England Meeting House," published in the *Atlantic Monthly*, that served as the first chapter of the book. *Sabbath* evoked the roughhewn texture of colonial life as well as the contours of religious piety. "Strange and grotesque decorations did the outside of the earliest meeting-houses bear," she wrote of the practice of collecting animal bounties; "grinning wolves' heads [were] nailed under windows and by the side of the door, while splashes of blood, which had dripped from the severed neck, reddened the logs beneath." She described the medley of sounds from drums, horns, bells, and conch shells that called the Puritans to public devotion. She related how worshipers "piously froze" in plain, unheated meetinghouses where services were often punctuated by moments of levity. One of the numerous dogs

FIGURE 22. Sampler-style cover of Alice Morse Earle's *Home Life in Colonial Days* (1898). Earle capitalized on the colonial revival fascination with authentic crafted historical artifacts.

owned by the Puritans disrupted worship by chasing a skunk into the meetinghouse. A frustrated minister yelled "Fire, fire, fire!" to awaken his dozing audience. A layman, uninspired by the sermon, observed that he would prefer to hear his "dog bark than Mr. Bellamy preach." By skillfully employing humor and re-creating the sights, sounds, and smells of the colonial world, Earle produced an informative yet readable, entertaining book that humanized the Puritans for an audience reared on the literary realism of magazines such as the *Atlantic Monthly*. As she put it, she offered up the Puritans, whose "blood stirs in my drowsy brain," in all their "rough grandeur." [35]

And the Puritans did possess a new moral and physical grandeur for Victorian colonial revivalists like Earle. *The Sabbath in Puritan New England* was a best-seller not only because of its aesthetic realism but also because it reflected and contributed to a new adaptation of Puritan-Pilgrim tradition. If that tradition persisted as a vital presence across three centuries of New England life, it did so by a continuing process of historical revision in which the religious past was adapted to the shifting interpretive needs and cultural politics of regional identity. Colonial revivalists such as Earle, even as they humanized New England's founders, restored moral and physical strenuosity (and some severity and repression) to the Puritan past and then invoked regional tradition as a tonic for the ailments of modern America. Thus, the approach of the Salem bicentennial did not dissuade Earle from producing a laudatory book about her religious ancestors. In fact, 1891 also witnessed the publication of Barrett Wendell's historical apologia for Cotton Mather. In *Cotton Mather: The Puritan Priest,* Wendell defended the often maligned minister against charges of fanaticism in the witchcraft hysteria. He showered praise on Mather for "strenuously" and "devoutly" pursuing what he thought was right and for "striving, amid endless stumblings and errors, to do his duty." [36]

From Moses Coit Tyler's ground-breaking American literature text through a spate of books published in the 1890s, the colonial revival stimulated an outpouring of Puritan studies. Earle cited and expressed her approval for Tyler's work, and, in her book on the Puritan Sabbath, she produced perhaps the most lively, engaging, and successful interpretation of New England's religious founders during the entire colonial revival era. While acknowledging the Puritans' imperfections, Earle and her contemporaries conveyed a Victorian appreciation for the virile character, rock-ribbed sense of duty, and spiritual aspirations embodied in the lives of their ancestors. The conclusion to *The Sabbath in Puritan New England* summed up the dominant colonial revival appraisal of the region's religious founders: "Patient, frugal, God-fearing, and industrious, cruel and intolerant sometimes, but never cowardly, sternly obeying the word of God in the spirit and the letter, but erring sometimes in the interpretation thereof,—surely they have no traits to shame us, to keep us from thrilling with pride at the drop of their blood which runs in our backsliding veins."[37] Earle's voice was that of a genteel, elegiac Jeremiah. Her books lamented the decline of Old New England and issued a moral summons to colonial descendants: through their leadership tradition could be preserved and drawn on as a fount of restorative values for the maladies of Victorian America.

The Sabbath in Puritan New England was a gendered text, but not because of the scenes of cozy domesticity that cheer the pages of most of Earle's other works. Rather, her first colonial revival study resonated with the discourse of "manliness," the strenuous life, and the moral muscularity of Puritan civic and religious leaders. When Earle described how "our grandfathers" displayed "tough fibre" and "vast powers of endurance, both mental and physical," her readers would have recognized that "neurasthenia" did not afflict Old New England.[38] A newly diagnosed disorder of Victorian America, neurasthenia was a nervous ailment that in the 1880s and 1890s became an alarming symptom of the decline of the Anglo-Saxon race. Neurasthenia, it was widely believed, signaled the physical and emotional enervation that accompanied the modern transition from bodily to mental labor. Surely Earle's celebration of the stamina of the colonial character inspired her readers to ward off neurasthenia and to reverse the trend toward moral and physical decline. But the colonial revival celebration of strenuous Puritan leaders involved far more than history as nostalgia and therapy. It recalled the manly moral and civic leadership that was increasingly being displaced by the ethnic bosses who so offended Earle and postwar Yankee reformers—the "goo-goos" or good government "chowder heads" ridiculed by James Michael Curley.[39]

During the years surrounding the publication and repeated reprinting of *The Sabbath in Puritan New England,* new, sympathetic biographies of stalwart moral leaders from John Winthrop to Jonathan Edwards appeared, along with volumes such as *The Puritan as a Colonist and Reformer.* One volume, *The New Puritanism,* emerged from a symposium in 1897 celebrating the fiftieth anniversary of the Plymouth Congregational Church in Earle's own Brooklyn Heights. Speakers endeavored to distill from the Puritanism of Old New England enduring elements of tradition for modern America. The moral energy and "social conscience" of Puritanism received high praise. One speaker called for a "revival of Puritanism" and berated Victorian America for its "vice," "luxury and effeminacy," stressing the importance of "character" and "clean living as a condition of public service."[40]

The Sabbath in Puritan New England, biographies of Puritan leaders, and volumes like *The New Puritanism* all commemorated Old New England's moralistic republicanism and called for its renewal. Moreover, the progress of Saint Anniversary led to the erection of impressive "manly" statues of Puritan-Pilgrim figures—visual odes to the moral vigor and civic watchfulness of Old New England's leaders who were enshrined in Earle's first book. These bronze monuments occupied public space in cities within and beyond the region that were undergoing dramatic ethnic change. In 1880, for instance, the 250th anniversary of Massachusetts's founding led to the erection of a statue of John Winthrop in downtown Boston (Figure 23). A muscular Winthrop tightly grips his Bible as he stares out toward the altered civic terrain of the city he helped establish. Seven years later Augustus Saint-Gaudens sculpted the impressive statue, *The Puritan,* which was unveiled in the center of Springfield (Figure 24). The nine-foot bronze both humanized and aggrandized his subject, creating a striding figure who exudes vitality, strength, conviction, and purpose. Saint-Gaudens's work clearly influenced subsequent Puritan statuary. The New England Society of Philadelphia commissioned him to sculpt a replica of *The Puritan* for its city. At about the same time the New England Society of New York erected in Central Park a large manly monument of the *The Pilgrim,* an armed, broad-shouldered sentinel who visually conflates Puritan and Pilgrim virtue and vigor. Even Rhode Island, ever inclined to challenge Puritan-Pilgrim narratives of American origins, participated in the celebratory civic discourse that exalted the manly virtue of Old New England. The virile figure of the *The Independent Man,* the bronze incarnation of Rhode Island's colonial spirit, was cast in 1899 for the dome of the new statehouse and peered down on encircling triple-decker ethnic neighborhoods.[41]

Colonial revivalists installed numerous smaller monuments, bronze plaques, and granite markers—the civic moorings of Old New England —on a changing landscape. Historic anniversaries and their commemorative artifacts aimed to inspire colonial descendants and to encourage respect for tradition and interest in Americanization among the surging ranks of immigrants. Monuments like Saint-Gaudens's *The Puritan* became

FIGURE 23. Richard S. Greenough, *John Winthrop* (1880), Boston. Photograph by Antonia Conforti.

FIGURE 24. Augustus Saint-Gaudens, *The Puritan* (1887), Springfield, Massachusetts. This muscular, energetic, and daunting figure suggests not Hawthorne's "black-browed" religious enthusiasts but the manliness, moral conviction, and civic determination that colonial revivalists saw in the Puritan past. Photograph by Antonia Conforti.

shrines to the spirit of Old New England—elements in an ongoing civil religion that, ironically, finally subverted the iconophobia and idol smashing of the region's founders.

Far from being an uncongenial date on which to launch a writing career with a study of the Puritan Sabbath, 1891 marked Earle's timely plunge into the cultural politics and heritage economy of colonial revival America. "I love to read of such vigorous, powerful lives," Earle enthused of her New England forebears with rhetoric suitable for inscription on newly cast Puritan statuary: "they seem to be of a race entirely different from our own." She directly returned to the Puritans in only one other book—her biography of *Margaret Winthrop* (1895), the governor's wife. But almost all of her publications were informed by the appreciation for Puritanism's civic-moral achievements displayed in her first book. The principal "foundation of the New England commonwealth was religion," she repeated in her works, and "the second was certainly neighborliness." [42] After *The Sabbath in Puritan New England* Earle trained her sights on the social texture of Old New England—the interstices of ordinary life where religious injunction and worldly challenge converged to shape regional character and community.

In its sheer volume, Earle's concentrated outburst of print rivals the work of major nineteenth-century custodians of regional identity such as Jedidiah Morse and Harriet Beecher Stowe. Like Morse, Earle represented Old New England as a coherent cultural region. For her, as for Morse, Puritanism served as the wellspring of New England's cultural essence. But Earle, influenced by the literary ethnography of local color writing and by the emergence of folk studies, offered a more anthropological rendering of regional distinctiveness than the politicized cultural geography of Morse's texts. The distinctiveness of Old New England resided in the folkways and customs of its people recorded in written documents but also inscribed in the artifactual remains of colonial life. Earle's work is closer to Stowe's domestic-centered re-creation of New England life. Far more than Stowe, of course, Earle reconstructed the material world of the past. Yet, in many respects her Old New England constitutes an imaginative progression from Stowe. Like Stowe's four New England novels (1859–78), which are set in different states, Earle, whose immediate family ties stretched from Massachusetts and Rhode Island to Vermont and Maine, produced volumes that re-created Old New England life with textual and artifactual evidence drawn from across the region. Women and domesticity persist at the center of Earle's evocation of Old New England in ways that addressed anxieties and cultural needs of an audience whose tastes Stowe had helped shape.

In the concluding pages of *Margaret Winthrop,* Earle extracted an abiding lesson of the Puritan woman's life that was "far more urgent today." Dame Winthrop illustrated "the beauty in woman's life of home-loving, home-keeping, home-influencing" and affirmed "the true dignity which comes from simplicity of living, simplicity in dress, in home-furnishing, in hospitality, in all social and domestic relations." [43] Earle's writings reconstructed Old New England not from the perspective of the pulpit or pew but from the warm glow of the hearth—the historical shrine of the colonial revival. She reassembled the artifacts of colonial domesticity and imbued them with the cultural politics of Victorian America.

Home Life in Colonial Days proved to be the most successful of Earle's domestic texts. The book was reprinted four times in its first two years of publication. More than 140 photographs of artifacts and staged colonial activities enhanced its appeal and influence. With its richly textured history of family life and its redolent images of domestic simplicity, industry, and warmth, *Home Life* became an indispensable volume for the growing house museum movement and for the historical pageantry associated with Old Home Week. Indeed, one creator of a colonial kitchen museum exhibit cut images and text from its pages and used them as labels for the artifacts on display. [44] *Home Life* was a nostalgic and ideologically freighted volume readily accessible to and filled with human interest for the colonial revival reading public. This work—like several of Earle's other studies—also functioned as a guidebook for enterprising heritage exhibitors.

Earle's colonial interiors reassembled the domestic material world of Old New England. But her domestic scenes were artifacts themselves, projections of the colonial revival imagination that were rooted in the cultural predicaments of her age. Buffeted by a new social order framed on one side by expanding ethnic tenement districts and on the other by the material display of industrial wealth, colonial revivalists lauded the balance and order of Georgian and neoclassical architecture, emblems of the proportioned world of Old New England. So, too, colonial revivalists imputed moral and cultural meaning to the simple and orderly domestic interiors of the past. Earle contrasted the plain interiors of colonial homes with "our bric-a-brac filled days," calling up the image of cluttered Victorian parlors. Such museumlike interiors were monuments to consumerism, symptoms of a devitalized American life and national character: the weakening of "self-sufficiency," "neighborliness," and "social ethics" that

FIGURE 25. Kitchen fireplace in the John Greenleaf Whittier House. The well-equipped colonial hearth served as an emblem of family intimacy, domestic self-reliance, and home crafts. Alice Morse Earle, *Home Life in Colonial Days* (1898).

Earle deplored.[45] The domestic interiors of Old New England, whether in the pages of Earle's books or in newly opened house museums, were not just nostalgic representations of an unrecoverable past. They prodded native-born Victorians to reaffirm tradition. As her concluding admonition to readers of *Margaret Winthrop* suggested, Earle's domestic history of Old New England advanced a simple but genteel cultural aesthetic—a colonial revival counterpoint to the "disorder" of ethnic tenement life and the material excesses of Victorian consumers.

The domestic rites of Old New England played out around the hearth. By the late nineteenth century the use of stoves and then central heating transformed the colonial hearth into a sentimental artifact of family intimacy and warmth. "The shutting up of the great fireplaces and the introduction of stoves marks an era," Lucy Larcom recalled, "[and] the abdication of shaggy Romance . . . at the New England fireside."[46] In *Home Life in Colonial Days,* Earle included a picture of the well-equipped fireplace in the restored John Greenleaf Whittier homestead in Haverhill, Massachusetts, where the nineteenth-century poet had been born (Figure 25). The

Whittier House was part of an emerging heritage circuit—restored homes of writers visited by tourists in search of Old New England. The Whittier House possessed perhaps the most famous colonial revival hearth, one immortalized in *Snowbound*. Earle was repeatedly drawn to Whittier for his poeticizing of the "homely contentment" of Old New England. She quoted *Snowbound* at length in her books:

> Between the andirons' straddling feet
> The mug of cider simmered slow . . . ,
> And, close at hand, the basket stood
> With nuts from brown October woods.
> What matter how the night behaved!
> What matter how the north wind raved!
> Blow high, blow low, not all its snow
> Could quench our hearth-fire's ruddy glow.

Earle rounded out the picture of what came to be known in museum circles as the "Old Tyme" kitchen exhibit: "Over the fireplace and across the top of the room were long poles on which hung strings of peppers, dried apples, and rings of dried pumpkin."[47]

Earle's photographic and verbal images of domesticity constituted a Currier and Ives representation of regional pastoral simplicity brought indoors. Her Old New England, as her use of Whittier's *Snowbound* suggests, acquired a historical elasticity; the era endured in her books as a stable and seemingly static past that extended from the seventeenth into the nineteenth century. Earle could not contain Old New England within the historical boundaries of the "colonial" era. *Home Life in Colonial Days* wandered into the nineteenth century for evidence and artifacts. In some books Earle talked about the world of "our grandmothers." Her volumes on the history of early American gardens and on *Stage Coach and Tavern Days* substituted the "Old-Time" era for the colonial age. For all the details and exactness of her volumes, her old-time New England was essentially a stationary imagined past—an epoch of continuity, stability, self-sufficiency, and cultural homogeneity. In short, Earle increasingly transmuted Old New England into the historically expansive "age of homespun."[48]

Her interpretive maneuvering reflected the larger historical contortions of the colonial revival movement. Old New England or the "old times" signified more than the colonial past; such terms conjured up images of nineteenth-century America before railroads, mill complexes, immigrant hordes, urban squalor, and conspicuous displays of wealth.

Looking back on the American past from the 1890s, Earle imagined the decades that lengthened from the colonial era to her grandmother's age in the early nineteenth century as an unbroken epoch of social intimacy and pastoral simplicity. In her nostalgia for Old New England, Earle, like other colonial revivalists, revealed the unmistakable symptoms of that cultural consort of neurasthenia—antimodernism. The self-sufficient, craft-centered household of Old New England sustained the energy and endurance of the regional character during the two centuries that comprised the imagined stable age of homespun.

Earle prided herself on the recovery of the "homespun vocabulary" of Old New England, the identification of now forgotten names for an array of ingenious household artifacts. Her description and display of these artifacts communicated a colonial revival cultural vocabulary of antimodernism—a discourse that treasured handmade objects as expressions and sources of character. The "vitality and strength" of colonial women "were woven into the warp and woof" of homespun linens, she observed in *Colonial Dames and Good Wives*. "With their close woven, honest threads, runs this finer beauty, which may be impalpable and imperceptible to a stranger, but which to me is real and ever-present, and puts me truly in touch with the life of my forebears." In *Home Life in Colonial Days,* Earle assailed the cheapening of material life and the devaluation of character that accompanied the nineteenth-century advance of industrialization. "The daughters who in our days of factories leave the farm for the cotton-mill, where they perform but one of the many operations in cloth manufacture, can never be as good home-makers or as helpful mates as the homespun girls of our grandmothers' days." [49]

Conflating the colonial with the age of homespun, Earle focused her anxieties over the decline of Old New England on domesticity and female character. Yet the home-forged virtue of men had also become a diminished thing. *Home Life in Colonial Days* exhibited a gallery of Yankee artifacts, from devices like corn shellers to a variety of tinware, that were inventive homemade objects or, presumably, products of local craftsmanship. Old New England was primarily a "wooden age," the era of "Jack-knife industries," the manly counterpart to the homespun activities of goodwives. "[T]he New England boy's whittling was his alphabet of mechanics," Earle observed, calling forth a familiar Yankee image and the inventive tinkering that supported the household self-sufficiency of the age of homespun. [50] But like the artifacts that resulted from his handicraft, the authentic Yankee, colonial revivalists worried, was increasingly a

FIGURE 26. Wool spinning, one of the numerous domestic crafts of women that were described and illustrated in Earle's books. Alice Morse Earle, *Home Life in Colonial Days* (1898).

quaint relic of a receding past, rather than the energetic, ubiquitous figure of the antebellum decades.

Earle's discussion and presentation of the material remnants of Old New England in her widely read books contributed to the colonial revival transformation of artifacts into antiques. Like the woven linens whose imaginative handling put Earle in touch with her forebears, antiques became artifacts that breathed the "spirit" of the past. Antiques were consecrated by the values understocked by Gilded Age America: character, craftsmanship, simplicity, good taste. Plain artifacts conspicuously displayed in upper-middle-class households like Earle's heralded a family genealogy descended from the age of homespun. The possession of an-

FIGURE 27. Making Thanksgiving pies, a three-generation hearthside industry. Work becomes craft, not drudgery, in Earle's women-centered households where busyness is enshrined. Alice Morse Earle, *Home Life in Colonial Days* (1898).

tiques announced a continuing allegiance to the values of Old New England; it also asserted a claim on "ownership" of the past.[51]

Earle's assiduous pursuit of her writing about the past, even to the point where she sought relief from a severe bout of neurasthenia, was partly inspired by the industrious exemplars of colonial womanhood who file through her books. Women are never at rest on the printed page or in photographs (Figures 26 and 27). Freed from household work by paid servants, Earle imagined the "fireside industries" of the homespun age not as domestic drudgery, which, as the now famous diary of Martha Ballard shows, became more burdensome with age. Instead, Earle's hearty, self-sufficient women inhabit a world where work almost always unfolds as craft, the antithesis to modern industrial labor and its "cheap" mass-produced commodities. Spinning, weaving, candle making, preserving, cheese making—such work comprises a satisfying ritual of fireside crafts with the nobility of Old New England wrought into the resulting artifacts. Earle's staged photographs and detailed descriptions of home crafts furnished a manual for museum reenactments of the age of homespun.[52]

The American Revolution, as Earle and her fellow DAR members fondly recalled, occasioned an impressive patriotic, public display of domestic virtue and skill. Dressed in homespun and transporting their linen wheels—that omnipresent and revered colonial revival artifact—women met in groups to spin goods for the rebel army. Earle was at pains to show that the self-sufficiency of the household did not mean that the colonial family dwelled in isolation from the community and the civic order. For Earle, the simple competency of the colonial household underscored how "modern luxuries" and bric-a-brac consumerism had eroded the hereditary New England character. She stressed, however, that a self-sufficient, home-based economy did not lead to social fragmentation in Old New England. Neighborliness resided next to Godliness in the age of homespun—an "old-time exalted type of neighborliness" that had been replaced with an impersonal "philanthropy."[53]

As a researcher familiar with colonial court records, Earle was certainly aware of the litigiousness of colonial "neighbors." But discounting evidence of acrimony, religious dissent, class conflict, and the acquisitiveness spawned by what we now recognize as the eighteenth-century "empire of goods," she portrayed a colonial world in social equilibrium, where the communal rites of interdependence complemented the economic autonomy of the household. The "walls and rafters" of Old New England were "held in place by the kind deeds and wishes of . . . friends and neighbors." Tree-chopping bees, stone-piling bees, barn and house raisings, "breaking out the town" after a snowstorm, "whangs" or collaborative annual housecleanings—these and other neighborly practices knit the social fabric of Old New England into an artifact as simple, beautiful, and durable as a homespun garment. But, alas, Earle regretted, "We [now] are independent of our neighbors. The personal element has been removed to a large extent from our social ethics."[54] Earle's imaginative and ideological attachment to one kind of historic community hindered her from appreciating the neighborliness and interdependence on display in the Petit Canadas and Little Italys in places like her native Worcester.

Earle descended from rhetorical flights of jeremiadlike moralizing to revel in the domestic and communal afterglow of Old New England. She re-created the age of homespun in all of its "cozy" quaintness and local color, though she lacked the literary skill and imagination of Stowe and Jewett. Still, she quoted Jewett and limned an old-time pastoral world— a way of life clung to by the elderly, self-sufficient herbalist of *The Country of the Pointed Firs,* Elmiry Todd, a fictional throwback to Earle's "age of our grandmothers." In *Customs and Fashions in Old New England,* Earle included herbal medicine among the domestic crafts of the period. Old-time New Englanders did not "run to a chemist or apothecary with a little slip of paper." From the contents of herbal gardens, they "picked, pulled, pounded, stamped, shredded, dropped, powdered and distilled" home remedies for ailments.[55]

Two of Earle's final books were devoted to colonial gardening. Colonial revival preservation encouraged the restoration of private and public gardens, and once again Earle furnished her audience with detailed historical information. Like the acquisition of antiques, colonial-style gardening promised to put people in touch with their ancestral past. A garden added to a city home or restored at a summer retreat re-created elements of the pastoral world of Old New England. Sundials, which became popular ornaments in colonial revival gardens, suggested a nostalgia for the premodern, organic life of the age of homespun.

In *Old Time Gardens* (1901), Earle turned to horticultural images to convey the simple beauty of traditional New England and to "botanize" regional identity. The lilac, "a flower welcomed by English-speaking folk since it first came to England," captured the cultural essence of New England. "Its very color seems typical of New England; some parts of celestial blue, with more of warm pink, blended and softened by that shading of sombre gray ever present in New England life into a distinctive color known everywhere as lilac—a color grateful, quiet, pleasing, what Thoreau called a 'tender, civil, cheerful color.'" So, too, the apple tree was a dignified English inheritance, bearer of "the social fruit of New England." Earle recalled the "earthy, appley smell," another New England "incense," that rose from well-stocked cellars and infiltrated the seldom-used parlors in old-time farmhouses. She described and offered staged pictures of the domestic production of apple cider and apple butter, hailing the fruit as "the beautiful rural emblem of industrious and temperate home life" in Old New England.[56]

Old Time Gardens was among Earle's most nostalgic books, filled with photographs of the beauty and rural simplicity of Old New England. She deplored the way the lawn, a modern invention spurred by the patenting of rotary mowers in 1868, increasingly displaced front yard flower gardens and thereby changed the landscape aesthetics of the region. But *Old Time Gardens* and a related book, *Sun Dials and Roses of Yesterday* (1902), were more than exercises in nostalgic escapism. They responded to and shaped a colonial revival historical agenda outdoors; the restoration of private gardens and the renovation of public space by village improvement societies cultivated the quest for Old New England on the landscape.[57]

Similarly, Earle's books on home life assisted the work of preservationists, museum exhibitors, and hereditary societies. The National Society of New England Women in Brooklyn, for example, based its reenactments of old-time customs such as quilting and corn-husking bees on Earle's work.[58] Her influential history of hearthside New England reaffirmed for such native-born women the moral responsibilities and burdens of domesticity. But her interiorized history cannot be reduced to a sign of the privatization of Victorian family life—a withdrawal into a new cultural edifice in which the domestic politics of Old New England occupied one floor. Earle's writing, lecturing, and hereditary society activities betray such a reading of her significance. For all of her hand wringing over the decline of Old New England, the past remained a source of renewal for Earle. Her books summoned native-born women both to a reaffirmation of domesticity and to leadership of heritage activities that were often nostalgic and nativist but also patriotic and civic minded. These commingled elements of the colonial revival were on display in Old York, Maine, a summer resort and village restoration that affords a view of the progress of Old New England at the local level.

The Colonial Revival and the Creation of Old York, Maine

York, Maine, was a cultural outpost of Old New England. Dona Brown has described how southern Maine coastal villages resembled other faded, "quaint" communities such as Litchfield, Connecticut, and Nantucket and Deerfield, Massachusetts, that attracted summer residents from the city who sought the small-town simplicity and ethnic homogeneity of the past.[59] York, like colonial revival summer resorts throughout the region, became an important site for heritage activities that revitalized a corner of Old New England seemingly unaltered by time.

In her books Earle made several references to the material remains of York's colonial past that continued to dominate the town's landscape. Moreover, she was acquainted with Mary Sowles Perkins, a wealthy New Yorker who descended from an old New England family and who took up summer residence in York in 1898. Perkins furnished Earle with at least one antique—a tinder box—that was photographed for *Home Life in Colonial Days*.[60] York, like the Wickford coastal village where the Earles summered, beckoned urbanites, some of whom traced their ancestry back to colonial Maine. Drawing on her wealth and family heritage as well as Earle's books, Mary Perkins quickly emerged as one of the leaders in the creation of Old York, a restoration and celebration of the colonial past that piled historic irony upon irony.

York was not the oldest settlement in Maine, but its first permanent resident arrived in 1630, before the landfall of John Winthrop's fleet. In 1639 Sir Ferdinando Gorges, the tireless promoter of English colonization of New England, received a proprietary charter for the "Province of Maine." Two years later he incorporated "Gorgeana" as the capital of his domain, with the Church of England as the official religion. By the time Gorges died in 1647, having never set foot in Maine, Gorgeana numbered perhaps three hundred settlers. It would soon be absorbed by Massachusetts and renamed York.[61]

The outbreak of civil war in England provided Puritan Massachusetts with an opportunity to deliver a blow to royal authority and the Anglican Church close to home. Massachusetts seized Gorgeana in 1652. Reenacting an earlier Puritan victory over the English city of York, Massachusetts renamed Gorgeana, neutralized considerable local resistance, and reorganized the town with a selectmen form of government.[62] Colonial revivalists would commemorate 1652 as marking the birth of York, downplaying the earlier history of the town. Curiously, the growing Episcopalian summer residents of Old York would celebrate the Puritan takeover that muscled aside the Church of England.

The first of York's two Congregational societies ordained a permanent minister in 1673. Four years later Massachusetts secured its authority over York and the Province of Maine by purchasing the claims of Gorges's heirs. York, which remained a frontier town, was subject to Native American attacks; in the Massacre of 1692, for instance, homes were burned and settlers fell victim to death or captivity.[63] Like the more famous Deerfield Massacre of a decade later, the York episode and the town's surviving "garrison" houses fostered the colonial revival "romance of Old York" — the story of hearty, pious, Anglo-pioneers advancing the New England frontier.

Continuing threats from Native Americans and their French allies slowed York's recovery and development in the early eighteenth century. But by 1732, when the population had grown to around 1,300, a second Congregational society was organized. In 1747 the First Church constructed a new meetinghouse in the center of town. York's closed field and increasingly dispersed pattern of development, however, left the town without a common or green.[64] The 1747 meetinghouse and its small lot would only be physically and imaginatively transformed into a "historic" village green by colonial revivalists such as Mary Perkins. Old York, a venerable patch of Old New England, required a village green to authenticate its identity even if history had not conferred one on the town.

Shortly after the French and Indian War ended in 1763, bringing new security to Maine, York's population stood at approximately 2,200. From the late eighteenth century through the first three decades of the nineteenth century, the town achieved a measure of prosperity, if not wealth, as a community of farmers, fishermen, and maritime traders. Shipbuilding and small-scale manufacturing also became part of the local economy. Though York seems never to have fully recovered from the commercial disruption associated with the War of 1812, its population reached a historic highpoint in 1830, when nearly 3,500 people resided in the town. But then York experienced six decades of decline, losing more than 10 percent of its population in the 1830s alone.[65]

Two important developments in the 1830s and 1840s added to the erosion of the town's economy. In 1832 the York courthouse, which had been completed in 1811, ceased serving as the principal legal forum for the county. Most legal proceedings, and the business they generated, were transferred to another town. A decade later, the Portland, Saco, and Portsmouth Railroad laid down tracks that transported travelers inland, completely bypassing York. The town began to slip ever more noticeably into decline.[66]

A stagnant waterfront, weather-beaten farmhouses, and migrating sons and daughters defined a post–Civil War York whose population bottomed out in 1890. Travelers' accounts of the 1870s describe an aged town but not the quaint Old York of the colonial revival imagination. In 1874 a writer in the *New Hampshire Gazette* acknowledged that York "once boasted a considerable commerce, of which no other evidence now remains than its decaying wharves, dilapidated warehouses, and few vessels of small tonnage." The town's colonial garrison houses were "remarkable in their decrepitude."[67] A year later, in his travel book *Nooks and Corners of the New England Coast* (1875), popular writer Samuel Adams Drake also noted disturbing signs of York's decline. The meetinghouse of 1747 had not been replaced with an up-to-date neoclassical churchly structure nor had it been modernized; it retained the old-fashioned side-to-side orientation and did not face the road. The meetinghouse was not attached to a handsome green but simply "placed on a grassy knoll, with the parsonage behind it." The nearby burial ground was in a deplorable state. "The place seemed wholly uncared for," Drake complained. "The grass grew rank and tangled, making the examination [of stones] difficult, and at every step I sank to the knee in some hollow."[68]

By the 1870s, however, new developments were under way that, by the turn of the century, would rescue the backwater village and transform it into Old York, a unique and authentic parcel of Old New England. Summer residents from the city served as the colonial revival cultural missionaries to York. Though a few summer cottages and one of York's first hotels were constructed in the late 1860s, it took three decades for the town to become an attractive resort. In particular, the influx of summer residents in the 1890s hastened York's physical and cultural transformation. Old houses were restored and new cottages built. For the first time since the 1820s, the town's year-round population grew—and it did so by 10 percent. Local folk found employment as carpenters, masons, painters, and gardeners serving the summer community, a presence that swelled York's population to 10,000 in July and August. Some residents took in boarders from the city who were seeking a taste of old-time country life.[69]

The town emerged as a resort comprised of old and new districts. The historic center of York—the first church, the courthouse, the burial ground, the oldest tavern—was situated at a protected location along the York River a mile from the coast. Twelve years after Massachusetts incorporated the settlement of Gorgeana in 1652 and renamed it York, the British seized New Netherlands and New Amsterdam from the Dutch and rechristened the colony and the seaport New York. The term "Old York" appears to have come into use in the eighteenth century, when ship captains and the makers of navigational maps used the name to distinguish the Maine town from the port of New York. References to Old York shifted in the nineteenth century. After midcentury "Old York" became a descriptive shorthand for the town's physical and economic decay. Near the end of the century, colonial revival tourists, summer residents, and local boosters reinvented Old York as an embodiment of unmodernized, picturesque Old New England.

This imaginative repossession of Old York coincided with the development of new summer communities in other parts of the town during the 1880s and 1890s. At the mouth of the York River a mile from the old village center, the rickety wharves, "dingy coal-sheds and fish-houses" of York Harbor gave way to colonial revival and shingle-style summer "cottages." York Harbor became a genteel summer haven for urban professionals and literati; writers William Dean Howells and Thomas Nelson

Page, for example, were literary ornaments of the *new* York. Three new Episcopal churches, two at York Harbor, were built during the decades of the town's transformation that stretched into the early twentieth century.[70]

North of York Harbor and two miles east of the old village, another summer community spread out along York Beach, where, in 1887, the railroad finally arrived in town and opened up the coastline to day excursionists. Howells identified with the urbaneness on display at York Harbor and among the old village restorationists; York Beach, he observed, attracted "people several grades of gentility lower than ours."[71] York Beach, where Roman Catholic masses were being offered by 1895, also attracted upwardly mobile Irish summer residents.

Recent historical work has shown how the growth of new coastal resort communities within the town bestowed on York Center, York Village, or Old York, as it was increasingly called, a quaint antiquity. The gray backwater village was transformed into an authentic relic of Old New England. Even before the founding in 1899 of the Old York Historical and Improvement Society, which became the town's heritage nerve center, the colonial revival imagination began to repossess the village as an outdoor museum that housed the physical remains, pastoral simplicity, and ethnic purity of Old New England. In 1882, for instance, an article in *Harper's,* titled "A Summer in York," lavished praise on the town. "Here meet four roads, with the usual adjuncts of a country village—post-office, variety store, town-hall, and schoolhouse, with the smithy lighted by the dusky glow of its [*sic*] forge," the author enthusiastically reported. "Three white steeples, looking hopeful and shining, point the way to another and a larger road, while close by stands that monument of justice, the ruins of the old jail." York's appeal lay not only in its natural beauty but also in "a most delightful vacuum in the way of shops, libraries, and indeed of almost all city incumbrances."[72]

Nine years later Samuel Adams Drake offered the public a similar appraisal of Old York. In a new travel book, *The Pine Tree Coast* (1891), Drake returned to the faded York he had described in *Nooks and Corners of the New England Coast* a decade and a half earlier. Drake's books are important because they suggest how the colonial revival "discovery" of Old York was part of a larger cultural encounter: the late-nineteenth-century imaginative reassessment of the Maine coast. We need to recall that explorers from Samuel Champlain to John Smith had portrayed the Maine coast as a scene of desolation. Champlain coined the name "Mount Desert" to describe what he saw as a barren place, not the location of the impressive natural scenery that would later be preserved as Acadia National Park. So, too, Smith dismissed the Maine coast as a desolate and frightening expanse. Much later, the pastoral-minded Timothy Dwight found little to praise in what nature had created on coastal Maine. It was not until the romantic movement of the mid-nineteenth century that artists like Thomas Cole, Frederick Church, and Fitzhugh Lane began to depict the Maine coast as a setting of sublime natural beauty.

Colonial revivalists, including travel writers like Drake, extended this imaginative discovery of the Maine coast. From the rock-bound shore and the lighthouse sentinels (most of which had only been built during the nineteenth-century golden age of trade) to the "old salts" who were so prominent in Sarah Orne Jewett's popular fiction and gray backwater villages like York, Maine was reimagined as a place with a heroic Yankee past, dramatic natural scenery, and undermodernized picturesque communities. (Late-nineteenth-century vacationers were responsible for the transformation of the lobster, which was not widely consumed by Mainers, into a "traditional" seafood and symbol of the state.) In 1884 Winslow Homer, New England's greatest maritime painter, moved to Prout's Neck, twenty-five miles north of York, and produced enduring images of the Maine coast and its hardy inhabitants.[73]

By the time Drake published *The Pine Tree Coast* in 1891, the cultural reinvention of both seaboard Maine and Old York had accelerated along with the colonial revival and the growth of tourism. The very title of Drake's chapter, "A Ramble in Old York," suggests a revised view of the village. "Old York, the country village, stretches itself out along the river banks, while modern York, a new plant in a strange soil, skirts the bluffs and beaches of the seashore," he wrote, leaving no ambiguity about his loyalties. "Old York was located with reference to the serious business of life; recent York, with regard to its idle pleasures only." Drake admired the aged, "typical New England farmhouses" of Old York, "low-walled, slant-roofed, big chimneyed affairs, half smothered in lilacs when I saw them, half hid beneath great masses of foliage that hung about the strong-limbed elms overhead." He saw the allure of Old York for genteel, genealogically minded urbanites. "What city people really like best about country villages," he offered, "is their natural charm, the fitness of things to their place and surroundings, the absence of all straining after effect." Still, Drake worried about the "fashion of universal renovation" that he observed in York. The summer residents of Old York "[are] taking pattern after the more modern houses around them, [and] are everywhere making over their old houses into new ones, so that our villages are in danger of being spoiled by the improving hand of carpenters and masons."[74]

As Drake's comments suggest, innovation and improvement—not just preservation—served as the midwives of Old York's physical and cultural rebirth. Outsiders transported the colonial revival, as well as modern plumbing, to York. Assisted by locals who now saw their past as a cultural and economic resource, summer residents restored homes, renovated public space, and began to organize and display Old York's history. The village was transformed into a cultural refuge—a quaint vestige of Earle's Old New England.

The history of the "village green" reveals the interplay of innovation and preservation in the colonial revival reinvention of Old York. The town had no green or common. Even the meetinghouse lot, which in many towns became the nucleus of a public green in the nineteenth century, was exceptionally small by New England standards. But a green authenticated regional identity; it symbolized communal history, aroused civic pride, and established physical order in the village. Old York required a village green to secure the community's new sense of itself as a genuine corner of Old New England. What came to be called a green developed in tandem with the growth of "summering" in York.

In 1882 the town took the first steps toward creating a green with the remodeling of "our ancient meetinghouse," which dated from 1747. Like many New England meetinghouses that had been placed on elevated terrain to remind Puritans of their priorities, York's First Parish rested on a knoll. But the building, with an old-fashioned side-to-side layout, faced away from the street. Both the interior and exterior of the meetinghouse were altered in 1882; a new, more stately steeple was constructed, for example, that soared twenty feet higher over the village. Most important, the meetinghouse was finally rotated so that it now had the more modern front-to-back design and faced the road and the old cemetery that Samuel Adams Drake had found so unkempt seven years earlier. The modest expanse of land between the front of the church and the road was increasingly referred to as the "village green."[75]

Other changes contributed to the invention of Old York's green. In 1893 the courthouse standing next to the meetinghouse was remodeled. The building, completed in 1811, had served primarily as a town hall after 1832, when York was no longer the legal center of the county. The town hall, perhaps symptomatic of York's declining fortunes, then fell into disrepair; it stood as "a disgrace to the town," one civic leader recalled. In

1893 the town hall was enlarged and substantially remodeled. Soon it was repainted from brown to stark white; indeed, throughout New England the colonial revival extended the "whitewashing" of the village landscape that had been part of the neoclassical visual aesthetic.[76]

By the 1890s, then, a new village was taking shape. The renovated meetinghouse and town house bordered a strip of public land that was beginning to be perceived as a village green. Summer residents, seeking respite from urban life, restored nearby historic homes, outfitting them with modern conveniences like central heating. The Old York Historical and Improvement Society, which was dominated by the mission and money of summer residents, assumed responsibility both for the continuing development of the green and for the preservation and celebration of Old York's colonial heritage.

Village improvement societies dated back to antebellum New England. Comprised of central village residents, these societies often spearheaded the first beautification of town commons in spite of resistance from "outlivers." Across the region in the late nineteenth century village improvement societies acquired a different character. In coastal and rural towns that were evolving into resorts, new or rejuvenated improvement societies received an influx of summer resident volunteers. The societies supplied a civic means through which "cultured" outsiders could promote change and implement a colonial revival agenda. Many of today's beautiful New England village centers bear the marks of "colonial" improvements that were installed in the late nineteenth and early twentieth centuries.[77] York's village green was largely an artifact of this movement.

In 1897, at the same time the *Atlantic Monthly* voiced apprehension over the decline of rural New England, it published a lengthy article touting the work of village improvement societies, supplying a blueprint for action, and rallying women to leadership of the cause. Summer residents, typically the "most highly civilized members of a community," promised to reverse the physical and cultural decay of backwater New England. They "awakened" civic spirit and injected new energy and civility into the communal lifeblood. "Village improvement," the *Atlantic* informed its readers, many of whom doubtless belonged to local societies, "is thus the offspring of the cities, and in most cases it is paid for and engineered by those who have enjoyed city advantages."[78]

Improvement societies labored to beautify and "pastoralize" villages — to enhance their timeless, unmodernized, picturesque qualities. This campaign altered town greens, a preoccupation of village improvers. With the planting of trees, shrubs, and flowers, the paving of walkways, the seeding and mowing of lawns, and the erection of benches, fountains, and historical monuments, the town green became a parklike site, a significant modification of the civic space that John Barber had visually documented.

The *Atlantic* detailed the village improvements that were sweeping through New England and traced their origins to the end of a broom handle. "Everywhere that village improvement takes active form we find women connected with it, for there is something about it congenial to the feminine temperament." Village improvement was an extension of orderly "house-cleaning," domesticity outdoors, with women capable of "neatly dust[ing] every continent."[79]

Almost as if they had memorized its lines, the members of the Old York Historical and Improvement Society enacted the program scripted in the *Atlantic* and launched a campaign to tidy up the village, especially its green. Though men and local residents played major roles in the organization, women and summer people dominated its work. In particular, Mary Sowles Perkins provided leadership and substantial funding for the civic improvement of Old York.

A contemporary of Alice Morse Earle, Mary Perkins (1845–1929) was the daughter of the well-to-do Sowles of St. Albans, Vermont. She met Newton S. Perkins on a trip to Europe. They married and lived in New York City, where Newton served as an Episcopalian minister. After visiting relatives in York in the summer of 1898, Mary and her daughter Elizabeth (1879–1952) purchased a colonial house there. Like other urban vacationers around them, mother and daughter then set about renovating and modernizing the structure, built during the mid-eighteenth century. Using Earle's *Old Time Gardens* as a guide, the two women restored the house's grounds. They ornamented the driveway with new apple trees, used millstones in the walkways, and organized flower beds around a sundial. Apparently, these historic artifacts did not sufficiently evoke Old York and New England's heroic past, so the Perkinses acquired a cigar store Indian. Placed on their property along a bank of the York River, it recalled the pioneer hardships of Old York.[80]

Mary Perkins's passion for York's history quickly thrust her into the leadership of the Historical and Improvement Society. The organization's articles of incorporation are spiced with tributes to the "sturdy, courageous, and God-fearing men and women, who, braving the perils of an unknown sea, abandoned the more fertile land of their fathers, to become the founders of a new people on a new continent." The founders' progeny

FIGURE 28. Old York, Maine, village green (ca. 1900). *Two Hundred and Fiftieth Anniversary: Gorgeana-York, 1652–1902* (1904).

had now scattered across the nation, but the "ancient buildings, landmarks, records and relics, the handicraft and acquisitions of those early settlers" demanded preservation "as memorials sacred to the memory of the honored pioneers and their immediate descendants."[81] The combined historical and village improvement society accelerated the colonial revival reinvention of Old York.

The society imposed new pastoral order on the village green. Elm trees were set out in straight rows with the promise that they would eventually form a canopy over the village green and its streets. Flowers and lilac bushes were planted. Walking paths and grass plots were designed. Indeed, the Chicago garden designer of one summer resident was commissioned to draft a plan for the green. The society was proud of its "turfing" of the village. On the green and between sidewalks and streets it supervised the installation of turf and monitored its mowing. The society also assumed responsibility for the upkeep of the old cemetery (Figure 28).[82]

With a spiffed-up pastoral landscape, a stately, modernized Congregational church, and an enlarged and newly painted white courthouse, York Village finally acquired what its history had not bestowed on the town: the likeness of a familiar regional icon. A 1902 article in the *New England Magazine,* titled "Old York, a Forgotten Seaport," described the progress of the past in "aristocratic York," where the "fragrance of old laces and brocade" made the town a "Mecca for artists, literary folk, and summer visitors." Standing in the village center, the writer took in the "unique charm of the place," with its "shady streets," ancient buildings, and venerable cemetery "bathed in sunshine." Old York endured as a "quaint" village "where it is always afternoon."[83]

Extending its beautification of York outside the green, the Improvement Society added new trees, shrubs, walking paths, and turf throughout the village and beyond. Members complained about advertisements nailed to trees or attached to large boulders in farmers' fields, jarring reminders of the summer trade that proved an economic boon to York. The society sought to camouflage offensive signs of modernity, prevailing on the railroad, for instance, to spruce up its station with shrubs and flowers. Even the name of Railroad Avenue was changed. After a Committee on Roads and Signs conducted research on the original names of streets and lanes, the society began renaming the landscape, mapping the colonial past of prominent families and important places. Railroad Avenue became Langdon Road; new names such as Harmon Lane and Sentry Hill dotted the town map. Perhaps half-humorously, the society resurrected the office of tithingman, the moral watchdog of colonial New England. Members who assumed responsibility for civic improvement in the town's precincts were referred to as "tithingmen."[84]

The Improvement Society also functioned as a historical organization. Throughout colonial revival New England, a changing social landscape and the progress of Saint Anniversary led to the creation of local historical societies. From its founding in 1899 the Old York Historical and Improvement Society worked not only to burnish the town's picturesque image but also to display its history. In the summer of 1899 Mary Perkins hosted a "colonial" party to raise money for the society. A new local newspaper, the *Old York Transcript,* detailed the goings-on of what proved to be the highlight of the summer social season. Nearly one thousand people, the paper claimed, attended the event at the Perkins retreat. Many guests arrived by liveried carriage decked out in colonial garb; well-appointed gentlemen were accompanied by "grand dames in powdered coiffures with huge shell combs." Members of York's summer elite imagined themselves as descendants of colonial gentry and reenacted social rituals that affirmed such an identity. "For the first time York has been infused with the spirit of research," the *Old York Transcript* reported. Residents were "burrowing into the depths of old chests and trunks," retrieving Old York's "ancient historic relics." Two rooms in the Perkins home offered a makeshift exhibit of donated historical items; guests at "Ye Old York Garden Party," as the newspaper described the summer gathering, examined these artifacts of the past.[85] Soon the renovated village acquired a museum. The town jail was restored as the "Old Gaol," a repository where the material remains of Old York were secured under lock and key.

The old jail had survived as yet another dilapidated vestige of York's colonial past. A bulky structure with a gambrel roof, two-inch planks of oak for lining, and a stone wall on one side, it was described by Samuel Adams Drake as a "queer old barrack." Directly across from the court-house, the jail recalled the era when York had been the county seat. Like the courthouse, it fell into disrepair in the late nineteenth century, but it fired the imagination of colonial revival travelers and vacationers. The building was owned by the town and rented out to tenants, who some-times allowed summer visitors to tour the structure for a fee. Given the quaint old jail's appeal to tourists, the town saw fit to complete its repairs in the early 1890s.[86]

By the end of the decade the Historical and Improvement Society had devised an ambitious plan for imaginatively integrating the jail into Old York, the new village center that was taking shape as a picturesque memo-rial to the town's colonial past. William Dean Howells suggested to Mary Perkins that the restored jail could also serve as a museum to house the kinds of artifacts on display at Ye Old York Garden Party. The Garden Party itself raised money for improvements to the town green and for res-toration of the jail, coordinated fronts in the campaign to fashion Old York—an outdoor museum of Old New England.[87]

Its reputed age conferred an aura of antiquity on the "Old Gaol," as it was increasingly and evocatively called. Though modern research con-vincingly shows that the structure was built, altered, and enlarged over nearly a century that stretched from its initial construction in 1719, the re-storers and their supporters claimed that the Old Gaol dated from 1653. In 1899 the local paper summarized the accepted historical wisdom: "Prob-ably the oldest public building now standing in this country north of the old Spanish possessions is the old jail at York village" (Figure 29).[88]

The Old Gaol Museum opened on July 4, 1900, with one speaker heap-ing praise on Mary Perkins for her "energy" "ability," and "magnificent efforts" to preserve Old York's heritage. The museum devoted several rooms to the artifacts and rituals of domestic life. Costumed women dem-onstrated linen and wool spinning and re-created teatime. It was precisely for such "portrayers of old colonial days" that Alice Morse Earle had pro-

FIGURE 29. Old Gaol, York, Maine (ca. 1902). *Two Hundred and Fiftieth Anniversary: Gorgeana-York, 1652–1902* (1904).

duced her handbook *Costume of Colonial Times*. Urbanites and their local supporters nudged Old York to the forefront of the colonial revival. The new "native museum," the *Old York Transcript* predicted with its characteristic boosterism, "will be for York what the Essex Institute is for Salem, the Old South Church for Boston, and Independence Hall for Philadelphia."[89]

In 1900 the newspaper repeatedly called for the addition of Old Home Week to the repertoire of colonial revival activities that were revitalizing Old York. "The Old Home Week idea appeals to one of the strongest of sentiments," the paper declared, "and its very mention seems a very inspiration to arouse feelings so long dormant." Apparently the Historical and Improvement Society was too preoccupied with the village green and the Old Gaol to assume responsibility for yet another heritage project. The *Old York Transcript,* claiming that Old Home Week was popular throughout Maine, found York's failure to adopt the celebration an embarrassment, especially because the governor of New Hampshire, who had introduced the idea, was a summer resident there.[90] Old Home Week finally arrived in York in 1902. It became part of the 250th anniversary of York's founding—a celebration whose rhetoric clarified the meaning of Old York for the colonial revival outsiders who served as the principal custodians of the town's heritage.

The Town of York and the Old York Historical and Improvement Society cosponsored the commemoration in August 1902. A parade, a concert, fireworks, and historical addresses filled the program. The village green served as the stage for most of these commemorative activities. The parade consisted of tableau floats depicting York's history from the seventeenth to the mid-nineteenth century. It wound its way from the new seaside summer communities to the village green, where commemorative rhetoric delineated Old York's historical significance. Only one year-round resident addressed the audience gathered on the green, indicating the extent to which local people had surrendered control of their history.[91]

That history dated back to the 1630s and to the establishment of Gorgeana with the Church of England as the official religion. But the commemoration honored the Puritan takeover in 1652 as the date of York's birth, though the bicentennial of that date in 1852 seems not to have occasioned celebration. Even the growing Episcopalian summer residents, many of whom, like Mary Perkins, were members of the Historical and Improvement Society, endorsed the Puritan conquest of Gorgeana as the beginning of Old York. Moreover, the Old Gaol, a hulking reminder of Puritan punitiveness, was embraced as a sacred relic.

James Phinney Baxter, president of both the Maine Historical Society and the New England Genealogical and Historical Society, delivered the principal address at York's anniversary celebration; he suggested that the colonial revival image of the morally strenuous Puritan was alive in York. "The rule of Massachusetts was severe, but it was beneficial," Baxter intoned, "and the order that it established, though far from perfect, led more settlers of a desirable kind to Maine, thereby improving the character of her citizenship." York developed as a Puritan offshoot, a community "fearing God, loving education, temperance and thrift." Dartmouth College president William J. Tucker, another commemorative speaker, echoed Baxter. "As someone has said about the Puritan," Tucker observed, " 'We may laugh at him when he isn't round, but if we happen to stumble on him we instinctively take off our hats.' "[92] Clearly, a colonial revival appreciation for the moral and physical vigor of New England's founders, lauded by Alice Morse Earle in her best-selling *The Sabbath in Puritan New England* and proclaimed by Puritan statuary, shaped how York's residents dated and retold the community's history. The Old Gaol was an emblem not of religious excesses but of the Puritan institutionalization of order, discipline, and social control. It was a fitting repository for the artifacts of Old York.

Commemorative speakers hailed the ethnic homogeneity that derived from York's Puritan roots. Though some Irish Catholics had invaded York Beach, Old York signaled the Yankee constancy of the town's population across time. York's ethnic purity enhanced its appeal as a refuge for summer residents from America's changing cities. "There is no foreign twang in the York tongue," the *Old York Transcript* boasted in 1899. "Thank God York has happily escaped being a dumping ground for the scum and riff-raff of other nations."[93] Anniversary orators voiced similar sentiments. York preserved its history and its Anglo-Saxon identity, Thomas Nelson Page exulted. "But elsewhere in our country are large numbers of people of other races and with other traditions; people who have not the past that we have, but who, bred under tyranny, have suddenly found themselves in a liberty which they know not how to appreciate or to preserve. They have become a part of our body politic, but are alien as yet to its principles. They must either be absorbed into it or must be held aloof from it." Dartmouth's President Tucker found it reassuring to come to York, "one of the homes of the old stock." The task before educators, he proposed, was "to make blue blood out of red blood" and "red blood out of blue blood."[94]

The Historical and Improvement Society, which had done so much so quickly to promote and consolidate the reinvention of Old York, published the anniversary addresses in its commemorative volume, *Two Hundred and Fiftieth Anniversary: Gorgeana-York, 1652–1902* (1904). Over the next decade two new comprehensive histories provided updated narratives of the town's distinctiveness as a crossroads of Old New England.[95] Colonial revivalists proved to be the imaginative pioneers of Old York.

Heritage and Americanization: "Restoring" the House of the Seven Gables

The commemorative rhetoric at Old York's 250th anniversary underscored how summer residents embraced the village as a haven from the changes vexing urban America. In the hands of the Old York Historical and Improvement Society, the past became a cultural refuge. Alice Morse Earle's nostalgia shaded into reaction and nativism. Yet her books and the work of groups such as the DAR also registered another side of the colonial revival's celebration of Old New England: a civic-minded, if often defensive, commitment to preserve and deploy the past in the service of Americanizing immigrants in the cities.

Salem, Massachusetts, became the site of the House of the Seven Gables Settlement Association, perhaps the most distinctive institutionalization of a useable past during the entire colonial revival era. Caroline Emmerton, Salem's version of Mary Perkins, transformed an extensively altered colonial structure into the most famous house in New England. The House of the Seven Gables, part of the growing colonial revival house museum movement at the turn of the century, mobilized Salem's past as a civic resource in two ways. First, the restored home became a heritage center—a museum and literary shrine of Old Salem within a densely packed ethnic neighborhood. And second, heritage tourists who visited the house generated money to finance the Americanization efforts and social services of the Settlement Association.

The dwelling that came to be known as the House of the Seven Gables dated from 1669. Its evolution over two and a half centuries into the legendary house museum testifies to the shifting currents of regional life, especially the vicissitudes of family and community fortunes. The house's gables, for example, which varied from four, to seven, to eight, to three, and finally back to seven with restoration, reflected the tastes and needs of the structure's multiple owners. When John Turner, identified as a "mariner," built the house on the Salem waterfront, it consisted of four rooms and four gables. Turner prospered, along with the expanding Salem waterfront, into a successful merchant with his own wharf and trading vessels. Profits translated into a larger home. In the late 1670s Turner built a wing that added three new gables to the house.[96]

The thirty-six-year-old merchant died in 1680, and his son and namesake eventually inherited the house. Following in the footsteps of his father, the second John Turner prospered as a merchant, and around 1720 he sought to remodel his residence to reflect his standing in Salem. In accord with eighteenth-century aesthetics, he modified its Gothic elements and enlarged the dwelling to fourteen rooms with eight gables.

The second Turner's oldest son inherited the house in 1769 and appears to have removed one gable. This John Turner fell on hard times, perhaps a result of the disruption of trade caused by the Revolutionary War. In 1782 he was forced to sell the house to merchant and ship captain Samuel Ingersoll, who proceeded to remove four more gables. The house with three gables remained in the Ingersoll family until 1879.[97]

Between 1811 and 1859 the house was the residence of Susannah Ingersoll, the reclusive daughter of the captain and a cousin of Nathaniel Hawthorne. The author undoubtedly visited the home that was located in a declining maritime neighborhood. He may have heard about or observed evidence of gables that had been removed. But during Hawthorne's lifetime and, indeed, until the Turner-Ingersoll house was restored by Caroline Emmerton in 1910, the dwelling possessed only three gables. The economic and cultural mission of Emmerton's restoration depended on securing the connection of Hawthorne and his novel to the house.

By the mid-nineteenth century the house and its surroundings—like Salem as a whole, which never fully recovered from the commercial dislocation surrounding the War of 1812—was far removed from the prosperous commercial world of the first two John Turners. From midcentury forward, the "Turner Lane" neighborhood was radically altered as maritime families and trades gave way to mills, immigrants, and tenements. By 1885 the Naumkeag Steam Cotton Company, established in the late 1830s adjacent to the Turner-Ingersoll house, had mushroomed into a complex of six buildings that employed more than three thousand workers.[98] These immigrant laborers inhabited a tenement district that reached to the doorstep of the old colonial "mansion," which, despite its appearance, some locals called the "House of the Seven Gables." When Susannah Ingersoll's adopted son sold the house to pay off his debts in 1879, it seemed possible that the structure might soon be leveled to make way for new working-class tenements. Largely unoccupied for several years, the house was next purchased by Henry Upton, a music teacher, in 1883. Upton, who would live in the house for twenty-five years, began to promote it as the actual setting of Hawthorne's novel. In 1892, for instance, he published the *House of the Seven Gables Series Dance Music.* Though the dwelling still retained only three gables, Upton encouraged Salem tourists who visited sites such as Hawthorne's birthplace to enter the House of the Seven Gables for twenty-five cents.[99]

In spite of his efforts, there remained considerable skepticism in Salem and beyond over Upton's claims. Consider Edwin M. Bacon's *Literary Pilgrimages in New England* (1902), a popular guide for heritage tourists. Bacon reproduced photographs of the Salem houses where Hawthorne had lived and described the Custom House on Derby Street where the famous author had worked. But he dismissed Upton's dwelling as "the so called 'Seven Gables' house." According to Bacon, "Other old Salem houses have been fixed upon as the house of the romance." The claim that "this Turner Street House," as he called it, was the location of Hawthorne's novel rested on "slender ground." The structure was primarily "interesting as one of the oldest houses in Salem, dating from 1662 [*sic*]." [100]

Bacon's skepticism concerning the authenticity of Upton's claims found support in Hawthorne's novel, which was published in 1851 when the author was living in the western Massachusetts town of Lenox. In the preface, Hawthorne insisted that *The House of the Seven Gables* was a "Romance," not a work of literary realism, and that the house was akin to imaginative "castles in the air." To be sure, Hawthorne had real houses in mind—including the Turner-Ingersoll place—when he described the gabled dwelling in his novel. But, as Bacon suggested, the fictional House of the Seven Gables was essentially "a reproduction in a general way of a style of colonial architecture, examples of which survived to the time of his youth." [101] Hawthorne represented the house as a brooding presence, a decaying emblem of the Puritan heritage, whose legacy he saw around him in antebellum religious revivalists and self-righteous reformers. The odd number of gables registered how the house lacked symmetry and balance, an architectural representation of the moral deformity that, Hawthorne believed, Puritanism had bred into the New England character and regional culture. Caroline Emmerton would have to "restore" the house and overhaul Hawthorne's interpretive furnishings.

Shortly after Edwin Bacon visited the house and four years before Emmerton bought it, Henry James traveled to Salem. James was touring New England after a twenty-five-year absence from America. "It never failed," he wrote of his travels in 1904, "that if moving about I made, under stress, an inquiry, I should prove to have made it of a flagrant foreigner." In pursuit of Old Salem and Hawthornean landmarks, James asked for directions to the House of the Seven Gables. A "crude" young man "stared at me as a remorseless Italian—as remorseless, at least, as six months of Salem could leave him." With the assistance of an "American" boy, James made it to Turner Street, only to discover "a large, untidy industrial quarter" and then the "anti-climax of the Seven Gables." He was led to a "shapeless object by the waterside," and his youthful host "invited me to take [it], if I could, for the Seven Gables." A disappointed James admitted, "The weak, vague domiciliary presence at the end of the lane may have been . . . the idea of the admirable book" by Hawthorne, but that conclusion required "a leap into dense darkness." [102]

Nevertheless, the enterprising Henry Upton's tours of the house generated more than two hundred dollars a year and suggested revenue-producing possibilities for Caroline Emmerton. She purchased the house from Upton in 1908, saved it once and for all from the threat of conversion to tenements, and refurbished it as "The House of the Seven Gables," a monument both for tourists and for the immigrants who lived in its shadow. Emmerton secured Hawthorne's ties to the house, capitalizing on his canonical literary status to further the work of heritage and social uplift in Salem. Her colonial revival "restoration" played several historical tricks on Hawthorne, not the least of which was to use the conservative writer's work and literary reputation in the cause of social reform — a topic that he so mordantly satirized in his fiction, including *The House of the Seven Gables*.

Emmerton's family background resembled that of Mary Perkins. Emmerton's paternal and maternal grandfathers had both profited handsomely from Salem's maritime trade. In particular, the investments in Western railroads of John Bertram, her maternal grandfather, laid the foundation of substantial cross-generational wealth. His daughter, Caroline Emmerton's mother, came to be known as "the richest woman in Salem."[103]

Emmerton's family bequeathed her not only wealth but also a legacy of engagement in Salem's civic life. When her grandfather Bertram died in 1882, the *Salem Evening News* described him as "one of the noblest benefactors Salem ever had." Emmerton's father and paternal grandfather both served as Salem aldermen. Her mother was active in Salem charitable organizations as a board member and a philanthropist. Caroline, who never married, followed in her mother's footsteps. In the early 1890s, while still in her twenties, she launched her extensive career of public service in Salem, joining the board of a home operated by the Family Service Association. Emmerton helped to found the first settlement association in Salem, which led to the creation of the House of the Seven Gables Museum.

In the winter of 1908, Emmerton and the other women of the newly established Salem Settlement Committee took over the Seaman's Bethel that stood next to Henry Upton's home, soon to be physically transformed into the House of the Seven Gables and promoted in ways that the music teacher could not have imagined. At the Bethel, the Settlement Association began offering classes in sewing, handicrafts, and dancing for the immigrant residents of the Turner Street neighborhood. "In passing and repassing the House of Seven Gables, on my way to and from the Bethel," Emmerton recalled, "the idea occurred to me that the old house would have many advantages as a Settlement headquarters." A restored house would serve as a literary shrine and museum of Salem's heritage for both tourists and immigrants and would produce revenue to support settlement work. Emmerton bought the house in 1908, began restoring it, and soon formed the House of the Seven Gables Settlement Association.[104]

Her efforts marked a unique convergence of two late nineteenth- and early twentieth-century developments: the growth of house museums and of social settlements. Between 1895 and 1910 the number of house museums in America increased fivefold, from twenty to one hundred.[105] Restored historic houses and homes of writers became sites for the colonial revival display of Old New England's domestic heritage that filled Alice Morse Earle's books. Emmerton was undoubtedly aware of Earle's work. She may have also been influenced by the domestic period rooms that opened in 1907 in Salem's Essex Institute, one of the first museum exhibits of its kind in the country. In addition to exhibiting domestic heritage, museums like the restored House of the Seven Gables captured the colonial revival's architectural antimodernism. A 1913 article in the *Boston Evening Transcript,* which someone clipped and saved at the House of the Seven Gables, summarized such antimodernism: "New England has been blessed with a wealth of fine old houses. They were built before the European traditions of the dignified and picturesque workmanship died out of the craft of American carpenters—when carpentry was a fine art." The newspaper went on to complain that, with the growth of former country towns, "these buildings come under the hammer. Honest timbers and choice architecture go to make room for shoddy walls of the jere-builder." [106] On several levels, from nostalgic domesticity to architectural antimodernism, old homes occupied the imaginative center of the colonial revival.

At the same time that house museums spread, settlements multiplied in America's burgeoning cities. The number of settlement houses providing social, educational, and recreational services in immigrant neighborhoods rose from six in 1891 to four hundred by 1910.[107] The house museum and social settlement movements had features in common. Both preached a gospel of domesticity, the settlement house, for example, teaching household skills and middle-class etiquette. Both expressed a colonial revival, antimodern appreciation for the domestic arts; immigrant handicrafts, for instance, represented one of the few elements of ethnic heritage that settlement workers deemed worthy of preservation. Moreover, both house museums and social settlements recalled the social intimacy and scale of life of an older small-town America. As Caroline Emmerton put it in 1910, "Our spirit is best expressed by the word 'fellowship'—that fellowship which is so natural a part of life in the villages and small towns, and which often gets lost sight of in the cities." An early annual report of the House of the Seven Gables Settlement Association characterized the organization as part of a restored neighborly New England village: "A settlement is, briefly expressed, a home composed of homes and located among homes. Like its prototype it is a place of intimate relationships and in the largest definition, a birthplace of loftiest ideals and aspirations."[108] A site of progressive reform, the settlement nevertheless reflected elements of the nostalgia for an earlier, simpler way of life characteristic of the colonial revival house museum movement.

The founders of house museums and settlements also shared an interest in propagating American heritage among immigrants. A leader of Boston's South End House, who also served as an executive of the Immigration Restriction League, observed in 1905 that settlements were "bits of neutral territory where the descendants of the Puritans may meet the chosen leaders among the immigrants from Italy, Russian, and the Levant."[109] But the "neutral" South End settlement house engaged in extensive Americanization efforts that included escorting immigrants to historic sites in Boston. "The historical and literary associations of old houses," Emmerton proclaimed, "must surely help in making American citizens of our boys and girls."[110] And Salem, whose population was approximately thirty-five thousand when Emmerton bought the property on Turner Street, was a heavily immigrant city whose future troubled longtime residents. As one native wrote in the *Salem Evening News,* immigrants "already hold the balance of power in city politics, and if they are not given the hand of fellowship and assimilated and inspired with respect for American ideals and American institutions, they will get absorbed and go to swell the columns of socialism, militant laborism, and other isms."[111] The House of the Seven Gables Settlement Association became a purveyor of heritage for colonial revival tourists and of social services and Americanization for Salem's immigrant workers.

In 1908 Emmerton hired Joseph Chandler, one of New England's leading restoration architects, who had worked on the Paul Revere House in Boston. He labored through 1909 under Emmerton's supervision. She had decided to recapture "the atmosphere of an old Salem house in 1840," when Hawthorne was already a successful writer and before mills, immigrants, and tenements rearranged the city's waterfront. To create a "home-likeness instead of the deadness of a museum," Emmerton allowed that the house's furnishings required "a blending of periods." The house would reflect Salem's post-Revolutionary era of maritime prosperity, a less problematic epoch of the community's past than the colonial period with its record of witchcraft. In pursuing her "restoration," Emmerton had to deflect the kind of doubts about the house's authenticity that Edwin Bacon had expressed several years earlier. She acknowledged the misgivings of "Salem people who were skeptical" that there was a real House of the Seven Gables or that the Turner-Ingersoll-Upton dwelling was that house.[112]

Yet her restoration and the financial prospects of her settlement hinged on securing Hawthorne's ties to the house. Chandler's work and the way the restored house was exhibited transformed literary romance into an architectural assertion of realism; the gabled dwelling became an authentic artifact of Hawthorne's life, not a projection of his imagination. Emmerton restored four gables to reach the requisite seven, insisting that Hawthorne observed evidence of or heard about the other gables during his visits to the house. Among other "restorations," Emmerton recreated Hepzibah's penny shop from the novel. On expanding his house in 1678, the first John Turner had converted a kitchen into a shop where he could merchandise small wares, a common practice of merchants at the time. Emmerton used this precedent to reconstruct Hawthorne's fictional store, but with a commercial purpose that extended beyond penny candy. "Old pictures, old china, old furniture," the *Salem Evening News* reported, "everything has been provided . . . , down to the [novel's] little tinkling door bell to announce the buyer."[113]

Through Emmerton, Hawthorne presided over the second birth of the House of the Seven Gables, not as literary conceit but as realistic museum (Figures 30 and 31). Whenever possible, Emmerton installed Hawthorne and his novel in the restored house. She conceded that Hawthorne's "exuberant fancy decks out the house with many details not to be found in the original, but fundamentally this was the house through which his characters moved."[114] Guides reinforced this message of the restoration. One early visitor described the interpretive realism that Emmerton had institutionalized. "This was Miss Hepzibah's bedroom: everything here is just as Hawthorne saw it last," a young female guide announced. "All that we do is to keep it well dusted. We never move or disturb anything." Emmerton produced a special edition of *The House of the Seven Gables* so that visitors could read the novel in the museum's colonial revival garden while sipping tea.[115]

FIGURE 30. The House of the Seven Gables before restoration. The Turner-Ingersoll-Upton house had only three gables before the structure was restored. Two of the gables are seen in this photograph. Courtesy of the Society for the Preservation of New England Antiquities.

Domestic classes for immigrants were held in the House of the Seven Gables during its first year of operation. Revenues from the house also supported settlement activities at the Seaman's Bethel, which Emmerton eventually bought, moved across the street from the museum, and renamed Turner Hall. In the first year admission fees to the house and sales in the tearoom generated nearly two thousand dollars, almost a third of the settlement's operating budget. In 1911 Emmerton purchased the Hathaway House (1682), one of Salem's ancient structures that served as the city's Old Bakery, where residents had taken their beans and brown bread. Moving the Old Bakery to the site of the House of the Seven Gables, she again linked preservation, heritage, and commercial opportunity. Classes in sewing, cooking, and housekeeping were transferred from the House of the Seven Gables to the Old Bakery. In the summer, the Old Bakery also provided lodging for visitors to the Hawthorne shrine.[116]

FIGURE 31. The House of the Seven Gables after restoration. Five of the gables are seen in this photograph, taken after Emmerton restored the house. Courtesy of the Society for the Preservation of New England Antiquities.

Emmerton eventually bought and moved another old dwelling to what had developed into the colonial revival heritage and social service complex of the House of the Seven Gables Settlement Association. Visitors to the site, which was rapidly becoming the most famous house museum in New England, not only purchased an encounter with the region's fabled literary heritage; they found lodging and food—eventually even shore dinners—as well as antiques for sale on the former property of John Turner. The money paid by tourists supported the social work and Americanization efforts of the settlement. Emmerton had created, a visiting journalist later accurately observed, "a neighborhood center to interpret America to the foreign-descended factory peoples of Salem." [117]

The restored House of the Seven Gables proclaimed Emmerton's goal of preserving the past for both native-born and immigrant Salemites. From the beginning the House of the Seven Gables Settlement Association functioned as a center of heritage and Americanization activities in Salem. Such civic work gained urgency in 1910. Within months of the opening of the museum, Salem was convulsed by strikes in the shoe industry. Labor unrest provoked fears of mounting violence and radical political protest.[118] Amid a rising tide of immigrants and growing alarm over labor unrest, a new monument to Salem's past was erected—a grand human figure that was a visual companion to the bulky, angular House of the Seven Gables and that hovered like a moral sentry over Salem's changed social order. In 1911 noted sculptor Henry Kitson completed a statue of Roger Conant, the first permanent settler in Salem (Figure 32). Situated next to the common in the center of the city, the magnificent figure rivaled Saint-Gaudens's statue of *The Puritan,* to which it bears a striking resemblance. Bestride an eight-foot boulder, the stern, manly Conant towered over pedestrians; like the restored House of the Seven Gables, the sculpture served to inspire the native-born minority and to encourage respect for Salem's heritage among the city's immigrant throng.

The Americanization and heritage appreciation work of the House of the Seven Gables Settlement Association did not acquire the severity that seemed to be cast into Conant's bronze figure. Settlements were envisioned as bridges across the class and ethnic divisions that eroded older experiences of community, though colonial Salem itself had been torn by strife. "We are not here to work *for* them but *with* them," the *First Annual Report* of Emmerton's settlement association noted of the Turner Street neighbors. The children and adults who participated in the settlement's classes and clubs represented nine different nationalities. Irish, Polish, and Russian residents dominated, the last two groups comprising the most recent immigrants with the greatest need for heritage and civic tutoring.[119]

In addition to the interest in the past stimulated by the restoration and operation of the house museum, the settlement pursued a variety of programs to Americanize the neighborhood. Classes and clubs welcomed more than seventy-five children and adults each day. Instead of "the old race prejudice," the *Salem Evening News* noted in 1911, these immigrants to the "quaint" settlement encountered the "realization that they are first of all Americans." Thanksgiving parties introduced newcomers to New England's heroic past. Children participated in patriotic plays with colonial revival subject matter. In 1912 the settlement's girls performed a *Pair of Scissors,* described as a play taking "one back to the time of Betsy Ross" and staged with "quaint costumes and manners of speech [that] are decidedly

FIGURE 32. Henry Kitson, *Roger Conant* (1911), Salem, Massachusetts. This striding, imposing figure harks back to earlier colonial revival Puritan statuary, especially the work of Saint-Gaudens. The statue became a visual companion to the restored House of the Seven Gables, both serving to link the Salem newly altered by immigrants to the city's early history. Photograph by the author.

picturesque." At the same time, the Polish, Irish, and Russian Jewish boys of the settlement performed *A True Patriot,* a play about Washington and the Revolutionary Army. "Long live George Washington, and may his country produce many like him!" the final lines declared.[120]

The Settlement Association offered American heritage lectures in Yiddish and Polish. In 1913 eighty people attended a Yiddish lecture, "A Trip through the United States," that exhibited "lantern slides" of the "different sections of the country." The same year Polish neighbors heard a lecture in their native language on "The Story of the American People." These presentations furthered the ongoing naturalization work of the settlement.[121]

Beyond such activities and the restoration of the House of the Seven Gables that helped fund them, the commitment of Caroline Emmerton and the settlement to the preservation of colonial revival heritage and Americanization is best exemplified by the spectacular *Pageant of Salem,* held in 1913. Community historical pageants emerged as one of the most popular heritage activities of the late colonial revival. During the first two decades of the twentieth century, pageants were staged in cities and towns across the country, with New England the site of a large number. Pageants represented a Progressive era use of the past. They endeavored to reaffirm—or create—a sense of community, a common history, and a public past in the face of the changes that buffeted Salem.[122] Linked to community uplift, pageants acted as another cultural vehicle for the colonial revival's heritage politics. Not surprisingly, then, the *Pageant of Salem* became a direct extension of Emmerton's work with the House of Seven Gables and its Settlement Association.

The association sponsored the pageant as a fund-raiser and Emmerton wrote the script. To produce the four-day extravaganza, Emmerton hired Margaret Maclaren Eager, an experienced pageant director whose credits included the Pilgrim festival *Old Plymouth Days and Ways.* The pageant of Old Salem proved to be one of the region's largest and earned two thousand dollars for the settlement. Its Americanizing narrative stopped well short of the era when immigrants began to dominate life in Salem.[123]

The pageant was staged on the grounds of a local country club over four afternoons and evenings in June. The cast consisted of more than a thousand people, among them representatives of numerous historical societies on Boston's North Shore. Salem's history unfolded in a series of scenes that began with Native Americans and their welcome of Roger Conant, followed by the arrival of English settlers. Caroline Emmerton, who was a Unitarian, could not avoid acknowledging, as the program described it, "The strain of superstition and intolerance which was in the Puritan character." Scenes were devoted to the banishment of Roger Williams from Salem, the persecution of Quakers, and the "delusion" of witchcraft. Emmerton seemed to be calling for a new tolerance in Salem, one that would extend to immigrants as they made strides toward Americanization.[124]

The privileged era in Emmerton's pageant of Old Salem extended from the Revolution to the age of Hawthorne, which was enshrined in the restored house. The pageant staged major events from Salem's Revolutionary history. It commemorated the "Commercial Days" in the decades that followed independence, then turned to "The Salem of Romance: Nathaniel Hawthorne." For dramatic presentation, Emmerton adapted the upbeat last chapter of *The House of the Seven Gables*—the departure of Clifford, Hepzibah, Phoebe, and Holgrave for the deceased Judge Pyncheon's country estate. "The name of Nathaniel Hawthorne is indissolubly connected with Salem and his birthplace," the pageant program proclaimed, "and the houses in which he lived and wrote his masterpieces of the language are Meccas for travelers and lovers of his books."[125] After the tribute to Hawthorne and *The House of the Seven Gables,* the pageant's history of Salem closed with the entrance of the Grand Army of the Republic.

It was estimated that as many as twelve thousand people saw the *Pageant of Salem*.[126] No one speculated on the number of immigrants in the audiences. But clearly the pageant's history of Old Salem was not intended just to raise money from the native-born to be used for immigrants. It was designed, like the restored House of the Seven Gables itself, to commemorate a public communal past—a cultural plane on which the native-born and assimilating immigrants could meet.

Emmerton's dedication to preserving and using the past for reformist ends included her membership on the board of the Society for the Preservation of New England Antiquities (SPNEA). Established by William Summer Appleton in 1910, SPNEA was the first regionwide historic preservation organization in the United States. It pursued restorations similar to the House of the Seven Gables, but with a closer adherence to historical authenticity. SPNEA eventually sponsored a journal, *Old-Time New England,* that extended the colonial revival's reconstruction of the region's early history.[127]

But the founding of SPNEA also signaled something new: the beginnings of the professionalization of heritage work, which would crowd out women and amateurs like Caroline Emmerton and Mary Perkins. These two colonial revival leaders, as well as Alice Morse Earle, represent a bygone period when women served as major guardians of regional cultural heritage and identity and when the celebration of Old New England underwrote the politics of domesticity, antimodernism, and Americanization.

The North Country and
Regional Identity
From Robert Frost to the Rise
of *Yankee* Magazine, 1914–1940

In *The Middle West: Its Meaning in American Culture,* James R.
Shortridge examines the westward migration of one region's heartland. Midwestern identity coalesced in the late
nineteenth and early twentieth centuries as a pastoral region of small towns and independent farmers. So rooted
was Midwestern identity in such pastoralism that, with the
emergence of an urban-industrial order represented by Chicago, Cleveland, and Detroit, the region's perceived core
migrated toward the Kansas-Nebraska plains to preserve
an image long cultivated by insiders and outsiders.[1]

As the history of Midwestern identity suggests, regions
are artifacts of the imagination as well as geographic and
cultural entities. Regions not only reflect the varied local
cultures that form part of the mosaic of American diversity;
they also bestow spatial and conceptual order on the sprawling continental United States. But to supply national geocultural order, regional identities require periodic imaginative upkeep. Shifts in the imagined centers of regional life
comprise one response to change that enables entrenched
images to persist and to perpetuate familiar perceptions of
America's geocultural order.

Between the turn of the twentieth century and the Great
Depression the "real" New England underwent an imaginative migration similar to the Midwest's. With the urban,
industrial, and ethnic transformation of southern New England, the regional heartland seemed to shift northward.
Old New England acquired an increasingly fixed geographic location; it endured in the Yankee towns and vil-

lages of Maine, New Hampshire, and Vermont. The regional periphery was reimagined as the new center of New England identity.[2]

During the colonial era eastern Massachusetts, the landfall for the bulk of participants in the Great Migration, served as the hub of New England and its clergy-driven culture of print. With access to printing presses and financial support from well-off parishioners, for example, Boston ministers dominated the Puritan world of print. Their publications far surpassed the writings of their colleagues in other parts of New England, enabling the clergy of Boston and its surroundings to shape Puritan piety and regional identity through printed sermons, jeremiads, and providential histories.[3] In the early republic, however, the New England heartland seemed to migrate to the Connecticut River Valley. Jedidiah Morse, Timothy Dwight, and Noah Webster—influential spokesmen for New England's national regionalism so provocatively dramatized by the Hartford Convention—imagined the pastoral villages of the Connecticut Valley as the region's republican heartland. A generation later, with the New England literary renaissance and the propagation of the Pilgrim epic, eastern Massachusetts reemerged as the regional heartland—though not without imaginative competition from the Connecticut Valley. The Yankee continued to be heavily identified with Connecticut, and image makers like Harriet Beecher Stowe and John Barber persisted in representing the state as New England's "land of steady habits." From the colonial era to the Civil War, then, the real New England shifted between competing imaginative strongholds in Massachusetts and Connecticut.

In the decades after the Civil War, the land of steady habits began to drift northward, a gradual geographic relocation that accompanied the colonial revival's cultural deployment of Old New England. In fact, as urban, industrial, and ethnic shifts transformed southern New England, colonial revivalists increasingly associated Old New England with a subregion less altered by change: the more rural and ethnically homogeneous northern states and the hill country of western New England that resembled them. Alice Morse Earle's antiquing forays into northern New England and her references to (and illustrations of) its old-fashioned customs, signaled the growing colonial revival imaginative investment in the geography that Robert Frost would poeticize beginning with his breakthrough book, *North of Boston* (1914). So, too, the summer colonization of Old York, Maine, represented a broader geographic discovery of the persistence in the north country of authentic New England—a world of Yankee villages where an agricultural way of life prevailed.

A slowly evolving identification of Old New England with the north country helps explain the alarmist essays of the 1890s that were filled with portentous descriptions of rural life in the region. Perceived as a cultural redoubt of Old New England, the rural North and its fortunes acquired a new visibility. Journalistic Jeremiahs worried over the plight of the agricultural economy, the migration of young people, and the physical and mental fitness of those who stayed behind. To be sure, northern New Englanders, long accustomed to harvesting rocks, faced new challenges in the late nineteenth century, particularly from Midwestern farmers. But urban commentators, already distressed by the changing face of Boston, Worcester, and Hartford, exaggerated the peculiar ailments of the traditional New England world north of Boston. Heavy migration from farming communities, after all, was occurring throughout the United States, not just in northern New England.[4]

By the turn of the century, the north country had achieved a measure of social and economic stability. The growth of commercial dairy farming (particularly in Vermont) sustained many rural families and communities. Harvey Pearley Hood, for instance, a Vermont native who moved to Derry, New Hampshire, where aspiring poet Frost took up residence in 1900, established the largest dairy corporation in New England in the late nineteenth century. From their Derry farm, H. P. Hood and his sons shipped southward to Boston milk and eggs purchased from New Hampshire farmers.[5]

Moreover, as the rebirth of Old York suggests, tourism also helped bring economic stability and even prosperity to numerous communities in northern New England. Beginning in the late nineteenth century, state economic development officials capitalized on colonial revival nostalgia for the pastoral world of Old New England. Old Home Week was only the most obvious of their innovations. From Vermont to Maine state officials took over fish and game management in the interest of tourism. Economic development and conservation merged to re-create and preserve pastoral elements of an imagined Old New England. States restocked waterways and forests and regulated hunting and fishing. They also widely advertised farm property for sale, encouraging turn-of-the-century urbanities to purchase a piece of Old New England.[6]

Indeed, through the early decades of the twentieth century, aggressive state-sponsored campaigns to promote the northern states countered reports of rural decline and shaped the image of the subregion as the unchanging, pastoral Yankee heartland. The rise of the automobile opened access to the north country for visitors and summer residents seeking temporary refuge from the spreading mills, immigrant neighborhoods, and triple-deckers of southern New England. By the 1920s state authorities in northern New England responded to increased automobile ownership and travel with improved roads, numbered routes, and promotional campaigns that were soon distilled into official slogans like "Unspoiled Vermont" and "Maine: Vacationland."[7]

In 1922 the *Nation* magazine initiated a series of essays in which established writers examined the individual American states. Three pieces on New England sketched a new geography of regional identity reaching back to the colonial revival. Dorothy Canfield Fisher, a successful fiction writer who abandoned New York City to reestablish family roots in Vermont, was the first contributor. "Vermont, like some of the remote valleys in the Pyrenees," Fisher gushed, "has always been too far out of the furiously swirling current of modern life to be much affected by it or to dread its vagaries." Two months later Robert Herrick published an essay on Maine that plotted the latitudes of the new regional heartland: "whatever may be left of that famous Old New England, some time Puritan, always Protestant, will be found today more purely and abundantly in Maine than elsewhere. The types of faces, the habits, and the ideas are much like those I remember in Massachusetts of thirty years ago." Maine stood as the "last stronghold of the Puritan," Herrick concluded, failing to note the surge of the Ku Klux Klan, whose ranks in the state would number fifty thousand by 1924. In support of Herrick's cultural reading of the regional landscape, a third essay on New England appeared in the *Nation* series in 1922 — a nativist screed on Massachusetts. "Massachusetts: A Roman Conquest" was written by John Macy, who regretted that "Irish and Catholic are roughly synonymous with the Bay State." He lamented that its cities were filled with "Italians, Canadian-French, Portuguese, [and] Poles, who are spiritually subject to the Celtic American cardinal."[8]

Robert Frost, at the time a recently acclaimed regional bard who was a poetic publicist for northern New England but certainly no nativist, had been asked to contribute to the *Nation*'s state series. He refused, expressing uneasiness with the tone of the essays.[9] But a year later Frost published *New Hampshire,* a Pulitzer Prize–winning book of verse that affirmed the people, folkways, and pastoral beauty of the state where he had located his poetic voice — and then moved on to Vermont. Between 1914 and 1928 Frost produced four books of poetry with titles rooted in the geography of northern New England. In those critically well-received and popular volumes and in his far-flung public performances, Frost increasingly assumed the persona of the Yankee farmer-poet speaking for northern New England. Frost was not only a versifier who appealed to literary sophisticates; he was also the poet of people not particularly fond of poetry. Yet in the learned paper trail that constitutes Frost criticism, the relationship of the popular and prolific Yankee poet-performer to shifts in regional identity remains unexplored.

For more than two decades from the publication of *North of Boston* through the American regionalist movement of the Great Depression, Frost performed important cultural work in the imaginative relocation of the New England heartland. *North of Boston,* the new cultural formation around which regional identity cohered, also received a boost from Calvin Coolidge, the first New Englander to occupy the presidency in nearly three generations. Silent Cal appeared to be the offspring of the same cultural terrain that produced Frost and the hill folk who were the subjects of his poetry. Furthermore, the Yankee values that Frost poeticized—often, to be sure, with irony and doubt—and that Coolidge seemed to embody emerged as a regional inheritance that promised to sustain northern New England in the depression.

In the midst of economic collapse, with southern New England in particular reeling from shutdown mills, high unemployment, and labor unrest, a New Hampshire–based magazine launched what would become an impressive publishing history. *Yankee,* which became enormously successful regionwide, initially riveted on the folkways of northern New England.

Robert Frost and the Imaginative Rise of the North Country

Robert Frost is one of the poetic giants of New England and American literature, though dissenters have argued that he deserves nothing more than advanced placement in the school of local color writers. Like Sarah Orne Jewett's more elegiac rendering of Maine in *The Country of the Pointed Firs,* a consummation of themes and aesthetics associated with local color writers, Frost's *North of Boston* represented the hill country as at once a diminished world and a location of physical beauty where the regional character, in all of its gnarled dignity and tautness, endured. It would be decades before critics unpacked Frost's poetry, fully disclosing the irony and the doubt—the vein of dark humanism—that ran through many of his poems and seemed to elevate the farmer-poet above the local color plane. Nevertheless, from the appearance of *North of Boston* critics reckoned that they were dealing with a new Walt Whitman: an indigenous and realistic American–New England poet who used blank verse to poeticize the prickly humanity of ordinary folk.

To segments of a new middlebrow reading public that helped make his books best-sellers and that swelled the audiences at his readings, Frost was something of the Calvin Coolidge of American poetry.[10] Colloquial, accessible, aphoristic, concretely evocative—Frost, in his poetry and public persona, refuted chronicles of regional decline and reaffirmed the historical tenacity of the Yankee character and the vitality of New England culture. After the surprising success of *North of Boston,* Frost increasingly warmed to the role of Yankee spokesman for New England, the Will Rogers of regional identity.

Frost published verse for six decades, and critics have erected their own towering edifice of print on top of the poet's oeuvre. New discoveries still spring from close readings of his poems. Critics continue to gauge the weight of the local and the universal in his work; others add to our understanding of the dark ambiguity beneath the poet's realistic and seemingly transparent surfaces. Such readings typically proceed with unexamined assumptions concerning his relationship to New England. Moreover, not a single critic has related Frost's emergence between World War I and the depression to changes in regional life and identity.[11]

Frost not only participated in a new regionalist movement that swept through American culture by the 1930s. He also increasingly capitalized on and, more important, contributed to the imaginative shift of the real New England to the north country. Frost fled from Lawrence, Massachusetts, the so-called immigrant city, an industrial smudge on the regional landscape where residents spoke more than three dozen languages by 1890, when the poet attended high school there. His flight to Derry, New Hampshire, and the poetry that ensued might be read as part of a larger imaginative withdrawal from industrial-ethnic New England. Just north of Derry stood Manchester—New Hampshire's version of Lawrence. Manchester was dominated by the Amoskeag Company, a complex of mills that comprised the largest textile operation in the world. Thus, although it was not as transformed as southern New England, the north country had its own industrial order and immigrant presence. Yet Frost's "realistic" poetic representation of the area all but obliterated evidence that undermined its rural, Yankee attributes.

Literary critics, who have been understandably preoccupied with the aesthetics of Frost's verse, have usually assumed that the poet was himself a Yankee farmer and not someone who began primarily as an observer of country ways. Seizing on biographical information that disputes such a facile assumption and on evidence that Frost deliberately cultivated the myth of the Yankee farmer-poet, a few critics have loosened his ties to New England, presumably making possible more universal readings of his poetry.[12] The cultural historian of regional identity is less interested in sifting through evidence for and against Frost's New England credentials or in appraising his literary achievement. Rather, struck both by the poet's increasing geographic rootedness in the Yankee north country and by his popularity as a versifier and performer, the interpreter of regional identity poses a different line of inquiry: What cultural work did Frost's poetry and his celebrity perform? How did his best-selling books and packed readings relate to shifts in regional identity and to the revival of regional feeling in American life that reached a peak in the 1930s and that, in New England, found expression in cultural productions like *Yankee* magazine?

New England and its Yankee ways constituted something of an acquired identity for Frost, not a direct birthright. He was born in San Francisco in 1874 to a father who despised and repudiated his New England roots. William Prescott Frost Jr. had been born in New Hampshire and raised in Lawrence, Massachusetts, where the poet's grandfather had sought work in the textile industry and eventually rose to mill overseer. When the Civil War broke out, young William became hardened in his Southern sympathies and ran away from home in a failed attempt to enlist in the Confederate army. Nearly a decade after the war, William reaffirmed his rejection of New England and his abiding Southern sentiments by naming his son Robert E. Lee Frost.[13]

By then William had fled to San Francisco with his wife Isabelle, an immigrant from Scotland whom he had met in Pennsylvania. William worked for several San Francisco newspapers and threw himself into California Democratic Party politics and into a life of frustration drowned in drink. When he died of consumption in 1885 at the age of thirty-four, William had accumulated no wealth for his wife, the ten-year-old future poet, or his younger sister. Grandfather Frost paid for the family to travel to Lawrence, where "Robbie" received a belated introduction to the New England his father had scorned.[14]

The California son hardly embraced the gritty cotton mill, immigrant world that constituted his father's boyhood home. Lawrence and all it represented would never find a place in Frost's poeticizing of New England. But even the rural Yankee world, which connected Frost to a Puritan-Yankee paternal heritage that reached back to the seventeenth century and for which he would become an "authentic" poetic voice, failed for years to stir an identification with New England. Shortly after their arrival in Lawrence, the Frosts moved just across the state border to Salem, New Hampshire, where Isabelle accepted a teaching position. "At first I disliked the Yankees," Frost recalled. "They were cold. They seemed narrow to me. I could not get used to them."[15]

Into early adulthood Salem and Lawrence largely defined the regional and familial world that Frost inhabited. He lived in Salem but attended school in Lawrence. In 1892 he graduated from Lawrence High School, serving as covaledictorian with the young woman he would marry three years later. With his grandfather's financial assistance, Frost enrolled at Dartmouth College but dropped out before the end of the first semester. He then worked at a series of jobs that included spells in Lawrence mills, where ten-hour days and six-day weeks were the norm.[16] Frost seems to have developed no bond with the immigrant laborers who toiled around him, and his experience in the mill failed to yield material for his poetry. Indeed, in the 1930s proletarianized critics, who accepted his preferred self-image as a farmer-poet and who were unfamiliar with his urban, industrial background, would take Frost to task for his avoidance of social criticism and for the homilies to rural self-reliance that they found in his verse.

In 1897 Frost made a second, more successful foray into the privileged world of New England collegiate life, which would further distinguish him from the ordinary Yankee farmers for whom he was later received as a spokesman. Once again with his grandfather's support, Frost enrolled at Harvard as a special student and spent two years studying the classics. When he left Cambridge in 1899, the twenty-five-year-old Frost, who had been writing poetry since high school, was still not a Yankee farmer-poet in the making. As one perceptive student of Frost has argued, the poet's "background was more urban, . . . literary and sophisticated than he usually indicated."[17]

Frost's claim on a farming background derived from his nearly decade-long experience raising chickens in Derry, New Hampshire, where in 1900 his grandfather bought him a farm. Derry, a small town just north of Salem, was heavily agricultural but also contained shoe factories. Though something less than an enthusiastic and energetic farmer, Frost sold the eggs from his chickens to H. P. Hood and Sons. When his grandfather died in 1901, he was the beneficiary of a five-hundred-dollar yearly annuity. He seemed to lose heart in farming, and by 1906 he turned to teaching at a private academy in Derry. Within a few years Frost moved into an apartment in Derry's central village and rented his farm. Under the provisions of his grandfather's will, he did not acquire full title to the property until 1911. As soon as the farm became his own, he sold it.[18] Thus, even in Derry Frost was not rooted to the soil. Yet he would soon be hailed as an indigenous Yankee voice, the farmer-poet of "those who stayed behind."

Like his father, Frost fled New England. He moved his family to England in 1912, and in a matter of months the thirty-eight-year-old poet placed his first book of verse with a London publisher. *A Boy's Will* was far removed from the regional life and sensibility that would soon dominate Frost's poetry; the volume has been accurately described as a late romantic fermentation, a lyrical account "of the artist as a young man."[19] Frost had been publishing poems and collecting rejections for nearly two decades with little recognition. Perhaps influenced by local color writers such as Sarah Orne Jewett, who published in the same journals where Frost struggled to place poems, his early work shows some evidence of the place-bound direction that his verse would take. Yet even as late as 1912, Frost had not yet discovered the creative possibilities of a poetic vision grounded in the Yankee rural world of northern New England. "If there is any virtue in Location—but don't think I think there is," he wrote to an American editor shortly after his arrival in England. "I know where the poetry must come from if it comes."[20]

But soon Frost was at work on *North of Boston*. His English experience sharpened his own sense of Yankee identity. As he admitted to the same American editor in mid-1913, "we are very homesick in this English mud. We can't hope to be happy long out of New England. I never knew how much of a Yankee I was till I had been out of New Hampshire a few months." Among sophisticated literary John Bulls Frost was received as a Yankee farmer-poet, Brother Jonathan as a competent, untutored bard. Frost was quick to embrace the persona, as he would in interviews and readings once he returned to the United States. At the end of 1913 he described his hope of eventually writing poetry "from a farm in New England where I could live cheap and get Yankier and Yankier." Frost's English experience helped him situate his personal identity and locate a source for his poetry in provincial America. "I never saw *New* England as clearly as when I was in Old England," he acknowledged in 1915.[21]

The poet who denied the importance of location in 1912 published *North of Boston* in London two years later. Frost considered other titles — *Farm Servants, New England Eclogues,* and *New England Hill Folk.* Years after, he explained his choice. *North of Boston* "gathered itself together in retrospect and found a name for itself in the real estate advertising of the Boston Globe. . . . I like its being locative." [22] Dominated by dramatic monologues and dialogues, *North of Boston* seemed like "short stories in verse," not poetry. Moreover, Frost used language that he described as "absolutely unliterary," drawing on the sparse vernacular of ordinary Yankee folk while avoiding a dialect that could degenerate into caricature. [23]

In early 1915, two days before the Frosts' return from their English sojourn, the American edition of *North of Boston* was published by Henry Holt and Company. A literary community with ties to northern New England brought the book to publication, revealing Frost's appeal to urban sophisticates, vacationing consumers of regionalism, and people with rural roots who found in the poet's work affirmation of the world they had left behind. Florence Holt, wife of the New York publisher, had read an English copy of *North of Boston* in 1914 while at the family's summer retreat in Vermont. She was struck by the realism of Frost's poetry and suspected that he was a Vermonter. "My mother knows the people about here better than I do," Holt wrote to Frost, "& she finds many similar to them in your verses: certainly you have New England in them!" Mrs. Holt sent the volume on to New York with a recommendation that her husband's firm publish an American edition. Editor Henry Harcourt, who also had a summer home in Vermont, sent the book to Dorothy Canfield Fisher for review. Fisher, who after earning a Ph.D. from Columbia had retreated to Vermont and wrote fiction and nonfiction about the state, responded enthusiastically to *North of Boston.* [24]

Frost would be boosted by other literary sophisticates with ties to northern New England. He would also introduce the hill country, as critics observed, to the many people who only knew it from "the cool verandas of summer boarding-houses." Southern New England had been conquered by immigrants, the north country "overrun by outsiders of another culture," that is, vacationers who had further marginalized "naturally" reticent Yankees, reviewers and critics noted. But Frost became the poetic tribune of authentic New Englanders, giving voice "to the true way of the old Yankees themselves, as if he were the last of the Yankees and their essence." [25]

Frost's new personal and creative identification with northern New England coincided with the emergence of the hill country as the imagined regional heartland. Frost eliminated Lawrence from his poetic representation of New England and downplayed his urban background, cultivating a narrative of rustic origins and identity. The poet-performer reassured audiences that the real New England continued to exist and that it could be located north of Boston—and north of Lawrence, too. He became the voice of a sometimes hidebound land of steady habits—a vital Yankee culture that seemed far more than a quaint relic in a region that was increasingly becoming Lawrence writ large.

Yet if, starting with *North of Boston,* Frost was received as an indigenous farmer-poet, an avatar of Old New England, it was not his north country Yankee neighbors who made his works best-sellers or who packed the public readings that he later staged at universities and in cities nationwide. Beyond the major literary significance and universal elements of his poetry, Frost's books and performances were implicated in the new cultural geography of New England identity. The "authentic" voice of the hill country wrote for outsiders, helping them fix the regional heartland's new physical coordinates. In a caustic remark long after Frost had become established, a critic charged that he was the "poet who celebrates the diminished but prosperous and self-respecting New England of the tourist home and the antique shop in the abandoned gristmill" and whose popularity was "somehow connected in one's mind with the search for ancestors and authentic old furniture."[26] Such a dismissive, reductionist assessment obscures the shifts in regional identity that enabled the poet, through his books and stage performances, to participate in a cultural commodification of northern New England that, however significant, comprises only one aspect of his importance for us.

Between *North of Boston* and his third, more precisely located collection, *New Hampshire,* Frost increasingly celebrated the Yankee character and the pastoral landscape of Old New England. In England he had discovered his bonds to the region and had awakened to the poetic potential of native materials. American critics, however, quickly affirmed Frost's Yankee authenticity, acclaiming him as the Whitmanesque voice of rural New England who also recalled the region's accessible and popular "fireside poets" of the mid-nineteenth century. "[W]here Lowell and Whittier observed and reported [on] the New England peasant," one reviewer argued, "Frost has become one."[27]

"Never larrup an emotion," Frost insisted in one of the newspaper interviews he welcomed immediately after the stir provoked by the publication of *North of Boston*. Cultivating the image of a guileless "Yank from Yankville," he deplored the "pocketsful of poetic adjectives like pocketsful of peanuts carried into a park for the gray squirrels" that filled so much poetry.[28] The dramatic poems and lyrics of *North of Boston* acquired their power and distinctiveness from sparse, seemingly unpoetic language derived from vernacular speech. A hardheaded realism and emotional restraint shaped the Yankee poetic persona that emerged from *North of Boston*. And so did Frost's memorable aphorisms, however much they were couched in irony and voiced by flawed or troubled characters. "Good fences make good neighbors," a fellow farmer repeats rotelike as he assists the poet repairing a stone wall dividing their property in "Mending Wall," *North of Boston*'s opening poem. "Home is the place where, when you have to go there, / they have to take you in," the husband in "The Death of the Hired Man" observes while resisting the final return of a former farmhand. "[T]he best way out is always through," the disturbed wife in "A Servant to Servants" quotes her stoic husband.[29]

Though drawn from his own observations of hill folk, Frost's gallery of Yankee types in *North of Boston* resembles the cast of regional characters one finds in the mid-nineteenth-century New England literature that the poet knew so well. In "The Mountain," an industrious, utilitarian farmer driving an oxcart, who recalls Thoreau's Yankee neighbors, confesses to the narrator that he has never climbed the majestic mountain that he has worked around his entire life. "What would I do? Go in my overalls . . ." (p. 48), he asks. In "The Code," farmhands refuse "to be druv," like Harriet Beecher Stowe's cranky Yankee character, Sam Lawson, in *Oldtown Folks*. One hayer walks off to protest the perceived imperiousness of the "town-bred farmer" (p. 71). The other worker stays but only to lecture the boss: "You've found out something. / The hand that knows his business won't be told / To do work better or faster—those two things" (p. 72). A genteel, professorial, high-minded Yankee who has lost his attachment to his simple north country rural roots receives his comeuppance at the hands of the voluble, democratic Lafe in "A Hundred Collars." Stranded in a small town late at night, the professor is forced to share a room with a "Vermont Democrat" (p. 82), a forced familiarity that exposes the enlightened professor's disdain for common folk.

The Yankee characters in *North of Boston* are both tragic and comic. Lafe, in a gesture of intimacy and equality, offers the repulsed professor one hundred size fourteen collars that he has outgrown: "I've been a-choking like a nursery tree / When it outgrows the wire band of its name tag"

(p. 51). Frost insisted that "A Hundred Collars" was one of the most whimsical poems in the collection, part of the substantial humor that offsets its serious elements. But *North of Boston* stands as Frost's most unsentimental book, with "Home Burial" among its most hard-boiled poems. A mother, grieving for her child who is buried in an old family graveyard, lashes out in her poem: "Friends make pretense of following to the grave, / But before one is in it, their minds are turned / And making the best of their way back to life . . ." (p. 58).

As one of Frost's most astute critics argues, in his breakthrough volume the poet had not yet fully positioned himself as a Yankee hill country insider, the sage and celebrant of New England so visible, for example, in the long title poem of *New Hampshire*.[30] In "Mending Wall," the narrator joins in the spring ritual of repair only to question the utility of New England's bounded landscape. The poet's reticent, tradition-minded neighbor is described as "an old-stone savage" who "moves in darkness" (p. 40). The reserve displayed by other characters shades into repression, with madness occasionally lurking behind the walls and pastures of a seemingly tranquil landscape. The female narrator of "A Servant to Servants," *North of Boston*'s grimmest dramatic monologue, describes the cage, "Or room within a room, of hickory poles" (p. 68), where a mad uncle was once confined.

In *North of Boston* Frost, the realistic poet still negotiating his personal ties to Yankee ways, satirized Old Home Week, the affirmative rite of colonial revival New England. The Stark family returns to Bow, New Hampshire, and to a landscape that actually matches their name: "A rock-strewn town where farming has fallen off, / And sprout-lands flourish where the ax has gone" (p. 74). Rain challenges and defeats the spirit of reunion; only two Starks meander to the ancestral homestead, now nothing more than an outlying cellar hole, and they question their investment in family stock. "But don't you think we sometimes make too much / of the old stock? What counts is the ideals, / And those will bear some keeping still about." Yet Frost increasingly identified with his Puritan-Yankee family roots and excluded "new stock" New Englanders from his poeticizing of the region and its people.

The tensions and emotional detachment of *North of Boston* suggest a poet who was still an "uncertain observer" of rural New England and not yet the self-assured "spokesman for the region" that he would soon become, with his poetic persona dominating his material.[31] Still, the critical reaction to *North of Boston,* like Frost's reception in England, bestowed a cultural authority on the poet that he quickly embraced: urban-based reviewers hailed him as "a Yankee of Yankees," an indigenous voice of Old New England. His collection revealed a bard who "was of New England in every fiber," a farmer-poet of native genius who exchanged the plow for the pen and produced brilliant "unliterary" verse that was an extension of his life and labors. The poet's "manly power" and emotional reserve, critics pointed out, united him to the Yankee characters whose stories he recorded. But *North of Boston* captured far more than the human geography of Frost's world, reviewers also noted. It evoked the landscape of northern New England: the mountain that blocked the stars at night; the scattered homesteads, some of them forsaken; the fields and orchards wedged between granite outcroppings and forests. *North of Boston,* one influential contemporary critic concluded, confers on the north country "the power of an immense and moving actor in the lives of the folk it overshadows." [32]

If most reviewers recognized that *North of Boston* depicted rural New England as "not unrelievedly grey" but composed of "a multitude of shades," one prominent critic—poet Amy Lowell—linked Frost to an earlier literature of regional decline. *North of Boston,* Lowell claimed, "reveals a disease which is eating into the vitals of our New England life, at least in its rural communities." [33] Frost's Yankees became variants on the characters in *Ethan Frome* (1911), lonely, morbid, enervated rural folk— the human detritus of a once vital way of life.

Frost repudiated such a reading of *North of Boston* and of rural New England's prospects. In an address—"What Became of New England?"— delivered well after he had fully developed his identification with and poetic affirmation of Yankee life, he recalled Lowell's response to *North of Boston* and rejected any "Spenglerian" interpretations of the region's rich culture. "I don't give up on New England too easily," Frost proclaimed. "I don't give up these words that I've cared for,—the phrases. I long to renew them." Situating himself squarely within a Puritan-Yankee tradition of cultural renewal, Frost spoke like the regional poetic publicist he had become. "And the thing New England gave most to America was the thing I am talking about: a stubborn clinging to meaning,—to purify words until they meant what they should mean." [34] *North of Boston* was precisely such a purification of poetry padded with pocketsful of adjectives, a fresh, original collection of verse that was received as evidence of the continuing cultural vitality of Yankee New England.

North of Boston burst on the American literary scene as a best-seller; it went through five printings in its first year alone. Frost became the subject of interviews, where he eased into his role as rustic New England sage that would become part of his Yankee celebrity. "My country is a milk and sugar country," a newspaper interviewer quoted the poet. "We get what runs from trees and what runs from cows."[35] As if to validate his new investment in the geography of *North of Boston,* Frost retreated deep into Yankee hill country. In 1915 he purchased a farm in Franconia, New Hampshire, at the head of the scenic White Mountains. A year later, he published *Mountain Interval,* a collection of verse in which he more clearly emerged as a Yankee farmer-poet, participating in and affirming the values of New England country life.

Telling shifts from *North of Boston* to *Mountain Interval* register Frost's progressive grounding of his life and poetic persona in the Old New England world of the north country. *Mountain Interval* softens the dark shades of *North of Boston.* Not the hill folk but the poet emerges as the central character of *Mountain Interval.* A record of the insider's movements and experiences, *Mountain Interval* evokes the New Hampshire landscape with far more photographic detail than does *North of Boston.*[36]

In "Christmas Trees," Frost is the Yankee horse trader dickering with the city sharpy over the sale of his trees. The enormously popular "Birches" summons both the poet's "rustic" youth and the beauty of the trees after an ice storm, when branches "click upon themselves" and await the sun to "shed crystal shells" like "heaps of broken glass" (p. 117). In "Pea Brush" the poet is a Yankee farmer in search of birch boughs "to bush my peas" (p. 119). "A Time to Talk" records Frost's acceptance of local neighborly conventions, which a town-bred farmer violates in *North of Boston*'s "The Code." From the road a friend calls to the poet hoeing in his field. Though busy, the poet does not simply shout back, eyeing "all the hills I haven't hoed." He plants his hoe "Blade-end up" (p. 120) and ambles to the edge of his field. Over the stone wall the neighbors engage in a friendly visit, not the stiff exchange of *North of Boston*'s "Mending Wall."

To be sure, *Mountain Interval* is not all pastoral images of the hill country landscape and affirmations of the poet's immersion in its rural life. " 'Out, Out — ,' " one of Frost's grimmest and most powerful poems, re-creates the "snarling" sound of a buzz saw in an otherwise placid, pastoral setting where the horizon outlines "Five mountain ranges one behind the other / Under the sunset far into Vermont" (p. 131). A young boy doing man's work cutting firewood severs his hand when he loses control of the saw and bleeds to death. " 'Out, Out — ' " is immediately followed by the humorous "Brown's Descent," a poem about the Yankee character that, like "Birches," became a favorite of audiences at Frost's public readings. Brown lives on a "lofty farm," and one winter day he gets blown down the icy hill, " 'cross lots, 'cross walls, 'cross everything" (p. 132). But Brown's "slide," far from being emblematic of the decline of the Yankee race, becomes a meditation on Frost's descent. Instead of the "Stark-stock" questions of *North of Boston*'s "Generations of Men," "Brown's Descent" leads to the affirmation of Frost's Yankee identity. Twice he refers to "our stock." To those who "say our stock was petered out," the poet's reply is straightforward: "Yankees are what they always were" (p. 133). Far more than *North of Boston, Mountain Interval* is something of a conversion narrative—the poetic testimony of a newborn Yankee. Culturally awakened in England, affirmed by the critical and popular reception of *North of Boston,* Frost embraces in *Mountain Interval* the gospel of rural Yankee virtue.

For the next two decades, in his poetry and performances, location served Frost as a literary resource and cultural commodity, never more so than in his second volume after *North of Boston,* the Pulitzer Prize–winning *New Hampshire* (1923). The long title poem of *New Hampshire* could have been easily adapted for the *Nation* magazine's series of articles on individual states launched the previous year. Though Frost refused to contribute, his poetry mapped the new geography of regional identity delineated by the *Nation*'s essays on Vermont, Maine, and Massachusetts. From *North of Boston* to *New Hampshire* and beyond to *West-Running Brook* (1928), his books and stage appearances helped relocate the real New England to the pastoral Yankee world of the north country. Beyond their major importance as literature, Frost's volumes are cultural artifacts. They are works of the imagination that emerged from a particular historical context and that performed, along with his theatrical readings, cultural work. As cultural texts Frost's books need to be related to other texts that shaped regional identity along similar lines: Dorothy Canfield Fisher's widely read fiction and nonfiction on Vermont such as *Hillsboro People* (1915), periodical literature like the *Nation*'s state series of 1922, Wallace Nutting's popular *New England Beautiful* books of the early 1920s, the *Autobiography of Calvin Coolidge* (1929), and, in the 1930s, *Yankee* magazine and Thornton Wilder's *Our Town,* the Pulitzer Prize–winning play set in New Hampshire.

Consider the work of the highly successful Wallace Nutting. In the same year that Frost published *New Hampshire,* Nutting, a retired Congregational minister, released *New Hampshire Beautiful.* The volume was part of his New England "States Beautiful" series, which had been launched in 1922 with the first volume on Vermont. Nutting also brought out volumes on Maine, Massachusetts, and Connecticut. Designed primarily for tourists, Nutting's books combined descriptive texts with three hundred photographs per volume. He consistently imaged the regional landscape as a Frostian quiltwork of rolling hills, clustered birches, and stone-walled orchards and farms. Even his books on Connecticut and Massachusetts filtered out evidence of urbanization and industrialization and selected images of rural Old New England that imaginatively linked these states to the Yankee hill country of the north. Nutting's volumes also included poems, or hymns to the landscape, that often dealt with Frostian subject matter but fell far short of the Yankee poet's verbal compactness and subtlety. The first poem in *New Hampshire Beautiful,* for example, was titled "Singing Birches." Nutting's volume celebrated not only the physical beauty of the north country but also its familiar Yankee farmer and "villager who looks out on the same fair landscape that has filled the eye of his fathers at least to the third and fourth generations." [37] As Nutting's popular books suggest, Frost's poetic images of the regional landscape circulated in a cultural setting filled with similar representations of the new geography of authentic Old New England.

New Hampshire offered Frost's own tribute to the state and furnished ammunition to those who wanted to assign his work to the local color literary suburbs. "She's one of the two best states in the Union. / Vermont's the other . . ." (p. 155), Frost boasts in the collection's title poem. United "like wedges, / Thick end to thin end and thin end to thick end," the two states "fit together" like "a figure of the way the strong / Of mind and strong of arm should fit together . . ." (p. 156). Recalling his flight from Lawrence to Derry, Frost claims that New Hampshire was only "The nearest boundary to escape across," not a place where the people were better "Than those I left behind. / I thought they weren't. / I thought they couldn't be. And yet they were" (p. 158). New Hampshire people did not need to be elevated, as some city slickers thought. "The only fault I find with old New Hampshire / Is that her mountains aren't quite high enough" (p. 159).

"New Hampshire" reveals "the public figure's relishing consciousness of himself," the contrarian Yankee farmer-poet performing on the stage of his own verse. [38] With critical acclaim and public admiration in his hip pocket, the Harvard-educated poet found his stride dismissing the new Freudian urban literary sophisticate, the "pseudo-phallic" "New York alec" (p. 160). The poet as Brother Jonathan revels in his resistance to literary and intellectual fashion: "I refuse to adapt myself a mite / To any change from hot to cold, from wet / To dry, from poor to rich, or back again" (p. 157). Frost dons the garb of the rustic bard of the north country with far more fanfare than he displayed in *Mountain Interval.* "I choose to be a plain New Hampshire farmer / With an income in cash of say a thousand / (From say a publisher in New York City)" (p. 162).

The long title poem of *New Hampshire* is important to students of regional identity even if it does not stand as a significant literary achievement. Of course, Frost offered in *New Hampshire* some of his most enduring and powerful poems, lyrics laced with irony, doubt, and a search for meaning in a pastoral world whose surfaces often seem so welcoming and picturesque. Yet, as one contemporary poet-critic admirer put it, "were one to see nothing but the picture, Frost would be the last to prod the point."[39] Certainly, the boosterish "New Hampshire" frames his affirmation of the pastoral beauty and Yankee simplicity of the north country, whatever veins of darkness run through some of the volume's other poems.

"The Ax-Helve" is among the most interesting compositions in *New Hampshire.* It is one of the preciously few Frost poems that acknowledge the presence of anyone but Yankees in the northern New England landscape. In an interview published in the *New York Times Book Review* in 1923, shortly before *New Hampshire* was released, Frost described how the "Irish, then the French, and now the Poles," had made their way into northern New England. The Yankee poet expressed his impatience with native-born neighbors who saw immigrants as invaders. The "constant flow of new blood," he insisted, would only "make America eternally young, which makes her poets sing of the songs of a young country."[40]

And yet Frost's poems were hymns to Old New England that virtually erased ethnics from a pastoral Yankee world. The poet drew on his immigrant mother's Scottish Presbyterian background to reinforce his identity with his father's Puritan-Yankee ancestors, not with newcomers like Baptiste, the French-Canadian neighbor of the "Ax-Helve" who does not even possess a first name in Frost's poem.[41] It is Baptiste who makes the overture of "neighborliness," inviting the poet to visit and crafting an ax handle for him. Frost narrates the story and turns to dialect, which leaves Baptiste as an exotic outsider in the homogeneous Yankee world of his poetry. "Come on my house and I put you one in / What's las' awhile — good hick'ry what's grow crooked" (p. 174). New England is not renewed by new blood in Frost's poetry; that would have made Lawrence or Manchester a central location of his verse. Rather, Old New England abides in the north country as Yankee stock and Yankee ways resist the "Roman conquest" of the region. Not surprisingly, Frost refused to join other literary luminaries in support of Sacco and Vanzetti, the Italian immigrant radicals whose trial and execution for robbery and murder in Massachusetts was a cause célèbre in the 1920s.

In his poetic paean to New Hampshire, Frost also paid tribute to neighboring Vermont. By the time he published *New Hampshire,* he had already been living in South Shaftsbury, Vermont, for three years with increasing acceptance as a spokesman for that state's Yankee traditions. Though college teaching and public readings provided the principal means of his support, Frost cultivated his hill country rustic identity. A familiar photograph from 1921, titled "The Farmer-Poet at the Stone Cottage," shows Frost in country attire posed against the backdrop of Vermont's rolling landscape, an image of bucolic Old New England and its enduring Yankee simplicity that would soon be popularized by photographs of President Calvin Coolidge's visits to his Plymouth Notch boyhood home, where, outfitted in his grandfather's woolen smock, he toiled in the fields (Figure 33). A year before Coolidge assumed the presidency in 1923, Frost was named the poet laureate of Vermont. In a short time, the Committee on Vermont Traditions and Ideals, part of a newly created and publicly funded Vermont Commission on Country Life established to define and preserve the state's distinctive culture and folkways, included some of his verse in its volume on Vermont poetry.[42]

Doubtless members of the Vermont commission, like many of Frost's readers, viewed him as a spokesman for the same old-fashioned flinty Yankee values lauded in the *Autobiography of Calvin Coolidge* (1929). Only recently have Silent Cal's popularity and achievements been rescued from a history that has been written by New Deal liberals. But President Coolidge's contribution to the shaping of regional identity, which seems intertwined with Frost's in the 1920s, remains unexamined. Biographers and journalists held up Coolidge as something of a political counterpart to Frost: an authentic product of and spokesman for Old New England. A biography, published by the Atlantic Monthly Press in 1923, praised the new president as representing the "conscience of the best that is in New England. We have a personification of basic American principles: thrift, caution, courage, balance, and a keen sense of what is right." This volume compiled a string of quotations, the prosaic Yankee wisdom of Coolidge that would be woven into his autobiography: "We need more of the office

FIGURE 33. Paul Waitt photograph, titled "The Farmer-Poet at the Stone Cottage," shows Robert Frost in South Shaftsbury, Vermont (1921). Blackington Collection. Courtesy of Yankee Publishing, Inc., Dublin, New Hampshire.

desk and less of the show-window in politics. Let men in office substitute the midnight oil for the limelight."[43]

Noted journalist William Allen White, in the first of his two biographies of Coolidge, published in 1925, described him as a loyal son of a state where "simplicity" and "the fundamentals of American life" survive — the Yankee virtues of "Thrift, frugality, punctuality, [and] precision" in this business twist on the moral universe of Frost's "New Hampshire."[44] Two years later *National Geographic* magazine offered a long essay on Coolidge's Vermont with photographs, including several of Plymouth Notch that Wallace Nutting would have approved. *National Geographic* dubbed it "the most truly American of our states," a place where "people have hardly changed in their essential elements in a century." The magazine attributed a Frost-like Yankee stoicism to Vermonters: "one meets a difficulty, subdues it, and goes on to the next day's work."[45]

We need not reduce Frost to the Coolidge of American verse to establish links between the northern New England poet and the Vermont-born president. These connections involve far more than related public personae and place-bound identities that shaped perceptions of the real New England. From *Mountain Interval* to *New Hampshire* and beyond to *West-Running Brook,* Frost produced many poems in which he spoke as an insider affirming Yankee ways. Other poems were often read, even by critics, without full appreciation of the irony and uncertainty that informed Frost's vision. Moreover, Frost admired Coolidge; he identified with his political and cultural conservatism, praised his "overthemountain nature," and respected his kindred descent from "a modest, frugal, and unpretentious line of Puritan farmers."[46] From the Sacco-Vanzetti case through the depression, Frost's political detachment and poetic rejection of social criticism provoked literary enemies who saw him as a product of the same stingy soil that gave birth to Coolidge. Another contemporary northern New England author — Maine poet and nonfiction writer Robert P. Tristram Coffin, who later served as book and poetry editor of *Yankee* magazine — defended Frost against such critics and summarized the Coolidge-like Yankee moral vision that emerges from much of his verse. "Frost likes his people in individual, not mass formation. He isn't blaming their troubles on the capitalists or the environment, but on the way life is built and the way they are built," a New England creed of tenacity and self-reliance that *Yankee* magazine would inscribe as depression-era regional scripture.[47]

By the mid-1920s, with the taciturn Coolidge a national emblem of the persistence of traditional New England values in the "flapper era," the formerly shy Frost had his own public stage. He had developed his role as a poet-performer, a popular adaptation of the nineteenth-century stage Yankee and rustic sage. In other words, Frost had become New England's version of Will Rogers, a folk figure who entertained audiences and defined the lineaments of an authentic American regional character.

Newspapers gave full reports of Frost's readings. At one reading in Texas in 1922, Frost began by citing Amy Lowell's comment, in response to *North of Boston,* that the Yankee poet Frost lacked a sense of humor. He proceeded to read "The Cow in Apple Time," a humorous poem from *Mountain Interval.* A Cow "scorns a pasture" and "runs from tree to tree" consuming fallen apples so that it "drools / A cider syrup" (p. 121). Perhaps, Frost advised the audience, Lowell thought the beast was a "tragic cow." He proceeded to regale his listeners with recollections and pointed observations. Local newspapers showered praise on the Yankee visitor. "A sense of humor is almost requisite to the poet—and we are pleased to discover that Robert Frost possesses this attribute in a manner droll and spontaneous," one reporter observed. "The impression that Frost left with most of us," another wrote, "was one of inexpressible gentleness, with humor and strength and whimsical sincerity."[48]

The farmer-poet from the hill country became a familiar figure before college and urban audiences in the North, particularly in New England. In the mid-1930s Frost offered a series of readings-lectures at Harvard. Packed audiences greeted a speaker whose style resembled a meandering country road or mountain trail. "He seems to wander here and there," the *Boston Transcript* reported, "as illustrations suddenly occur to him, and as convictions rise suddenly in him," all the while making "forward progress" in spite of many "sideward excursions." Humor and aphorism peppered Frost's remarks and kept the audience enthralled. The poet's comments, the reporter for the *Transcript* observed, often seemed "famous on the instant; epigrammatic; sound; wise. All over the hall people . . . are busily taking notes." When it came time to read poems, Frost preferred selections from *A Further Range,* a new collection not yet published. The title was a play on the regional geography that had given Frost his materials and that had shaped his reputation as a poet and performer. He sought a further range "beyond the mountains of New England; new subjects; fresh fields." But his Harvard audiences kept requesting the "older and familiar poems."[49] His audiences sought ongoing affirmation of the identity that Frost had fashioned for himself and for New England in the four books of poetry he published between 1915 and 1928 and in his Yankee performances.

His best-selling books appear to have broadened the audience of poetry readers. As one prominent contemporary critic argued, the Yankee poet spoke to "several audiences" and was "appreciated on various levels." If Frost could not be "all things to all men," he seemed to offer "something for almost anybody."[50] His influence as a regional poet was thus enhanced not only by his fame but also by his appeal to readers unfamiliar with poetry who welcomed his accessible verse, attended his readings, and helped underwrite his celebrity. In fact, Frost both helped create and benefited from a new audience for the poetry he produced. An increase in high school and college graduates between World War I and the depression encouraged the growth of a new middlebrow reading public. In New England, for example, the rate of seventeen-years-olds in the population who graduated from high school grew from 16 to 60 percent between 1910 and 1938. The founding of the Book-of-the-Month Club in 1925 was one response of the publishing industry to a new audience of readers created by the increase in high school and college graduates. Dorothy Canfield Fisher, one of Henry Holt's most successful writers and a literary friend and supporter of Frost, served on the editorial selection committee of the Book-of-the-Month Club. In the mid-1930s Frost became a Book-of-the-Month Club author; the promotional article in *Club News* announcing his selection was titled "A Yankee Sage."[51]

As the Book-of-the-Month Club recognition and the poet's public performances suggest, in spite of proletarian criticism of his verse Frost's popularity seemed to surge as the depression deepened. His *Collected Poems* (1930) won the Pulitzer Prize in 1931; *A Further Range* (1936) garnered the same honor six years later. In 1937 Henry Holt brought out *Recognition of Robert Frost,* a volume of laudatory reviews and essays, each approved by the poet, that stretched across two and a half decades of criticism. "They would not find me changed from him they knew— / Only more sure of all I thought was true," proclaimed the book's inscription.[52] Frost's earthy verities and down-home celebrity found new resonance among his depression-era audiences. Indeed, his importance in the cultural history of American regionalism is twofold: he not only contributed to the northward imaginative shift of the real New England; he also participated in a larger resurgence of regional thinking and feeling that gained momentum in the 1920s and pervaded American life during the tumultuous years of the depression.

Frost became a spokesman for a "higher provincialism," a cross-regional search for the indigenous sources of an essential American culture. In the title poem of *West-Running Brook,* Frost strikingly summarized the cultural quest that animated the regional impulse of the 1920s and 1930s:

It is this backward motion toward the source,
Against the stream, that most we see ourselves in,
The tribute of the current to the source.
It is from this in nature we are from.
It is most us (p. 238).

Regional life represented the wellspring of the real America and was a source of renewal for a culture contending with the corrosive, artificial, modernizing forces of the twentieth century: urbanization, industrialization, standardization, mass culture, and imported ideas like Freudianism.[53]

If the Yankee sage became, as *Recognition of Robert Frost* announces, more "sure of all I thought was true" in the 1920s and 1930s, it was in part because cultural currents moved in his direction. From the Midwest, to the South, to the Southwest, regional cultures, folk, communities, and landscapes were rediscovered in art, literature, and historical writing as the "bedrock of America." In New England, one reborn regional artist argued, writers and painters proved to place-bound partisans from other parts of the country that the region was not simply "the fag end of Europe."[54] Frost's enormous contribution to this regional project reassured audiences that an authentic Yankee way of life persisted in the north country.

Frost's personal and cultural rebirth as a Yankee poet embodied precisely the American renewal that regionalist rhetoric summoned in the 1920s and 1930s. When Frost repudiated "guide book poetry" laden with picturesque words in favor of simple language grounded in the everyday local world, he voiced a larger regionalist dissatisfaction with genteel and academic poetry that had lost its moorings in the fundamental realities of American life. When the contrarian poet ridiculed a "pseudo-phallic" "New York alec," he expressed the regionalist cultural resistance to European modernist ideas. And when Frost located the New England heartland of Yankee folk, traditions, and small communities in the north country, he discovered one corner of the regionalist holy grail — the real America of authentic natives, place-bound lives, and unspoiled landscapes.

The depression, of course, accelerated both the regionalist movement's espousal of a higher provincialism as an alternative to modernization and its search for landscapes not "washed out by the inundating tide of city life," as one literary admirer of Frost put it in the mid-1930s.[55] The Yankee poet's popularity expanded with the regionalist agenda during the depression: a real and imaginative quest to recover local islands of stability that would reassure Americans struggling through a decade of social turbulence. Frost's Yankees, like the poet who presented himself to the public, had not succumbed to the blandishments of modern life. Frost spoke for indigenous, tradition-minded folk with deep roots in seemingly stable, even intimate communities—New England atavists who appeared better equipped than many Americans to cope with the depression.

The founding of *Yankee* magazine was one northern New Englander's response to the challenges of the depression. *Yankee* celebrated and worked to preserve the New England country ways that Frost's poetry and performances increasingly esteemed. Furthermore, like Frost, *Yankee* promoted the identification of the real New England with the north country and reflected the high tide of regionalist sentiment in the 1930s.

Yankee Magazine, 1935–1940

Early in 1932 writer-critic Bernard DeVoto, a friend and literary supporter of Frost, published an essay in *Harper's Magazine* that measured the pulse of depression-era New England. DeVoto's article, "New England: There She Stands," won Frost's praise for its affirmation of the region's Yankee cultural reserves that the poet had been examining for years. DeVoto found little to celebrate in the "ulcerous growths of industrial New England" that stretched, he noted, from Lawrence and Lowell, Massachusetts, to Pawtucket, Rhode Island, and beyond. "To spend a day in Fall River," DeVoto observed, "is to realize how limited were the imaginations of the poets who have described Hell."[56]

A winter trip to Vermont's Northeast Kingdom, where he maintained a summer home, supplied DeVoto with evidence that many New Englanders, and perhaps the region as a whole, had stockpiled experience and traditions that would enable them, better than other Americans, to ride out the depression. "How, indeed, should hard times terrify New England?" DeVoto asked. Much of the region had confronted "hard times," a "perpetual depression," for generations. "It began to look as though the bankrupt nation might learn something from New England."[57]

DeVoto's essay offered his Vermont neighbor, a resourceful Yankee undefeated by the state's thin soil and short growing season, as a regional cultural exhibit. "Jason" was an exemplar of New England's customary survival skills. He grew and preserved his own vegetables, hunted for rabbits and deer, sold his maple syrup for cash, and provided handyman services to summer residents. Though the depression was tightening its grip on the nation and though Jason's efforts only amounted to an existence "far below 'American standards,'" DeVoto found his neighbor living in "comfort and security," hardly affected by the economic devastation of 1932. "There are thousands like Jason on the hillside farms of Vermont, New Hampshire, and northwestern Massachusetts," DeVoto observed. "They have never thrown themselves upon the charity of the nation. They have never assaulted Congress, demanding a place at the national trough."[58]

DeVoto's Jason is one of those "real" New Englanders who people Frost's verse—authentic Yankees who refuse to blame their problems on capitalism or the environment and whose heritage of self-reliance and tenacity suggested that the region might endure the depression without political and social upheaval. Such a depression-era ideology of New England uplift inspired New Hampshire–based *Yankee* magazine, founded in 1935. *Yankee* delivered its own version of Frostian New England to thousands of readers each month. Its second issue contained a tribute to the poet titled "Robert Frost: The Realist," which stressed his "acceptance of the world as it is." Two months later the magazine renewed its praise of Frost as the greatest Yankee poet and continued to cite his achievement through the depression years.[59]

Yankee's readership expanded significantly between 1935 and 1940, years when Frost was immensely popular. The magazine made its own major contributions to the imaginative relocation of the New England heartland to the north country and, like Frost, expressed the regionalist sensibility that swept through America in the 1930s. Moreover, *Yankee* shared Frost's political conservatism and mounted a regionalist critique of the nationalizing thrust of the New Deal.

Yankee developed into one of the best-known and most successful regional magazines in America, part of a lucrative publishing operation that came to include *The Old Farmer's Almanac*. By 1985, fifty years after its birth, *Yankee*'s circulation exceeded one million, with two-thirds of its subscribers residing outside New England.[60] Well before then *Yankee* had established its winning formula; eschewing politics and controversy, the magazine examined the history, customs, and people of New England, recognizing the contributions of the region's six states. But *Yankee* initially focused on northern New England, and more than the cultural politics of the regionalist movement rippled through its early pages. *Yankee* invoked the politics of Calvin Coolidge to attack the New Deal.

Robb Sagendorph, a thirty-four-year-old native of Newton, Massachusetts, a suburb of Boston, launched *Yankee* from his Dublin, New Hampshire, home in September 1935. Sagendorph did not possess long New England roots. His parents were from Philadelphia; they moved to Newton so that his father could run the family manufacturing firm, Penn Metal Company, in Boston. After graduating from the exclusive Noble and Greenough School in 1918, Sagendorph attended Harvard, gaining valuable magazine experience with the *Harvard Lampoon* and earning a bachelor's degree in 1922. Two years later he received a master's degree from the university's Business School. He then went to work as a salesman for the Penn Metal Company in New York City. Sagendorph married Beatrix Thorne of Chicago in 1928, and the young couple took up residence in fashionable Greenwich, Connecticut, the course of their lives seemingly on a predictable trajectory.[61]

In 1930, however, Sagendorph left the family company and bought a house and thirteen acres in Dublin, New Hampshire, next to Peterborough, the site of his parents' summer home. Worsening economic conditions that seriously affected Penn Metal apparently prompted Sagendorph's move to New Hampshire, where he planned to farm and write. Countless other refugees from depression-marred modern America found their way to northern New England in the 1930s, including back-to-the landers, artists, and writers. Helen and Scott Nearing, for instance, purchased a rundown sixty-five-acre homestead in Vermont in 1932; E. B. White fled New York to North Brooklin, Maine, in 1938, about the time that Norman Rockwell retreated to Arlington, Vermont, and began to use his Yankee neighbors as subjects for his reassuring images of ordinary American life. Scores of far less prominent people, driven by economic necessity or a longing for old-time America, made their way to northern New England during the depression decade. By 1940 *Yankee* magazine praised this invasion of city-born "neo-Yankees" for their work revitalizing the cultural life of the hill country. "Almost all the new invaders of the country towns are college graduates," *Yankee* reported, "and the majority are professional people, with writers, painters, and teachers predominating."[62]

Sagendorph, like Frost, was something of a neo-Yankee, but he wisely chose not to use that title for his regional magazine. During his first years in Dublin Sagendorph wrote short stories and novels set in New England, but he seems to have had little if any success publishing his work. By 1935 at least, he had turned to nonfiction. In that year he completed a book-length manuscript with the ominous title "Before Armageddon," his observations on the mounting national distress sown by the depression. Yet economic and social turmoil did not operate as a solvent on Sagendorph's Republican Party loyalties. He voted for Herbert Hoover over Franklin D. Roosevelt in 1932, commenting in "Before Armageddon," that "former business associates, old friends, and family were too strong for me to resist."[63] For Sagendorph and many other regionalists, including Frost, the New Deal would chafe as a centralizing, bureaucratic juggernaut— a political expression of the growing corporate and cultural standardization that so defaced American life and threatened to level regional and local cultures. *Yankee* was born in an act of cultural, and increasingly political, resistance to what was perceived as the assault of flatlanders on New England's distinctive heritage.

Shortly after *Yankee*'s first decade of publication, Sagendorph completed yet another book manuscript that he was never able to publish: a history of the magazine's founding and early years. That volume and Sagendorph's editorials in the 1930s define *Yankee* as a sort of Baedeker of Old New England enlivened with a defiant appeal for cultural preservation similar to the higher provincialism of *I'll Take My Stand* (1930), the noted Southern regional manifesto. *Yankee* was dispatched into a world, Sagendorph complained, of "WPA leaf raking and crop destruction, salacious literature and salacious movies, inane radio programs and aimless automobile races," all of which seemed to threaten "the *real* foundations of American living—ingenuity, inventiveness, private enterprise, reward for an honest day's labor, penalty for sloth." Consequently, he reported, the real New Englander, "this 'white man' whom I choose to call the YANKEE . . . , wasn't doing so well" in 1935.[64]

For inspiration Sagendorph looked back to the cultural heyday of the Yankee in the antebellum decades. In his history of *Yankee*'s founding, Sagendorph documented the existence of nineteenth-century magazines that bore the same name. He recounted the brief history of John Neal's *Yankee,* founded in Portland, Maine, in 1828, and he described his copy of an even earlier *Yankee* that dated from around 1815. Though Sagendorph, like Frost, served as a self-appointed spokesman for the reticent Yankee, his editorial voice was not simply the product of observation of and participation in New England hill country life; it was also shaped by his knowledge of nineteenth-century literary and cultural history, the period we now know "invented" the Yankee. Sagendorph installed a popular "Swoppers' Column" that enabled subscribers to advertise items for trade free of charge. As an illustration for the column Sagendorph used William Sidney Mount's *Coming to a Point,* an antebellum painting of two whittling Yankee rustics that was almost identical to the artist's *Farmers Bargaining* for a horse.[65]

Sagendorph's counterattack on the twin evils of mass commercial culture and centralized governmental power began with the first issue of *Yankee,* which was sent to twenty-five hundred subscribers in September 1935. Sagendorph published *Yankee* from his Dublin farmstead; the magazine's office, a newspaper reported in 1935, consisted of "a delightful shack between two pine trees." Production of the first issue, Sagendorph recalled, resembled an old-fashioned New England barn raising. "All of us — neighbors, friends, relatives, — turned to and helped bind that issue." Circulation grew steadily, reaching ten thousand by 1937 and nearly thirty thousand by the early 1940s.[66]

Yankee was introduced as a New Hampshire magazine. To attract his first subscribers, Sagendorph sent publication announcements to all the names in New Hampshire telephone books. The cover of the first issue shows a baby with the name "Yankee"; the "infant" is placed at the front steps of a home with "New Hampshire" emblazoned on the door (Figure 34). "It has been left on New Hampshire's doorstep," Sagendorph explained, "because we know it will find a congenial home there." With material such as a history of Concord, a play about early Keene, and a poem titled "New Hampshire," *Yankee* began as a monthly devoted to the Granite State. Perhaps, Sagendorph speculated in the first issue, the magazine would grow to include "Yankee relatives" in the other New England states as well as "millions of kin . . . across the continent."[67]

In fact, *Yankee* quickly broadened its geographic scope; it appealed to readers throughout New England, to natives residing beyond the region's borders, and to summer vacationers. From a New Hampshire–focused publication "for Yankee readers, by Yankee writers, about Yankeedom" the magazine became a more geographically, though not ethnically, inclusive monthly "for Yankees Everywhere." Sagendorph came to discuss Yankeedom as New England's seventh state, "a state of mind." But such market-driven Yankee inclusiveness did not overshadow the privileged cultural

FIGURE 34. *Yankee*'s first cover identifies it as a New Hampshire magazine. Illustration by Joseph Stern. Courtesy of Yankee Publishing.

ground that northern New England occupied in the magazine's geography of regional identity. Readers from Connecticut and Rhode Island complained about the shortage of material on their states. Yet even as he widened *Yankee*'s coverage in response to his readership, Sagendorph became more ideologically invested in those parts of northern New England that had not yet succumbed to the Democratic Party and the New Deal. As a relative of Sagendorph who later joined the magazine remarked, the popular image of the real Yankee remained a male who was "*never* young and lived in either Maine or Vermont" (Figure 35).[68]

In the first issue Sagendorph explained that the purpose of his magazine was "the expression and perhaps, indirectly, the preservation of that great culture in which every Yank was born and by which every real Yank must live." From his journalistic pulpit in depression-era regionalism's house of worship, Sagendorph assumed the pose of a contrarian Yankee and cultural Jeremiah. He bewailed "mass production, mass distribution, mass advertising, and mass almost-everything-you-can-think-of." The New England Yankee's "individuality, initiative, and natural ingenuity" were on the verge of being " 'swallered inter' a sea of chain stores, national releases, and nation wide hookups." Furthermore, an intrusive national government offered relief programs that eroded Yankee traditions of industry and self-reliance.[69]

In his editorials and in one newspaper interview that appeared a month after *Yankee* began publishing, Sagendorph fleshed out the regional creed that guided the magazine's production and his understanding of the real New England. Provincial America was the location of the nation's moral and cultural strengths and vital traditions. "I have an idea," Sagendorph told a reporter for the *Boston Sunday Herald,* "that New England, taken alone, is stronger than New England taken with the rest of the country—so is the Middle West, and so is the South."[70] In an editorial several months later, his growing confidence in his enterprise found expression in a twentieth-century New England "Calvinism" whose spiritual capital was located in Plymouth Notch, Vermont. "Thrift," "Faith," "Individuality," "Ingenuity," "Community Interest"—the terms resounded in Sagendorph's editorials not just as a prescription for literary and cultural renewal but as a party line. "There is reason to believe," *Yankee* asserted, "that, with less pampering by the national economists of our unemployed, native ingenuity might once again come to the fore."[71]

But *Yankee* was not founded as a political organ. Fiction, poetry, history, folk culture, and profiles of contemporary New Englanders dominated its pages. Over the first few years Sagendorph experimented with and modified the magazine's format. A typical issue carried two short stories, several poems, perhaps a reminiscence, a history of a New England community, news on the regional economy, and feature articles, especially on Yankee customs. A regular column focused on New England country dancing. *Yankee* reprinted detailed instructions for various types of dance, recording folk tradition in the interest of preservation. Stories

Definition of a Yankee:

A MAN WHO AIN'T LEANIN' ON NOTHIN'

YANKEE

August 1939   *25 Cents*

FIGURE 35. The magazine's preferred image of the real Yankee: an aged male from Vermont or Maine who subscribed to the politics of self-reliance summarized by the definition proclaimed on this cover.
Photograph by A. W. Pressley. Courtesy of Yankee Publishing.

on Vermont maple sugaring and on Maine potato farming included long lists of recipes showing how Yankees put their bounty to good use. When *Yankee* looked at a New England industrial city, as early issues did with Manchester and Nashua, New Hampshire, it usually concentrated on the Yankee ingenuity behind the community's development and the educational and cultural contributions of Yankee entrepreneurs.[72]

The "ulcerous sores" of industrial New England, however, did not blight the pages of *Yankee* in the 1930s. Rather, bucolic images and accompanying accounts of covered bridges, stone walls, town meetings, Old Home Days, and self-reliant rural customs complemented the magazine's more literary elements. Beatrix Sagendorph, the publisher's artist wife, designed *Yankee*'s covers and contributed illustrations for poems and stories. Other artists also provided images for the magazine, including J. J. Lankes, Frost's illustrator.

The dominant visual narrative that emerges from *Yankee* captures both the Old New England landscape of the hill country and the capacity of Yankee folk to prevail over the depression. The first major "artistic" cover appeared in December 1935. It was the creation of Maxfield Parrish, an established illustrator from Philadelphia who had settled in a small New Hampshire town. Parrish's "White Birch—Winter" was part of a popular series of nostalgic calendar images of Old New England that he began in the 1930s (Figure 36). Another December cover, published two years after Parrish's Frostian illustration, presents a more domesticated image of winter in the hill country. It depicts a vernacular connected New England farmhouse protected by a hill, a cozy fire that obviously warms the dwelling's interior, and young and old shovelers working together to clear a path to the door (Figure 37). All of these visual elements suggest tradition, stability, simplicity—precisely the Yankee virtues that Bernard DeVoto celebrated in his winter visit to his Vermont neighbor.[73]

Some suggestive images, like *Yankee*'s reproduction of Mount's whittling Yankees "Coming to a Point," became fixtures for regular columns. When *Yankee* established a "Job Exchange" in 1938, a painting by Molly Luce was chosen as the illustration. Luce was yet another popular image maker of Old New England in the 1930s; among her works is the painting *Reading from Robert Frost* (1932), a depiction of young devotees of the poet gathered in a pastoral setting while one of them recites the Yankee sage's verse. The Luce painting that graced *Yankee*'s Job Exchange portrays a New England comprised of small, neat villages nestled in hill country hollows.[74] No sign of modern life, let alone of the mass culture that

YANKEE

Jl. 1 No. 4   Dec. 1935

WHITE BIRCH - WINTER by Maxfield Parrish

WHAT IS A YANKEE?
by
Claude Moore Fuess

PRICE   TWENTY   FIVE   CENTS

FIGURE 36. This was the first "artistic" cover of *Yankee*. Popular illustrator Maxfield Parrish depicts a Frostian setting and calendarlike image of enduring Old New England. Courtesy of Yankee Publishing.

Yankee deplored, disrupts the pastoral village scene. The automobile does not intrude, the horse serving as the preferred mode of transportation (Figure 38).

There are striking parallels between *Yankee*'s uplifting images of the real New England during the depression and the work of the photographic division of the New Deal's Farm Security Administration (FSA). Across

YANKEE

DECEMBER 1937
25 Cents

DOES OLD AGE BEGIN AT THIRTY? By MAUDE PARKER

FIGURE 37. Another reassuring image of sturdy hill country folk who, like Bernard DeVoto's "Jason," go on with their lives, undaunted by winter or the depression. Illustration by Beatrix Sagendorph. Courtesy of Yankee Publishing.

America, FSA photographers documented the hardships of the depression at the same time that they expressed the new artistic interest in the indigenous folk, local places, and vernacular cultures that constituted an essential America. But displaying the poverty of Southern sharecroppers, Dust Bowl farmers, and similar human casualties of the depression decade

YANKEE'S JOB EXCHANGE

is free of charge to all subscribers. If you want a job, or have a job to give, use this column to state your wants or needs. YANKEE assumes no responsibility except that of placing jobbers in touch with jobbers. Let us know when you've got your job — or the position has been filled, so we can stop the ad. One six line ad per month allowable.

Painting by Molly Luce, courtesy of Grace Horne Galleries

FIGURE 38. Molly Luce's image of small-town old New England was one of many that appeared in *Yankee* and in regional art and photography of the 1930s. Courtesy of Yankee Publishing.

seemed to many in and outside of Congress to communicate a defeatist story whose purpose, as *Yankee* had already protested, was to marshal support for more federal relief.[75]

Under political pressure, Roy Stryker, head of the FSA's historical section from 1935 to 1943, went in search of *Yankee*-like images of Americans' capacity to preserve their local institutions and customs against the ravages of the depression. Stryker may have been familiar with *Yankee* and with Sagendorph's espousal of a self-reliant creed for the region. What seems clear is that Stryker turned to New England, particularly the Yankee hill country, for affirmative photographs of familiar icons and small-town community life. New England often served as the first circuit for new FSA photographers, who usually carried explicit instructions from Stryker. He told one New England–bound photographer to focus on reassuring regional material — "autumn, pumpkins, raking leaves, roadside stands. . . .

You know, pour maple syrup on it, . . . mix well with white clouds and put on a sky-blue platter." Stryker provided some members of his staff, such as the well-known Marion Post Wolcott, with detailed shooting scripts organized by season. "View of the village taken from low place showing church against a background of snow-covered spruce hills," one winter script outlined for Wolcott. "Emphasize the church steeple." This script also called for a "farmhouse and barns near road—winter is a good time to emphasize why New Englanders built their houses, etc., near by the road."[76] In its cultural brew of regionalist sentiment, positive images of New England life, and strong interest in the northern states, much of the work of the FSA photographers could have easily made its way into *Yankee* instead of the newspapers and magazines where it did appear.

Of course, though political pressure influenced their aesthetic choices, the FSA photographers' documentary work in New England was more than a confection of regionalist sentiment. Moreover, even *Yankee* sometimes acknowledged rents in the social fabric of regional life. As early as September 1936, the magazine published an anonymous piece titled "Nice Clean Little Town." It purported to be written by someone who had moved from a suburb of New York City to a small New England town and whose expectation of clean country living was challenged by the discovery of high school pregnancies and lax morality among families in the outback. *Yankee* presented the article with apologies and the hope that "it will lead to correction."[77] Two years later the magazine contained a report on "Gangdom's Threat to New England," which described the spread of gambling, prostitution, and business corruption in Massachusetts, Rhode Island, and Connecticut cities, in an attempt to provoke moral outrage: "When the New England Yankee is aroused—something happens." According to the article, northern New England appeared untainted by mobsters. "All of them consider Maine, New Hampshire and Vermont (particularly Vermont) as the sticks or 'missionary country.'"[78]

"Gangdom's" rise, *Yankee* suggested, coincided with the ethnic transformation of urban southern New England. Ethnic issues played out in the magazine the way they figured in Frost's poetry: native-born Yankees comprised the authentic New Englanders; rhetorical genuflections before the altar of ethnic assimilation did not translate into stories about Yankee newcomers. Promoting Yankeedom as a state of mind proved rather more geographically than ethnically liberating. As *Yankee* broadened its New England coverage, it added a new regular column, "Six Smart Yanks," consisting of profiles usually drawn from each of the states. At first, ethnic names and faces never appear; later non-Yankees occasionally make their way into the feature.

Sagendorph, like Frost, was no nativist; on his father's side he descended from eighteenth-century German immigrants. Yet he worried that ethnic change, not just corporate commercialism, would "swaller" up Yankee tradition. His magazine joined in the regionalist search for indigenous "American folk" that sorted out people according to their origins. In the first issue, Sagendorph responded to a recent article that compared the Yankee's fate to the decline of the ultimate representative of an authentic, indigenous America. "The Yankee, like the Red Man, has become the vanishing American," he quoted *Scribner's Magazine*.[79]

From *Yankee*'s inaugural issue, the cultural politics of ethnic and regional identity shaped Sagendorph's representation of New England and its people. Four months into its existence, the magazine contained a piece, "What Is a Yankee," that, Sagendorph recalled, "really put us on the publishing map." Written by Claude Moore Fuess, headmaster of Andover Academy, the "article was quoted in newspapers and reprinted all over the United States." Fuess, who praised Frost's verse, located the Yankee heartland in relation to Boston. "I think I know what a Yankee is," he wrote with confidence, "and I am certain that I can find within less than a hundred miles of Boston many perfect specimens of the type." Yankeeness comprised far more than a state of mind available through cultural assimilation. "No Latin or Slav, even in the second generation, can properly be called a Yankee," Fuess insisted. "The true Yankee comes down from Anglo-Saxon stock and from branch to branch of the family tree."[80]

For Fuess, Calvin Coolidge loomed as the perfect specimen of the "Yankee type," a judgment that, if references in *Yankee* to the recently deceased president are any indication, Sagendorph shared. Fuess's genuine Yankee also toed a traditional political line. "The Yankee prefers familiar roads and tested policies." Not only did the Yankee refuse to support communism, fascism, socialism "or any other 'ism,'" Fuess maintained, but also "until recently the Yankee in rural New England seldom went 'on the town.'"[81]

Two years after publishing Fuess's widely read essay, *Yankee* addressed the "native" New Englander's relationship to the region's immigrant and ethnic populations. And if the treatment fell short of nativism, it nevertheless defined the bounds of the magazine's cultural horizon. "Immigrants or Americans?" was the work of Chris J. Agrafiotis, who wrote as an ethnic spokesman appealing to Yankees for greater engagement with New England's newcomers. In essence, Agrafiotis offered a brief for the Yankeefication of New England ethnics. Drawing a distinction between naturalization and Americanization, he urged Yankees to undertake a complete assimilation of the more than 60 percent of New Englanders who were first- or second-generation newcomers to the region. If the ethnic New Englander remained insufficiently assimilated, it was "because after we have made him a citizen, we stopped." Such a failure produced "the creeping of the many 'isms' which are today a menace to American liberty." [82]

Agrafiotis prodded Yankees to give up their "scorn and suspicion" of immigrants, even urging intermarriage as a solution to the question of assimilation.[83] But his entire argument only reinscribed native-born stereotypes of immigrants. He linked immigrants to radicals, that is, to the legacy of Sacco and Vanzetti that festered in the labor turmoil of the 1930s. And he depicted immigrants as the subjects of Yankee uplift, not as contributors in their own right to New England culture. Reinforcing these entrenched perceptions of ethnics, *Yankee* illustrated Agrafiotis's article with the image of a hooked-nose, skullcap–clad immigrant who looks as if he has just washed ashore (Figure 39). In addition, juxtaposed with Agrafiotis's plea for assimilation is another essay, titled "I Married a Yankee." The author, Mary Kay, describes herself as the daughter of an Irish family that knew neither domestic order nor financial discipline. Marriage to a Yankee brought about cultural and economic salvation. "I rejoice that I married a Yankee who knew the meaning of real thrift," Kay writes, "and had the strength of mind enough to practice it." [84] *Yankee* represented immigrants almost exclusively as subjects for ongoing moral and political tutoring. It failed to acknowledge what mill operators had long recognized and what is readily documented in New England ethnic autobiographies: immigrants such as the Franco-Americans, who made up the largest non-Yankee population of the northern states, brought their own work ethic and traditions of family enterprise and frugality to the region.[85]

Coolidge's self-reliant creed and Frost's unsentimental realism may have triumphed on *Yankee*'s pages, but the political currents of depression-era New England seemed increasingly to prevail against the order that Sagendorph sought to celebrate, preserve, and use as the basis for ethnic assimilation. Except for Massachusetts, which had gone Democratic in 1928, New England remained solidly Republican into the 1930s. In 1932 Roosevelt claimed only the Bay State. Four years later Connecticut, New Hampshire, and Rhode Island fell to the Democrats. Beyond its periodic

FIGURE 39. Joseph Pistey Jr.'s image of an immigrant, a stereotype that seemed
to undermine the magazine's call for Yankees to reach out to newcomers
(December 1937). Courtesy of Yankee Publishing.

calls for ethnic assimilation, *Yankee* responded to these political shifts in two ways. First, in the late 1930s it adopted an acerbic, defensive political stand. And second, Maine and Vermont, Yankee-Republican holdouts, acquired a new cultural cachet in the magazine's pages as a living museum of Old New England.

By the fall of 1937, Sagendorph could no longer restrain his hostility to FDR and the New Deal. To be sure, *Yankee* had germinated in an ideological hothouse, as Sagendorph's "Before Armageddon" suggests. A growing political undertow had consistently threatened to drag the magazine away from its primary mission as a literary and cultural journal during its first two years of operation. Furthermore, from its inception *Yankee* was immersed in the cultural politics of the regionalist movement. But *Yankee* posed as a nonpartisan publication and resisted direct political commentary. Sagendorph dropped the pretense of nonpartisanship in September 1937, exactly two years after *Yankee*'s founding.

"Editorially and personally we are fed up with the New Deal, — fed up to the eyes," Sagendorph erupted. "We just can't take it any more. *Yankee* is going Republican." The New Deal stood for a set of policies and programs "unutterably opposed to the Yankee tradition." Roosevelt's attempt in 1937 to pack the Supreme Court helped *Yankee* define what was at stake: "it is nothing less than American individualism versus a transplanted brand of European collectivism." Sagendorph urged readers to defend their rights against "a John L. Lewis" and the non-Yankee "Frankfurter-Corcoran-Cohen Brain Trust." (*Yankee* published a genealogical essay to explain that Delano, Roosevelt's middle name, was an Anglicization of a name derived from a French ancestor, De La Noye, which meant that the president had no claim on a Yankee ancestry.)[86]

Sagendorph published letters that supported *Yankee*'s political stand. He claimed that "an overwhelming majority of readers" endorsed its anti–New Deal position. Other readers were disappointed by the intrusion of bald partisan politics into the magazine's heavily nostalgic fare. Sagendorph feared that if *Yankee* posted open season on the New Deal, he would "antagonize" rather than "convert" readers who disagreed with his politics. Thus he quickly restrained his partisan outburst.[87]

Instead, he floated the idea of a "Yankee Party" that would rescue America from the perils represented by Republicans as well as Democrats. For *Yankee*'s Republicanism, like its imaging of New England, was rooted in the small-town America that gave the nation Calvin Coolidge. Imbued with the regionalist affirmation of ordinary folk, *Yankee* espoused a New England populism that the Republican Party was sometimes accused of betraying. Sagendorph complained in 1937 that the party of Coolidge represented "a little too much of New York–white collar–Newport–summer resident attitude to be very effective."[88] A Yankee Party, he suggested, might be the only alternative.

In the summer and fall of 1938, Sagendorph explored the question "Is There a Yankee Party?" in several issues of his magazine. He believed there were "thousands of Yankees . . . scattered all over the country today . . . who are not finding just what they want in either the Elephant or the Donkey." He asked readers to submit presidential nominations; he drew up a seventeen-point platform; and he proposed the bald eagle, emblem of American liberty, as the party's symbol. Sagendorph's campaign was more than a publicity stunt, but it was also less than a well-thought-out plan to create a bloc of voters who might influence the two major parties. Moreover, like the magazine itself, Sagendorph's Yankee Party was entangled in the politics of identity. In his crusade to preserve and celebrate Yankee culture, Sagendorph often sounded like an ethnic cheerleader exploiting resentments to shore up group identity. Yankees unfortunately lacked "the solidarity of race-consciousness," he wrote in one of his 1938 political editorials. "The melting pot is smelting not the foreigner but the native. Our traditions are yielding to Old World propaganda. Blood is no longer thicker than water."[89]

Still, Yankee-Republican Vermont and Maine seemed to endure, though growing numbers of ethnic Democrats were stirring in those states as well. During the years when Sagendorph politicized *Yankee,* the magazine devoted increasing attention to Vermont and Maine. Even more than New Hampshire, where the magazine began and remained headquartered in expanded "shacks" on Sagendorph's farm, Vermont and Maine seemed to represent authentic Old New England. Stories and images enshrined the virtuous Yankeeness of the two states. In October 1938, for example, *Yankee* ran a story about enterprising, self-reliant Vermont fern pickers. These Vermont Yankees from the town of Warren, the magazine reported, earned a "good living" from the commercial harvesting of ferns, farming, and lumbering. "They're all good Vermont Republicans," *Yankee* proclaimed, "not too sympathetic to the present political order, and boast that Warren hasn't yet drawn a cent from its $1,800 WPA allotment."[90]

Another major article lauded Vermonters as embodiments of New England common sense and self-reliance for their rejection of the so-called White Elephant Road. In 1936 the federal government proposed to finance a parkway that would travel the length of the state parallel to the Green Mountains. Voters turned down the offer in a statewide referendum. New England's most thinly populated state stood tall against the federal Goliath, an expression of Yankee independence and contrariety that the magazine commended to its readers. The Vermonter's fierce attachment to the Green Mountain State resembled the place-bound loyalty of a "Balkan peasant." Such a Yankee considered Vermont "more his country that his state." This provincial patriotism was born of history; the state, after all, began as an independent republic, and Vermonters continued to honor the spirit of Ethan Allen. In the White Elephant Road controversy, Yankee Vermont rose up to defend its traditions and pastoral simplicity against governmental and commercial intrusion. The Vermont author of the account framed the issue in terms familiar to *Yankee* readers: "are we going to keep the greatest, and perhaps the only asset we have, our unique scenic beauty . . . or are we going *loco*, like Florida and California, and 'develop,' commercialize, exploit and 'improve' this asset for the benefit of the tin-can tourist?"[91]

Of course, tourists, recreationists, and summer residents had already made substantial inroads into Vermont life. Skiing, for example, first emerged as an important source of income in northern New England during the 1930s; the industry's marketing added to the appeal and recreational romance of the hill country. Even *Yankee* created a winter sports issue. In many ways, *Yankee* was involved in the "selling" of northern New England. By the late 1930s, the magazine had opened advertising offices in Boston, Chicago, New York, and Maine.[92] While city-based and national advertisers appeared in *Yankee,* its commercial pages were dominated by businesses and pastoral images of northern New England. Country inns, summer camps, real estate companies, ski resorts, and producers of items like maple syrup—*Yankee*'s advertisers, in one way or another, offered readers a connection to Old New England.

In the *Yankee* of the late 1930s the heartland of traditional New England seemed to straddle the political holdouts of Vermont and Maine, "a national park for the preservation of Republican wild life," the magazine mordantly noted in early 1937.[93] In Maine as in Vermont, Sagendorph found strong evidence that Yankeedom survived. "Maine Whips CIO," *Yankee* crowed in August 1937. When the union tried to organize shoe workers in Lewiston and Auburn, Mainers crossed the picket lines in a display of "good Yankee horse sense," though the report failed to note that

many of these workers were Franco-Americans. The Congress of Industrial Organizations (CIO) gave up its campaign. Two years later *Yankee*
confirmed its strong affection for the state when it published an unusual
number—a "Special Maine Christmas Issue" devoted to the "Downeast"
corner of New England.[94] The magazine's imagery of Old Maine was reinforced in the 1930s by the catalog covers of L. L. Bean, the tradition-
minded Yankee manufacturer of outdoor items—products whose purpose and craftsmanship recalled Old New England.

Maine writers played a prominent role in *Yankee*. Robert P. Tristram
Coffin, in his capacity as book and poetry editor, not only reviewed many
Maine works; he also published his own poetry that celebrated the state
and its people. In 1936 *Yankee* published his long poem "Tipsham Foreside," which offered up the Mainer as the salt of New England:

> The Foreside people, being Maine folks, stay
> Full of juice and do not dry away
> Into Yankees of the harder kind,
> Such as local-color artists find
> Under the mountains called the Green and White.

John Gould was another Maine writer who contributed regularly to *Yankee*.
In 1939, for instance, Gould published two pieces demonstrating that
small-town Maine continued to uphold New England tradition. "Perambulating the Town Bounds" explained how Brunswick still adhered to
the colonial requirement that a circuit of the town boundary be made
every five years to ensure that there had been no encroachment from
neighboring jurisdictions. The author quoted Frost's "Good fences make
good neighbors" as a venerable Yankeeism.[95]

Gould's second piece, appearing in March 1939, celebrated town meeting time in New England. Gould compiled a photographic essay of the
ordinary folk in coastal Harpswell engaged in the rituals of local democracy (Figure 40). His photographs closely resemble the images of the Vermont town meetings that were such an important part of Marion Post
Wolcott's FSA documentary work in New England. With totalitarianism
advancing in Europe and the fear of assorted "isms" at home, the New England town meeting had become a reassuring symbol of American democratic traditions and stability. Gould incorporated his *Yankee* material into
an important book, *New England Town Meeting: Safeguard of Democracy*, published in 1940.[96]

Just as Sagendorph's magazine reimagined the nineteenth-century

FIGURE 40. Images of town meeting day in Harpswell, Maine. Photographer John Gould celebrates rituals of community and grassroots democracy (*Yankee,* March 1939). Courtesy of Yankee Publishing.

Yankee for a new era, so too it redeployed the New England town as a regional icon for new political and cultural purposes. Stories on town meetings appeared frequently in *Yankee,* and in 1938 the magazine established a new feature, "Town Reports," offering news from across New England. The first installment included a full-page picture of a Freeport, Maine, citizen reading his annual report, an evocative image of grassroots democracy.[97] As in Molly Luce's painting that accompanied the "Job Exchange," the traditional imagery of stable, pastoral small-town New England was part of *Yankee*'s imaginative stock-in-trade. Even *Yankee*'s advertisers sometimes contributed to the revitalization of the iconographic New England town. Howard Johnson was one of the magazine's important advertisers. This New England Yankee built restaurants on major highways in the 1930s that responded to nostalgia for Old New England. His restaurants, with their cupola, dormers, and shutters, were modeled on the architecture of the classic white village; customers were not allowed to tip in a setting that evoked small-town New England.

Yankee's politically charged stories, FSA photographs, and the architectural motifs of Howard Johnson's all suggest how regionalist sentiment in the 1930s enshrined the small New England town as an artifact of the real America. In the white village, regional cultural archaeologists of the 1930s unearthed American "primitives"—Yankee folk whose simple place-bound lives preserved community stability and local tradition. *Our Town,* Thornton Wilder's Pulitzer Prize–winning play of 1938, sentimentalized this provincial Yankee world and advanced its identification with the magnetic North of the regionalist imagination. Wilder spent many summers at the MacDowell Colony for artists in Peterborough, New Hampshire, next door to Dublin. He was at MacDowell in the summer of 1937, shortly before he began work on *Our Town.* He undoubtedly knew Sagendorph's operation and saw *Yankee* on local newsstands. Dublin is mentioned in the play, though Peterborough served as its model.[98]

Like *Yankee* magazine, *Our Town* is a bittersweet tribute to Old New England. It nostalgically recalls homespun life in Grover's Corners, New Hampshire, between 1901 and 1913, the horse-and-buggy era. Grover's Corners is *Yankee*'s idealized region in miniature. Its "Polish Town" and "Canuck families" are mentioned at the beginning of the play and then disappear for good across the village railroad tracks. Grover's Corners represents the essential New England that Sagendorph saw slipping away. As the publisher and editor of the *Grover's Corners Sentinel* explains: "Politically, we're eighty-six per cent Republicans; six percent Democrats; four per cent socialists; rest indifferent. Religiously, we're eighty-five per cent Protestants; twelve percent Catholics; rest indifferent." In response to a question about "social injustice and industrial inequality," the down-to-earth publisher-editor explains the town's Coolidgean social ethic: "we do all we can to help those that can't help themselves and those that can we leave alone." [99] One wonders if Wilder had been reading the work of a real-life publisher-editor in small-town New Hampshire.

Yankee continued to grow until 1941, when Sagendorph moved to New York City to work for the wartime Office of Censorship. The magazine stopped publishing in 1942. As war approached Sagendorph had altered *Yankee* to acknowledge threatening world events and to promote American patriotism. "A Yankee is an American," he stressed shortly before Pearl Harbor, "and in the present crisis, thank God, the North, South, East and West are together, working and fighting for the same principles and ideals." [100] World War II and its aftermath inaugurated an era of American cultural nationalism that would undercut the regionalist sentiment that developed through the 1920s and 1930s.

Yankee began publishing again in July 1945. The magazine and Robert Frost, who remained enormously popular until his death in 1963, continued to contribute to the perception of the north country as the real New England, aided by ever more important state tourist offices. But regionalism as a category of identity confronted serious cultural challenges in the 1950s and 1960s. A new revival of regional feeling would not surge through American culture until the 1970s.

Epilogue

Toward Post-Yankee
New England

The regionalist sentiment of the 1920s and 1930s receded in the decades after peace was achieved in Europe as Cold War nationalism infused American culture. With much of Europe in ruins, the nation appeared on the verge of fulfilling the economic and political promise of what commentators increasingly referred to as "the American century." Even Republican administrations, responding to Cold War politics, advanced the New Deal's nationalizing, integrating agenda. Whether through the Federal Highway Act (1956) or the National Defense Education Act (1958), which followed the launching of Sputnik, Americans were offered policies and rhetoric that pulled them together in a national crusade against Godless totalitarianism and the threat of nuclear annihilation. The National Endowments for the Arts and the Humanities, federal initiatives of the tumultuous 1960s, were rooted in a Cold War nationalism that sought to celebrate American "exceptionalism" — the idea that the nation's experience was unique in the annals of world history — and to unite citizens through an appreciation of the country's historical and cultural achievements.

New England reasserted its national regionalism during the Cold War decades. Benefiting from the new patriotic interest in America's exceptional past, New England submitted an updated claim as the American homeland. A series of new outdoor museums showcased the regional origins of America's unique heritage. Plimoth Plantation was founded in 1947, the same year that the re-created Old Sturbridge Village opened to the public. Massachusetts's Historic Deerfield and Vermont's Shelburne Museum began official operation in 1952. In New Hampshire, Portsmouth's reassembled colonial village, Strawbery Banke, opened in 1958. Small, older village museums, such as Connecticut's Mystic Seaport, entered a new era of growth during the postwar decades, and Boston organized and promoted its "Heritage Trail," where the "Spirit of America" was born.[1]

At the same time, as higher education entered an era of expansive growth, New England's influential colleges and universities helped position the region as the seedbed of American culture. Harvard's formidable Perry Miller dominated the revival of Puritan studies and offered New England's founders as tough-minded realists, shapers of national character and culture who provided lessons for the postwar challenges confronting America. One of Miller's Harvard colleagues, F. O. Mathiessen, rechristened the mid-nineteenth-century literary flowering—the New England Renaissance—as the "American Renaissance." Miller's and Mathiessen's bulky, authoritative volumes shaped a new postwar reading of the New England origins of American culture.[2]

Unlike earlier expressions of national regionalism, New England's heritage was enlisted more in the service of American than regional patriotism. As the founder of Historic Deerfield put it in 1952, "our young and powerful nation finds itself engaged in an ideological conflict with Communism." Re-creating the life of "a New England village can be the most eloquent response to the strident falsehoods poisoning the air today."[3]

Cold War nationalism helped reaffirm New England's image as the American homeland. But during the postwar years New England, America's oldest industrial region, was also perceived as a place in economic decline. The historic plight of the textile industry is as familiar to New Englanders as the protracted futility of the Boston Red Sox. The region's textile centers never fully recovered from the depression. The shoe industry then followed the downward trajectory of textile mills. From the 1950s through most of the 1970s, New England as a whole lagged the rest of the nation in population and employment growth. In fact, between 1950 and the energy crisis of the 1970s, the unemployment rate in New England was above the national average nearly every year. We now know that New England was in the forefront of deindustrialization, which would lead to a new, strong postindustrial economy. But for much of the last fifty years deindustrialization was typically perceived as evidence of a region in decline. As the major economic development commission for the region reported in 1976, "[T]he New England economy, in general, has faltered since World War II. The downturn in the nation's economy accentuated the 1975 basic problem: a slow but steady and pervasive deterioration of its economic base."[4]

Some commentators, particularly in the 1950s, suggested that New England's demise extended beyond its economic problems to the "hollowing out" of its Yankee culture. For two centuries following the Great Migration of the 1630s, New England endured as America's most culturally homogeneous region. But by the early twentieth century, European and French Canadian immigrants had transformed it into America's most ethnically diverse region. This historical status is now often obscured by the heavy Hispanic and Asian immigration of the last three decades that has disproportionately altered states and regions outside of New England. Yet statistics suggest how European and Canadian immigrants dramatically changed New England. In 1950, for example, Rhode Island, Connecticut, and Massachusetts were ranked as the three states with the highest percentage of their population consisting of white foreign-born residents and their children. Even New Hampshire, Maine, and Vermont were above the national average, though their significantly lower ethnic percentage helps explain why the northern tier of states abided as the perceived home of the real New England (see Table 1).

By the 1950s ethnic New Englanders had begun to make significant inroads into the region's political and professional circles. Perhaps this helps explain the reaction to New England's ethnic transformation of George Wilson Pierson. In 1954 the prominent Yale historian delivered an address to the American Historical Association titled "The Obstinate Concept of New England: A Study in Denudation." A year later his presentation appeared in the *New England Quarterly,* a scholarly journal founded in 1928 as part of the regionalist movement. Surveying the region's history, Pierson concluded that New England had exhausted its moral and cultural assets in three endeavors: efforts to missionize and "control" the West, to reform the South, and to industrialize the East. "New England's future looks dark," he lamented. "It is, as they say, a 'finished' region — or at least a region whose products must be given a fine finish."[5]

Pierson examined New England's ethnic alteration as part of the region's "denudation." Yankee New England had been "overwhelmed" by immigrants. "In the seaports are the South Boston Irish and the Grand Avenue Italians," he observed, "in the interior, the 'hopping frogs' from Canada and immigrants from Poland." New England, Pierson seemed to bemoan, "is no longer the home of the Yankee but the Yankee *ghetto.*"[6]

His essay is significant not just because it summarizes a familiar postwar perspective on New England's economic decline. Pierson also related a

TABLE I.

States with the Highest Percentage of White
Foreign Born and Children of White Foreign
Born, 1950

Rank	State	Percentage of Total White Population
I	Rhode Island	49.9
2	Connecticut	49.5
3	Massachusetts	49.5
4	New York	49.2
5	New Jersey	44.8
6	North Dakota	39.6
7	New Hampshire	36.1
8	Minnesota	34.7
9	Illinois	33.4
10	Michigan	33.3
17	Maine	27.1
18	Vermont	25.6
	United States	25.0

Source: Robert W. Eisenmenger, *The Dynamics of
Growth in New England's Economy, 1870–1964* (Middletown,
Conn., 1967).

history of Puritan-Yankee cultural dissolution, seemingly unaware that his discourse on regional decline was itself a venerable trope of New England identity. From second-generation Puritans, to nineteenth-century Federalists, to post–Civil War colonial revivalists, to readers of *Yankee* magazine—New England was persistently viewed as a region on the skids. Only the putative sources of its cultural decay changed over time.

Pierson, like the founder of *Yankee,* excluded ethnics from his narrative of regional identity and assigned them considerable responsibility for the erosion of New England's cultural distinctiveness. He imagined a stable Puritan-Yankee past from which he could chart the disintegration of the "real" New England. In response to such declension models of regional culture, David Hackett Fischer proposed, in *Albion's Seed,* an alternative, overdrawn genetic approach that located New England's essence in an *enduring* Puritan past. Fischer offered a kind of transhistorical Puritan tradition that, he argued, has been remarkably persistent as the shaping force of New England culture down to the present.[7]

Fischer started working on *Albion's Seed* during a period of renewed scholarly and popular interest in regionalism. Beginning in the 1970s, a regional revival gathered momentum in the nation's cultural life. Cold War politics ultimately produced not national unity but Vietnam and a new skepticism about American exceptionalism. Suburban sprawl led to the uncontrolled development of the rural landscape; suburbanism spawned Levittown and Strip Mall, USA. The progress of the "American century" gave birth to the environmental movement and reinvigorated historic preservation, both of which preached the importance of place. At the same time the suburban, corporate transformation of American life made heritage and historical quaintness a valued commodity. Heritage tourism became a major postindustrial "industry." Well-funded state tourist bureaus aggressively marketed regions to growing numbers of travelers in search of authentic places and pasts. Indeed, beginning in the 1980s car license plates became traveling billboards with state slogans and icons that mapped a new geographic awareness and demonstrated how place had become a consumer commodity. Moreover, the energy crisis of the 1970s and early 1980s underscored continuing regional variations in American life. Terms like Frost Belt, Sun Belt, and Rust Belt described a new postindustrial geography of regional difference and of uneven economic promise. The South's rapidly growing population and new political clout summoned visions of the "Southernization" of American life.

For a variety of reasons and in various ways the 1970s thus inaugurated a regional revival in American life. In that decade the National Endowments established state humanities and arts councils across the country — cultural analogues to the "New Federalism" that emerged in Washington, D.C., and that has remained influential in debates about returning power and authority to state governments. State humanities and arts councils became conduits for federal money that supported local heritage activities that became part of the regional revival. By the late 1990s the National Endowment for the Humanities, conceived largely as an agency of cultural nationalism, proposed the creation of ten regional heritage centers across the country funded with federal and private money. Such an initiative, along with the spread of academic regional studies centers in recent years, suggests the high tide of a new regionalism in American life. "The study of regional culture and politics, folkways and eccentricities, long dismissed as the minor leagues of academic scholarship," the *New York Times* reported in 1999, "is fashionable at American universities as it has not been since at least the 1930's."[8]

Scholars have recently issued calls for a new approach to regional studies, one that recognizes how regions have always been dynamic places. Such an understanding encourages historians to move beyond declension and genetic models of regional cultures. For New England, historians of regional identity confront a clear agenda. I have tried to explain how both on the ground and in the country of the imagination New England has been an ever-changing region. Perhaps this knowledge will help us move beyond the layered historical narratives and the canonical icons that fix New England's essence in some stable, pure, and imagined Puritan or Yankee past. We need a new, post-Puritan/Yankee narrative of New England distinctiveness that will address the interpretive needs of the region in the twenty-first century. The ethnic transformation of New England should be positioned at the center of a new narrative of regional distinctiveness.

But both declension and genetic interpretations of a fabled Puritan-Yankee past consign ethnics to the cultural periphery, portraying them either as underminers or, in the case of *Albion's Seed,* as passive recipients of the real New England's authentic traditions. Yet immigrants and their offspring helped create the New England that advances toward its quadricentennial. Immigrants brought their own work ethic to the region rather than simply needing to be tutored in Yankee industriousness. Immigrants gave New England the highest workforce participation rate in the country, as women toiled in factories to support their families. Immigration gave New England rich human capital that not only helped industrialize the region, but also remained vital in the postindustrial era. New England benefited from the presence of large numbers of second- and third-generation ethnics—ambitious and upwardly mobile sons and daughters of blue-collar workers who learned from family experience that there was no future in the mills and the economy they represented and who flocked into higher education. Indeed, a dose of New England mill work often served as a tonic for aimless ethnic youth. The father of Terrence Murray, now the head of Fleet, the largest bank in New England, sent his seemingly unambitious son into a Woonsocket, Rhode Island, mill to teach him the importance of education. Murray, a high school dropout, eventually went on to Harvard and became the dominant figure in New England banking, a field long impervious to ethnic inroads.

Above all, immigrants altered the political culture of New England, modifying the moralistic republicanism of Yankee tradition. "All politics is local," Massachusetts representative and house speaker Tip O'Neil famously announced. In much of the region, traditional New England moralism merged with competitive ethnic ward politics to shape regional political culture, an often fragile synthesis that went asunder, for instance, when Senator Ted Kennedy was spit upon in South Boston during the busing turmoil of the early 1970s.

Perhaps the sustained immigration of recent decades and the current revival of interest in the study of regionalism will encourage advocates of a new regional studies to revise standard narratives of New England's distinctive past. If rhetoric is to be matched by results, practitioners of a new regional studies will have to go beyond documenting how familiar New England stories and icons emerged at particular historical moments, addressed changing interpretive needs, and rested on silences about the region's past. We need a new narrative of how New England developed not only as a Puritan-Yankee city on a hill but also as an ethnic city by the mill.

Notes

INTRODUCTION

1. Ernest Hebert, *The Dogs of March* (New York, 1979), pp. 58–59.
2. Hawthorne quoted in Michael C. Steiner and Clarence Mondale, eds., *Region and Regionalism in the United States: A Source Book for the Humanities and Social Sciences* (New York, 1988), p. x.
3. David Hackett Fischer, *Albion's Seed: Four British Folkways in America* (New York, 1989). See the excellent "Forum" on Fischer's volume in *William and Mary Quarterly* 48 (April 1991): 224–308.
4. I am using the language of David Harlan to describe the state of American historical writing. See *The Degradation of American History* (Chicago, 1997), p. 67.
5. For a classic interpretation of change and the decline of New England's cultural distinctiveness, see George Wilson Pierson, "The Obstinate Concept of New England: A Study in Denudation," *New England Quarterly* 28 (March 1955): 3–17. For a guide to regionalist sentiment, see Steiner and Mondale, *Region and Regionalism*.
6. On the substitution of regional for national cultural holism, see Katherine G. Morrissey, *Mental Territories: Mapping the Inland Empire* (Ithaca, N.Y., 1997), p. 9.
7. I am adapting this phrase from James Clifford, "Introduction: Partial Truths," in Clifford and George Marcus, eds., *Writing Culture: The Poetics and Politics of Ethnography* (Berkeley, Calif., 1986), p. 22. See also Clifford, *The Predicament of Culture: Twentieth-Century Ethnography, Literature, and Art* (Cambridge, Mass., 1988), and Victoria E. Bonnell and Lynn Hunt, eds., *Beyond the Cultural Turn: New Directions in the Study of Society and Culture* (Berkeley, Calif., 1999). Bonnell and Hunt's introduction (pp. 1–32) is especially helpful.
8. Mark A. Peterson, *The Price of Redemption: The Spiritual Economy of Puritan New England* (Stanford, Calif., 1997), p. 8; David D. Hall, "Narrating Puritanism," in Harry S. Stout and D. G. Hart, eds., *New Directions in American Religious History* (New York, 1997), pp. 73–74.
9. Edward L. Ayers and Peter S. Onuf, eds., *All Over the Map: Rethinking American Regions* (Baltimore, 1996), p. 4. On the "new regional studies," see David Jordan, ed., *Regionalism Reconsidered: New Approaches to the Field* (New York, 1994); Glen E. Lich, ed., *Regional Studies: The Interplay of Land and Peoples* (College Station, Tex., 1992); and Morrissey, *Mental Territories*. See also the "Forum" on

"Bringing Regionalism Back to History," *American Historical Review* 104 (October 1999): 1156–1239. The only book-length example of new approaches applied to New England is Dona Brown, *Inventing New England: Regional Tourism in the Nineteenth Century* (Washington, D.C., 1995). Brown's excellent book is very suggestive, as is Stephen Nissenbaum's essay "New England as Region and Nation," in Ayers and Onuf, *All Over the Map,* pp. 38–61. A recent art history book based on a Smithsonian exhibition also contains a few essays that might be considered examples of a new regional studies. See especially the essays by William H. Truettner in Truettner and Roger B. Stein, eds. *Picturing Old New England: Image and Memory* (New Haven, Conn., 1999). To date, the so-called new regional studies approach has only had a modest impact on our understanding of New England.

10. Ayers and Onuf, *All Over the Map,* p. 8.

11. Richard White, *"It's Your Misfortune and None of My Own": A New History of the American West* (Norman, Okla., 1991), p. 616. I have also benefited from critiques of the "new western history" that discuss the interpenetration or merging of imagined and historic regions. See, e.g., Forrest G. Robinson, "Clio Bereft of Calliope: Literature and the New Western History," in Robinson, ed., *The New Western History* (Tucson, Ariz., 1998), pp. 74–75.

12. White, *"It's Your Misfortune,"* p. 613.

13. David Jaffee, *People of the Wachusett: Greater New England in History and Memory* (Ithaca, N.Y., 1999), p. 17.

14. On the imagined pasts and historical narratives of community identity, see T. H. Breen, *Imagining the Past: East Hampton Histories* (Reading, Mass., 1989); see also Clifford, "Partial Truths." Of course, the widely cited text that explores the processes of identity formation is Benedict Anderson, *Imagined Communities: Reflections on the Origin and Spread of Nationalism,* rev. ed. (London, 1991).

15. See Richard Brodhead, *The School of Hawthorne* (New York, 1986), p. 5, and Breen, *Imagining the Past,* chap. 1.

16. For the two-hundred-year (1790–1990) trajectory of New England's population decline within the nation as a whole, see, e.g., Laurence Becker, "New England as a Region," in Jerome M. Mileur, ed., *Parties and Politics in the New England States* (Amherst, Mass., 1997), p. 9, and Joshua L. Rosenbloom, "The Challenges of Economic Maturity: New England, 1880–1940," in Peter Temin, ed., *Engines of Enterprise: An Economic History of New England* (Cambridge, Mass., 2000), p. 155.

CHAPTER ONE

1. Roger Thompson, *Mobility and Migration: East Anglian Founders of New England, 1629–1640* (Amherst, Mass., 1994), p. 203.

2. On the peopling of early New England, in addition to Thompson, *Mobility and Migration,* see David Cressy, *Coming Over: Migration and Communication between England and New England in the Seventeenth Century* (New York, 1988), chaps. 2–4; Virginia D. Anderson, *New England's Generation: The Great Migration and the Formation of Society and Culture in the Seventeenth Century* (New York, 1991), chaps. 1–3; and Robert Charles Anderson, comp., *The Great Migration Begins: Immigrants to New England, 1620–1633,* 3 vols. (Boston, 1995).

3. David D. Hall, "Literacy, Religion, and the Plain Style," in Hall and David Grayson Allen, eds., *New England Begins: The Seventeenth Century,* 3 vols. (Boston, 1982), 1:5; Harry S. Stout, *The New England Soul: Preaching and Religious Culture in Colonial New England* (New York, 1986), pp. 3–10; Kenneth A. Lockridge, *Literacy in Colonial New England* (New York, 1974).

4. Virginia Anderson (*New England's Generation*) underscores the distinctiveness of colonial New England's collective self-consciousness; see esp. chap. 5. See also Phillip H. Round, *By Nature and Custom Cursed: Transatlantic Civil Discourse and New England Cultural Production* (Hanover, N.H., 1999).

5. Nicholas Canny and Anthony Pagden, eds., *Colonial Identity in the Atlantic World, 1500–1800* (Princeton, N.J., 1987), p. 9.

6. William Hubbard, *A General History of New England from the Discovery to 1680* (1682), in Massachusetts Historical Society, *Collections* 2 (1815): 545.

7. On Locke and the broad European background for Smith's vision of New England, see Jack P. Greene, *The Intellectual Construction of America: Exceptionalism and Identity from 1492 to 1800* (Chapel Hill, N.C., 1993), esp. p. 52.

8. Smith quoted in Douglas R. McManis, *European Impressions of the New England Coast, 1497–1620* (Chicago, 1972), pp. 54–55.

9. On Norumbega and European knowledge and perceptions of New England, see Emerson W. Baker et al., eds., *American Beginnings: Exploration, Culture, and Cartography in the Land of Norumbega* (Lincoln, Nebr., 1994); Cressy, *Coming Over,* chap. 1; and McManis, *European Impressions,* chaps. 1–5.

10. John Canup, *Out of the Wilderness: The Emergence of an American Identity in Colonial New England* (Middletown, Conn., 1990), pp. 10–13.

11. Karen Ordahl Kupperman, "Climate and Mastery of the Wilderness," in David D. Hall and David Grayson Allen, eds., *Seventeenth-Century New England* (Boston, 1984), p. 5.

12. Smith, *Description of New England,* in *The Complete Works of Captain John Smith, 1580–1631,* edited by Philip L. Barbour, 3 vols. (Chapel Hill, N.C., 1986), 1:329–30, 339–40.

13. Brian Harley, "New England Cartography and the Native Americans," in Baker et al., *American Beginnings,* p. 297.

14. See, e.g., Smith, *New England's Trials* (1620), in Barbour, *Works,* 1:386–406, and Smith, *Advertisements for the Unexperienced Planters of New England, or Any Where* (1631), in *Works,* 3:253–302.

15. Smith, *Description of New England,* p. 347.

16. Smith, *Advertisements for the Unexperienced Planters,* p. 270. For an excellent discussion of the economic perspectives of Smith and the Puritans, which has influenced my analysis, see Stephen Innes, *Creating the Commonwealth: The Economic Culture of Puritan New England* (New York, 1995), esp. chaps. 1–3; see also Margaret Ellen Newell, *From Dependency to Independence: Economic Revolution in Colonial New England* (Ithaca, N.Y., 1998), chaps. 1–5.

17. [Robert Cushman], "Reasons and Considerations touching the lawfulness of removing out of England into the parts of America" (1622), in Dwight Heath, ed., *Mourt's Relation: A Journal of the Pilgrims at Plymouth* (New York, 1963), pp. 89–90. The *Mayflower* Compact (1620) is printed in *Mourt's Relation,* pp. 17–18. See also William Bradford, *Of Plymouth Plantation,* edited by Harvey Wish (New York, 1962), esp. pp. 69–75.

18. On the history of Plymouth, see John Demos, *A Little Commonwealth: Family Life in Plymouth Colony* (New York, 1969), and George D. Langdon Jr., *Pilgrim Colony: A History of New Plymouth, 1620–1691* (New Haven, 1966).

19. Thompson, *Mobility and Migration,* p. 12.

20. Canup, *Out of the Wilderness,* chap. 1. The work of David Grayson Allen is at the center of the revisionist scholarship that sees New England as a transplantation of English culture and practices. See Allen, *In English Ways: The Movement of Societies and Transferral of English Local Law and Customs to Massachusetts Bay in the Seventeenth Century* (Chapel Hill, N.C., 1981). Allen summarizes his argument in "Both Englands," in Hall and Allen, *Seventeenth-Century New England,* pp. 55–82. See also Martyn J. Bowden, "Culture and Place: English Sub-Cultural Regions in New England in the Seventeenth Century," *Connecticut History* 35 (1994): 68–146, and Bowden, "Invented Tradition and Academic Convention in Geographical Thought about New England," *GeoJournal* 26 (1992): 187–94.

21. T. H. Breen, "Persistent Localism: English Social Change and the Shaping of New England Institutions," in Breen, *Puritans and Adventurers: Change and Persistence in Early America* (New York, 1980), pp. 3–23.

22. On colonial degeneration, see Canup, *Out of the Wilderness,* esp. chap. 1.

23. Arthur Krim, "Acculturation of the New England Landscape: Native and English Toponymy of Eastern Massachusetts," in Peter Benes, ed., *New England Prospect: Maps, Place Names and the Historical Landscape* (Boston, 1980), pp. 69–88; Smith, *Advertisements for the Unexperienced Planters,* p. 275.

24. Bradford, *Of Plymouth Plantation,* p. 78.

25. Higginson, "New-Englands Plantation, or A short and True Description of the Commodities and Discommodities of that Countrey," in Everett Emerson, ed., *Letters from New England: The Massachusetts Bay Colony, 1629–1638* (Amherst, Mass., 1976), p. 30; William Wood, *New England's Prospect,* edited with an introduction by Alden T. Vaughan (Amherst, Mass., 1977), pp. 57–58.

26. Heath, *Mourt's Relation,* p. 53. On Native American improvements to the land

and seasonal village life, see William Cronon, *Changes in the Land: Indians, Colonists, and the Ecology of New England* (New York, 1983), chap. 3.

27. Michael Wigglesworth, "God's Controversy with New England" (1662), in Alan Heimert and Andrew Delbanco, eds., *The Puritans in America: A Narrative Anthology* (Cambridge, Mass., 1985), p. 232.

28. David Grayson Allen, "*Vacuum Domicilium:* The Social and Cultural Landscape of Seventeenth-Century New England," in Hall and Allen, *New England Begins,* 1:18; Cecilia Tichi, *New World, New Earth: Environmental Reform in American Literature from the Puritans through Whitman* (New Haven, 1979), esp. p. 6.

29. On English knowledge of Spanish cruelty and on Puritan historical narratives and the refighting of Indian wars in print, see the excellent study of Jill Lepore, *The Name of War: King Philip's War and the Origins of American Identity* (New York, 1998), pp. 8–12. On the Pequot War, see Francis Jennings, *The Invasion of America: Indians, Colonialism, and the Cant of Conquest* (New York, 1975), quotations on pp. 182, 223.

30. On competency, see Virginia Anderson, *New England's Generation,* chap. 4.

31. John White, *The Planters Plea* (1630), in Massachusetts Historical Society, *Proceedings* 62 (1929): 391; James K. Hosmer, ed., *Winthrop's Journal: "History of New England," 1630–1649,* 2 vols. (New York, 1908), 1:116, 133.

32. Regulation quoted in Peter N. Carroll, *Puritanism and the Wilderness: The Intellectual Significance of the New England Frontier, 1629–1700* (New York, 1969), p. 183. See also Tichi, *New World, New Earth,* chap. 1.

33. Edward Trelawny to Robert Trelawny, October 10, 1635, in Emerson, *Letters from New England,* p. 176.

34. For the best analysis of orthodox, popular, and folk elements in Puritan religious culture, see David D. Hall, *Worlds of Wonder, Days of Judgment: Popular Religious Belief in Early New England* (New York, 1989). For provocative analyses of the exercise of Puritan political and cultural authority that shaped an orthodox New England, see Darren Staloff, *The Making of an American Thinking Class: Intellectuals and Intelligentsia in Puritan Massachusetts* (New York, 1998), and Jane Kamensky, *Governing the Tongue: The Politics of Speech in Early New England* (New York, 1997).

35. Marian Card Donnelly, *The New England Meeting Houses of the Seventeenth Century* (Middletown, Conn., 1968); Edmund W. Sinnott, *Meeting House and Church in Early New England* (New York, 1963); Peter Benes, ed., *New England Meeting House and Church, 1630–1850* (Boston, 1980), pp. 124–28.

36. Thomas Dudley to Lady Bridget, March 28, 1631, in Emerson, *Letters from New England,* p. 72. On remigration, see Cressy, *Coming Over,* p. 192.

37. Bulkeley quoted in David D. Hall, *The Faithful Shepherd: A History of the New England Ministry in the Seventeenth Century* (Chapel Hill, 1972), p. 172.

38. See Gary Gertsle, "Liberty, Coercion, and the Making of Americans," *Journal of American History* 84 (September 1997): 534–36.

39. Wood, *New England's Prospect,* pp. 31–32. See also Kupperman, "Climate and Mastery of the Wilderness," pp. 6–15.

40. Wood, *New England's Prospect,* pp. 31–32. See also Canup, *Out of the Wilderness,* pp. 10–12, 15–17.

41. Wood, *New England's Prospect,* p. 32.

42. Higginson, "New-Englands Plantation," p. 34.

43. *New England's First Fruits* (1643), reprinted in Samuel Eliot Morison, *The Founding of Harvard College* (Cambridge, Mass., 1935), p. 441.

44. As Stephen Carl Arch points out, Richard Mather explained how his son's name was chosen for the "never-to-be forgotten *Increase,* of every sort, wherewith God Favoured the Country, about the time of his Nativity." See *Authorizing the Past: The Rhetoric of History in Seventeenth-Century New England* (DeKalb, Ill., 1994), p. 96.

45. Wood, *New England's Prospect,* p. 28; Higginson, "New-Englands Plantation," p. 35; Cronon, *Changes in the Land,* p. 120.

46. Edward Johnson, *Wonder-Working Providence of Sions Savior in New England, 1628–1651* (1654), edited by J. Franklin Jameson (New York, 1910), p. 84. See also Kupperman, "Climate and Mastery of the Wilderness," p. 20.

47. Johnson, *Wonder-Working Providence,* p. 210.

48. Avihu Zakai, *Exile and Kingdom: History and Apocalypse in the Puritan Migration to America* (New York, 1992), p. 68.

49. Sacvan Bercovitch became the most influential exponent of this view in *The Puritan Origins of the American Self* (New Haven, Conn., 1975) and *The American Jeremiad* (Madison, Wis., 1978). See David Harlan, "A People Blinded from Birth: American History according to Sacvan Bercovitch," *Journal of American History* 79 (December 1991): 949–71.

50. Winthrop, "A Model of Christian Charity," in Heimert and Delbanco, *Puritans in America,* p. 91.

51. For the political use of Winthrop's address from the 1960s to the 1980s, see Joseph M. McShane, "Winthrop's 'City upon a Hill' in Recent Political Discourse," *America* (October 1, 1988): 194–98, and Michael Reagan, *The City on a Hill* (Nashville, Tenn., 1997).

52. Theodore Dwight Bozeman, *To Live Ancient Lives: The Primitivist Dimension in Puritanism* (Chapel Hill, N.C., 1988), p. 114. Bozeman is the leading critic of the Americanist interpretation of the Puritan migration. My discussion of the founding generation's religious orientation is heavily indebted to his analysis and to the revisionist work of Andrew Delbanco, *The Puritan Ordeal* (Cambridge, Mass., 1989) and "The Puritan Errand Re-viewed," *Journal of American Studies* 18 (1984): 343–60. See also David Scobey, "Revising the Errand: New England's Ways and the Puritan Sense of the Past," *William and Mary Quarterly* 41 (1984): 3–31.

53. Winthrop quoted in Emerson, *Letters from New England,* p. 41.

54. Winthrop, "Reasons to Be Considered for . . . the Intended Plantation in New England" (1629), in Heimert and Delbanco, *Puritans in America,* p. 73. See also Bozeman, *To Live Ancient Lives,* pp. 90–95, and Delbanco, *Puritan Ordeal,* chap. 3. On Winthrop's famous address being delivered before departure from England, see Hugh J. Dawson, "John Winthrop's Rite of Passage: The Origins of the 'Christian Charitie' Discourse," *Early American Literature* 26 (1991): 219–31.

55. Cotton, "God's Promise to His Plantations" (1630), in Heimert and Delbanco, *Puritans in America,* pp. 79–80.

56. Higginson quoted in Cotton Mather, *Magnalia Christi American, or The Ecclesiastical History of New England,* 7 vols. (1702; reprint, New York, 1967), 3:362; Winthrop quoted in Emerson, *Letters from New England,* p. 41; Hooker, "The Danger of Desertion" (1631), in Heimert and Delbanco, *Puritans in America,* p. 69.

57. The theme of exile runs through the revisionist work of Bozeman and Delbanco that has already been cited. For a balanced assessment of this scholarship, see Charles L. Cohen, "The Post-Puritan Paradigm of Early American Religious History," *William and Mary Quarterly* 54 (October 1997): 704.

58. John Cotton to an Unidentified Clergyman, December 3, 1634, in Emerson, *Letters from New England,* p. 129.

59. Scobey, "Revising the Errand," pp. 13, 15.

60. Bozeman's *To Live Ancient Lives* (chap. 3) offers the best discussion of the Puritans' religious mission.

61. Nathaniel Ward, "The Simple Cobbler of Aggawam" (1647), in Perry Miller and Thomas H. Johnson, eds., *The Puritans: A Sourcebook of Their Writings,* 2 vols. (1938; reprint, New York, 1963), 1:227.

62. William G. McLoughlin, *Rhode Island: A Bicentennial History* (New York, 1978), p. viii.

63. *The Works of Anne Bradstreet,* edited by John Harvard Ellis (Gloucester, Mass., 1962), pp. 339–40.

64. Hooke, *New England's Tears for Old England's Fears* (1641), in Heimert and Delbanco, *Puritans in America,* p. 105.

65. Nathaniel Mather (1651) quoted in Donnelly, *New England Meeting Houses,* p. 61.

66. Cressy, *Coming Over,* chap. 10.

67. John Cotton, Foreword to John Norton, *The Answer to . . . Mr. William Appolonius* (1648), in Heimert and Delbanco, *Puritans in America,* p. 107. See also Stout, *New England Soul,* pp. 50–53.

68. *New England's First Fruits,* p. 430. On missionary motivation for Puritan colonization, see, e.g., Winthrop, "Reasons to Be Considered for Justifying the Undertakers of the Intended Plantation in New England" (1629), in Heimert and Delbanco, *Puritans in America,* p. 71.

69. *New England's First Fruits,* p. 445.

70. J. A. Leo Lemay, *"New England's Annoyances"* (Newark, Del., 1985), pp. 1–3. Lemay identifies Edward Johnson as the author of the song and argues for the Americanized New England identity that it suggests (chap. 3).

CHAPTER TWO

1. Edward Johnson, *Wonder-Working Providence of Sions Savior in New England, 1628–1651* (1654), edited by J. Franklin Jameson (New York, 1910), pp. 21–23, 61, 151, 271.

2. Ibid., p. 52.

3. Nicolas Canny and Anthony Pagden, eds., *Colonial Identity in the Atlantic World, 1500–1800* (Princeton, N.J., 1987), p. 9.

4. Michael Wigglesworth, "God's Controversy with New England" (1662), quoted in Alan Heimert and Andrew Delbanco, eds., *The Puritans in America: A Narrative Anthology* (Cambridge, Mass., 1985), p. 253.

5. Johnson, *Wonder-Working Providence,* p. 85.

6. Ibid., p. 210. See also Virginia D. Anderson, *New England's Generation: The Great Migration and the Formation of Society and Culture in the Seventeenth Century* (New York, 1991), chap. 5, and Theodore Dwight Bozeman, *To Live Ancient Lives: The Primitivist Dimension in Puritanism* (Chapel Hill, N.C., 1988), chap. 9. Recent revisionist scholars examining the second generation's interpretation of the Puritan past build on the insights of Robert Middlekauff, *The Mathers: Three Generations of Puritan Intellectuals, 1596–1728* (New York, 1971). In a superb analysis of "The Invention of New England," Middlekauff argues that "the fathers may have founded the colonies but the sons invented New England" (p. 98).

7. Nathaniel Morton, *New Englands Memoriall,* edited by Howard J. Hall (1669; reprint, New York, 1937), quotation found in "Dedication to the Christian Reader. See also Harry S. Stout, *The New England Soul: Preaching and Religious Culture in Colonial New England* (New York, 1986), chap. 3.

8. David Cressy, *Coming Over: Migration and Communication between England and New England in the Seventeenth Century* (New York, 1988), p. 69.

9. Mather quoted in Conrad Cherry, "New England as Symbol: Ambiguity in the Puritan Vision," *Soundings: An Interdisciplinary Journal* 58 (1975): 354. For demographic pressure on expansion, see David Jaffee, *People of the Wachusett: Greater New England in History and Memory, 1630–1860* (Ithaca, N.Y., 1999), esp. chaps. 1–2 for the second generation, and Philip Greven, *Four Generations: Population, Land, and Family in Colonial Andover, Massachusetts* (Ithaca, N.Y., 1970).

10. Jack P. Greene, *Pursuit of Happiness: The Social Development of Early Modern British Colonies and the Formation of American Culture* (Chapel Hill, N.C., 1988), p. 64.

11. Cotton Mather, quoted in William G. McLoughlin, *Rhode Island: A Bicentennial History* (New York, 1978), p. viii.

12. Christine Leigh Heyrman, *Commerce and Culture: The Maritime Communities of Colonial Massachusetts, 1690–1750* (New York, 1984), p. 223.

13. David W. Conroy, *In Public Houses: Drink and the Revolution of Authority in Colonial Massachusetts* (Chapel Hill, N.C., 1995), pp. 58–62. On the profane, see Richard P. Gildrie, *The Profane, the Civil, and the Godly: The Reformation of Manners in Orthodox New England, 1679–1749* (University Park, Pa., 1994), and Bruce C. Daniels, *Puritans at Play: Leisure and Recreation in Colonial New England* (New York, 1995), esp. chap. 8.

14. This is Bradford's subdued description in *Of Plymouth Plantation,* edited by Harvey Wish (New York, 1962), p. 67, offered long after the settlement of Plymouth and the early descriptions of its openness. Bradford makes one passing reference to Native American "cornfields." For the Native American impact on the land, see William Cronon, *Changes in the Land: Indians, Colonists, and the Ecology of New England* (New York, 1983).

15. Anderson, *New England's Generation,* pp. 15–16; Cressy, *Coming Over,* pp. 68–70.

16. John Higginson, *The Cause of God and His People in New England* (Cambridge, Mass., 1664), pp. 10–11; William Stoughton, *New-Englands True Interest* (Cambridge, Mass., 1670), pp. 9, 19. For an insightful analysis of the Great Migration, see Anderson, *New England's Generation,* chap. 5.

17. Samuel Danforth, *A Brief Recognition of New-Englands Errand into the Wilderness* (Cambridge, Mass., 1671), p. 19. Danforth, however, was not the first to use the phrase. See, e.g., Jonathan Mitchell's sermon, delivered in 1667 and published four years later, *Nehemiah on the Wall* (Cambridge, Mass., 1671), p. 28. On the second generation's "theology of place," see Cherry, "New England as Symbol," pp. 349–52; see also Perry Miller, *Errand into the Wilderness* (1956; reprint, New York, 1964), chap. 1, and the updating of Miller in Bozeman, *To Live Ancient Lives;* Andrew Delbanco, *The Puritan Ordeal* (Cambridge, Mass., 1989) and "The Puritan Errand Re-viewed," *Journal of American Studies* 18 (1984): 343–60; and David Scobey, "Revising the Errand: New England's Ways and the Puritan Sense of the Past," *William and Mary Quarterly* 41 (January 1984): 3–31. On the meanings of the New Israel, see the discussion of Increase Mather's views in Middlekauff, *The Mathers,* pp. 107–8. Also important are the revisionist arguments of Reiner Smolinski, "Israel Redivivus: The Eschatological Limits of Puritan Typology in New England," *New England Quarterly* 63 (September 1990): 357–95. Smolinski reattaches Puritan rhetoric about the New Israel to eschatology, thereby limiting New England's claim to moral exclusivity. Yet even he concedes that the New Israel extended to America; moreover, Puritan preaching encouraged a collective identity rooted in an emergent sense of New England moral superiority.

18. See James Clifford, "Introduction: Partial Truths," in Clifford and George Marcus, eds., *Writing Culture: The Poetics and Politics of Ethnography* (Berkeley,

Calif., 1986), pp. 1–26, and Timothy Breen, *Imagining the Past: East Hampton Histories* (Reading, Mass., 1989).

19. Anne Bradstreet, "To My Dear Children," in Heimert and Delbanco, *Puritans in America,* pp. 138–39. See also Anderson, *New England's Generation,* esp. p. 220, and Delbanco, *Puritan Ordeal,* chap. 6.

20. Order regulating settlement quoted in Joseph Wood, *The New England Village* (Baltimore, 1997), p. 45. On Connecticut, see Bruce C. Daniels, *The Connecticut Town: Growth and Development, 1635–1790* (Middletown, Conn., 1979). On land hunger and town founding, see John Frederick Martin, *Profits in the Wilderness: Entrepreneurship and the Founding of New England Towns in the Seventeenth Century* (Chapel Hill, N.C., 1991). On geographic dispersal, see Douglas R. McManis, *Colonial New England: A Historical Geography* (New York, 1975), pp. 41–66.

21. Keayne's offense quoted in Bernard Bailyn, *The New England Merchants in the Seventeenth Century* (1955; reprint, New York, 1964), p. 42. See also Bailyn, *The Apologia of Robert Keayne: The Self-Portrait of a Puritan Merchant* (New York, 1965).

22. James K. Hosmer, ed., *Winthrop's Journal: History of New England,* 2 vols. (New York, 1908), 2:20. The best recent discussion of the Keayne affair is in Stephen Innes, *Creating the Commonwealth: The Economic Culture of Puritan New England* (New York, 1995), chap. 4. My analysis is shaped by Innes's interpretation.

23. Mary Rowlandson, *The Soveraignty and Goodness of God, Together with the Faithfulness of His Promises Displayed: Being a Narrative of the Captivity and Restauration of Mrs. Mary Rowlandson* (Cambridge, Mass., 1682). The classic work on the captivity narrative is Richard Slotkin, *Regeneration through Violence: The Mythology of the American Frontier, 1600–1860* (Middletown, Conn., 1973). For a good brief introduction, see Alden T. Vaughan and Edward W. Clark, eds., *Puritans among the Indians: Accounts of Captivity and Restoration, 1676–1724* (Cambridge, Mass., 1981), pp. 1–28. For a recent treatment, see Jill Lepore, *The Name of War: King Philip's War and the Origins of American Identity* (New York, 1998), chap. 5.

24. Charles F. Hambrick-Stowe underscores this "geographical correlate." See *The Practice of Piety: Puritan Devotional Disciplines in Seventeenth-Century New England* (Chapel Hill, N.C., 1982), p. 256. On the "vast and furious ocean" journey of the founders, see Cressy, *Coming Over,* chap. 6.

25. Rowlandson, *The Soveraignty and Goodness of God,* in Vaughan and Clark, *Puritans among the Indians,* pp. 37, 44–45, 49, 59. I have used this widely available edition of Rowlandson's narrative.

26. Ibid., p. 69. For a helpful discussion of the captivity narrative in the context of New England social history, see Laurel Thatcher Ulrich, *Good Wives: Image and Reality in the Lives of Women in Northern New England, 1650–1750* (New York, 1980), chap. 11.

27. For the English background of the jeremiad, see Bozeman, *To Live Ancient Lives,* pp. 287–98. What I am suggesting is that the rhetoric of the jeremiad brought about the imaginative relocation of the national covenant, especially

in relation to England's post-Restoration religious state. But in terms of millennialism and eschatology, New England was only one part of the New Israel. See Smolinski, "Israel Redivivus," pp. 369–78.

28. For my discussion of the Americanization of the jeremiad, I am heavily indebted to Bozeman, *To Live Ancient Lives,* pp. 298–310. See also Stout, *New England Soul,* chap. 4, and, of course, the seminal work of Perry Miller, *The New England Mind: From Colony to Province* (Boston, 1953), chaps. 1–10. Sacvan Bercovitch, in *The American Jeremiad* (Madison, Wis., 1978), extends Miller in a less persuasive way than do Bozeman and Stout. For a powerful critique of the way the jeremiad and the theme of declension have shaped interpretations of early New England history, see Mark A. Peterson, *The Price of Redemption: The Spiritual Economy of Puritan New England* (Stanford, Calif., 1997), pp. 1–22.

29. For "civic preaching," see Stout, *New England Soul,* p. 92, and A. W. Plumstead, ed., *The Wall and the Garden: Selected Massachusetts Election Sermons, 1670–1775* (Minneapolis, 1968), pp. 3–37.

30. John Calvin, quoted in Karen Ordahl Kupperman, "Climate and Mastery of the Wilderness," in David Hall and David Grayson Allen, eds., *Seventeenth-Century New England* (Boston, 1984), pp. 26–27; for the climate changes toward the end of the century, see p. 25.

31. Samuel Hooker, *Righteousness Rained from Heaven* (Cambridge, Mass., 1677), p. 18.

32. Wigglesworth, "God's Controversy with New England," pp. 239, 236.

33. Stout, *New England Soul,* pp. 111–15. On the earlier afflictions, see Gildrie, *The Profane, the Civil, and the Godly,* chap. 1.

34. [Increase Mather], "Epistle Dedicatory," *The Necessity of Reformation . . .* (Boston, 1679), p. 7.

35. Ibid. On covenant renewals, see esp. Stout, *New England Soul,* pp. 96–97, and Hambrick-Stowe, *The Practice of Piety,* pp. 248–51.

36. Stoughton, *New-Englands True Interest,* pp. 7, 35; Urian Oakes, *New England Pleaded with . . .* (Cambridge, Mass., 1673), p. 24; Increase Mather, *Pray for the Rising Generation* (Boston, 1679), p. 17.

37. Cotton Mather, *The Way to Prosperity* (1689), in Plumstead, *The Wall and the Garden,* p. 137. I have benefited from John Canup's *Out of the Wilderness: The Emergence of an American Identity in Colonial New England* (Middletown, Conn., 1990), chap. 6, which discusses "Criolian degeneracy" in a colonial context, though my connections to the jeremiad and my reading of Mather differ from his interpretation. See also Canny and Pagden, *Colonial Identity,* p. 9.

38. [Increase Mather], *The Necessity of Reformation,* p. 7; Cotton Mather, *The Way to Prosperity,* p. 132.

39. Cotton Mather, *Magnalia Christi Americana, or The Ecclesiastical History of New England,* 7 vols. (1702; reprint, New York, 1967), 1:25.

40. Mather quoted in Plumstead, *The Wall and the Garden,* p. 144.

41. Cotton Mather, *Things for a Distressed People* (Boston, 1696), p. 13; Nicholas Noyes, *New Englands Duty and Interest* . . . (Boston, 1698), p. 77; Increase Mather, *The Doctrine of Divine Providence* . . . (Boston, 1684), p. 43.

42. Hambrick-Stowe, *The Practice of Piety,* p. 255. For an excellent analysis of the conflicts in Mather's identity and in the *Magnalia,* see Kenneth Silverman, *The Life and Times of Cotton Mather* (New York, 1985), esp. pp. 157–66; see also Middlekauff, *The Mathers,* chap. 12.

43. Mather, *Magnalia,* 1:27; Stephen Carl Arch, *Authorizing the Past: The Rhetoric of History in Seventeenth-Century New England* (DeKalb, Ill., 1994), p. 146.

44. Morton, *New Englands Memoriall,* p. 84.

45. Ibid., pp. 137, 140; Johnson, *Wonder-Working Providence,* pp. 47–48, 67–68, 72–76, 82–86; Hambrick-Stowe, *The Practice of Piety,* p. 253.

46. Mather, *Magnalia,* 1:40, 69, 107.

47. Ibid., 40, 69, 81, 118; Mather quoted in Plumstead, *The Wall and the Garden,* p. 144.

48. Silsbe quoted in T. H. Breen, "Ideology and Nationalism on the Eve of the American Revolution: Revisions Once More in Need of Revising," *Journal of American History* 84 (June 1997): 28n.

49. On the process of cultural Anglicization or re-Anglicization, see Richard L. Bushman, *The Refinement of America: Persons, Houses, and Cities* (New York, 1993); James Deetz, *In Small Things Forgotten: The Archaeology of Early American Life* (New York, 1977); and T. H. Breen and Timothy Hall, "Structuring Provincial Imagination: The Rhetoric and Experience of Social Change in Eighteenth-Century New England," *American Historical Review* 130 (December 1998): 1411–39. For a different interpretation of eighteenth-century culture, see Jon Butler, *Becoming American: The Revolution before 1776* (Cambridge, Mass., 2000).

50. Peterson (*The Price of Redemption,* pp. 178–80) points out how in Boston the Dominion initially provoked reaffirmation of New England's Puritan tradition. But invocations of English rights soon followed.

51. Richard R. Johnson, *Adjustment to Empire: The New England Colonies, 1675–1715* (New Brunswick, N.J., 1981), chap. 3; David S. Lovejoy, *The Glorious Revolution in America* (New York, 1972), pp. 347–77; T. H. Breen, *The Character of the Good Ruler: A Study of Puritan Political Ideas in New England, 1630–1730* (New Haven, Conn., 1970), chap. 4.

52. Johnson, *Adjustment to Empire,* pp. 4, 307–27.

53. The best introductions to the reshaping of regional identity in the eighteenth century, which have influenced my analysis, are Bruce Tucker, "The Reinvention of New England, 1691–1770," *New England Quarterly* (1985): 315–40, and Stout, *New England Soul,* chaps. 6–7.

54. Mather quoted in Tucker, "Reinvention of New England," p. 318.

55. Mather, *Magnalia,* 1:65, 2:200.

56. Ibid., 1:75–76. See also Silverman, *Life and Times of Cotton Mather,* pp. 161–68.

57. Thomas Prince, *The Peopling of New England* (Boston, 1730), p. 24. See also Prince, *A Chronological History of New England* (Boston, 1736).

58. Thomas Foxcroft, *Observations Historical and Practical on the Rise and Primitive State of New England* (Boston, 1730), pp. 2, 14–15, 17, 45. See also Mather, *Magnalia,* 1:86.

59. John Barnard, *The Throne Established by Righteousness* (1734), in Plumstead, *The Wall and the Garden,* pp. 230, 240, 249; Breen, *Character of the Good Ruler,* p. 183.

60. Massachusetts House quoted in Breen, *Character of the Good Ruler,* p. 199. See also Richard L. Bushman, *King and People in Provincial Massachusetts* (Chapel Hill, N.C., 1985), chaps. 1–3.

61. Breen, *Character of the Good Ruler,* chap. 6; Stout, *New England Soul,* chaps. 7, 9; Tucker, "Reinvention of New England," pp. 322–23.

62. Jonathan Mayhew, *A Sermon Preached in the Audience of His Excellency William Shirley, Esq. . . . , (1754),* in Plumstead, *The Wall and the Garden,* pp. 299, 302. See also Nathan Hatch, *The Sacred Cause of Liberty: Republican Thought and the Millennium in Revolutionary New England* (New Haven, Conn., 1977), chap. 1.

63. John Rogers, *A Sermon Preached before His Excellency the Governour . . .* (Boston, 1706), pp. 29–31.

64. Benjamin Colman, *David's Dying Charge to the Rulers and People of Israel* (Boston, 1723), p. 29. I am indebted to Michael P. Winship, *Seers of God: Puritan Providentialism in the Restoration and Early Enlightenment* (Baltimore, 1996), for calling my attention to the Rogers and Colman texts.

65. Prince, *The Peopling of New England,* p. 21.

66. Foxcroft, *Observations Historical and Practical,* pp. 11, 16, 22–23. See also Prince, *Chronological History of New England* and *Annals of New England* (Boston, 1755). Stout (*New England Soul,* pp. 166–67) argues that election speakers in Massachusetts and Connecticut Anglicized ancient Israel and saw the Jewish covenant as a kind of constitution.

67. Jeremiah Dummer, *A Defense of the New England Charters* (1721), in Heimert and Delbanco, *Puritans in America,* p. 68. Dummer's *Defense* had actually been written in 1715.

68. On the consumer revolution, see T. H. Breen, "An Empire of Goods: The Anglicization of Colonial America, 1690–1776," *Journal of British Studies* 25 (October 1986): 467–99; Breen, " 'Baubles of Britain': The American and Consumer Revolutions of the Eighteenth Century," *Past and Present* 119 (May 1988): 73–104; and Bushman, *The Refinement of America.* On New England's population, see Robert V. Wells, *The Population of the British Colonies in America before 1776* (Princeton, N.J., 1975), chap. 3. On the slave trade within the overall pattern of American commerce, see Jay Coughtry, *The Notorious Triangle: Rhode Island and the African Slave Trade* (Philadelphia, 1981), pp. 3–22.

69. Breen, "An Empire of Goods," pp. 484–93. See also Robert Blair St. George, "Artifacts of Regional Consciousness in the Connecticut River Valley," in St. George, ed., *Material Life in America, 1600–1860* (Boston, 1988), pp. 335–56.

70. Bushman, *The Refinement of America,* esp. chaps. 2, 4; Breen, "An Empire of Goods," p. 478; Deetz, *In Small Things Forgotten,* chaps. 3, 5; Wayne Craven, *Colonial American Portraiture* (New York, 1986), chap. 8; Conroy, *In Public Houses,* pp. 93–96.

71. *Boston Gazette,* quoted in Conroy, *In Public Houses,* p. 95.

72. Deetz, *In Small Things Forgotten,* p. 38. See also James Deetz and Patricia Scott Deetz, *The Time of Their Lives: Life, Love, and Death in Plymouth Colony* (New York, 2000), esp. p. 10.

73. Marian Card Donnelly, *The New England Meeting Houses of the Seventeenth Century* (Middletown, Conn., 1968), esp. pp. 74–77.

74. Bushman, *The Refinement of America,* pp. 169–80; Bettina A. Norton, "Anglican Embellishments: The Contributions of John Gibbs, Junior and William Price to the Church of England in Eighteenth-Century Boston," in Peter Benes, ed., *New England Meeting House and Church, 1630–1850* (Boston, 1980), pp. 70–85.

75. On the Hingham Church, see Robert J. Wilson III, *The Benevolent Deity: Ebenezer Gay and the Rise of Rational Religion in New England, 1696–1787* (Philadelphia, 1984), pp. 196–97. On the trend toward changes to interiors of meetinghouses, see Jane C. Nylander, "Toward Comfort and Uniformity in New England Meeting Houses, 1750–1850," in Benes, *New England Meeting House and Church,* pp. 82–100.

76. On these developments and the growth of an "Anglican" understanding of the ministry, see J. William T. Youngs Jr., *God's Messengers: Religious Leadership in Colonial New England, 1700–1750* (New York, 1976), pp. 30–39.

77. John Corrigan, *The Prism of Piety: Catholick Congregational Clergy at the Beginning of the Enlightenment* (New York, 1991), pp. 5–8.

78. Ibid., pp. 28–30.

79. John Frederick Woolverton, *Colonial Anglicanism in North America* (Detroit, 1984), pp. 128–29. Woolverton (p. 28) points out that in 1750 there were only forty-four Anglican churches in New England.

80. See Frank Lambert, *Inventing the "Great Awakening"* (Princeton, N.J., 1999) and *Pedlar in Divinity: George Whitefield and the Transatlantic Revivals, 1737–1770* (Princeton, N.J., 1993); Harry S. Stout, *The Divine Dramatist: George Whitefield and the Rise of Modern Evangelism* (Grand Rapids, Mich., 1991); and Timothy D. Hall, *Contested Boundaries: Itineracy and the Reshaping of the Colonial American Religious World* (Durham, N.C., 1994). On Edwards, see Joseph A. Conforti, *Jonathan Edwards, Religious Tradition, and American Culture* (Chapel Hill, N.C., 1995), esp. pp. 36–37.

81. Charles Hambrick-Stowe, "The Spirit of the Old Writers: The Great Awakening and the Persistence of Puritan Piety," in Francis J. Bremer, *Puritanism: Trans-*

atlantic Perspectives on a Seventeenth-Century Anglo-American Faith (Boston, 1993), pp. 277–91.

82. For Edwards's sermon rhetoric, see Gerald R. McDermott, *One Holy and Happy Society: The Public Theology of Jonathan Edwards* (University Park, Pa., 1992), p. 23n.

83. Edwards's unpublished sermons are quoted in Mark Valeri, "The Economic Thought of Jonathan Edwards," *Church History* 60 (March 1991): 43, 49. The new church covenant is in C. C. Goen, ed., *The Great Awakening,* vol. 4 of *The Works of Jonathan Edwards,* 19 vols (New Haven, Conn., 1972), pp. 551–54 (quotation, p. 554).

84. Edwards quoted in McDermott, *One Holy and Happy Society,* p. 22.

85. Stephen J. Stein, ed., *A Humble Attempt* (1747), vol. 5 of *The Works of Jonathan Edwards,* 19 vols. (New Haven, Conn., 1977).

86. Edwards quoted in McDermott, *One Holy and Happy Society,* p. 20.

87. Hatch, *Sacred Cause of Liberty,* chap. 1; Stout, *New England Soul,* chap. 12.

88. Charles Chauncy quoted in Stout, *New England Soul,* p. 237; Edwards quoted in McDermott, *One Holy and Happy Society,* p. 93.

89. Mayhew, *A Sermon Preach'd in the Audience of His Excellency William Shirley, Esq. . . . ,* reprinted in Plumstead, *The Wall and the Garden,* pp. 308, 310; Solomon Williams, *The Relations of God's People to Him . . .* (New London, Conn., 1760), p. 19.

90. Samuel Langdon, *Joy and Gratitude to God . . .* (Portsmouth, N.H., 1760), pp. 23–24; Thomas Foxcroft, *Grateful Reflections on the Signal Appearances of Divine Providence* (Boston, 1760), pp. 10–12; Hatch, *Sacred Cause of Liberty,* chap. 1.

91. Belknap quoted in George B. Kirsch, *Jeremy Belknap: A Biography* (New York, 1982), p. 49; editor quoted in Breen, "Ideology and Nationalism on the Eve of the American Revolution," p. 28.

92. Woolverton, *Colonial Anglicanism in North America,* p. 34; Stephen Nissenbaum, *The Battle for Christmas* (New York, 1996), pp. 32–33.

93. See Breen, "Ideology and Nationalism on the Eve of the American Revolution," pp. 29–33.

CHAPTER THREE

1. Sam Adams quoted in Gordon S. Wood, *Creation of the American Republic, 1776–1787* (Chapel Hill, N.C., 1969), p. 118. The literature on republicanism is voluminous. Helpful overviews include Daniel T. Rodgers, "Republicanism: The Career of a Concept," *Journal of American History* 79 (June 1992): 11–38, and Joyce Appleby, "Republicanism in Old and New Contexts," *William and Mary Quarterly* 43 (January 1986): 20–34.

2. Connecticut minister quoted in Nathan O. Hatch, *The Sacred Cause of Liberty: Republican Thought and the Millennium in Revolutionary New England* (New Haven, Conn., 1977), p. 60.

3. Charles Francis Adams, ed., *The Works of John Adams,* 10 vols. (1850–56; reprint, New York, 1969), 9:366.

4. Jefferson quoted in James Roger Sharp, *American Politics in the Early Republic* (New Haven, Conn., 1993), p. 189.

5. On New England's moralistic republicanism and the conflicting Southern perspective, see ibid., esp. p. 21, and Robert Kelley, *The Cultural Pattern in American Politics: The First Century* (New York, 1979), pp. 83–86. On sectional conflict under the Articles of Confederation, see Peter S. Onuf, "Federalism, Republicanism, and the Origins of American Sectionalism," in Edward L. Ayers and Onuf, eds., *All Over the Map: Rethinking American Regions* (Baltimore, 1996), chap. 1. Onuf refers to New Englanders as "precocious sectionalists" (p. 25).

6. David Waldstreicher, *In the Midst of Perpetual Fetes: The Making of American Nationalism, 1776–1820* (Chapel Hill, N.C., 1997), chap. 5. Waldstreicher's superb analysis of national regionalisms in the early republic has helped shape my interpretation of Morse's geographies and New England regionalism.

7. On Morse's life and clerical career, see Richard J. Moss, *The Life of Jedidiah Morse: A Station of Peculiar Exposure* (Knoxville, Tenn., 1995); Joseph W. Phillips, *Jedidiah Morse and New England Congregationalism* (New Brunswick, N.J., 1983); James King Morse, *Jedidiah Morse: A Champion of New England Orthodoxy* (New York, 1939); and William Buell Sprague, *The Life of Jedidiah Morse, D.D.* (New York, 1874). Phillips offers a few pages on Morse's geographies. Moss devotes a chapter to Morse's geography as a personal vision. The most helpful examination of Morse's work is by a geographer; see Ralph H. Brown, "The American Geographies of Jedidiah Morse," *Annals of the Association of American Geographers* 31 (September 1941): 145–217. Less helpful are the brief treatments of Morse in Robert Lawson-Peebles, *Landscape and Written Expression in Revolutionary America* (New York, 1988), pp. 64–73, and Martin Bruckner, "Models of World-Making: The Language of Geography in American Literature" (Ph.D. diss., Brandeis University, 1997), pp. 107–12. A revised chapter of Bruckner's dissertation is more insightful; see "Lessons in Geography: Maps, Spellers, and Other Grammars of Nationalism in the Early Republic," *American Quarterly* 51 (June 1999): 325–33.

8. Federalist slogan quoted in James M. Banner Jr., *To the Hartford Convention: The Federalists and the Origins of Party Politics in Massachusetts, 1789–1815* (New York, 1970), p. 87.

9. T. H. Breen, "Ideology and Nationalism on the Eve of the American Revolution: Revisions Once More in Need of Revising," *Journal of American History* 84 (June 1997): 37.

10. Gordon S. Wood, ed., *The Rising Glory of America, 1760–1820* (New York, 1971), p. 1; Waldstreicher, *Perpetual Fetes,* esp. chap. 3; Len Travers, *Celebrating the Fourth: Independence Day and the Rites of Nationalism in the Early Republic* (Amherst, Mass., 1997).

11. Jedidiah Morse, *The American Geography* (1789; reprint, New York, 1970), pp. 65, 68. I have used this widely available facsimile of Morse's first major geography text.

12. Webster quoted in Timothy Dwight, *Travels in New England and New York,* edited by Barbara Miller Solomon, 4 vols. (Cambridge, Mass., 1969), 1:xxii. Stephen Nissenbaum uses the term "New England's New England" in a different context. See "New England as a Region and Nation," in Ayers and Onuf, *All Over the Map,* p. 39.

13. On the Woodstock and Yale backgrounds of Morse's life, see Moss, *Morse,* chaps. 1–2, and Phillips, *Morse and New England Congregationalism,* chap. 1.

14. Morse quoted in Brown, "American Geographies of Jedidiah Morse," p. 153.

15. Jedidiah Morse, *Geography Made Easy* (New Haven, Conn., 1784), pp. 39, 41.

16. Morse quoted in Brown, "American Geographies of Jedidiah Morse," p. 153.

17. Morse, *American Geography,* p. vi.

18. Both Phillips (*Morse and New England Congregationalism,* esp. p. 31) and Moss (*Life of Jedidiah Morse,* esp. chap. 3) offer helpful suggestions about Morse's temperamental and intellectual predilections.

19. Some of these changes are discussed in Onuf, "Federalism, Republicanism," pp. 14–15.

20. Morse, *American Geography,* p. vii. On Vermont, Maine, and regional mobility, see Michael A. Bellesiles, *Revolutionary Outlaws: Ethan Allen and the Struggle for Independence on the Early American Frontier* (Charlottesville, Va., 1993); Alan Taylor, *Liberty Men and Great Proprietors: Revolutionary Settlement on the Maine Frontier, 1760–1820* (Chapel Hill, N.C., 1990); and Stewart Holbrook, *The Yankee Exodus: An Account of Migration from New England* (New York, 1950).

21. Phillips, *Morse and New England Congregationalism,* pp. 20–21.

22. Morse quoted in ibid., pp. 27–28, and in Moss, *Morse,* p. 35.

23. Webster quoted in Joseph J. Ellis, *After the Revolution: Profiles of Early American Culture* (New York, 1979), p. 183. See also Richard M. Rollins, *The Long Journey of Noah Webster* (Philadelphia, 1980), p. 48.

24. Phillips, *Morse and New England Congregationalism,* pp. 34–35; Brown, "American Geographies of Jedidiah Morse," p. 176.

25. William J. Gilmore, *Reading Becomes a Necessity: Material and Cultural Life in Rural New England, 1780–1835* (Knoxville, Tenn., 1989), p. 64.

26. Jedidiah Morse and Elijah Parish, *A Compendious History of New England* (1804; 3d ed., enlarged and improved, Charlestown, Mass., 1820), pp. 87, 286–92; Morse, *The American Gazetteer* (Boston, 1797).

27. Morse, *American Geography,* p. vii. On the post-Revolutionary culture of print, see esp. David Jaffee, *People of the Wachusett: Greater New England in History and Memory* (Ithaca, N.Y., 1999), chap. 6, and "The Village Enlightenment in New England, 1760–1820," *William and Mary Quarterly* 47 (July 1990): 327–46. Also helpful are Robert Gross, *The Minutemen and Their World* (New York, 1976),

chap. 7, and Michael Warner, *The Letters of the Republic* (Cambridge, Mass., 1990), esp. chap. 5.

28. On Webster's *Speller* and *Dictionary,* see Ellis, *After the Revolution,* pp. 172–78, and Rollins, *Long Journey of Noah Webster,* esp. chap. 8. On the *Farmer's Almanack,* see Jaffee, "Village Enlightenment," pp. 328–33. For Pike's so-called American Arithmetic, see Nicholas Pike, *New and Complete System of Arithmetick . . . Adapted to the Commerce of Citizens of the United States* (Newburyport, Mass., 1788). For Bingham, see Caleb Bingham, *The American Preceptor: Being a New Selection of Lessons for Reading and Speaking Designed for the Use of Schools* (Boston, 1794).

29. Louis Leonard Tucker, *Clio's Consort: Jeremy Belknap and the Founding of the Massachusetts Historical Society* (Boston, 1989); David D. Van Tassel, *Recording America's Past: An Interpretation of the Development of Historical Societies in America, 1607–1884* (Chicago, 1960), p. 181.

30. Samuel Williams, historian of Vermont, quoted in Jeremy Belknap's *New Hampshire,* edited with an introduction by G. T. Lord (Hampton, N.H., 1973), p. xxii.

31. Ibid., p. 251. The other state histories included Samuel Williams, *The Natural and Civil History of Vermont* (1794); James Sullivan, *The History of the District of Maine* (1795); Benjamin Trumbull, *A Complete History of Connecticut,* vol. 1 (1797); and George Minot, *Continuation of the History of the Massachusetts Bay Colony* (1798).

32. Morse, *American Geography,* p. 48.

33. Jedidiah Morse, *The American Universal Geography,* 2 vols. (Boston, 1793), 1:416–17, 519. By the 1812 edition Morse had added another "Division," "The Louisiana Territory." In 1819 he changed this fourth division to the "Western States and Territories" but kept only his general description of New England. For a helpful discussion of these changes, see Fulmer Mood, "The Origin, Evolution, and Application of the Sectional Concept, 1750–1900," in Merrill Jensen, ed., *Regionalism in America* (1951; reprint, Madison, Wis., 1965), pp. 41–46.

34. For a suggestive analysis of the difference between regionalism, the product of a "consciousness of fixed, essential differences," and sectionalism, the product of more fluid economic and political interests, see Onuf, "Federalism, Republicanism," p. 22.

35. Morse, *American Geography,* pp. 144, 149.

36. Ibid., p. 146.

37. Ibid., pp. 145, 148, 219.

38. Cephas Brainerd and Eveline Warner Brainerd, eds., *The New England Society Orations,* 2 vols. (New York, 1901), 1:6.

39. Before he became a nativist, Morse invited immigrants to New England. In 1793 he helped found and served as the corresponding secretary of the Massachusetts Society for the Information and Advice of Immigrants. His geography texts appear to have attracted the attention of prospective immigrants. Morse believed that homogeneous New England could absorb and assimilate

immigrants. But they did not settle in New England in significant numbers, the immigrant society soon went out of existence, and Morse and his fellow Federalists became increasingly nativist in their views of the diversity of other regions. See Sprague, *Life of Jedidiah Morse,* pp. 137–39.

40. Morse, *American Geography,* pp. 140, 147.

41. L. H. Butterfield, ed., *The Diary and Autobiography of John Adams,* 5 vols. (Cambridge, Mass., 1961), 3:195.

42. Dwight, "Greenfield Hill," reprinted in V. L. Parrington, ed., *The Connecticut Wits* (1926; reprint, New York, 1969), pp. 184–85, 220.

43. Morse, *American Geography,* p. 241.

44. Ibid., pp. 147–48. See also Morse and Parish, *Compendious History of New England,* pp. 115–19.

45. Morse, *American Geography,* p. 145.

46. Ibid. Timothy Dwight offers a breakdown of New England's leadership of newspaper publishing. See *Travels,* 4:252; see also Charles Clark, *The Public Prints: The Newspaper in Anglo-American Culture, 1665–1740* (New York, 1994).

47. Morse, *American Geography,* p. 145.

48. Jaffee, "Village Enlightenment." See also Gilmore, *Reading Becomes a Necessity,* and Richard D. Brown, *Knowledge Is Power: The Diffusion of Information in Early America, 1700–1865* (New York, 1989).

49. Phillips, *Morse and New England Congregationalism,* p. 216.

50. Morse, *American Geography,* pp. 145–46.

51. Ibid., pp. 144, 147.

52. Ibid., pp. 206, 210, 212.

53. Ibid., pp. 164, 192, 198, 200, 471.

54. Ibid., pp. 177, 241. See also Morse's treatment of Connecticut in *American Universal Geography* and *American Gazetteer.*

55. *American Geography,* p. 142.

56. Ibid., p. 241. For an excellent analysis of Revolutionary Connecticut, see Christopher Grasso, *A Speaking Aristocracy: Transforming Public Discourse in Eighteenth-Century Connecticut* (Chapel Hill, N.C., 1998). Richard J. Purcell's *Connecticut in Transition, 1775–1818* (Middletown, Conn., 1963) is also still useful.

57. Morse, *American Geography,* p. 219.

58. Yale student quoted in Noble E. Cunningham, *The Jeffersonians in Power, Party Operations, 1801–1809* (Chapel Hill, N.C., 1963), p. 132. A still helpful volume on the state's religious establishment is Charles R. Keller, *The Second Great Awakening in Connecticut* (New Haven, Conn., 1942). For a good recent treatment of one part of Connecticut, see David W. Kling, *A Field of Divine Wonders: The New Divinity and Village Revivals in Northwestern Connecticut, 1792–1822* (University Park, Pa., 1993). Morse was a strong advocate of revivals as a means of cultivating virtue and ordered liberty.

59. Morse, *American Geography,* p. 219. For a helpful discussion of this perspective,

see K. Alan Snyder, "Foundations of Liberty: The Christian Republicanism of Timothy Dwight and Jedidiah Morse," *New England Quarterly* 56 (September 1983): 382–97.

60. Morse, *American Geography,* p. 241.

61. Ibid., p. 218; Dwight, "Greenfield Hill," pp. 184–85. For an excellent essay on Dwight's landscape aesthetics, which has influenced my thinking, see Peter Briggs, "Timothy Dwight 'Composes' a Landscape for New England," *American Quarterly* 41 (September 1988): 359–77.

62. Belknap quoted in Brown, "American Geographies of Jedidiah Morse," p. 157, which also contains information (pp. 160–66) on Morse's data-gathering activities. In addition to his residency in Georgia, Morse briefly filled a pulpit in New York City in 1788. See Moss, *Morse,* pp. 35–36.

63. Morse, *American Geography,* pp. 251, 258.

64. Ibid., p. 257. On the economic motives of Dutch settlers, Morse was quoting Swedish botanist Peter Kalm's *Travels into North America* (1771).

65. Morse, *American Geography,* pp. 292, 313.

66. Ibid., pp. 383, 387–88.

67. Ibid., p. 387. These figures are drawn from Christine Leigh Heyrman's excellent analysis of the pre–Bible Belt South in *Southern Cross: The Beginnings of the Bible Belt* (New York, 1997), p. 23.

68. Morse, *American Geography,* pp. 417, 451.

69. Ibid., pp. 432–33.

70. Ibid., p. 418. For an outstanding analysis of the male-centered folk culture of the South and Protestantism's accommodations to it, see Heyrman, *Southern Cross,* esp. chap. 3.

71. The term "America's Latin America" is adapted from Edward L. Ayers; see "What We Talk about When We Talk about the South," in Ayers and Onuf, *All Over the Map,* p. 73. In applying the term to *Uncle Tom's Cabin,* I have in mind especially Stowe's construction of an exotic moral and physical landscape in a South that she had never visited.

72. St. George Tucker, *A Letter to the Reverend Jedidiah Morse* (Richmond, Va., 1795), p. 8; James Freeman, *Remarks on the American Universal Geography* (Boston, 1793), pp. 59, 61. For the positive reception of Morse's work, see Brown, "American Geographies of Jedidiah Morse," pp. 183–85.

73. Brainerd and Brainerd, *New England Society Orations,* 1:4–5.

74. Phillips, *Morse and New England Congregationalism,* pp. 33, 163; Brown, "American Geographies of Jedidiah Morse," p. 137; Dwight, *Travels,* 1:150.

75. Dwight, *Travels,* 1:123. Barbara Miller Solomon's introduction to *Travels* is very helpful, as is the perspective of Briggs's "Timothy Dwight 'Composes' a Landscape" and Lawrence Buell's *New England Literary Culture: From Revolution through Renaissance* (New York, 1986), esp. chap. 13.

76. Morse quoted in Dwight, *Travels,* 1:xxvii.

77. Ibid., 1:33, 121, 150, 2:73, 353, 3:245.

78. Ibid., 1:156–57, 257.

79. Ibid., pp. 7, 209. John B. Jackson offers a helpful analysis of Dwight in "A Puritan Looks at Scenery," in *Discovering the Vernacular Landscape* (New Haven, Conn., 1984), pp. 56–64.

80. Dwight, *Travels,* 1:8, 2:230.

81. Ibid., 2:230.

82. Ibid., p. 321.

83. Ibid., pp. 161, 165. On the land war, see Taylor, *Liberty Men and Great Proprietors.*

84. Dwight, *Travels,* 1:xxxiv–xxxviii. In her introduction, Solomon offers a very good account of Dwight's ethnic awareness and notes (xlvii) his deletion of "Yankee."

85. Ibid., 1:121, 214, 4:327.

86. Ibid., 1:122.

87. Ibid., 4:327–28.

88. Ibid., 3:186, 372.

89. Ibid., 4:373.

90. Prospectus for the *Palladium* quoted in Phillips, *Morse and New England Congregationalism,* p. 94. See also Robert Edson Lee, "Timothy Dwight and the Boston Palladium," *New England Quarterly* 35 (June 1962): 229–38. Lee (p. 233) points out that free copies were sent to the clergy. For a recent introduction to Dwight's thought, see John R. Fitzmier, *New England's Moral Legislator: Timothy Dwight, 1752–1817* (Bloomington, Ind., 1998).

91. Boston paper quoted in Onuf, "Federalism, Republicanism," p. 25.

92. Morse, *American Geography,* p. 146; Phillips, *Morse and New England Congregationalism,* chap. 2.

93. On New England federalism and the politics of the early republic, see Waldstreicher, *Perpetual Fetes,* esp. chap. 3; Sharp, *American Politics in the Early Republic,* esp. chap. 1; and Ronald P. Formisano, *The Transformation of Political Culture: Massachusetts Parties, 1790s–1840s* (New York, 1983), esp. chaps. 1–2. I have also found two older works valuable: Linda K. Kerber, *Federalists in Dissent: Imagery and Ideology in Jeffersonian America* (New York, 1970), esp. chap. 1, and Banner, *Hartford Convention,* esp. chaps. 1–4.

94. Morse quoted in Moss, *Morse,* p. 84. See also Morse's earlier jeremiad delivered on Thanksgiving, *A Sermon, Preached at Charlestown, November 29, 1798...* (Boston, 1798), pp. 11–13, app., and Waldstreicher, *Perpetual Fetes,* p. 267. In chapter 5 of his insightful revisionist study, Waldstreicher discusses the different national regionalisms of New England, the South, and the West.

95. Thomas Boylston Adams and Josiah Quincy quoted in Kerber, *Federalists in Dissent,* pp. 23–26, 31.

96. Joanne Pope Melish, *Disowning Slavery: Gradual Emancipation and "Race" in New England, 1780–1860* (Ithaca, N.Y., 1998), chaps. 1–2; Jackson Turner Main, *Society*

and Economy in Colonial Connecticut (Princeton, N.J., 1985), p. 177; William D. Piersen, *Black Yankees: The Development of an Afro-American Subculture in Eighteenth-Century New England* (Amherst, Mass., 1988). On Rhode Island's continuing involvement in the slave trade, see Jay Coughtry, *The Notorious Triangle: Rhode Island and the African Slave Trade, 1700–1807* (Philadelphia, 1981), chap. 6.

97. Boston paper quoted in Kerber, *Federalists in Dissent,* p. 36. See also Banner, *Hartford Convention,* pp. 104–9.

98. Uriah Tracy and Timothy Pickering quoted in Henry Adams, *History of the United States during the First Administration of Thomas Jefferson, 1801–1805* (1889–91; reprint, New York, 1986), pp. 374–75; Morse quoted in Moss, *Morse,* p. 84.

99. Federalists quoted in Banner, *Hartford Convention,* pp. 93, 95.

100. Phillips, *Morse and New England Congregationalism,* pp. 98–99; Banner, *Hartford Convention,* pp. 98–99; Waldstreicher, *Perpetual Fetes,* pp. 200–209.

101. Kerber, *Federalists in Dissent,* p. 32; Waldstreicher, *Perpetual Fetes,* p. 254. Waldstreicher is particularly suggestive in analyzing the patriotic "sectional nationalism" of the Federalists.

102. Kittredge quoted in Samuel Eliot Morison, *The Maritime History of Massachusetts, 1783–1860* (1921; reprint, Boston, 1961), p. 212; Pickering quoted in Banner, *Hartford Convention,* p. 117. Morison (p. 21) also mentions the flag of secession.

103. Morse quoted in Phillips, *Morse and New England Congregationalism,* p. 164. See also Rollins, *Long Journey of Noah Webster,* p. 126.

104. Banner, *Hartford Convention,* chap. 8.

105. Opponents of Federalist Party quoted in David M. Roth, *Connecticut: A Bicentennial History* (New York, 1979), p. 111.

106. Alexis de Tocqueville, *Democracy in America,* edited by Phillips Bradley, 2 vols. (New York, 1945), 1:304; Susan E. Grey, *The Yankee West: Community Life on the Michigan Frontier* (Chapel Hill, N.C., 1996), p. 4; John Leighly, "Town Names of Colonial New England in the West," *Annals of the Association of American Geographers* 68 (June 1978): 233–48.

CHAPTER FOUR

1. D. W. Meinig, "Symbolic Landscapes: Models of American Community," in Meinig, ed., *The Interpretation of Ordinary Landscapes* (New York, 1979), p. 167.

2. The best discussion of these settlement patterns is David Grayson Allen, *In English Ways: The Movement of Societies and Transferral of English Local Customs to Massachusetts Bay in the Seventeenth Century* (Chapel Hill, N.C., 1981). See also Summer Chilton Powell, *Puritan Village: The Formation of a New England Town* (Middletown, Conn., 1963); Edward T. Price, *Dividing the Land: Early American Beginnings of Our Private Property Mosaic* (Chicago, 1995), chap. 2; and Martyn J.

Bowden, "Culture and Place: English Sub-Cultural Regions in New England in the Seventeenth Century," *Connecticut History* 35 (1994): 68–146.

3. William Bradford, *Of Plymouth Plantation,* edited by Harvey Wish (New York, 1962), p. 213. On the dispersed pattern of settlement, see the numerous essays of Joseph Wood collected in *The New England Village* (Baltimore, 1997). On the entrepreneurial impulse behind town founding, see John Frederick Martin, *Profits in the Wilderness: Entrepreneurship and the Founding of New England Towns in the Seventeenth Century* (Chapel Hill, N.C., 1991).

4. Charles E. Clark, *The Eastern Frontier: The Settlement of Northern New England, 1610–1763* (New York, 1970), chaps. 12–13; James L. Garvin, "The Range Township in Eighteenth-Century New Hampshire," in Peter Benes, ed., *New England Prospect: Maps, Place Names, and the Historical Landscape* (Boston, 1982), pp. 47–68.

5. Regulation quoted in Clark, *Eastern Frontier,* p. 207.

6. Wood, *New England Village,* esp. chap. 2; John R. Stilgoe, "Town Common and Village Green in New England, 1620–1981," in Ronald Lee Fleming and Lauri A. Halderman, eds., *On Common Ground* (Harvard, Mass., 1982), pp. 7–36; Charles A. Place, "From Meeting House to Church in New England," *Old-Time New England* 13 (October 1922): 69–77, (January 1923): 111–23, and (April 1923): 149–65; Peter W. Williams, *Houses of God: Region, Religion, and Architecture in the United States* (Urbana, Ill., 1997), chap. 1.

7. Traveler quoted in John D. Cushing, "Town Commons of New England, 1640–1840," *Old-Time New England* 51 (Winter 1961): 92. See also William Butler, "Another City upon a Hill: Litchfield, Connecticut, and the Colonial Revival," in Alan Axelrod, ed., *The Colonial Revival in America* (New York, 1985), pp. 15–51.

8. Cushing, "Town Commons," pp. 88–90. On "horseshed Christians," see David D. Hall, *Worlds of Wonder, Days of Judgment: Popular Religious Belief in Early New England* (New York, 1989), p. 15.

9. Jedidiah Morse, *The American Geography* (1789; reprint, New York, 1970), p. 141. Wood (*New England Village*) offers the best discussion of the commercial and physical transformation of New England communities. See also Richard M. Candee, "Maine Towns, Maine People: Architecture and Community, 1783–1820," in Charles E. Clark, James S. Leamon, and Karen Bowden, eds., *Maine in the Early Republic* (Hanover, N.H., 1988), pp. 26–61; Christopher Clark, *The Roots of Rural Capitalism: Western Massachusetts, 1780–1860* (Ithaca, N.Y., 1990); Robert Gross, *The Minutemen and Their World* (New York, 1976), chap. 7; and Jonathan Prude, *The Coming of the Industrial Order: A Study of Town and Factory Life in Rural Massachusetts, 1813–1860* (New York, 1983).

10. For an excellent analysis of how the commercialism and neoclassicism of the white village migrated into the hinterland and shaped the distinctive organization of northern New England's connected farm complexes, see Thomas

Hubka, *Big House, Little House, Back House Barn: The Connected Farm Buildings of New England* (Hanover, N.H., 1984); see also J. Ritchie Garrison, *Landscape and Material Life in Franklin County, Massachusetts, 1770–1860* (Knoxville, Tenn., 1991).

11. Stilgoe, "Town Common and Village Green," pp. 17–21.

12. Ibid., pp. 25–29; Cushing, "Town Commons," pp. 87–90; Rudy J. Favretti, "The Ornamentation of New England Towns, 1750–1850," *Journal of Garden History* 2 (1982): 325–42.

13. Dickens quoted in Stephen Nissenbaum, "New England as Region and Nation," in Edward L. Ayers and Peter S. Onuf, eds., *All Over the Map: Rethinking American Regions* (Baltimore, 1996), p. 45. On Tocqueville's reactions to the New England village, see *Democracy in America,* edited by J. P. Mayer (New York, 1996), pp. 62–70.

14. Though his engravings are frequently used as illustrations, Barber remains a neglected figure. On his life and work, see the pamphlet by Chauncey Cushing Nash, *John Warner Barber and His Books* (Milton, Mass., 1934), and William J. Linton, *American Wood Engraving: A Victorian History* (Watkins Glen, N.Y., 1976), pp. 11–12.

15. Barber quoted in Nash, *Barber and His Books,* p. 37.

16. Ibid.

17. John Barber, *Historical Collections of Massachusetts* (Worcester, 1839), preface. See also Barber, *Historical Collections of Connecticut* (New Haven, 1836). My "reading" of Barber's engravings has been influenced by Robert St. George's analysis of Ralph Earl's paintings of a generation earlier. See St. George, *Conversing in Signs: Poetics of Implication in Colonial New England* (Chapel Hill, N.C., 1998), pp. 329–35.

18. Wood, *New England Village,* chap. 3; Garrison, *Landscape and Material Life,* esp. p. 151.

19. For a suggestive discussion of fences, see Garrison, *Landscape and Material Life,* pp. 117–21.

20. Connecticut resident quoted in William Cronon, *Changes in the Land: Indians, Colonists, and the Ecology of New England* (New York, 1983), p. 120.

21. Timothy Dwight, *Travels in New England and New York,* edited by Barbara Miller Solomon, 4 vols. (Cambridge, Mass., 1969), 1:273. Dwight also appears to have been the first person to describe distinctive New England dwellings, which, he said, "may be called with propriety Cape Cod houses" (3:50–51).

22. Ibid., 1:272.

23. Connecticut resident quoted in Susan Allport, *Sermons in Stone: The Stone Walls of New England and New York* (New York, 1990), p. 65. Allport also discusses (pp. 106–11, 161–65) non-Yankee workers who built stone walls. On Thoreau's punning on the name of the pond, see *Walden* (1854; reprint, New York, 1962), p. 241.

24. On fences, in addition to Garrison, *Landscape and Material Life,* pp. 117–21, see Allport, *Sermons in Stone,* chap. 2.

25. Favretti, "Ornamentation of New England Towns," p. 333; Stilgoe, "Town Common and Village Green," pp. 27–28.

26. For promenades, see Favretti, "Ornamentation of New England Towns," pp. 334–36, On Brunswick's common and mall, see George A. Wheeler and Henry W. Wheeler, *History of Brunswick, Topsham, and Harpswell, Maine* (Boston, 1878), p. 538.

27. Henry David Thoreau, "Walking," *Excursions* (1863; reprint, New York, 1962), p. 169.

28. See, e.g., *Historical Collections of Connecticut,* p. 66, and *Historical Collections of Massachusetts,* p. 78.

29. On Lowell as an experiment in nonurban industrialization, see Thomas Bender, *Toward an Urban Vision: Ideas and Institutions in Nineteenth-Century America* (Lexington, Ky., 1975), chap. 2. For a provocative nationalistic reading of antebellum New England landscape paintings, see Angela Miller, *Empire of the Eye: Landscape Representation and American Cultural Politics, 1825–1875* (Ithaca, N.Y., 1993), esp. pp. 167–68, 188–96.

30. Harriet Beecher Stowe, *Stories, Sketches, and Studies* (New York, 1967), pp. 1–2; Joan D. Hedrick, *Harriet Beecher Stowe: A Life* (New York, 1994), p. 78 (Stowe's letter to her sister). Stowe's story was later retitled "Uncle Lot." My discussion of Stowe and the white village draws on the excellent analysis of Lawrence Buell, *New England Literary Culture: From Revolution to Renaissance* (New York, 1986), chap. 13, "The Village as Icon."

31. Buell, *New England Literary Culture,* p. 297.

32. Harriet Beecher Stowe, *Uncle Tom's Cabin* (1852; reprint, New York, 1966), p. 172. Stowe had only visited northern Kentucky while living in Cincinnati.

33. Ibid., p. 179.

34. Ibid.

35. On the nineteenth-century imaging of Vermont, see Robert L. McGrath, "Ideality and Actuality: The Landscape of Northern New England," in Benes, *New England Prospect,* pp. 114–16.

36. Stowe, *Uncle Tom's Cabin,* pp. 362, 389.

37. Ibid., pp. 367, 369.

38. Harriet Beecher Stowe, *Oldtown Folks* (1869), edited by Dorothy Berkson (New Brunswick, N.J., 1987), p. 3.

39. Ibid., p. 10.

40. Ibid., pp. 23–24, 31.

41. Hedrick's excellent *Life* of Stowe details her mobility and her literary entrepreneurialism.

42. Stowe, *Oldtown Folks,* pp. 46, 288.

43. Ibid., pp. 11, 297.

44. Buell, *New England Literary Culture,* pp. 305–6.

45. Henry Ward Beecher, *Norwood, or Village Life in New England* (New York, 1867), p. 2; Stowe, *Oldtown Folks,* p. 3.

46. Thomas J. Schlereth, "The New England Presence on the Midwest Landscape," *Cultural History and Material Culture* (Charlottesville, Va., 1990), pp. 195–217.

47. Sarah Burns, *Pastoral Inventions: Rural Life in Nineteenth-Century American Art and Culture* (Philadelphia, 1989), p. 152.

48. The classic work on this interregional conflict is William R. Taylor, *Cavalier and Yankee: The Old South and American National Character* (New York, 1961). Taylor's volume remains a very suggestive work that informs aspects of my analysis.

49. On the origins of the term "Yankee," see H. L. Mencken, *The American Language,* supp. 1 (New York, 1945), pp. 194–97; "Yankees," *The Harvard Encyclopedia of American Ethnic Groups* (Cambridge, Mass., 1980), p. 1028; and "Yankee," in *A Dictionary of American English on Historical Principles,* 4 vols. (Chicago, 1944), 4:2514–15.

50. "Yankee Doodle, or (as now Christened by the Saints of New England) The Lexington March" (1777), Harris Rare Books, John Hay Library, Brown University. See also J. A. Leo Lemay, "The American Origins of 'Yankee Doodle,'" *William and Mary Quarterly* 33 (1976): 435–64, and Cameron C. Nichols, *New England Humor from the Revolutionary War to the Civil War* (Knoxville, Tenn., 1993), pp. 33–38.

51. Edwin T. Bowden, ed., *The Satiric Poems of John Trumbull* (Austin, Tex., 1962), p. 103.

52. English observer quoted in Nichols, *New England Humor,* p. 34. See aslo Winnifred Morgan, *American Icon: Brother Jonathan and American Identity* (Newark, Del., 1988).

53. English visitor quoted in *Dictionary of American English,* 4:2514.

54. Morse, *American Geography,* p. 147.

55. Royall Tyler, *The Contrast* (1787; reprint, New York, 1970), pp. 54, 55.

56. Dwight, *Travels,* 1:223.

57. Dwight offers the best description of the peddler's travels and bargaining in ibid., 2:33–34. Helpful discussions of Yankee peddlers are found in David Jaffee, "Peddlers of Progress and the Transformation of the Rural North, 1760–1840," *Journal of American History* 78 (1991): 511–35; Shirley Spaulding DeVoe, *The Tinsmiths of Connecticut* (Middletown, Conn., 1968), pp. 149–53, app. 6 (includes a peddler's contract); and Diana Ross McCain, "Yankee Peddlers," *Early American Life* 20 (1989): 6–15.

58. Thomas Haliburton, *The Clockmaker, or The Sayings and Doings of Samuel Slick, of Slicksville* (Philadelphia, 1837).

59. "A Real Patriot" quoted in McCain, "Yankee Peddlers," p. 14.

60. David Humphreys, *The Yankee in England* (n.p., 1816), pp. 14–15. This essay introduced Humphreys's play.

61. Taylor, *Cavalier and Yankee,* esp. chap. 3. See also Buell, *New England Literary Culture,* pp. 335–43; Daniel G. Hoffman, *Form and Fable in American Fiction* (New York, 1961), pp. 44–56; and Constance Rourke, *American Humor* (New York, 1931), chap. 1.

62. Washington Irving, "Rip Van Winkle," *The Sketch Book* (1819–20; reprint, New York, 1954), pp. 41, 44.

63. Irving, "The Legend of Sleepy Hollow," *The Sketch Book,* pp. 353, 355.

64. Ibid., p. 361.

65. Ibid., p. 384.

66. English lady quoted in Taylor, *Cavalier and Yankee,* p. 47.

67. Ralph Waldo Emerson, "Self-Reliance," *Essays and Lectures* (New York, 1983), p. 275.

68. James Russell Lowell, *Poetical Works,* 5 vols. (New York, 1966), 2:46–47; editor John Neal, quoted in Rourke, *American Humor,* p. 27. On the nationalistic rise of the Yankee in American culture during the antebellum decades, see Burns, *Pastoral Inventions,* chap. 7, and Elizabeth Johns, *American Genre Painting: The Politics of Everyday Life* (New Haven, Conn., 1991), chap. 2. On the proliferation of Yankees on stage and in print, see Nichols, *New England Humor,* chaps. 3–6.

69. Johns, *American Genre Painting,* p. 31.

70. Emerson, "Self-Reliance," pp. 273, 281.

71. The examinations of the Yankee character identified in the other notes offer gendered views that exclude women. And yet the notion of "republican motherhood," as defined by Linda Kerber, reserved for women the role of shapers of character. See Kerber, *Women of the Republic: Intellect and Ideology in Revolutionary America* (Chapel Hill, N.C., 1980), and Rosemarie Zagarri, "Morals, Manners, and the Republican Mother," *American Quarterly* 44 (June 1992): 192–215.

72. Lydia Maria Child, *The American Frugal Housewife* (1832 ed., reprint, Cambridge, Mass., n.d.). On the volume's publishing history, see Carolyn L. Karcher, *The First Woman of the Republic: A Cultural Biography of Lydia Maria Child* (Durham, N.C., 1994), pp. 126–31. Of course, Ben Franklin's *Autobiography,* written between 1771 and 1790 but not completely published until the early nineteenth century, became, as Child suggests, a great "Yankee" text. Franklin presented himself as a simple American republican struggling with conflicts that would be central to the Yankee and American character in the antebellum decades when the book was widely read.

73. Child, *American Frugal Housewife,* pp. 1, 33, 116.

74. Ibid., p. 91.

75. Ibid., pp. 6, 95, 99. In *Cavalier and Yankee* (p. 120), William Taylor discusses Sarah Josepha Hale's important novel *Northwood* (1827) and the need to show the Yankee male as more of a family man. I am talking about a domestica-

tion of the Yankee that is differently gendered from Taylor's exclusively male analysis of regional character.

76. Child, *American Frugal Housewife,* pp. 8–9.

77. Stowe, "A New England Sketch," p. 7.

78. Ibid., pp. 8–9.

79. Stowe, *Uncle Tom's Cabin,* pp. 175, 224. See also David Grant, "*Uncle Tom's Cabin* and the Triumph of Republican Rhetoric," *New England Quarterly* 81 (September 1998): 429–48.

80. A helpful introduction to the spinster in the regional literary imagination is Barbara A. Johns, "Some Reflections on the Spinster in New England Literature," in Emily Toth, ed., *Regionalism and the Female Imagination* (University Park, Pa., 1985), pp. 29–64.

81. Stowe, *Uncle Tom's Cabin,* p. 398.

82. Ibid.

83. Stowe, *Oldtown Folks,* pp. 22–23.

84. Ibid., pp. 40, 221–22, 288.

85. Henry David Thoreau, "A Plea for Captain John Brown," in *Reform Papers,* edited by Wendell Glick (Princeton, N.J., 1973), pp. 112–13, 119.

86. For a detailed breakdown of the settlers who journeyed to Plymouth in the 1620s, see George F. Willison, *Saints and Strangers* (New York, 1945), app. A. On Plymouth's founding and early history, see George D. Langdon Jr., *Pilgrim Colony: A History of New Plymouth, 1620–1691* (New Haven, Conn., 1966), and John Demos, *A Little Commonwealth: Family Life in Plymouth Colony* (New York, 1970).

87. Bradford, *Of Plymouth Plantation,* pp. 69–70. See also Dwight B. Heath, ed., *Mourt's Relation: A Journal of the Pilgrims at Plymouth* (New York, 1963), pp. 17–18, and Mark L. Sargent, "The Conservative Covenant: The Rise of the Mayflower Compact in American Myth," *New England Quarterly* 61 (June 1988): 233–51.

88. See, e.g., Cotton Mather, *Magnalia Christi Americana, or The Ecclesiastical History of New England,* 7 vols. (1702; reprint, New York, 1967), 1:54–65, and Thomas Prince, *A Chronological History of New England* (Boston, 1736), pp. 84–85, 180–254.

89. Neither Bradford's *Of Plymouth Plantation* nor *Mourt's Relation* mention Plymouth Rock; see also Mark L. Sargent, "Plymouth Rock and the Great Awakening," *Journal of American Studies* 22 (August 1988): 249–55. As I was nearing completion of this analysis of Plymouth, John Seelye published his exhaustive examination of Plymouth Rock's place in American culture. *Memory's Nation: The Place of Plymouth Rock* (Chapel Hill, N.C., 1998) is an encyclopedic study from which I have learned much. Though I use many of the same sources as Seelye, my short analysis focuses on Plymouth in the context of the creation of an antebellum regional identity. A year after Seelye's work appeared, art historian Ann Uhry Abrams published *The Pilgrims and Pocahontas: Rival Myths*

of Origins (Boulder, Colo., 1999). Abrams's study nicely complements Seelye's because of its strong analysis of visual representations of Plymouth's history and its comparative perspective. Again, I cover some of the same ground but with a focus on Plymouth's role in the formation of New England identity.

90. See, e.g., Heath, *Mourt's Relation,* pp. 89–90.

91. Nathaniel Morton, *New Englands Memoriall,* edited by Howard J. Hall (1669; reprint, New York, 1937), p. 5; Mather, *Magnalia Christi Americana,* 1:54.

92. Langdon, *Pilgrim Colony,* esp. p. 55; Demos, *Little Commonwealth,* esp. pp. 142–44.

93. Hannah Adams, *A Summary History of New England, from the First Settlement of Plymouth to the Acceptance of the Federal Constitution* (Dedham, Mass., 1799), p. 25. On the designation "Pilgrim," see Albert Mathews, "The Term Pilgrim Fathers and Early Celebrations of Forefathers' Day," *Publications of the Colonial Society of Massachusetts* 17 (1914): 293–391.

94. Adams, *Summary History of New England,* p. 21.

95. In *Memory's Nation,* Seelye examines nineteenth-century Forefathers' Day rhetoric. Terms such as "cornerstone," "doorstep," and "granite foundation" of America were widely used to describe Plymouth Rock.

96. James Thacher, *History of the Town of Plymouth, from Its First Settlement in 1620, to the Present Time* (Boston, 1835), p. 29; Sargent, "Plymouth Rock and the Great Awakening," p. 250.

97. "Records of the Old Colony Club," *Proceedings of the Massachusetts Historical Society* 3 (1887): 389, 400, 404–5. On the origins of the New England clambake, see Kathy Neustadt, *Clambake: A History and Celebration of an American Tradition* (Amherst, Mass., 1992), chaps. 1–2.

98. Charles Turner, *A Sermon Preached at Plymouth, December 22, 1773* (Boston, 1774), p. 12; Mathews, "The Term Pilgrim Fathers," p. 305 (Boston paper). Mathews's lengthy essay provides an excellent description of the development of Forefathers' Day.

99. "Records of the Old Colony Club," pp. 442–43; Mathews, "The Term Pilgrim Fathers," pp. 305–6; Sargent, "Plymouth Rock and the Great Awakening," p. 250; Seelye, *Memory's Nation,* pp. 31–33.

100. Morse, *American Geography,* pp. 150, 152–53, 156.

101. Jeremy Belknap, *American Biography, or An Historical Account of Those Persons Who Have Been Distinguished in America...,* 2 vols. (Boston, 1794, 1798), 2:192. Belknap devotes one hundred pages to biographies of Plymouth's leaders.

102. Commemorators' toast quoted in Mathews, "The Term Pilgrim Fathers," p. 311. On the Federalists' appropriation of Plymouth Rock, see Seelye, *Memory's Nation,* chap. 3, and Abrams, *Pilgrims and Pocahontas,* chap. 5.

103. Mathews, "The Term Pilgrim Fathers," pp. 312, 317–18.

104. Morton, *New Englands Memoriall,* p. 14; Bradford, *Of Plymouth Plantation,* pp. 69–70.

105. Chandler Robbins, *A Sermon Preached at Plymouth, December 22, 1793* (Boston, 1794), p. 33; Belknap, *American Biography,* 2:191–92; John Quincy Adams, *An Oration Delivered at Plymouth, December 22, 1802* (Boston, 1802), pp. 20–22; Rufus Choate, "The Age of the Pilgrims, the Heroic Period of Our History" (1843), in Cephas Brainerd and Eveline Warner Brainerd, eds., *The New England Society Orations,* 2 vols. (New York, 1901), 1:336. See also Sargent, "Conservative Covenant," pp. 242–51.

106. Mathews, "The Term Pilgrim Fathers," p. 324.

107. Dwight, *Travels,* 3:72–74.

108. Richmond citizen quoted in David Waldstreicher, *In the Midst of Perpetual Fetes: The Makings of American Nationalism* (Chapel Hill, N.C., 1996), pp. 267–68. On Plymouth and Jamestown as the mainsprings of contending national historical narratives, see Abrams, *Pilgrims and Pocahontas,* esp. chaps. 5–7; Mark L. Sargent, "Rekindled Fires: Jamestown and Plymouth in American Literature, 1765–1863" (Ph.D. dissertation, Claremont Graduate School, 1985), esp. chap. 4 for the bicentennial of Jamestown; and Wesley Frank Craven, *The Legend of the Founding Fathers* (New York, 1956), chap. 5.

109. Forefathers' Day toast quoted in Mathews, "The Term Pilgrim Fathers," p. 337.

110. Ibid., pp. 325, 332, 339, 341.

111. Ibid., pp. 336–37; Abrams, *Pilgrims and Pocahontas,* pp. 90–95, 98–103; Seelye, *Memory's Nation,* pp. 11–12.

112. Webster, "First Settlement of New England," *The Works of Daniel Webster,* 4 vols. (Boston, 1856), 1:7, 12, 22.

113. Ibid., pp. 14, 26.

114. Ibid., pp. 30–31. For a good discussion of the ongoing national regionalism of Webster's New England, see Harlow Sheidley, *Sectional Nationalism: Massachusetts Conservative Leaders and the Transformation of America* (Boston, 1998).

115. Barber, *Historical Collections of Massachusetts,* p. 519.

116. Tocqueville, *Democracy in America,* p. 38n. On Weir's painting, see Seelye, *Memory's Nation,* pp. 252–54, and Abrams, *Pilgrims and Pocahontas,* pp. 146–52.

117. Daniel Walker Howe, *The Political Culture of the American Whigs* (Chicago, 1979), p. 9. See also Sheidley, *Sectional Nationalism,* and Dean C. Hammer, "The Puritans as Founders: The Quest for Identity in Early Whig Rhetoric," *Religion and American Culture* 6 (Summer 1996): 161–94.

118. Webster, "First Settlement of New England," pp. 34–35.

119. Mathews, "The Term Pilgrim Fathers," p. 337; Winthrop, "Address" (1839), and Charles Brickett Hadduck, "The Elements of National Greatness" (1841), in Brainerd and Brainerd, *New England Society Orations,* 1:259, 273.

120. Philip Melancthon Whepley, "The Memory of the Blessed" (1822), and Samuel Knapp, "Address" (1829), in Brainerd and Brainerd, *New England Society Orations,* 1:116, 153–54.

121. Winthrop, "Address," pp. 252–53.

122. Quoted in Joanne Pope Melish, *Disowning Slavery: Gradual Emancipation and Race in New England, 1780–1860* (Ithaca, N.Y., 1998), p. 233.

123. Harriet Beecher Stowe, *The Mayflower, or Sketches of Scenes and Characters among the Descendants of the Pilgrims* (Boston, 1843), and *Oldtown Folks,* pp. 3, 9.

124. George Perkins Marsh, "Address" (1844), in Brainerd and Brainerd, *New England Society Orations,* 1:373.

125. Hadduck, "Elements of National Greatness," p. 279.

126. Leonard Bacon, "Address" (1838), and John Prescott Hall, "Discourse" (1847), in Brainerd and Brainerd, *New England Society Orations,* 1:193–94, 2:66.

127. Lydia Maria Child, *Hobomok and Other Writings,* edited by Carolyn L. Karcher (New Brunswick, N.J., 1991), p. 6.

128. Catharine Sedgwick, *Hope Leslie, or Early Times in Massachusetts* (1827; reprint, New York, 1969), p. 31. For excellent discussions of literary and historical interpretations of New England's religious heritage in the nineteenth century, see Buell, *New England Literary Culture,* chaps. 8–11, and Philip Gould, *Covenant and Republic: Historical Romance and the Politics of Puritanism* (New York, 1996), chaps. 1–4.

129. Ralph Waldo Emerson, *Historical Discourse at Concord* (1835), in Emerson, *Miscellanies* (Boston, 1878), pp. 30, 33, 35.

130. Ibid., pp. 76, 84.

131. Ibid., p. 45.

132. On Winthrop's reputation, see James G. Moseley, *John Winthrop's World* (Madison, Wis., 1992), chap. 7. In *Covenant and Republic,* Philip Gould offers a suggestive discussion of Winthrop and the "republicanization" of Puritan tradition; see esp. pp. 41–46. I would argue that the Pilgrims helped mediate this process.

133. John Winthrop, *The History of New England from 1630–1649,* edited by James Savage, 2 vols. (Boston, 1825).

134. See *Massachusetts Historical Society Collections* 7 (1838): 31–48.

135. Alexander Young, *Chronicles of the Pilgrim Fathers* (Boston, 1841) and *Chronicles of the First Planters of Massachusetts Bay* (Boston, 1846). On the discovery of Bradford's manuscript, see Willison, *Saints and Strangers,* pp. 61–62.

136. Mathews, "The Term Pilgrim Fathers," p. 322; George Bancroft, *History of the United States of America: From the Discovery of the Continent,* 10 vols. (1859; reprint, New York, 1882), 1:233–34.

137. Robert C. Winthrop, *Life and Letters of John Winthrop,* 2 vols. (Boston, 1864, 1867), 2:2–3, 107.

138. *Prose Writings of William Cullen Bryant,* edited by Parke Godwin, 2 vols. (New York, 1964), 2:221, 224. On Plymouth Rock and the antislavery crisis, see Seelye, *Memory's Nation,* chaps. 11–13.

139. For a good introduction to the history of Thanksgiving, see Jane Nylander, *Our Own Snug Fireside: Images of the New England Home, 1760–1860* (New York, 1993), chap. 10.

140. Henry David Thoreau, *Walden,* pp. 133–34. I have found particularly helpful discussions of Thoreau in Buell, *New England Literary Culture,* chap. 14, and Robert Gross, "Culture and Cultivation: Agriculture and Society in Thoreau's Concord," *Journal of American History* 69 (1982): 42–61.

141. Samuel Greene Arnold, *The Spirit of Rhode Island* (Providence, 1853), p. 10. See also Arnold, *History of the State of Rhode Island and Providence Plantations,* 2 vols. (New York, 1859), 1:10–46.

142. William Apess, *A Son of the Forest: The Complete Writings of William Apess: A Pequot,* edited with an introduction by Barry O'Connell (1829; reprint, Amherst, Mass., 1992), p. 11. O'Connell's introduction is a very suggestive interpretation of Apess's work.

143. Apess, *Eulogy on King Philip, Complete Writings of William Apess,* p. 297.

144. Ibid., pp. 278, 286.

145. Ibid., p. 286.

146. See Jill Lepore, *The Name of the War: King Philip's War and the Origins of American Identity* (New York, 1998), pp. 227–32, though Lepore does not explore Mount Hope Rock's connection to Plymouth Rock.

147. Harriet Wilson, *Our Nig, or Sketches from the Life of a Free Black,* edited with an introduction by Henry Louis Gates Jr. (1859; reprint, New York, 1983), quotation from title page.

148. For a good discussion of the racial exclusions from New England's sense of history, see Melish, *Disowning Slavery,* chap. 6.

149. Wilson, *Our Nig,* preface.

150. Ibid., pp. 65–66.

151. Ibid., p. 129.

CHAPTER FIVE

1. Lucy Larcom, *A New England Girlhood* (1889; reprint, Boston, 1986), p. 251. Other authors of autobiographies in the postwar decades included Thomas Bailey Aldrich, Harriet Beecher Stowe, and Edward Everett Hale. On nostalgia for antebellum childhood in art, see Sarah Burns, "Barefoot Boys and Other Country Children: Sentiment and Ideology in Nineteenth-Century American Art," *American Art Journal* 22 (1988): 25–50.

2. Larcom, *New England Girlhood,* pp. 93, 96, 98, 117. For a survey of visual images of Old New England between 1865 and 1945, see William H. Truettner and Roger B. Stein, eds., *Picturing Old New England* (New Haven, 1999).

3. On antebellum New England's progressivism, see Dona Brown, *Inventing New England: Regional Tourism in the Nineteenth Century* (Washington, D.C., 1995), p. 8. For a suggestive contrast between Northern progressivism and exceptionalism

and Southern conservatism in the antebellum era, see James M. McPherson, *The Battle Cry of Freedom: The Civil War Era* (New York, 1988), pp. 6–21.

4. Celia Betsky, "Inside the Past: The Interior and the Colonial Revival in American Art and Literature, 1860–1914," in Alan Axelrod, ed., *The Colonial Revival in America* (New York, 1985), p. 251.

5. Julia Ward Howe, "The Battle Hymn of the Republic," *Atlantic Monthly* 9 (February 1862): 228; Hale quoted in George M. Frederickson, *The Inner Civil War: Northern Intellectuals and the Crisis of Union* (New York, 1965), p. 118.

6. George Bancroft, "Lincoln's Place in History," *Atlantic Monthly* 15 (June 1865): 764. For a good discussion of the *Atlantic*'s postwar nationalism and optimism, see Ellery Sedgwick, *The Atlantic Monthly, 1857–1909: Yankee Humanism at High Tide and Ebb* (Amherst, Mass., 1994), pp. 106–8.

7. Henry Adams, *The Education of Henry Adams* (1918; reprint, Cambridge, Mass., 1961), p. 266; "Politics," *Atlantic Monthly* 32 (August 1873): 252. Adams originally made the remark on ethical lapses in 1869.

8. Harriet Beecher Stowe, *Poganuc People* (1878; reprint, Hartford, Conn., 1987), p. 319.

9. For Tyler, see Kermit Vanderbilt, *American Literature and the Academy* (Philadelphia, 1986), chap. 6.

10. Moses Coit Tyler, *A History of American Literature,* 2 vols. (1878; reprint, New York, 1887), 1:94, 101.

11. For a helpful discussion, see Nina Baym, "Early Histories of American Literature: A Chapter in the Institutionalization of New England," *American Literary History* 1 (Fall 1989): 459–84, and Joseph A. Conforti, *Jonathan Edwards, Religious Tradition, and American Culture* (Chapel Hill, N.C., 1995), chap. 6.

12. Oliver Wendell Holmes, *Pages from an Old Volume of Life: A Collection of Essays, 1857–1881* (Boston, 1883), p. 361.

13. John Fitzgerald quoted in James M. Lindgren, *Preserving Historic New England: Preservation, Progressivism, and the Remaking of Memory* (New York, 1995), p. 33.

14. For a helpful overview of French Canadian immigrants in New England, see the introduction to C. Stewart Doty, ed., *The First Franco-Americans: New England Life Histories from the Federal Writers Project, 1938–39* (Orono, Maine, 1985), pp. 1–10. The classic work on the ethnic transformation of the region is Barbara Miller Solomon, *Ancestors and Immigrants: A Changing New England Tradition* (1956; reprint, Chicago, 1972). For an excellent study of Anglo-Saxon racialism and the "new immigration," see Mathew Frye Jacobson, *Whiteness of a Different Color: European Immigrants and the Alchemy of Race* (Cambridge, Mass., 1999), chaps. 2–3.

15. Oliver Wendell Holmes, *Our Hundred Days in Europe* (1887; reprint, New York, 1971), p. 313; Samuel Adams Drake, *Our Colonial Homes* (Boston, 1893), p. 19.

16. Wendell quoted in Lindgren, *Preserving Historic New England,* p. 18.

17. *American Landmarks: A Collection of Pictures of Our Country's Historic Shrines* (Boston, 1893), p. vii; Solomon, *Ancestors and Immigrants,* p. 107.

18. James Michael Curley, *I'd Do It Again* (1957; reprint, New York, 1976), pp. 31, 34. There is no satisfactory study of the triple-decker. Two books touch on its history: Douglass Shand-Tucci, *Built in Boston: City and Suburb, 1800–1950* (Boston, 1978), and Sam Bass Warner Jr., *Streetcar Suburbs: The Process of Growth in Boston, 1870–1900* (Cambridge, Mass., 1962). I have also drawn on an unpublished paper of one of my graduate students: Mitzi Cerjan, "Colonial Revival in the Air: New England Urban Symbols, 1870–1910," seminar paper, University of Southern Maine, 1998.

19. John R. Stilgoe, *Metropolitan Corridor: Railroads and the American Scene* (New Haven, Conn., 1983), pp. 328–30.

20. Clifton Johnson, *The New England Country* (Boston, 1893), pp. 36–37. As Hal Barron argues, rural decline was probably exaggerated. Population shifts stabilized communities such as the Chelsea, Vermont, of his study. See *Those Who Stayed Behind: Rural Society in Nineteenth-Century New England* (New York, 1984).

21. These and other articles are discussed in Brown, *Inventing New England,* pp. 150–54.

22. Richard H. Brodhead, *The Cultures of Letters: Scenes of Reading and Writing in Nineteenth-Century America* (Chicago, 1993), p. 133. Brodhead's volume contains two excellent essays on late nineteenth-century literary regionalism and its audience.

23. Frank Rollins, "New Hampshire's Opportunity," *New England Magazine* 16 (July 1897): 542; Brown, *Inventing New England,* pp. 138–42, 155–57.

24. Editorial writer quoted in James R. Shortridge, *The Middle West: Its Meaning in American Culture* (Lawrence, Kans., 1989), p. 34. Shortridge offers an excellent introduction to the development of Midwestern regional identity.

25. The only significant study of Earle is Susan R. Williams, "In the Garden of New England: Alice Morse Earle and the History of Domestic Life" (Ph.D. diss., University of Delaware, 1992).

26. Alice Morse Earle, *Colonial Dames and Good Wives* (New York, 1895).

27. Alice Morse Earle, *Customs and Fashions of Old New England* (New York, 1893), p. 126, and *Home Life in Colonial Days* (New York, 1898), p. 40.

28. Alice Morse Earle, *Costume of Colonial Times* (New York, 1894), p. xiii. See also Earle's engaging study of *Stage Coach and Tavern Days* (New York, 1900), which emphasizes New England. On the romantic realism of local color writers, see Josephine Donovan, *New England Local Color Literature: A Woman's Tradition* (New York, 1983), and Brodhead, *Cultures of Letters,* esp. chap. 5.

29. Williams, "In the Garden of New England," offers the most detailed biographical information on Earle. For her family background, see chap. 2.

30. For a good study of Worcester in the post–Civil War decades, see Roy Rosen-

zweig, *Eight Hours for What We Will: Workers and Leisure in an Industrial City* (New York, 1983).

31. Williams, "In the Garden of New England," pp. 107–12.

32. Earle quoted in ibid., p. 227.

33. Ibid.

34. On Earle's negotiations with her publishers and investment in the stock market, see ibid., pp. 145–51.

35. Alice Morse Earle, *The Sabbath in Puritan New England* (New York, 1891), pp. 11, 70–71, 96, 187, 259.

36. Barrett Wendell, *Cotton Mather: The Puritan Priest* (1891; reprint, Cambridge, Mass., 1926), pp. 1, 78–79, 301, 305. 6. In *Child Life in Colonial Days* (New York, 1899), a heavily illustrated book stressing the hardihood of early New England, Earle defended Cotton Mather's child-rearing practices (p. 209). On the colonial revival interest in the Puritans, see Conforti, *Jonathan Edwards,* chap. 6.

37. Earle, *The Sabbath in Puritan New England,* p. 327. She quoted Tyler in *Customs and Fashions,* p. 264.

38. Alice Morse Earle, *Stage Coach and Tavern Days* (New York, 1900), p. 365. On neurasthenia, see T. J. Jackson Lears, *No Place of Grace: Antimodernism and the Transformation of America* (New York, 1981), pp. 47–58.

39. Curley, *I'd Do It Again,* p. 27.

40. Lyman Abott, ed., *The New Puritanism* (New York, 1898), pp. 85, 96, 99; Ezra Byington, *The Puritan as a Colonist and Reformer* (Boston, 1899). John Winthrop, Thomas Hooker, Cotton Mather, Samuel Sewall, and Jonathan Edwards were all subjects of new sympathetic biographies in the late 1880s and 1890s.

41. On Puritan-Pilgrim statuary, see Conforti, *Jonathan Edwards,* chap. 6; John Seelye, *Memory's Nation: The Place of Plymouth Rock* (Chapel Hill, N.C., 1998), pp. 475–80; Michael Kammen, *Mystic Chords of Memory: The Transformation of Tradition in American Culture* (New York, 1991), pp. 206–15; and Roger B. Stein, "Gilded Age Pilgrims," in Truettner and Stein, *Picturing Old New England,* pp. 43–78. Other Puritan leaders who were memorialized in statues and bronzes included John Harvard, John Eliot, and Jonathan Edwards.

42. Earle, *Home Life,* pp. 318, 388; *Customs and Fashions,* p. 361.

43. Alice Morse Earle, *Margaret Winthrop* (New York, 1895), p. 335.

44. Melinda Young Frye, "The Beginnings of the Period Room in American Museums: Charles P. Wilcomb's Colonial Kitchens, 1896, 1906, 1910," in Axelrod, *Colonial Revival,* p. 238.

45. Earle, *Customs and Fashions,* p. 109, and *Home Life,* pp. 158, 388–90. On domesticity in the colonial revival, see Karal Ann Marling, *George Washington Slept Here: Colonial Revivals and American Culture, 1876–1986* (Cambridge, Mass., 1988), esp. chap. 6, and William H. Truettner and Thomas Andrew Denenberg, "The Discreet Charm of the Colonial," in Truettner and Stein, *Picturing Old New England,* pp. 79–109.

46. Larcom, *New England Girlhood*, p. 23.

47. Earle, *Home Life*, pp. 56, 75. See also Rodris Roth, "The New England, or 'Olde Tyme,' Kitchen Exhibit at Nineteenth-Century Fairs," in Axelrod, *Colonial Revival*, pp. 159–83, and Marling, *George Washington Slept Here*, pp. 164–71.

48. Earle, *Home Life*, esp. p. 166; Marling, *George Washington Slept Here*, pp. 161–74.

49. Earle, *Home Life*, pp. viii, 244, and *Colonial Dames and Good Wives*, pp. 314–15.

50. Earle, *Home Life*, pp. 305, 307–8.

51. For a helpful discussion of antiques, see Marling, *George Washington Slept Here*, pp. 86–88.

52. Earle, *Colonial Dames and Good Wives*, chap. 12, and *Home Life*, chaps. 8–11; Laurel Ulrich, *A Midwife's Tale: The Life of Martha Ballard, Based on Her Diary, 1785–1812* (New York, 1991). On Earle's neurasthenia, see Williams, "In the Garden of New England," p. 151.

53. Earle, *Colonial Dames and Good Wives*, pp. 240–43, and *Home Life*, pp. 103, 247–48, 390.

54. Earle, *Home Life*, pp. 310, 410, 417.

55. Earle, *Customs and Fashions*, p. 338. Marling (*George Washington Slept Here*, p. 34) stresses the cozy domestic images of the colonial revival.

56. Alice Morse Earle, *Old Time Gardens* (New York, 1901), pp. 147–48, 202, 214.

57. Ibid., chap. 2. See also Alice Morse Earle, *Sun Dials and Roses of Yesterday* (New York, 1902). On the rise of the front lawn, see Virginia Scott Jenkins, *The Lawn: A History of an American Obsession* (Washington, D.C., 1994), esp. pp. 29–31.

58. Williams, "In the Garden of New England," p. 218.

59. Brown, *Inventing New England*, chap. 6.

60. Earle, *Home Life*, p. 27; Earle to Mary Sowles Perkins, Elizabeth Perkins Papers, Old York Historical Society, York, Maine.

61. The best history of York is Charles Edward Banks, *History of York, Maine*, 2 vols. (Boston, 1931–35).

62. Ibid., 1:193.

63. Ibid., 1:254–308, 2:99–142.

64. Ibid., 1:15, 2:78–79.

65. Population figures are in ibid., 1:15.

66. Ibid., 2:228–29, 316.

67. "Old York," *New Hampshire Gazette*, January 22, 1874, p. 50.

68. Samuel Adams Drake, *Nooks and Corners of the New England Coast* (New York, 1875), pp. 134–35.

69. Banks, *History of York*, 1:15; Brown, *Inventing New England*, pp. 179–83; Jennifer Cutts, "Community in York, Maine: A Study of Tourism and Its Effects, 1870–1902" (typescript, Old York Historical Society, 1997).

70. Samuel Adams Drake, *The Pine Tree Coast* (Boston, 1891), p. 59; Edward Moody, *Agamenticus, Gorgeana, York, 1623–1914* (Augusta, Maine, 1914), pp. 236–37.

71. Howells quoted in Brown, *Inventing New England*, p. 175.

72. Sarah D. Clark, "A Summer in York," *Harper's New Monthly Magazine,* September 1882, pp. 487, 490. The essays in Sarah L. Giffen and Kevin D. Murphy, eds., *"A Noble and Dignified Stream": The Piscataqua Region in the Colonial Revival, 1860–1930* (York, Maine, 1992), offer numerous ideas and suggestions about the colonial revival influence on York. I have cited the essays I found most helpful. I am interested in relating York's early history to the colonial revivalists' imagined past, to the work of Alice Morse Earle, and, above all, to a commemorative narrative of York's Puritan origins that has been ignored. Even Dona Brown (*Inventing New England,* esp. p. 188), in her otherwise excellent analysis of southern Maine coastal resorts, argues that Puritanism was in "disrepute" among historically minded summer residents and colonial revivalists.

73. For a classic account of this mid-nineteenth-century imaginative discovery of the Maine coast, see the travel reports from a trip in 1858 that were serialized in the *New York Tribune* by Robert Carter and then published as *A Summer Cruise on the Coast of New England* (Boston, 1864). See also Pamela J. Belanger, *Inventing Acadia: Artists and Tourists on Mount Desert* (Rockland, Maine, 1999), and John Wilmerding, *The Artist's Mount Desert: American Painters on the Maine Coast* (Princeton, N.J., 1984). On late-nineteenth-century vacationers and the rise of the lobster as a fashionable food and Maine symbol, see George H. Lewis, "The Maine Lobster as Regional Icon: Competing Images over Time and Social Class," *Food and Foodways* 3 (1989): 306–16.

74. Drake, *Pine Tree Coast,* pp. 47, 59. See also Richard Candee, "The New Colonials: Restoration and Remodeling of Old Buildings along the Piscataqua," in Giffen and Murphy, *"A Noble and Dignified Stream,"* chap. 2.

75. The meetinghouse had actually been remodeled in 1838–39 but not fully modernized; see Moody, *Agamenticus, Gorgeana, York,* pp. 90–95. I have benefited from Sarah Giffen's suggestive comments in "Old York Historical and Improvement Society," in Giffen and Murphy, *"A Noble and Dignified Stream,"* pp. 91–93.

76. Moody, *Agamenticus, Gorgeana, York,* p. 98. The first remodeling of the town hall was completed in 1874.

77. For suggestive discussions, see William Butler, "Another City upon a Hill: Litchfield, Connecticut, and the Colonial Revival," in Axelrod, *Colonial Revival,* pp. 15–51, and John R. Stilgoe, "Town Common and Village Green in New England, 1620–1981," in Ronald Lee Fleming and Lauri A. Halderman, eds., *On Common Ground: Caring for Shared Land from Town Common to Urban Park* (Harvard, Mass., 1982), pp. 30–35. See also Parris Thaxter Farwell, *Village Improvement* (New York, 1913).

78. Mary Caroline Robbins, "Village Improvement Societies," *Atlantic Monthly* 79 (February 1897): 213–14, 222.

79. Ibid., p. 212.

80. Thomas Johnson, Curator, and Virginia Spiller, Librarian, Old York Histori-

cal Society, have supplied me with information on the Perkins family. See also Johnson, "Elizabeth Perkins House," and Amy W. Hufnagel, "Elizabeth Perkins House Gardens," in Giffen and Murphy, *A Noble and Dignified Stream,* pp. 67–76, 96–97.

81. "Articles of Incorporation," Old York Historical and Improvement Society, Records (Old York Historical Society), p. 1.

82. Ibid., pp. 36, 69–70. See also Giffen, "Old York Historical and Improvement Society," p. 92, and Lucinda Brockway, " 'Tempus Fugit': Capturing the Past in the Landscape of the Piscataqua," in Giffen and Murphy, *A Noble and Dignified Stream,* pp. 83–86.

83. Pauline Carrington Bouve, "Old York, a Forgotten Seaport," *New England Magazine* 26 (August 1902): 694, 696.

84. Old York Historical and Improvement Society, Records, pp. 70–71.

85. "Old York Garden Party," *Old York Transcript,* August 17, 1899, p. 1. Mary Perkins contributed her own money to the society as well. See, e.g., "Report of Treasurer," Old York Historical and Improvement Society, Records, p. 134.

86. Drake, *Pine Tree Coast,* p. 47. See also Kevin Murphy, "Old Gaol Museum," in Giffen and Murphy, *A Noble and Dignified Stream,* pp. 205–7.

87. "For the Sake of Old York," *Old York Transcript,* May 3, 1900, p. 2.

88. "Old York," *Old York Transcript,* July 6, 1899, p. 1; John Hecker, "Historical and Structural Analysis, Old Gaol, York, Maine" (typescript, Old York Historical Society, 1976).

89. "For the Sake of Old York," p. 2, and "Old Jail Museum," *Old York Transcript,* July 5, 1900, p. 1; Earle, *Costume of Colonial Times,* p. xi; Murphy, "Old Gaol Museum," pp. 205–7.

90. *Old York Transcript,* July 19, 1900, p. 2, and August 2, 1900, p. 2.

91. *Two Hundred and Fiftieth Anniversary: Gorgeana-York, 1652–1902* (York, Maine, 1904), pp. 85–95.

92. James Phinney Baxter, "Agamenticus, Bristol, Gorgeana, York: An Oration," and William J. Tucker, "Address," in ibid., pp. 25, 32, 108. Tucker was quoting an unidentified commentator on the Puritans.

93. *Old York Transcript,* June 8, 1899, p. 2.

94. Thomas Nelson Page, "Address," and Tucker, "Address," in *Two Hundred and Fiftieth Anniversary,* pp. 109–10, 117.

95. Moody, *Agamenticus, Gorgeana, York;* Herbert Milton Sylvester, *Old York* (Boston, 1909). For an excellent study of commemoration and historical memory, see John Bodnar, *Remaking America: Public Memory, Commemoration, and Patriotism in the Twentieth Century* (Princeton, N.J., 1991).

96. Caroline O. Emmerton, *The Chronicles of Three Old Houses* (Salem, 1935), pp. 8–11. Emmerton's book serves as a basic history of the house and of its restoration. It is written, at least in part, as a defense of her work and should not be accepted at face value. Though her restoration receives brief mention in studies

such as Lindgren, *Preserving Historic New England,* pp. 74–76, 142–43, there are no scholarly assessments of Emmerton's life and work.

97. Emmerton, *Chronicles of Three Old Houses,* pp. 12–23.

98. There is no satisfactory modern history of the changing industrial world of Salem and the Turner-Derby Street area. I have found helpful insights in K. David Moss, "Outline for the Life and Times of Caroline Emmerton" (typescript, House of the Seven Gables, n.d.), p. 1. I have also found useful information in Frances Diane Robotti, *Chronicles of Old Salem* (Salem, 1948).

99. Eleanor Putnam, *Old Salem* (Boston, 1891), pp. 79–82; Emmerton, *Chronicles of Three Old Houses,* pp. 25–26; Henry Upton, "House of the Seven Gables Series Dance Music" (Salem, 1892), copy in the House of the Seven Gables Archives (hereafter cited as HSG Archives).

100. Edwin M. Bacon, *Literary Pilgrimages in New England* (Boston, 1902), pp. 212–13.

101. Nathaniel Hawthorne, *The House of the Seven Gables* (1851; reprint, New York, 1981), pp. vii–viii; Bacon, *Literary Pilgrimages,* p. 213.

102. Henry James, *The American Scene* (1907; reprint, New York, 1967), pp. 265, 269, 271. For an excellent discussion of Hawthorne's literary reputation and influence at the time, including the institutionalization of his works in schools, see Richard H. Brodhead, *The School of Hawthorne* (New York, 1986), esp. chap. 3.

103. The best sources of information on Emmerton are the obituaries with her papers in box 19B, HSG Archives. See "The Death of John Bertram" (March 3, 1882), "The Death of Jennie Emmerton" (August 15, 1912), and "The Death of Caroline Emmerton" (March 18, 1942), *Salem Evening News.* See also Moss, "Life and Times of Caroline Emmerton," pp. 1–2, and Irene V. Axelrod, "No Small Matter: A Biographical Sketch of the Life and Times of Caroline Emmerton" (typescript, House of the Seven Gables, 1996).

104. Emmerton, *Chronicles of Three Old Houses,* pp. 26–30.

105. Laurence Vail Coleman, *Historic House Museums* (Washington, D.C., 1933), p. 18.

106. " 'Preserved' New England: What the Antiquarian Societies are Doing," *Boston Evening Transcript,* November 22, 1913, in "Newspaper Clippings, 1909–1916," HSG Archives.

107. For the growth of settlements, the standard work is Allen F. Davis, *Spearheads for Reform: The Social Settlements and the Progressive Movement, 1890–1914* (New York, 1967), p. 12. Of course, Jane Addams, who grew up in a small Midwestern town, wrote the classic work on the settlement. *Twenty Years at Hull-House* (New York, 1910) suggests the way settlements combined professional social work with nostalgia for a lost social world.

108. Caroline Emmerton, "History of the House of Seven Gables," *Salem Evening News,* May 10, 1910, in "Newspaper Clippings, 1909–1916," HSG Archives; House of the Seven Gables Settlement Association, *Fifth Annual Report, 1914–15* (Salem, 1915), p. 3.

109. South End House leader quoted in Solomon, *Ancestors and Immigrants,* p. 143.

110. Emmerton, *Chronicles of Three Old Houses,* p. 39.

111. Salem native quoted in Lindgren, *Preserving Historic New England,* p. 73.

112. Emmerton, *Chronicles of Three Old Houses,* pp. 36–37. See also "House of Seven Gables Sold for Settlement Work Purposes," *Salem Evening News,* June 22, 1909, in "Newspaper Clippings, 1909–1916," HSG Archives.

113. "Restoration of Famous Building," *Salem Evening News,* March 21, 1910, ibid.

114. Emmerton, *Chronicles of Three Old Houses,* p. 36.

115. The guide's statement is quoted from a suggestive critical evaluation of the museum that was published in the *Craftsman* and pasted into "Newspaper Clippings, 1909–1916," HSG Archives. On the house's development as a resort, see Moss, "Life and Times of Caroline O. Emmerton," p. 5, and Coleman, *Historic House Museums,* p. 102.

116. House of the Seven Gables Settlement Association, *First Annual Report, 1910–1911* (Salem, 1911), p. 13; Emmerton, *Chronicles of Three Old Houses,* pp. 46–47.

117. Leon Whipple, "Hawthorne Gives Alms," *Survey* 55 (October 1, 1925): 45.

118. See Robotti, *Chronicles of Old Salem,* pp. 94–95.

119. *First Annual Report,* p. 13, and *Fifth Annual Report,* p. 4. For a helpful essay, see William B. Rhoads, "The Colonial Revival and the Americanization of Immigrants," in Alan Axelrod, *Colonial Revival,* pp. 341–61.

120. "House of Seven Gables," April 4, 1911, March 23, 1912, *Salem Evening News,* in "Newspaper Clippings, 1909–1916," HSG Archives.

121. "House of Seven Gables," January 12, 1913, and "Lecture in Polish to Every School Student," June 8, 1913, *Salem Evening News,* ibid.; House of the Seven Gables Settlement Association, *Third Annual Report, 1912–13* (Salem, 1913), p. 12.

122. See David Glassberg, *American Historical Pageantry: The Uses of Tradition in the Early Twentieth Century* (Chapel Hill, N.C., 1990), esp. pp. 1–5.

123. "Pageant Will Be Greatest Historical Spectacle Ever Held in City of Salem," *Salem Evening News,* April 28, 1913, in "Newspaper Clippings, 1909–1916," HSG Archives.

124. *Program, Pageant of Salem,* June 13–14, 16–17, pp. 16–17. For a copy of the program, see HSG Archives. See also Moss, "Life and Times of Caroline Emmerton," p. 7, and Irene V. Axelrod, "Biographical Sketch of . . . Caroline Emmerton," p. 9.

125. *Program, Pageant of Salem,* p. 42. Handwritten and typed drafts of Emmerton's adaptation of the chapter from Hawthorne's novel are in box 19A, HSG Archives.

126. For a report, see *Salem Evening News,* June 18, 1913, in "Newspaper Clippings, 1909–1916," HSG Archives, and House of the Seven Gables Social Settlement, *Fourth Annual Report, 1913–1914* (Salem, 1914), p. 4.

127. On the history of SPNEA, see Lindgren, *Preserving Historic New England.*

1. James R. Shortridge, *The Middle West: Its Meaning in American Culture* (Lawrence, Kans., 1989), chaps. 3–6.

2. Conversations with Stephen Nissenbaum have influenced my thinking about shifts in the perceived geographic centers of New England. He touches on the subject and on the northward drift of the New England heartland in "New England as Region and Nation," in Edward L. Ayers and Peter S. Onuf, eds., *All Over the Map: Rethinking American Regions* (Baltimore, 1996), p. 39.

3. See, e.g., George Selement, "Publication and the Puritan Minister," *William and Mary Quarterly* 37 (1980): 219–41.

4. See the revisionist work of Hal S. Barron in *Mixed Harvest: The Second Great Transformation in the Rural North, 1870–1930* (Chapel Hill, N.C., 1997), and *Those Who Stayed Behind: Rural Society in Nineteenth-Century New England* (New York, 1984); see also the helpful comments in Dona Brown, *Inventing New England: Regional Tourism in the Nineteenth Century* (Washington, D.C., 1995), esp. pp. 135–38, 151–53. For hereditarian concern about Yankees and rural New England, see Nancy L. Gallagher, *Breeding Better Vermonters: The Eugenics Project in the Green Mountain State* (Hanover, N.H., 1999), esp. chap. 2.

5. Lawrance Thompson, *Robert Frost: The Early Years, 1874–1915* (New York, 1966), pp. 315–16.

6. Richard Judd, *Common Lands, Common People: The Origins of Conservation in Northern New England* (Cambridge, Mass., 1997), pp. 206–22.

7. See, e.g., J. Kevin Graffagnino, "Arcadia in New England: Divergent Visions of a Changing Vermont, 1850–1920," in Nancy Price Graff, ed., *Celebrating Vermont: Myths and Realities* (Middlebury, Vt., 1991), pp. 45–60. Vermont's and Maine's slogans were officially adopted in the 1930s.

8. Dorothy Canfield Fisher, "Our Rich Little Poor State," *Nation,* May 31, 1922, p. 644; Robert Herrick, "The State of Maine — Down East," *Nation,* August 23, 1922, p. 122; John Macy, "Massachusetts: A Roman Conquest," *Nation,* December 27, 1922, p. 709.

9. Lawrance Thompson, *Robert Frost: The Years of Triumph, 1915–1938* (New York, 1970), p. 231.

10. Hostile critics in the 1930s and 1940s deplored the social and political philosophy of Frost's poetry as Coolidgean. See, e.g., Granville Hicks, "The World of Robert Frost" (1930), and Malcolm Cowley, "Frost: A Dissenting Opinion" (1944), both in the *New Republic* and reprinted in Philip L. Gerber, ed., *Critical Essays on Robert Frost* (Boston, 1982), pp. 89–92, 95–103.

11. On Frost criticism, in addition to Gerber, *Critical Essays,* see Edwin H. Cady and Louis J. Budd, eds., *On Frost: The Best from AMERICAN LITERATURE* (Durham, N.C., 1991). For the most recent biography of Frost and interpretation of his poetry, see Jay Parini, *Robert Frost: A Life* (New York, 1999).

12. In *Robert Frost and New England* (Princeton, N.J., 1979), John C. Kemp draws on Lawrance Thompson's exhaustive biographical project to reinterpret Frost as a regional poet. Kemp's book is filled with excellent close readings of the poet's early work. I have learned much from his informative use of Thompson and from his effort to sort out the regional and the more universal elements in Frost's poetry. But Kemp represents only one approach to Frost as a New England poet. He does not relate Frost's work or his popularity to shifts in regional identity or to the rise of regional sentiment in American culture.

13. Thompson, *Frost: The Early Years,* chap. 1.

14. Ibid., chaps. 3–4.

15. Frost quoted in ibid., p. 49.

16. Ibid., chaps. 13–14.

17. Ibid., chap. 20. Kemp (*Frost and New England,* p. 42) offers the assessment of the poet's background.

18. Thompson, *Frost: The Early Years,* chaps. 25–27.

19. Kemp, *Frost and New England,* p. 85.

20. Frost to Susan Ward Hayes, September 15, 1912, in Lawrance Thompson, ed., *Selected Letters of Robert Frost* (New York, 1964), p. 52.

21. Frost to Susan Ward Hayes (May 13, 1913), Frost to Ernest L. Silver (December 8, 1913), and Frost to William Stanley Braithwaite (March 22, 1913), ibid., pp. 73–74, 103, 160.

22. Robert Frost, *North of Boston Poems,* edited by Edward Connery Lathem (New York, 1983), pp. v–vi; Frost to John T. Bartlett (August 7, 1913) and Frost to Thomas B. Mosher (October 24, 1913), ibid., pp. 89, 96.

23. Thompson's *Frost: The Years of Triumph* summarizes critical commentary on the short story quality of the poet's verse. Frost characterized the "unliterary" language of *North of Boston Poems* in a letter to John T. Bartlett, December 8, 1913, in Thompson, *Selected Letters,* p. 102.

24. Holt to Frost, August 7, 1914, in Thompson, *Selected Letters,* pp. 130–31, 133; Thompson, *Frost: The Years of Triumph,* pp. 5–6.

25. Carl Van Doren, "Soil of the Puritans," in Gerber, *Critical Essays,* pp. 69, 72, 75. Cornelius Weygandt, Professor of English at the University of Pennsylvania, was a summer resident of New Hampshire who promoted Frost. John Farrar, an important New York editor from Vermont, was yet another admirer; Farrar wrote a number of essays praising Frost.

26. Cowley, "Frost: A Dissenting Opinion," p. 103.

27. John Farrar, "From *The Literary Spotlight*" (1924), in Richard Thornton, ed., *Recognition of Robert Frost* (New York, 1937), p. 169; Sylvester Baxter, "New England's New Poet" (1915), in Gerber, *Critical Essays,* p. 29. These two volumes contain much of the early Frost criticism, though the poet approved the selections included in the volume edited by Thornton and sponsored by publisher Henry Holt.

28. "Of Axe-Handles and Guide-Book Poetry," *Philadelphia Public Ledger* (1916), in Gerber, *Critical Essays,* pp. 48, 50. Frost began referring to himself as a "Yank from Yankville" in England. See Thompson, *Frost: The Early Years,* p. 415.

29. Robert Frost, *Collected Poems, Prose, and Plays* (New York, 1995), pp. 39, 43, 66. Hereafter page references to this edition will be made in the text.

30. Kemp, *Frost and New England,* p. 104.

31. Ibid., pp. 25–26.

32. "Of Axe-Handles and Guide-Book Poetry," p. 48; Baxter, "New England's New Poet," p. 28; William Dean Howells, "Editor's Easy Chair" (1915), in Thornton, *Recognition of Frost,* p. 45; Louis Untermeyer, *American Poetry since 1900* (New York, 1923), p. 21.

33. Amy Lowell, "North of Boston" (1915), in Gerber, *Critical Essays,* p. 22.

34. Robert Frost, "What Became of New England?" (1937), in Edward Connery Lathem and Lawrance Thompson, eds., *Robert Frost: Poetry and Prose* (New York, 1972), pp. 385, 387–88.

35. "Of Axe-Handles and Guide-Book Poetry," p. 49. On the early publishing history of *North of Boston* and other Frost volumes, see the first biography of the poet, Gorham B. Munson, *Robert Frost: A Study in Sensibility and Good Sense* (New York, 1927), p. 70.

36. Kemp, *Frost and New England,* offers a good analysis of how Frost's poetry after *North of Boston* registers the movement from outsider to insider.

37. Wallace Nutting, *New Hampshire Beautiful* (Framingham, Mass., 1923), pp. 4, 14. Within two years, 1922–24, Nutting completed volumes on all the New England states except Rhode Island, imaging the region as a Yankee pastoral world of small towns and villages. He then expanded his States Beautiful series to other parts of the country. But he held special affection for Old New England. See, e.g., *Maine Beautiful* (Framingham, Mass., 1924), pp. 3, 8.

38. Randall Jarrell quoted in William H. Pritchard, *Frost: A Life Reconsidered* (New York, 1984), p. 157. Pritchard's discussion of New Hampshire is not as helpful as Kemp's *Frost and New England,* esp. pp. 199–200.

39. Untermeyer, *American Poetry since 1900,* p. 16.

40. Frost, "An Interview" (1923), in Lathem and Thompson, *Frost: Poetry and Prose,* p. 295.

41. For Frost's identification with Puritan tradition, see "What Became of New England?," pp. 385, 388, and Thompson, *Frost: Years of Triumph,* chap. 17. On concern about the Franco-American corruption of the Yankee character in northern New England, see Gallagher, *Breeding Better Vermonters,* pp. 95–97.

42. William C. Lipke, "From Pastoralism to Progressivism: Myth and Reality in Twentieth-Century Vermont," in Graff, *Celebrating Vermont,* pp. 63–67; Frost to Richard H. Thornton, October 1, 1930, in Thompson, *Selected Letters,* p. 368.

43. Edward Elwell Whiting, *President Coolidge: A Contemporary Estimate* (Boston, 1923), pp. xi, 26; *The Autobiography of Calvin Coolidge* (London, 1929).

44. William Allen White, *Calvin Coolidge: The Man Who Is President* (New York, 1925), pp. 238–45. White's second biography appeared thirteen years later: *A Puritan in Babylon: The Story of Calvin Coolidge* (New York, 1938).

45. Herbert Corey, "The Green Mountain State," *National Geographic,* March 1927, pp. 333, 343.

46. Thompson, *Frost: Years of Triumph,* pp. 257, 607n.

47. Robert P. Tristram Coffin, *New Poetry of New England: Frost and Robinson* (Baltimore, 1938), p. 70.

48. The quotations and full reports of Frost's performance are in Thompson, *Frost: Years of Triumph,* pp. 212–13.

49. See the account from the *Boston Transcript* (1936) reprinted in Thornton, *Recognition of Frost,* pp. 117–18.

50. Mark Van Doren, "The Permanence of Robert Frost," ibid., p. 5.

51. Padraic Colum, "A Yankee Sage" (1936), ibid., pp. 162–65. On the Book-of-the-Month Club and the growth of middlebrow culture, see Janice A. Radway, *A Feeling for Books: The Book-of-the-Month Club, Literary Taste, and Middle-Class Desire* (Chapel Hill, N.C., 1997), esp. chap. 5. For the increase in high school graduates in New England, see Joshua L. Rosenbloom, "The Challenges of Economic Maturity: New England, 1880–1840," in Peter Temin, ed., *Engines of Enterprise: An Economic History of New England* (Cambridge, Mass., 2000), p. 186.

52. Thornton, *Recognition of Frost.*

53. For Frost's relationship to a "higher provincialism," see Cornelius Weygandt, "New Hampshire," an excerpt from his book on the White Mountains (1934), in ibid., pp. 65–66. For a good introduction to regional thinking in the 1930s, see Michael C. Steiner, "Regionalism in the Great Depression," *Geography Review* 73 (October 1983): 430–46. Michael Steiner called my attention to the passage from "West-Running Brook" and its relationship to regional sentiment in the 1930s.

54. Robert L. Dornan, *Revolt of the Provinces: The Regionalist Movement in America, 1920–1945* (Chapel Hill, N.C., 1993), esp. pp. 1–25 (quotation, p. 24); Donna M. Cassidy, " 'On the Subject of Nativeness': Marsden Hartley and New England Regionalism," *Winterthur Portfolio* 29 (1994): 232.

55. Weygandt, "New Hampshire," p. 73.

56. Bernard DeVoto, "New England: There She Stands," *Harper's Magazine,* March 1932, p. 411. For DeVoto's defense of Frost, see "The Critics and Robert Frost," *Saturday Review of Literature* 17 (January 1, 1938): 3–4, 14–15. For Frost's admiration of DeVoto's New England essay, see Thompson, *Frost: Years of Triumph,* p. 671n.

57. DeVoto, "New England: There She Stands," p. 407.

58. Ibid., pp. 407–8.

59. Shubrick Clymer, "Robert Frost: The Realist," *Yankee,* October 1935, p. 22; Clyde Moore Fuess, "What Is a Yankee?," *Yankee,* December 1935, p. 15.

60. C. Robertson Trowbridge and Judson D. Hale Sr., *Yankee Publishing Incorporated* (New York, 1985), p. 9; Hale, *The Education of a Yankee* (New York, 1987), p. 209.

61. Biographical and family information was furnished by Lorna Trowbridge, Sagendorph's daughter and the retired archivist of *Yankee* magazine. Also helpful were the "Biographical Sketch" of Sagendorph in his papers in *Yankee* Archives, Dublin, New Hampshire, and Hale, *Education of a Yankee,* esp. chap. 2. Hale, who became editor of *Yankee,* was Sagendorph's nephew.

62. Chard Powers, "New Yankeedom," *Yankee,* February 1940, p. 26.

63. Robb Sagendorph, "Beyond Armageddon" (1935), unpublished ms., Sagendorph Papers, *Yankee* Archives, pp. 58–59.

64. Robb Sagendorph, "This Is *Yankee*" (1947), unpublished ms., Sagendorph Papers, p. 2.

65. Ibid., p. 1. Introduced in December 1935, the "Swoppers' Column" grew in popularity and was a source of considerable humor. It soon became a radio show sponsored by H. P. Hood and Sons.

66. Sagendorph, "This Is *Yankee,*" pp. 6, 8, 140, 512. The magazine's office is described by Laurie Hillyer, "Tradition behind *Yankee* Magazine," *Boston Sunday Herald* (October 20, 1935), and reproduced without page numbers in Sagendorph, "This Is *Yankee.*"

67. Robb Sagendorph, "Introducing *Yankee,*" *Yankee,* September 1935, p. 2.

68. For a change in the magazine's billing, see *Yankee,* September 1935, August 1936, July 1937, March 1938. For requests for more material on southern New England, see, e.g., *Yankee,* May 1936, p. 49, and November 1939, p. 4. On the magazine's image of the Yankee, see Hale, *Education of a Yankee,* p. 208.

69. Sagendorph, "Introducing *Yankee,*" p. 2.

70. Hillyer, "Tradition behind *Yankee* Magazine."

71. Editorial, *Yankee,* May 1936, p. 2.

72. Fred W. Lamb, "Early Manchester," *Yankee,* October 1935, pp. 1–10; Howard F. Thompson, M.D., and Ella Shannon Bowles, "The Yankee Threads of Nashua," *Yankee,* November 1935, pp. 10–13.

73. For the larger context of artists' imaging of New England during the 1930s, see William H. Truettner, "Small-Town America," in Truettner and Roger B. Stein, eds., *Picturing Old New England* (New Haven, 1999), pp. 111–41.

74. On Luce, her painting of Frost, and her depiction of rural New England, see Roger D. Howlett, *Molly Luce: Eight Decades of the American Scene* (Boston, 1981). Paul Sample was another important painter who created Yankee-like images of northern New England. See Robert L. McGrath and Paul F. Glick, *Paul Sample: Painter of the American Scene* (Hanover, N.H., 1988).

75. For a suggestive discussion of the FSA's work in New England, see William F. Robinson, *A Certain Slant of Light: The First Hundred Years of Photography in New England* (Boston, 1980), pp. 188–89.

76. Stryker quoted in F. Jack Hurley, *Portrait of a Decade: Roy Stryker and the Develop-*

ment of *Documentary Photography in the 1930s* (Baton Rouge, La., 1974), p. 148; FSA shooting script from Stryker to Wolcott, Winter 1939–40, Roy Stryker Papers, Archives of American Art, Smithsonian Institution, Washington, D.C. Donna Cassidy of the University of Southern Maine supplied me with a copy of the script and with information about the political context of FSA photographers' work in New England.

77. "Nice Clean Little Town," *Yankee,* September 1936, p. 19.

78. Joseph Dineen, "Gangdom's Threat to New England," *Yankee,* February 1938, pp. 9, 37.

79. Sagendorph, "Introducing *Yankee,*" p. 2.

80. Sagendorph, "This Is *Yankee,*" p. 9; Fuess, "What Is a Yankee?," pp. 14–16. Fuess wrote a biography of Coolidge; see *Calvin Coolidge: The Man from Vermont* (Boston, 1940).

81. Fuess, "What Is a Yankee?," pp. 14–16.

82. Chris J. Agrafiotis, "Immigrants or Americans?," *Yankee,* December 1937, p. 10.

83. Ibid., pp. 10–12.

84. Mary Kay, "I Married a Yankee," *Yankee,* ibid., p. 11.

85. While *Yankee* was urging assimilation, the Work Projects Administration was collecting ethnic life histories that illustrated this immigrant work ethic. See, e.g., C. Stewart Doty, *The First Franco-Americans: New England Life Histories from the Federal Writers Project, 1938–39* (Orono, Maine, 1988).

86. "*Yankee* Goes Republican," *Yankee,* September 1937, p. 9; "2537 Years of Franklin Delano Roosevelt," *Yankee,* May 1937, pp. 11–12.

87. Sagendorph, "This Is *Yankee,*" p. 227. See also Letters to the Editor, *Yankee,* October 1937, pp. 32–33.

88. "*Yankee* Goes Republican," p. 9.

89. Robb Sagendorph, "Is There a Yankee Party?," *Yankee,* August 1938, p. 5, September 1938, pp. 5–6, October 1938, pp. 6–7.

90. "Fern Picking in Vermont," *Yankee,* October 1938, p. 8. See also David Gale, "From Proctorville to Proctor," *Yankee,* February 1939, pp. 40–43.

91. Vrest Orton, "The White Elephant Road," *Yankee,* February 1936, pp. 37–39.

92. Robb Sagendorph, "This Is *Yankee,*" p. 512; *Yankee,* February 1939, p. 7.

93. Leonard Morrison, "Sunflower Seedlings," *Yankee,* January 1937, p. 15.

94. R. B. Skinner, "Maine Whips CIO," *Yankee,* August 1937, p. 19; *Yankee* Special Maine Christmas Issue, December 1939.

95. Robert P. Tristram Coffin, "Tipsham Foreside," *Yankee,* March 1936, p. 25; John Gould, "Perambulating the Town Bounds," *Yankee,* September 1939, p. 18.

96. John Gould, "Town Meeting," *Yankee,* March 1939, pp. 24–25, and *New England Town Meeting: Safeguard of Democracy* (Brattleboro, Vt., 1940).

97. "Town Reports" began during town meeting month in 1938. See *Yankee,* March 1938, pp. 5–7, 26.

98. Thornton Wilder, *Our Town* (1938; reprint, New York, 1975), p. 110. For a helpful

discussion of *Our Town* and of the imaging of Grover's Corners, see Truettner, "Small Town America," pp. 111–15.

99. Wilder, *Our Town,* pp. 32–35.

100. For Sagendorph's nationalism and his modification of the magazine, see "Permanent Change in Policy," *Yankee,* July 1940, p. 6. For the quotation on Americanism, see the cover of *Yankee,* October 1941.

EPILOGUE

1. For helpful discussions of such postwar heritage activities, see Dona Brown and Stephen Nissenbaum, "Changing New England, 1865–1945," in William Truettner and Roger Stein, eds., *Picturing Old New England: Image and Memory* (New Haven, Conn., 1999), p. 12; Michael Kammen, *Mystic Chords of Memory: The Transformation of Tradition in American Culture* (New York, 1991), esp. pp. 556, 566; and Jane Holtz Kay, *Preserving New England* (New York, 1986), chap. 2.

2. Perry Miller, *The New England Mind: From Colony to Province* (Cambridge, Mass., 1953); F. O. Mathiessen, *The American Renaissance* (New York, 1941).

3. Quoted in Brown and Nissenbaum, "Changing New England," pp. 12–13. A group of prominent scholars convened at the University of Wisconsin in 1949 to examine regional studies. The volume that emerged from the conference seemed to underscore the problems and complexity of regional studies and might be read as something of a valedictory to the movement. See Merrill Jensen, ed., *Regionalism in America* (Madison, Wis., 1951).

4. Economic development commission quoted in *The New England Regional Plan: An Economic Development Strategy* (Hanover, N.H., 1981), pp. 1, 117 (employment figures). For a recent, more optimistic assessment of the course of deindustrialization, see Lynn Elaine Browne and Steven Sass, "The Transition from a Mill-Based to a Knowledge-Based Economy: New England, 1940–2000," in Peter Temin, ed., *Engines of Enterprise: An Economic History of New England* (Cambridge, Mass., 2000), chap. 5.

5. George Wilson Pierson, "The Obstinate Concept of New England: A Study in Denudation," *New England Quarterly* 29 (March 1955): 11–15. See also Oscar Handlin, "The Withering of New England," *Atlantic Monthly* 185 (April 1950): 49. Another Harvard faculty member, Howard Mumford Jones, took a different position, arguing that, at least on a cultural level, the region was not withering.

6. Pierson, "Obstinate Concept of New England," pp. 4, 11.

7. David Hackett Fischer, *Albion's Seed: Four British Folkways in America* (New York, 1989).

8. Peter Applebome, "Out from under the Nation's Shadow," *New York Times,* February 20, 1999, p. A15.

Index

Page references in italics refer to illustrations

Crane, Ichabod, 160–61

Creolization, 52–54

Culture: Yankee, 7, 154–55, 158; New England replication of English, 22–23, 320 (n. 20); of memorializaton, 56; hearth of, 93, 122; middlebrow, 285, 360 (n. 51). *See also* Holism, cultural; Identity, cultural

—print: republican, 83–91, 97–98; self-improvement in, 89; profit in, 98; of Massachusetts, 175, 264; post-Revolutionary, 333 (n. 27)

Curley, James Michael, 210, 221

Dairy farming, 265

Danforth, Samuel: *A Brief Recognition of New-Englands Errand into the Wilderness,* 42, 325 (n. 17)

Dartmouth College, 270

Daughters of the American Revolution, 214

Defense Education Act, 310

Degeneration, 18, 40, 52–55, 114, 320 (n. 22), 327 (n. 37)

Deindustrialization, 311, 363 (n. 4)

Delbanco, Andrew, 322 (n. 52), 323 (n. 57)

Depression: New England during, 267, 285, 287–88, 295, 296, 301; regionalism in, 287, 360 (n. 53); FSA photographs of, 297–99, 308; images of New England in, 361 (n. 73)

Derry, N.H., 271

DeVoto, Bernard, 295; "New England: There She Stands," 287–88

Dickens, Charles, 129, 204

Dickinson, Emily, 205

Diet, 25, 34

Dissenters, religious, 15–16, 18, 120, 172

Domesticity: cult of, 166; in colonial revival, 226–28, 229, 351 (n. 45), 352 (n. 55); of Revolution, 231–32; in settlement movement, 253

Dominion of New England, 51–52, 58–59, 62, 328 (n. 50)

Doolittle, Amos: "Brother Jonathan Administering a Salutary Cordial," *154*

Douglass, Frederick, 189, 200–201

Drake, Samuel Adams, 245; *Our Colonial Homes,* 209; *Nooks and Corners of the New England Coast,* 236–37, 238; *The Pine Tree Coast,* 238, 239

Drunkenness, 40

Dudley, Thomas, 24

Dummer, Jeremiah: *A Defense of the New England Charters,* 67, 329 (n. 67)

Durham, Conn., 132, *133*

Dutch: J. Morse on, 105–6, 159; view Yankees, 154; economic motives of, 336 (n. 64)

Dwight, Sereno, 109

Dwight, Timothy, 84, 97, 264; "Greenfield Hill," 95–96, 103–4; landscapes in, 103–4, 336 (n. 61); J. Morse influences, 109, 110, 113; as president of Yale, 109; *Travels in New England and New York,* 109–15, 135, 156; republicanism of, 110; federalism of, 110, 115, 116; in Puritan literary tradition, 113; on white villages, 128; on ethnicity, 150; on regional character, 154, 155, 160; visits Plymouth, 181–82, 184; on Maine, 239; on newspaper publishing, 335 (n. 46); on housing, 340 (n. 21); on peddlers, 342 (n. 57)

Eager, Margaret Maclaren, 260

Earl, Ralph, 103

179, 183; and Yankee virtue, 188; and South, 189, 190; and Puritans, 190–91; and J. Winthrop, 194; rhetoric of, 345 (n. 95); development of, 345 (n. 98)

Foster, John: "Map of New England," *46*

Fourth of July, 208

Foxcroft, Thomas, 63–64, 66–67; on conquest of Canada, 76

Framingham, Mass., 138, 139

Franco-Americans, 301, 306, 359 (n. 41)

Franklin, Benjamin, 87, 165; *Autobiography*, 89, 343 (n. 72)

French Canadians, 209, 210, 349 (n. 14)

Frost, Isabelle, 269, 270

Frost, Robert, 8, *282;* popularity of, 10, 287; *North of Boston*, 264, 274–77, 358 (n. 23); New Hampshire residence of, 265, 268, 270–71, 277; *New Hampshire*, 266, 273, 275, 278, 279–81; landscape in, 267; as farmer-poet, 267, 269, 271, 273, 277, 279–80, 281, 359 (n. 28); and rise of northern New England, 267–87; success of, 268; regionalism of, 268, 275, 285–86, 358 (n. 12); on Yankee character, 268, 273, 274–76; celebrity of, 269; early life of, 269–70; farming experience of, 270–71; composition of, 271; Yankee identity of, 271; teaching career of, 271, 281; publication of, 272, 359 (n. 35); public readings of, 273, 278, 281, 284, 360 (n. 48); realism of, 274, 275, 301; Yankees in, 274–75; cultural authority of, 276; "What Became of New England," 276; *Mountain Interval*, 277–78, 280, 284; on immigrants, 280; as Vermont poet laureate, 281; and Coolidge, 283; *West-Running Brook*, 283; politi-

cal views of, 283, 288; humor of, 284; *A Further Range*, 284, 285; Harvard lectures of, 284–85; audience of, 285; *Collected Poems*, 285; "higher provincialism" of, 286, 360 (n. 53); sociopolitical philosophy of, 357 (n. 10); criticism of, 357 (nn. 10–11), 358 (n. 27); as New England insider, 359 (n. 36); and Puritan tradition, 359 (n. 41)

Frost, William Prescott, 269

Fuess, Claude Moore, 362 (n. 80); "What is a Yankee?," 300

Fugitive Slave Law (1851), 195

Gardening, 233

Georgia, 107

Giffen, Sarah, 353 (n. 75)

Gilded Age, 215, 218

Glorious Revolution, 59, 60, 62, 175

Gorgeana, Maine, 235, 247. *See also* Old York, Maine

Gorges, Sir Ferdinando, 235

Gould, John: *New England Town Meeting*, 306

Gould, Philip, 347 (n. 132)

Governors, royal, 64

Grant administration, 207

Great Awakening, 67; re-Anglicization in, 72–74; jeremiads of, 73; Second, 192

Great Britain: folkways of, 3; cultural imperialism of, 65; war with France of, 75–76; constitution of, 79

Greater New England, 122, 123; Federalists on, 119; following Civil War, 124

Great Migration, 11–12, 38, 41–42, 325 (n. 16); middle class in, 12, 13, 36; rhetoric of, 42, 43; mythology of, 44; in verse, 50; C. Mather on, 56, 57, 62; centennial of, 63; and re-Anglicization, 65; eighteenth-century narratives of, 66; in American literature, 208; in Massachusetts, 264; Americanist interpretation of, 322 (n. 52)

Green Mountains, 305

Greenough, Richard S.: *John Winthrop,* *223*

Hale, Edward Everett, 206

Hale, Sarah Josepha, 343 (n. 75)

Haliburton, Thomas, 157

Harcourt, Henry, 272

Hartford Convention, 81, 116, 121–22, 159, 264

Harvard, John, 351 (n. 41)

Harvard College/University, 35, 53, 55; latitudinarianism of, 72; founding of, 190; Frost at, 270

Hawthorne, Nathaniel: *The House of* *the Seven Gables,* 170, 251, 261; on religious zealotry, 189, 190; and Turner-Ingersoll House, 249–52, 255; literary reputation of, 355 (n. 102)

Hebert, Ernest: *The Dogs of March,* 1

Hedrick, Joan D., 341 (n. 41)

Heritage activities: of colonial revival, 234; professionalization of, 261–62; and tourism, 314; post–World War II, 363 (n. 1)

Heritage Trail, 311

Herrick, Robert, 266

Heyrman, Christine Leigh, 336 (n. 67)

Higginson, Francis, 19, 30

Higginson, John: *The Cause of God and* *His People in New England,* 42

Hingham, Mass., 70, 71, 330 (n. 75)

Historic Deerfield, 310, 311

Holism, cultural, 4, 11, 84, 95, 105, 317 (n. 6)

Holmes, Oliver Wendell, 208, 209

Holt, Florence, 272

Holt, Henry, 272, 358 (n. 27)

Homer, Winslow, 239

Hood, Harvey Pearley, 265, 271, 361 (n. 65)

Hooke, William: *New England's Tears for* *Old England's Fears,* 32

Hooker, Thomas, 30

Hoover, Herbert, 290

House of the Seven Gables, *256, 257;* restoration of, 206, 248–62, 354 (n. 96); history of, 249–50; and Hawthorne, 250–52; as resort, 356 (n. 115)

House of the Seven Gables Museum, 10, 255

House of the Seven Gables Settlement Association, 249, 253, 256, 257; Americanization activities of, 257–61

Houses: triple-decker, 210–11, *212,* 350 (n. 18); historic, 228, 253

Howard Johnson restaurants, 308

Howells, William Dean, 237, 245

Identity, American: New England's role in, 27–29; assimilationist model of, 84. *See also* Identity, regional

Identity, cultural
—New England, 92–104, 317 (n. 5); Puritan-Yankee influence on, 5, 314; production of, 8, 89; in J. Morse, 82–83, 92–95. *See also* Nationalism, cultural; Identity, regional—New England
—Southern, 107–8

Identity, regional: defined, 1–2; cultural construction of, 5–6; differentiation in, 104; Southern, 107, 117, 200; politics of, 115–22; Midwestern, 213–14, 263, 350 (n. 24)
—New England: revision of, 4, 172;

alism of, 110, 115, 116; in Puritan
literary tradition, 113; *American Geography,* 116; Revolution in, 116–17;
on slavery, 118; retirement of, 122;
on white villages, 128; on ethnicity,
150; on regional character, 154, 155,
160; intellectual predilections of,
333 (n. 18); nativism of, 334 (n. 39);
on revivals, 335 (n. 58); reception of
works of, 336 (n. 72); villages in, 339
(n. 9)

Morse, Richard, 109

Morse, Samuel F. B.: *Landing of the
Forefathers,* 183

Morton, Nathaniel: *New Englands
Memoriall,* 55–56, 174–75, 180; reissue
of, 193

Moss, James King, 332 (n. 7)

Motherhood, republican, 166, 343
(n. 71)

Mount, William Sidney: *Farmers Bargaining, 163,* 163–64, 291; *Coming to a
Point,* 291, 295

"Mount Desert," 238–39

Mount Holyoke, Mass., 111

Mount Hope Rock, 199, 348 (n. 146)

Mourt's Relation, 344 (n. 89)

Murray, Terrence, 315

Museums: historical house, 253–54;
outdoor, 310; village, 310–11

Mystic Seaport, 310

Narragansetts, 21, 31

Nashua, N.H., 295

Natick, Mass., 147

National Endowments for the Arts
and the Humanities, 310, 314

National Geographic, 283

Nationalism: tension of with regionalism, 84; of New Deal, 310. *See also*
Regionalism, national
—cultural, 84, 162; during Cold War,

3, 310, 311, 314; during World War II,
309; of NEH, 314

National Society of New England
Women, 216, 234

Nation magazine, 266, 278

Native Americans: depopulation of,
19–20, 33; Spanish cruelty to, 20,
321 (n. 29); Puritan attitude toward,
20–21; Puritan accounts of, 21, 321
(n. 29); conversion of, 33; in Stowe's
writings, 148, 149; on regional identity, 198–99; impact of on land, 320
(n. 26), 325 (n. 14)

Nativism, 119, 207; and immigrants,
209; in colonial revival, 248;
Morse's, 334 (n. 39)

Natural rights, 83

Naumkeag, 19

Naumkeag Steam Cotton Company,
250

Navigation acts, 58, 60

Neal, John, 290

Nearing, Helen, 289

Nearing, Scott, 289

The Necessity of Reformation, 51

Neoclassicism, 129, 136, 339 (n. 10)

Neo-Yankees, 289

Neurasthenia, 221, 229, 231, 352 (n. 52)

New Canaan, Conn., 138, *140*

New Deal: regionalist critique of, 288;
Yankee on, 289, 290–91, 303; Farm
Security Administration in, 296–99,
361 (n. 75); nationalism of, 310

New England: cultural holism of, 4,
11, 84, 95, 105, 317 (n. 6); as imagined
region, 6, 263; as second England,
8, 17, 18, 21, 30; cultural imperialism
of, 9, 15, 156, 159; Revolutionary,
9, 79–81, 96; Federalism of, 9, 83;
triumphalism of, 9, 196, 202, 204,
206; depopulation in, 9, 318 (n. 16);
naming of, 11, 13–14, 15; population

of, 11, 39–40, 118; ethnic identity of, 11, 94–95, 113–14, 156, 312–13, 315; and England, 12–14, 15; exploration of, 13–14; colonization of, 14, 15, 19–20, 22; J. Smith's promotion of, 14–15, 16; J. Smith's map of, *16;* decentralized institutions of, 18; place names of, 19, 125; as vacuum domicilium, 20; in moral imagination, 21–22; remigration from, 23–24, 32, 34, 44; healthfulness of, 25; as wilderness, 26–27, 36, 37–38, 41–43, 47–48, 57, 62, 63, 77, 175, 190; moral regeneration in, 27, 38; as city upon hill, 27–29, 30, 43, 123, 316; religious liberty in, 30, 31, 60, 74, 185; Puritan disillusionment with, 32; religious mission of, 33, 42–44, 323 (n. 68); emigration from, 39, 117; moral identity of, 40, 81–82, 215; commercial empire of, 42, 58, 68, 74, 156; and "theology of place," 42, 325 (n. 17); re-integration into Britain of, 58, 63–64; London agents of, 60; slavery in, 68, 118–19; geopolitics of, 78, 117; during Revolutionary War, 79–81, 96; and South, 81, 95, 332 (n. 5), 342 (n. 48); disunionist sentiment in, 81–82, 96, 115, 116–17, 120; as cultural region, 82–83, 92–104, 119; in J. Morse, 86, 89; geographic change in, 87; literacy in, 88, 97–98; cultural geography of, 89, 109–15, 111; state histories of, 90–91; as national model, 91; civic culture of, 95–97, 111; newspapers of, 97, 335 (n. 46); racism in, 118–19, 198, 199–200; civil religion of, 184, 192; imagined past of, 228–29; heartland of, 264, 267; in Frost, 266–67; during Depression, 267, 285, 287–88, 295, 296, 301; literature of, 278–79;

high school graduates of, 285, 360 (n. 51); FSA photographs of, 296–99, 308, 361 (nn. 73, 75); supports Republican Party, 301, 303; Franco-Americans in, 301, 306; populism of, 304; winter sports in, 305; town meetings in, 306, *307;* during Cold War, 310–11; post-Yankee, 310–16; higher education in, 311; deindustrialization in, 311, 363 (n. 4); postwar economy of, 311–12; cultural decay in, 313; European perception of, 319 (n. 9); social history of, 326 (n. 26); southern, 361 (n. 68). *See also* Old New England

—antebellum: identity of, 9, 123; commerce in, 98; in Dwight, 109–15; cultural production in, 123–24; ethnic changes in, 124; white villages of, 124–50; religious liberals of, 191–92; commemoration in, 192, 198; racism in, 200–201; progress in, 204; regionalism of, 213

—colonial: and England, 10; identity of, 13; re-Anglicization in, 57–78; nationalist sentiment in, 77; central villages of, 127; self-consciousness of, 319 (n. 4). *See also* Colonial revival; Old New England; Re-Anglicization

—northern: rural life of, 265; tourism in, 265–66; during Depression, 267; as heartland, 267, 357 (n. 2); imaginative rise of, 267–87; Frost identifies with, 272–73; cultural commodification of, 273; neo-Yankees in, 289; farm complexes of, 339 (n. 10)

—postbellum: identity of, 203–6; during 1876 centennial, 205; immigrants to, 209–10; rural-urban migration in, 211; summer residents

on, 251; cultural dissolution of, 313; republicanization of, 347 (n. 132); and Frost, 359 (n. 41)

Puritans: of East Anglia, 3; literacy of, 4, 12, 90; intellectual, 12; economic activity of, 16, 44–45, 58, 320 (n. 16); and New England's identity, 17; English heritage of, 18; promotional literature of, 19, 25, 26, 36, 45; nineteenth-century view of, 22; religious culture of, 22–23, 321 (n. 34); diet of, 25, 34; eschatology of, 27; transatlantic community of, 29–30, 38, 42; as religious reformers, 30–31, 33; in English civil war, 31; Americanization of, 35; ocean imagery of, 47, 326 (n. 24); re-Anglicization of, 57; republication of texts of, 73, 193–94; town plans of, 125; communalism of, 128; Pilgrimization of, 172, 189–93, 195, 222; intolerance of, 182, 190, 191–92; in colonial revival, 220–21, 351 (n. 36), 353 (n. 72); monuments to, 222–25, 258, 351 (n. 41); female, 226; cultural authority of, 321 (n. 34); biographies of, 351 (n. 40)
—first-generation, 17–18; national identity of, 28–29; missionary motivation of, 33, 323 (n. 68); as exiles, 34, 42, 323 (n. 57); founding mission of, 37; avarice among, 45; imperial motives of, 63; as proto-republicans, 80. See also Great Migration
—second-generation: wilderness motifs of, 26–27, 36, 37–38, 41–43, 47–48, 57, 63, 77; regional identity of, 35, 38, 43; patriotism of, 37–38, 42; narratives of, 38, 40, 54–56, 77, 324 (n. 6); isolation from England of, 39; and secular development, 40, 42; mythologizing of, 41, 43–

45, 47–48, 53, 55, 61; jeremiads of, 48–55; under Dominion, 59

Putnam, George, 207

Quakers, 179, 191, 261
Quincy, Mass., 19

Racialism, 118–19, 198, 199–200, 348 (n. 148), 349 (n. 14)
Railroads, 129, 147
Reading public, 89–90, 285
Reagan, Ronald, 28
Realism, 217, 350 (n. 28)
Re-Anglicization, 8, 328 (n. 49); of regional identity, 35–36; eighteenth-century, 57–78; in Great Migration, 65; in Congregational Church, 66; consumption in, 68–69; political, 69, 74; and Puritanism, 69–72; in election sermons, 70; in architecture, 70–71; and clergy, 71; social consequences of, 73; during Seven Years' War, 75–76. See also Anglicanism

Reasons and Considerations, 17
Recognition of Robert Frost, 285, 286
Reformation, Protestant, 24, 32–34; backsliding from, 40, 49, 74
Reforming Synod, 51, 53
Regionalism, 317 (n. 5); revival of, 3–4; in J. Morse, 82, 84, 86; and nationalism, 84; in literature, 217, 278–79, 350 (n. 22); in Frost, 268, 275, 285–86; consumers of, 272; and modernism, 286; in American culture, 286, 358 (n. 12); during Depression, 287, 360 (n. 53); in *Yankee,* 303; post–Cold War, 309, 314–15, 316; popular interest in, 314; and sectionalism, 334 (n. 34)
—national, 81, 96, 106; in Stowe's works, 150; Yankee character in, 158;

of Federalists, 181, 185; Webster's, 183–84, 346 (n. 114); Whig, 187; post-bellum, 208; antebellum, 213, 332 (n. 6); during Cold War, 310

Regions: studies of, 4, 5, 314–15, 317 (n. 9), 363 (n. 3); imagined, 6, 10, 263, 318 (n. 11). *See also* Identity, regional

Remigration, 23–24, 32, 34, 44

Republicanism, 331 (n. 1); Revolutionary, 79–80, 89–90, 177; and Puritanism, 80, 86; in J. Morse, 93–94, 96–104, 106, 108; town-centered, 98–99; competency in, 99; and religion, 102; Yankee corruption of, 151, 156, 158, 161, 164; motherhood in, 166, 343 (n. 71); Pilgrim, 172, 175, 176, 179, 180, 182, 185; rhetoric of, 187

Republican Party, 207, 304; New England support for, 301, 303

Restoration, English, 35, 38, 39, 327 (n. 27)

Revivalism, 72–74, 75, 189, 192, 335 (n. 58)

Revolutionary War, 79–81, 96; and Puritanism, 9; clergy in, 102; J. Morse on, 116–17; Yankee character during, 152–53; Plymouth Rock in, 176, 178; domestic virtue in, 231–32; Connecticut during, 335 (n. 56)

Rhode Island: regionalism of, 7; Puritan view of, 30, 31; charter of, 60, 67; slave trade in, 68, 338 (n. 96); pluralism in, 100; in J. Morse, 100, 108; in Dwight, 111–12; in narratives, 197

Robbins, Chandler, 180–81

Robinson, John, 179

Rockwell, Norman, 289

Rogers, John, 65–66

Rollins, Frank, 213

Roosevelt, Franklin D., 290, 301, 303

Rowlandson, Mary: *The Sovereignty and Goodness of God,* 46–48

Rum, 40

Rust Belt, xi

Sabbatarianism, 23

"Sabbath day" houses, 127–28

Sacco and Vanzetti, trial of, 281, 283, 301

Sagadahoc colony, 14, 24

Sagendorph, Beatrix Thorne, 289, 295; covers by, *297*

Sagendorph, Robb, 8; editorials of, 283, 290–91; early life of, 289; "Before Armageddon," 290, 303; jeremiads of, 293; ancestry of, 300; "Is there a Yankee Party?," 304; in Office of Censorship, 308; nationalism of, 363 (n. 100)

Saint-Gaudens, Augustus: *The Puritan,* 222, *224,* 258

St. George, Robert, 340 (n. 17)

Salem, Mass.: founding of, 191; bi-centennial of, 220; waterfront of, 249; Custom House of, 250; "Turner Lane" neighborhood of, 250; in War of 1812, 250; immigrants to, 251, 254, 256; Seaman's Bethel in, 252, 256; Essex Institute in, 253; maritime prosperity of, 255; Hathaway House in, 256; Old Bakery in, 256; labor unrest in, 258; historical pageants in, 260–61; Frost's residence in, 270; industrialization in, 355 (n. 98). *See also* House of the Seven Gables

Salem Settlement Committee, 252

Sample, Paul, 361 (n. 74)

Sargent, Henry: *The Landing of the Fathers,* 183, *184,* 186

Secessionism, 81–82, 96, 115, 116–17; of

Yale College, 72

Yankee, character of, 197, 202; emergence of, 9, 123; feminization of, 10; stereotypes of, 113; in Stowe's writings, 150, 151, 274; traits of, 150–51; invention of, 150–71; urban audience for, 151; and republicanism, 151, 156, 158, 161, 164; postbellum, 152; during Revolution, 152–53; as icon, 154–55, 158; Federalist view of, 154–56; in Irving, 159–62; Emerson on, 162, 164; as national character, 162–63, 165, 171; stabilization of, 166; discourse of, 170; complexity of, 171; Thoreau on, 171; Pilgrim origins of, 185; in Frost, 268, 273, 274–76; in *Yankee,* 300, 361 (n. 68); gendered view of, 343 (n. 71), 344 (n. 75); Franco-American corruption of, 359 (n. 41)

Yankee (magazine), 8, 269, 278, 287–309; success of, 10; self-reliance in, 283; founding of, 287; regionalism in, 287, 303; circulation of, 288, 291; readership of, 288, 291–93; on New Deal, 289, 290–91, 303; cultural resistance in, 290; covers of, 291, *292, 296, 297;* "Swoppers' Column," 291, 361 (n. 65); office of, 291, 361 (n. 66); format of, 293, 295; on industrialization, 295; Job Exchange in, 295, *298,* 308; art of, 295–96; "Nice Clean Little Town," 299; ethnic issues in, 299–300; "Six Smart Yanks," 299–300; Yankee character in, 300, 361 (n. 68); immigrants in, 300–303, *303,* 362 (n. 85); advertisers in, 305; during World War II, 308

Yankee, The (periodical), 162, 290

Yankee-Doodle (comic figure), 151, 155, 161

"Yankee-Doodle" (tune), 152–53

"Yankee Party," 303–4

Yankees: cultural representations of, 150–51, 166; as peddlers, 151, 156–58, 161, 165, 171; mobility of, 151, 159, 165, 168, 185; etymology of term, 152, 342 (n. 49); dramatic representation of, 155–56, 165; female, 164–70, 205–6; of Connecticut, 264; *Yankee* depiction of, *294;* nationalistic rise of, 343 (n. 68); domestication of, 343 (n. 75). *See also* Old New England

York. *See* Old York, Maine

York Beach, Maine, 238, 248

Young, Alexander, 194